SAT

& College Preparation Course for the Christian Student

- Test-taking insights and strategies
- Timely tips for thriving academically
- 50+ sample essays sharpen your skills

JAMES P. STOBAUGH

First printing: June 2011

Master Books®, P.O. Box 726, Green Forest, AR 72638

Master Books® is a division of the New Leaf Publishing Group, Inc.

ISBN: 978-0-89051-624-9
Library of Congress Number: 2011928935
Cover by Diana Bogardus

Please consider requesting that a copy of this volume be purchased by your local library system.

Printed in the United States of America

Please visit our website for other great titles:
www.masterbooks.net

For information regarding author interviews,
please contact the publicity department at (870) 438-5288

Master Books®
A Division of New Leaf Publishing Group
www.masterbooks.net

This book is gratefully dedicated to my wife,
Karen Elizabeth Stobaugh

"Come! Glorify the Lord with me!
And let us exalt His name forever!"
—Psalm 34:3

Table of Contents

Every student who is planning on, or thinks there may be the possibility of, attending college should take the Scholastic Aptitude Test (SAT I). *The SAT and College Preparation Course for the Christian Student* is specifically designed for Christian students—in homeschools, in Christian schools, or among individual families—to strengthen their faith as well as increase their knowledge.

Why should a Christian student prepare for the SAT I any differently than a nonbeliever? SAT preparation must be understood in the context of our spiritual journey. In 2 Timothy 2, Paul urges the young pastor Timothy to study hard and to do his work as if he were working for the Lord. So must we do all that God calls us to do with all the strength, vitality, and courage we can. This book challenges you to work hard and to study to show yourself approved of the Lord.

My prayer for you is this:

"For this reason I kneel before the Father, from whom his whole family in heaven and on earth derives his name. I pray that out of his glorious riches he may strengthen you with power through his Spirit in your inner being, so that Christ may dwell in your hearts through faith. And I pray that you, being rooted and established in love, may have power, together with all the saints, to grasp how wide and long and high and deep is the love of Christ, and to know this love that surpasses knowledge—that you may be filled to the measure of all the fullness of God. Now to him who is able to do immeasurably more than all we ask or imagine, according to his power that is at work within us, to him be glory in the church and in Christ Jesus throughout all generations, for ever and ever! Amen." (Ephesians 3:14-21)

What Is the SAT I?

The SAT I is an aptitude test not an achievement or intelligence test. It does not measure your information acquisition or assimilation skills. It measures your potential success in college, but it has absolutely nothing to do with your worth in God's eyes.

Nevertheless, it is an important test, particularly for homeschoolers who do not have diplomas from an accredited school. It is the most common resource on which colleges—both secular and Christian—base their offers of admission and financial aid. Although most students can get into college even with low SAT scores, financial aid and scholarships will be more readily available for those students with higher SAT scores.

The SAT I is offered seven times a year in the United States and six times at international sites. The test:
—Takes three hours and 45 minutes but you should allow four hours
—Consists of 10 separately timed sections:
    Three sections test writing (60 minutes)
    Three sections test critical reading (70 minute)
    Three sections test mathematics (70 minutes)
    One unscored section tests critical reading, mathematics, or writing (25 minutes). Normally the CollegeBoard uses this section to create future tests.
—Assesses critical thinking and problem solving skills in three areas:
    Critical reading
    Mathematics
    Writing
—Includes three kinds of questions:
    Multiple-choice questions
    Student-produced responses (mathematics only)
    Essay questions
—Is machine-scored, except for the essay

Each section is worth 800 points. Thus, a perfect score is 2400. CollegeBoard reports that, on average, students answer 50 to 60 percent of questions correctly, 80 percent finish nearly the entire test, and most students complete at least 75 percent of the questions.

The verbal section consists of analysis questions, vocabulary questions (based on context), comparison questions (based on reading passages), and reading comprehension. The math section consists of arithmetic, algebra, geometry, quantitative comparisons, and grid-ins. In other words, the SAT I is essentially a critical reading, vocabulary, and arithmetic word problem test.

Should I Take Practice SAT I Tests?

Unfortunately, the SAT I is coaching resistant. Likewise, there is no correlation between frequency of taking the SAT I and increased scores. In fact, several studies have implied that repeat scores are equally low or high (+ or -8 points).

Nonetheless, my 30+ years of coaching the exam have conclusively shown me that taking practice tests (not real test) can be very helpful under the following condition: you must spend three to six months in some sort of coaching course between tests.

Thus, I recommend that you take a mock SAT every two months during your preparation. If you wish to purchase actual CollegeBoard mock SATs and to receive other

SAT preparation material, including free live instructional videos, text your name and e-mail to (870) 568-0072 or visit www.WhatIsTheBestTest.com. If you have questions feel free to phone 814-479-7710. In my opinion, it is best to take mock, not real, SAT I exams. Why? Recently CollegeBoard published a confidential study that showed that 10 percent of colleges averaged SAT I scores. I personally think that the number is larger. Therefore, it would be better to take eight to ten mock exams, and only two or three real exams. That way you do not have to explain any embarrassing initial low scores. One final note: in the past, CollegeBoard sent all official scores to colleges. Recently, though, CollegeBoard now will send only your requested scores.

What Are the PSAT and NMSQT?

The PSAT (Preliminary Scholastic Aptitude Test) is a shortened version of the SAT taken during the junior year and is generally recognized as a "practice" SAT. It is also referred to as the NMSQT (National Merit Scholarship Qualifying Test) because the scores of the PSAT are used to determine if a student can qualify for a National Merit Scholarship, a prestigious honor.

Unlike the SAT, the verbal section of the PSAT includes questions evaluating writing ability. These multiple choice questions will evaluate your ability to identify good writing by asking you to detect faults in usage and grammar.

The PSAT is scored differently than the SAT. Scores for each section on the PSAT range from 20 to 80. You may take the test any time prior to your junior year, but only the junior year PSAT score will count toward the NMSQT. In my years of coaching experience, I have found that the first score on the PSAT is oftentimes the best score, so I recommend only taking it your junior year.

During October of each year, the PSAT is administered in your local high school. In early December your scores will be mailed to you. After all the scores have been analyzed, your score will be compared to others and you may be designated a Recommended National Merit Semifinalist. Only the top scores—1.5 percent—reach a recommended National Merit Semifinalist status and only .7 percent actually win a scholarship.

In March, May, or June all Recommended National Merit Semifinalists must take the SAT I if they wish to be considered for a National Merit Scholarship. In early September of the senior year, PSAT scores and transcripts will be evaluated, and National Merit Scholarships will be awarded. Most scholarships come from corporations. NMSQT scholars are required to attend colleges that corporations choose to support if they wish to receive a National Merit Scholarship. Most colleges will award an equal or higher scholarship anyway, so go to where God is telling you to go regardless of where corporations want you to go.

For more information, see the PSAT/NMSQT Student Bulletin. Call (847) 866-5100.

Should I Take the PSAT?

Not necessarily. There is no correlation between frequency of aptitude test taking and increased scores; indeed, the opposite may happen. In fact, many students are discouraged by low PSAT scores and find that their SAT preparation is hindered. Therefore, I recommend that all students take a mock SAT to get an idea how well they will do on the PSAT. If in fact the student scores high (above 2250) then take the PSAT.

How Important Is Stress Reduction?

My thirty years of coaching remind me how important stress reduction is to high SAT I scores. In fact, in my opinion, it is the most important preparation variable. For Christians, at least, stress reduction is best accomplished by a frequent and thorough devotional and Bible memorization program. The SAT and College Preparation Course for the Christian Student amply discusses this point and provides preparation exercises that will equip the student to be ready for the SAT I.

What About Learning Disabled Students?

A student at any grade level with a documented disability is eligible for special arrangements for the PSAT and SAT. For further information, visit the CollegeBoard at www.collegeboard.org.

FREE Download!

Visit **nlpg.com/SATwkbk** to download your free copy of Dr. Stobaugh's *Workbook For The CollegeBoard© SAT I Essay.* This handy resource will give you additional tips and samples you can work on to hone your essay skills!

The SAT and College Preparation Course for the Christian Student is designed to prepare you academically and spiritually for the challenge ahead of you. There are four components to this course: 1) a daily devotion, 2) reading and vocabulary exercises, and 3) math and verbal exercises and 4) test taking strategies.

The lessons include:

- **A Comprehensive Reading Program.** Reading good books is the single best preparation for the SAT verbal section. You should try to read one book each week. Also, within the lessons are reading excerpts from various disciplines—art, music, social sciences, and natural sciences. These will help expand your vocabulary and improve your critical thinking skills. (Note: There is a suggested reading list in Appendix B which contains both Christian and secular works. Christian and public colleges read many of the same titles—especially the classics—but feel free to substitute other books as you deem appropriate.) It is also important to keep a reading journal. There is an outline for this in Appendix C.
- **Intentional Vocabulary Development.** As you work your way through the reading list, you will encounter unfamiliar words. For each word, you will then make a vocabulary card that you can later review to reinforce the definitions. Each lesson, then, encourages vocabulary development through the use of these vocabulary cards. There is an explanation and example in Appendix A.
- **Test-Taking Strategies.** Practical techniques for test-taking are given throughout the book, and more are listed in Appendix F.
- **Intentional Faith Building.** Through the use of a devotional journal (Appendix D) and target Scriptures (choose from examples in Appendix E), you will implement the spiritual disciplines of Bible reading and study, Scripture meditation and memorization, and prayer. In my experience, I have found that the best SAT scores come from students who have serious, disciplined prayer and devotional lives. These spiritual truths will be a great reservoir of strength from which you can draw not only on the day of the SAT exam, but throughout your life.
- **Essay Writing.** This section will introduce and explain several essay styles. You will be assigned to write various essays, which will be great preparation for the SAT I. Examples of each type will be given in the answer key. Essay assignments in this book will vary in length. However, during the actual SAT I test you will have 25 minutes to write your essay. A typical SAT essay is 300-400 words in length so keep this in mind as you write your practice essays.

This book is built around 150 lessons that can be completed in one, two, or three years. Each student should decide with his or her parents the best way to implement these lessons. Assuming students will take the exam in May or June of their junior year, families have found the implementation schedules on the following pages to be most successful.

Important Note to Parents:

You and your family are encouraged to join your student in this time of preparation. For example, everyone can join in learning new vocabulary words. Also, in some lessons I have included MindTrap® dilemmas (from the board game of the same name). I recommend you buy this game, and, as a family, try to solve one each day. They are fun and will help your student learn how to think.

Also, consider having your child learn Latin and/or Greek instead of a modern language. Modern languages can be picked up fairly easily in college. Greek and Latin will help in vocabulary preparation and grammar skills.

A vital part of SAT preparation is taking an actual SAT I exam. I recommend your student take a mock SAT every two months. If you wish to purchase actual CollegeBoard mock SATs and to receive other SAT preparation material, including free live instructional videos, text your name and e-mail to (870) 568-0072 or visit www.WhatIsTheBestTest.com. If you have questions feel free to phone 814-479-7710.

Finally, you are asked to spend time with your child in prayer and review of their vocabulary cards. Do not take this lightly. Encourage your student to work hard. Make sure your child memorizes Scriptures. Keep them reading. And, most importantly, pray for them!

The SAT Day

Here is one example of a typical test-day schedule. Times will vary depending on the actual time of the test, how far away the test site is, etc.

6:00 a.m.

Students: Wake up and eat a healthy breakfast. You should have been arising at this time for at a week or two before the exam to prepare your body. The whole family should gather and pray for the student.

6:30 a.m.

Last minute check-up: six sharpened #2 pencils, calculator with fresh battery, snack (no candy), ticket, picture ID, watch

7:00 a.m.

Parents should take the student to the test site, and then stay and pray for the student through the morning. It is a good idea to scout out the location the week before. Pray over the building. Relax in the car and meditate on Scriptures.

7:30 a.m.

As soon as the test site opens, go get a seat. Then return to the car. Do not hang around in the test site. Save a seat on the end of the row fairly distant from high traffic areas (doorways and bathrooms).

8:00 a.m.

By this time you should leave the car and go back into the test site. Parents should pray for the student one last time.

9:00 a.m.–12:30 p.m.

Take the exam. Be sure to use the exam to work the problems, not the answer sheet. I do not recommend sending your scores to a college until you get the score you want.

12:30 p.m.

Celebrate! Celebrate God's faithfulness! Meditate on what God has done in your life through this preparation process. Consider Joshua 4. You will receive your scores in six weeks.

The 3-Year Plan (highly recommended)

Beginning in 9th grade

Year 1:

Monday	Tuesday	Wednesday	Thursday	Friday
• Read lesson • Answer questions • Devotional journal • Begin book	• Devotional journal • Continue book	• Devotional journal • Continue book	• Devotional journal • Continue book	• Devotional journal • Finish book (use weekend if necessary) • Reading journal

Year 2:

Monday	Tuesday	Wednesday	Thursday	Friday
• Read lesson • Answer questions • Devotional journal • Begin book	• Devotional journal • Continue book	• Read lesson • Answer questions • Devotional journal • Continue book	• Devotional journal • Continue book	• Devotional journal • Finish book (use weekend if necessary) • Reading journal

Year 3:

Monday	Tuesday	Wednesday	Thursday	Friday
• Read lesson • Answer questions • Devotional journal • Begin book	• Devotional journal • Continue book	• Read lesson • Answer questions • Devotional journal • Continue book	• Devotional journal • Continue book	• Read lesson • Answer questions • Devotional journal • Finish book (use weekend if necessary) • Reading journal

The 2-Year Plan

Beginning in 10th grade

Year 1 and 2:

Monday	Tuesday	Wednesday	Thursday	Friday
• Read lesson • Answer questions • Devotional journal • Begin book	• Devotional journal • Continue book	• Read lesson • Answer questions • Devotional journal • Continue book	• Devotional journal • Continue book	• Read lesson • Answer questions • Devotional journal • Finish book (use weekend if necessary) • Reading journal

The 1-Year Plan

Beginning in 11th grade

Monday	Tuesday	Wednesday	Thursday	Friday
• Read lesson • Answer questions • Devotional journal • Begin book	• Read lesson • Answer questions • Devotional journal • Continue book	• Read lesson • Answer questions • Devotional journal • Continue book	• Read lesson • Answer questions • Devotional journal • Continue book	• Read lesson • Answer questions • Devotional journal • Finish book (use weekend if necessary) • Reading journal

Senior Year

The senior year should be devoted to college admission; however, that process may need to be delayed for an SAT retake during the senior year. If your score in May/June junior year is completely unsatisfactory, you may need to retake the exam early in your senior year. Take the test as soon as possible during the next year. This will leave open several options: early admission to the college of your choice (which will open more financial aid options); regular admission (complete applications as soon as possible); or delayed admission to a college, taking a year off to save money or to go on a mission trip. Your and your parents/guardians together need to consider prayerfully these options.

TIP
Active Reading

In the next one hundred & fifty lessons you will practice active reading. In other words, you will not merely read "words." You will understand or comprehend what the passage is saying. As I have already mentioned, reading is the single most important skill that you will need to receive a high score on the SAT I.

Active readers ask themselves questions and make predictions about what will happen next. These predictions make it easier to understand what comes next and significantly add to comprehension.

Here are some more suggestions:

- Mark up your text.

- Ask yourself pertinent questions and predict outcomes as you read.

- Why did the author choose a certain title? Identify evidence that supports this title.

- Determine the value of information and disregard that which is irrelevant.

- Be flexible. Adjust your conclusions as new information is presented.

- Suspend judgment until all facts are gathered and considered.

- Draw conclusions as you read.

- What is the author's purpose? Who is his audience? What is his main idea? How does he support it?

- Pay close attention to:
    the first sentence and last sentence of each paragraph.
    the first and last paragraph of each passage/essay.

Then they said to each other, "Let's build for ourselves a city and a tower. And let's make the top of the tower reach high into the sky. We will become famous. If we do this, we will not be scattered over all the earth." —Genesis 11:4 (NCV)

Scripture: Genesis 11:1-9

Lost Horizons by James Hilton is a story of four people brought against their will to a mythical place called Shangri-La. It is a magical place hidden in the mountains where no one grows old. The story is about Hugh Conway, who finds himself trapped by the fascination of eternal life. Humankind has always sought to create a perfect society; the Tower of Babel is one notable example. But God had other plans… "this is only the beginning of what they will do" (Genesis 11:6). Ultimately, all plans to create a perfect society fail—unless one centers that society on the Lordship of Jesus Christ. Plans to create a life without worry fail without a life centered on the Lordship of Jesus Christ.

What is a perfect world to you? What is a perfect world to God? Organize your thoughts!

Topic	My View	God's View
1. Obeying my parents		
2. Lying and stealing		
3. Loving my brothers/sisters		

Devotional Journal

A daily devotional time is valuable as you prepare for the SAT. To accomplish this implement a thirty-minute time each day by using Appendix D. Use the following passage as a sample meditation.

> Then Joseph could no longer control himself before all his attendants, and he cried out, "Have everyone leave my presence!" So there was no one with Joseph when he made himself known to his brothers. And he wept so loudly that the Egyptians heard him…. Joseph said to his brothers, "I am Joseph!" (Genesis 45:1-3)

Read/Vocabulary Cards

A. I recommend that you read *Lost Horizons* or choose a book from the book list on page 320, reading thirty to fifty pages per day.
B. Keep a list of vocabulary words that you do not know. First, define the words on your own, and then check your definitions in the dictionary. Keep the words on 3 by 5-inch cards and review them on Friday with your parents or guardians.

Reading Journal

When you finish reading each book, be sure to use the reading journal in Appendix C. This will help you identify and remember the author's ideas and worldview.

Solve

How many ways can a team win a best-of-five-games play-off?

Create a Reading Habit

- Discuss your reading material with your parents.
- Set aside a designated reading time each day.

Summary

Active Readers connect, question, predict, visualize, clarify, expect, and evaluate.

Connect with what you are reading.

Question what you read.

Predict what will happen next

Visualize details.

Clarify and review what you understand,

Expect to see your comprehension increase.

Evaluate (form opinions) about what you read.

As he went, he cried out, "My son Absalom, my son Absalom! I wish I had died for you. Absalom, my son, my son!" —2 Samuel 18:33 (NCV)

Scripture: 2 Samuel 18

During the Civil War, a Pennsylvania Dutch Quaker father disagreed vehemently with his son about his son's decision to enlist in the Union army. Nonetheless, the son enlisted and participated in many battles. During late 1862, the Quaker father had a dream that his son was wounded in battle. Knowing that a battle had been fought recently at Antietam Creek, Sharpsburg, Maryland, only a few miles from home, the Quaker father made his way by horse-drawn buggy until he came to the battlefield. His son was nowhere to be found. After receiving permission to search the battlefield, the worried father set out. It was now dark and the father lit a lantern. While searching for his son, he came across many wounded young men. Some cried for help; others merely whimpered. Growing discouraged, the Quaker father began to cry, "Jonathan Smythe, thy father seeketh after thee!" For several hours he cried. Many sons answered, but none of them were his Jonathan Smythe. But the man kept diligently at his task until he heard a very faint, barely audible reply, "Father, over here." And the son finished, "I knew that you would come." The Quaker father knelt down, took Jonathan in his arms, comforted him with his presence, dressed his wounds, and took him home. Jonathan recovered….In our Bible story today we meet rebellious, disturbed Absalom. Disobedient, disloyal Absalom led a rebellion against his father. Many of us will not understand why David was so upset when Absalom was killed.

Why do you think David was sad? Ask your father or another adult why he thinks David was willing to give his own life for his recalcitrant son.

Devotional Journal

Read/Vocabulary Cards

Grammar

The word *swimming* in this sentence is what part of speech?

Swimming is great fun.

Vocabulary

Define these words: precocious, deprecation.

Solve

Convert 1,451,500 milliliters (ml) to liters.

The SAT is essentially a vocabulary and critical thinking exam. Both the verbal and mathematic portions focus on the ability to solve problems and process information. Therefore, organized, consistent reading is critical to a high SAT score.

3
Life with Father

A man named Jairus came to Jesus….He bowed down at Jesus' feet and begged him to come to his house. Jairus had only one daughter. She was 12 years old, and she was dying. —Luke 8:41,42 (NCV)

Scripture: *Luke 8:40-56*

Recently a test sample of teenagers was asked this question: "Would you rather give up your father or television?" The young people chose television over their fathers at a rate of three to one! Given that fact, at a time when it is rare indeed to hear a young person speak of his father with affection, Clarence Day's book *Life With Father* is especially needed. Clarence Day's father was a firm man, but deeply appreciated and adored by his son. He was a good father. Jairus is a good father, too. But Jairus' daughter is dying. Jairus is an important official, and it is not judicious for him to grovel before the scandalous rabbi from Nazareth. In fact, Jairus could lose everything if he did. But his daughter is dying. She needs the Master's touch. So Jairus risks everything for his little one….

Tell your dad or your Heavenly Father that you love him. Thank him for all that he has done for you. You and your dad should read and discuss Life With Father *together.*

Devotional Journal

Read/Vocabulary Cards

Do you know the following vocabulary words from *Life With Father*? If not, define them, and make 3 by 5-inch cards.

A. apex
B. gusto
C. phlegmatic
D. avaricious
E. pertinacious
F. voluminous
G. idiosyncrasies
H. sardonic
I. inveigle
J. impresario
K. expostulate
L. wizened
M. apoplexy
N. astute
O. suavely

Solve

A. Convert 30 cubic meters (m3) to cubic centimeters (cm3).
B. Convert 1200 cubic meters to liters.

It is a waste of time for students to memorize the 500 most frequently used words on the SAT I. The best way to increase your vocabulary is to read widely and to remember what you have read (a list of books is included on page 320). Remember the three-step method of increasing your vocabulary: READ; KEEP 3 BY 5-INCH CARDS; USE THESE WORDS IN SPEECH AND WRITING.

22

Critical Reading

Read the passage on the next page and answer the questions following:

> We have as yet hardly spoken of the infant that little creature, whose innocent life had sprung, by the inscrutable decree of Providence, a lovely and immortal flower, out of the rank luxuriance of a guilty passion. How strange it seemed to the sad woman, as she watched the growth, and the beauty that became every day more brilliant, and the intelligence that threw its quivering sunshine over the tiny features of this child! Her Pearl—for so had Hester called her; not as a name expressive of her aspect, which had nothing of the calm, white, unimpassioned lustre that would be indicated by the comparison. But she named the infant "Pearl," as being of great price—purchased with all she had—her mother's only treasure! How strange, indeed! Man had marked this woman's sin by a scarlet letter, which had such potent and disastrous efficacy that no human sympathy could reach her, save it were sinful like herself. God, as a direct consequence of the sin which man thus punished, had given her a lovely child, whose place was on that same dishonored bosom, to connect her parent forever with the race and descent of mortals, and to be finally a blessed soul in heaven! Yet these thoughts affected Hester Prynne less with hope than apprehension. She knew that her deed had been evil; she could have no faith, therefore, that its result would be good. Day after day she looked fearfully into the child's expanding nature, ever dreading to detect some dark and wild peculiarity that should correspond with the guiltiness to which she owed her being (*The Scarlet Letter*, Nathaniel Hawthorne).

I.   This famous passage from Nathaniel Hawthorne's *The Scarlet Letter* introduces the memorable character Pearl. From the passage the reader knows that Pearl is
    A. the daughter of an illicit love affair between Hester Prynne and Arthur Dimmesdale
    B. a supernatural demon sent to punish Hester Prynne for her sin of adultery
    C. the daughter of Hester Prynne sent by God
    D. an example of bad choices

II. Pearl functions in this story as a(n)
    A. antagonist
    B. protagonist
    C. narrator
    D. foil

TIP

An Active Reading Example:

The Scarlet Letter by Nathaniel Hawthorne, 1850

Chapter 1
The Prison-Door

A throng of bearded men, in sad-colored garments and gray, steeple-crowned hats, intermixed with women, some wearing hoods, and others bareheaded, was assembled in front of a wooden edifice, the door of which was heavily timbered with oak, and studded with iron spikes.

The founders of a new colony, whatever Utopia of human virtue and happiness they might originally project, have invariably recognized it among their earliest practical necessities to allot a portion of the virgin soil as a cemetery, and another portion as the site of a prison. In accordance with this rule, it may safely be assumed that the forefathers of Boston had built the first prison-house, somewhere in the vicinity of Cornhill, almost as seasonably as they marked out the first burial-ground, on Isaac Johnson's lot, and round about his grave, which subsequently became the nucleus of all the congregated sepulchres in the old church-yard of King's Chapel. Certain it is, that, some fifteen or twenty years after the settlement of the town, the wooden jail was already marked with weather-stains and other indications of age, which gave a yet darker aspect to its beetle-browed and gloomy front. The rust on the ponderous iron-work of its oaken door looked more antique than any thing else in the new world. Like all that pertains to crime, it seemed never to have known a youthful era. Before this ugly edifice, and between it and the wheel-track of the street, was a grass-plot, much overgrown with burdock, pig-weed, apple-peru, and such unsightly vegetation, which evidently found something congenial in the soil that had so early borne the black flower of civilized society, a prison. But, on one side of the portal, and rooted almost at the threshold, was a wild rose-bush, covered, in this month of June, with its delicate gems, which might be imagined to offer their fragrance and fragile beauty to the prisoner as he went in, and to the condemned criminal as he came forth to his doom, in token that the deep heart of Nature could pity and be kind to him.

This rose-bush, by a strange chance, has been kept alive in history; but whether it had merely survived out of the stern old wilderness, so long after the fall of the gigantic pines and oaks that originally overshadowed it,--or whether, as there is fair authority for believing, it had sprung up under the footsteps of the sainted Ann Hutchinson, as she entered the prison-door,--we shall not take upon us to determine. Finding it so directly on the threshold of our narrative, which is now about to issue from that inauspicious portal, we could hardly do otherwise than pluck one of its flowers and present it to the reader. It may serve, let us hope, to symbolize some sweet moral blossom, that may be found along the track, or relieve the darkening close of a tale of human frailty and sorrow.

Noah did everything that God commanded him. —Genesis 6:22 (NCV)

Scripture: Genesis 6–8

Thor Heyerdahl, an explorer working on a Pacific Island, heard about a mythical hero named Kon-Tiki, who allegedly migrated to the island from the East, perhaps even from South America. Dr. Heyerdahl thought that the myth was true. But no one would believe him. So he tried to prove it by building a balsa log raft and floating across the Pacific. The book *Kon-Tiki* is the result. It is one of the most extraordinary journey books ever written. In a similar way, Noah and his family were some of the last people of his age to believe in God. To many, God was a joke. To others, He was a myth. But this God told Noah to do a crazy thing—to build an ark. And Noah obeyed.

Describe a time when you took a stand for Christ and others thought you were crazy. To be Christlike in everyday life is an increasingly unique phenomenon!

Devotional Journal

Read/Vocabulary Cards

Critical Thinking: Analysis

Even after Heyerdahl succeeded, many scientists doubted that the Polynesians came from Peru. They firmly believed that they had migrated from Asia. They argued that all Heyerdahl had proved was that he could float on a raft across the Pacific Ocean. What do you think? What sort of evidence would he need to find to support his claim?

Vocabulary

Define italicized words in context:
A. While the "Tamara" was avoiding *myriad* submerged reefs and eddies…
B. …the girls squirmed and greeted us *coquettishly* yet shyly… (from *Kon-Tiki* by Thor Heyerdahl)

Solve

A. 6.241 + .044 =
B. 6.241 - .044 =
C. 4.14 x 63.2 =

Critical Thinking: Essay

Definition Essay

As the name implies, the definition essay defines or explains what a particular word or idea means. It often combines several essay styles to create a complete definition of a complex subject. It involves more than the typical dictionary definition of a word, and includes the meaning that a particular word has come to have in society, its history, and its various meanings.

In a 75-word essay, describe your favorite vacation spot.

5 Wings Like Eagles

They will be able to rise up as an eagle in the sky. They will run without needing rest. They will walk without becoming tired. —Isaiah 40:31 (NCV)

> ## Scripture: Isaiah 40:29-31

While vacationing on an island off the coast of Maine, I observed a bald eagle flying over a stand of fir trees. He was magnificent! Suddenly, without warning, he was attacked by a score of angry crows. What happened next surprised me. The eagle was obviously the stronger adversary. But he chose not to fight: He chose to run! Like a rocket he shot up to the sun! The crows were unable to follow and the eagle escaped. It is sagacious to know when to fight—and when to run. If others attack you, stand firm on the Word of God. But be careful not to return evil for evil. Fly into the sky! Go to the Father! There is no dishonor in calling your parents to pick you up at a party where others are drinking or doing other ungodly things. Soar with the eagles!

Describe a time when a situation was so bad that you had nowhere to turn. Did you turn to God?

Devotional Journal

Read/Vocabulary Cards

Vocabulary

Define italicized words from context:

A. One morning, as we sat at breakfast, an unexpected sea splashed into our gruel and taught us quite *gratuitously* that the taste of oats removed the greater part of the sickening taste of sea water!

B. …octopuses …came up on the surface at night…they were so *voracious* that, if one of them fastened on to a piece of meat and remained on the hook, another came and began to eat its captured kinsman. (from *Kon-Tiki* by Thor Heyerdahl)

What kind of arithmetic operations will be on the SAT? Addition, subtraction, multiplication, division, percentages, averages, odd and even numbers, prime numbers, divisibility, basic algebra, algebra 2, and geometry.

Solve

    A. 31.42 divided by 1000

    B. 0.005514 divided by 0.032

    C. 0.41632 divided by 0.0214

Critical Thinking: Evaluation

The following chart examines immigration from 1861-1930 (U.S. Bureau of the Census).

Period	Total Immigrants Admitted	Northern and Western Europe		Southern and Eastern Europe	
1861-70	2,314,824	2,031,624	87.4%	33,628	1.4%
1871-80	2,812,191	2,070,373	73.6%	201,889	7.2%
1881-90	5,246,613	3,778,633	72.0%	958,413	18.3%
1891-1900	3,687,564	1,643,492	44.6%	1,915,486	51.9%
1901-10	8,795,386	1,910,035	21.7%	6,225,486	51.9%
1911-20	5,735,811	997,438	17.4%	3,379,126	58.9%
1920-30	4,107,209	1,284,023	31.3%	1,193,830	29.0%

What statements are true about this graph?

    A. Immigration increased most dramatically from 1880 to 1900 and 1980-2000.

    B. 1,100,000 people immigrated in 1900.

    C. Immigration rates in 1860 were greater than in 1960.

    D. A and B are true.

    E. All are true.

    F. None are true.

    G. C is true.

But Ruth said, "Don't ask me to leave you! Don't beg me not to follow you! Every place you go, I will go. Every place you live, I will live. Your people will be my people. Your God will be my God." —Ruth 1:16 (NCV)

Scripture: *The Book of Ruth*

The Book of Ruth is one of the most inspiring books of the Old Testament. Courage, fortitude, charity—they are all present in this remarkable book. Ruth's husband is dead. She by all rights can return to the comfort and safety of her own family. But Ruth has met her deceased husband's strange God, the God of Abraham, Isaac, and Jacob, the God who gives and demands so much. She can never leave this God or His people.

Do you know the God of Ruth? The God who gives and demands so much? Is He your Lord and Savior?

Devotional Journal

Read/Vocabulary Cards

Instead of reading thirty–fifty pages in a novel, read the Book of Ruth. Continue to record vocabulary words that you do not know on 3 by 5-inch cards.

Solve

3 ft.

4 ft.

A. 42 students can ride on a bus. There are 1264 students who want to go to a football game. How many buses will be needed to take all the students to the game?
B. How many 1-inch tiles would it take to cover the figure at right?

Grammar

How could the following sentence be improved?

The football game was played by wiry youth of impeccable character.

A. Wiry youth of impeccable character played the football game.
B. The football game was played by wiry, youth of impeccable character.
C. The football game was played by wiry youth with impeccable character.
D. The football game were played by wiry youth of impeccable character.

It is important to understand that the SAT is an aptitude test—not an achievement test (like the Iowa Basics or Stanford Tests). You will take it during the second semester junior year or first semester senior year. It measures your potential success in college; it does not necessarily measure your information acquisition and assimilation skills. It has absolutely nothing at all to do with your worth in God's eyes! God always has and always will love you!

The people complained to the Lord about their troubles. When he heard them, he became angry. Fire from the Lord burned among the people. It burned the edge of the camp. — Numbers 11:1 (NCV)

Scripture: *Numbers 11*

Mutiny on the Bounty by Charles Nordhoff and James Norman Hall is one of the most popular true stories in Western literature. Who can ever forget Captain Bligh and his mutinous sailors? But before we are too quick to judge… mutiny and rebellion are very dangerous pastimes. They should be undertaken with the utmost care and trepidation. In Numbers 11 we read that the Jewish nation has rebelled against Moses' leadership. God is displeased, not because Moses is a good or bad leader—no doubt he was not an easy leader to follow—but when Israel rebelled against Moses they were rebelling against God. There are times when disobedience is necessary—in Exodus, the Egyptian midwives refused to abort Hebrew babies—but the rebels must be willing to accept the penalty for breaking the law.

Are you submitted to the authority God has placed over you? Do you willingly obey your parents? Why or why not?

Devotional Journal

Read/Vocabulary Cards

Critical Thinking: Comparison

I recommend that you read *The Caine Mutiny* by Herman Wouk and compare it to *Mutiny on the Bounty*. Be sure to discuss similarities and differences.

The vocabulary words used throughout this course frequently occur on SAT exams.

Solve

A. The ratio of the number of boys to girls was 13 to 2. There were 26 boys. How many girls were there?
B. If 60 pounds of beans sold for $12.00, what was the price per pound of beans?

Critical Reading

A. Being thus left to our fortunes, it fortuned that within ten dayes scarce ten amongst us could either goe, or well stand, such extreame weaknes and sicknes oppressed us. And thereat none need marvaile, if they consider the cause and reason, which was this; whiles the ships stayed, our allowance was somewhat bettered, by a daily proportion of Bisket, which the sailers would pilfer to sell, give, or exchange with us, for money, Saxefras, furres, or love. But when they departed, there remained neither taverne, beere house, nor place of reliefe, but the common Kettell. Had we beene as free from all sinnes as gluttony, and drunkennesse, we might have been canonized for Saints; But our President would never have beene admitted, for ingrossing to his private, Oatmeale, Sacke, Oyle, Aquavitae, Beefe, Egges, or what not, but the Kettell; that indeed he allowed equally to be distributed, and that was halfe a pint

Lesson continues on the next page.

of wheat, and as much barely boyled with water for a man a day, and this having fryed some 26 weekes in the ships hold, contained as many wormes as graines; so that we might truely call it rather so much bran then corne, our drinke was water, our lodgings Castles in the ayre: with this lodging and dyet, our extreame toile in bearing and planting Pallisadoes, so strained and bruised us, and our continuall labour in the extremities of the heat had so weakned us, as were cause sufficient to have made us as miserable in our native Countery, or any other place in the world. . . . The new president and Martin, being little beloved, of weake judgement in dangers, and less industrie in peace, committted managing of all things abroad to Captaine Smith: who by his owne example, good words, and faire promises, set some to mow, others to binde thatch, some to build houses, others to thatch them, himselfe always bearing the greatest taske for his own share, so that in short time, he provided most of them lodgings, neglecting any for himselfe. This done, seeing the Salvages superfluitie beginne to decrease (with some of his workmen) shipped himselfe in the Shallop to search the Country for trade. The want of the language, knowledge to mannage his boat without sailes, the want of a sufficient power, (knowing the multitude of the Salvages) apparell for his men, and other necessaries, were infinite impediments, yet no discouragement (*The General History of Virginia*, Captain John Smith, 1624).

B. These troubles being blowne over, and now all being compacte togeather in one shipe, they put to sea againe with a prosperous winde, which continued diverce days togeather, which was some incouragement unto them; yet according to the usuall maner many were afflicted with sea-sicknes. And I may not omite hear a spetiall worke of Gods providence. There was a proud and very profane yonge man, one of the sea-men, of a lustie, able body, which made him the more hauty; he would allway be contemning the poore people in their sicknes, and cursing them dayly with greevous execrations, and did not let to tell them, that he hoped to help to cast halfe of them over board before they came to their jurneys end, and to make merry with what they had; and if he were by any gently reproved, he would curse and swear most bitterly. But it pleased God before they came halfe seas over, to smite this yong man with a greevous disease, of which he dyed in a desperate maner, and so was him self the first that was throwne overbord. Thus his curses light on his owne head; and it was an astonishment to all his fellow, for they noted it to be the just hand of God upon him. After they had injoyed faire winds and weather for a season, they were incountred many times with crosse winds, and mette with many feirce stormes, with which the shipe was shroudly shaken, and her upper works made very leakie; and one of the maine beames in the midd ships was bowed and craked, which put them in some fear that the shipe could not be able to performe the vioage. . . . (*The History of Plimoth Plantation*, William Bradford, 1620).

From the above passages the reader can conclude that
 A. John Smith was a collaborator with Native Americans.
 B. John Smith was a braver man than William Bradford.
 C. While the reader is unsure of John Smith's faith journey, he is sure that William Bradford
  contextualizes events according to acts of God.
 D. William Bradford and John Smith were married to sisters.

But God said to that man, "Foolish man! Tonight you will die. So who will get those things you have prepared for yourself?" —Luke 12:20 (NCV)

Scripture: *Luke 12:16-21*

Silas Marner, by George Eliot, is a great English novel that explores the consequences of pride and the benefits of forgiveness. The protagonist Marner had everything he needed, then lost it, and found something more valuable. In our Bible text today, we read about another man who has everything—or so he thinks. He is rich, healthy, and strong. But Jesus cautions His listeners in this parable to be careful about counting one's chickens before they hatch. What He is addressing is our priorities—what is most important to us? Gathering material possessions? Or obeying Him?

You may receive an allowance. Do you give part of that money to the Lord? Do you give Him part of your day in a devotion time? Purpose to do so if you do not.

Devotional Journal

Read/Vocabulary Cards

Make sure you review your vocabulary cards with your parents on a regular basis.

Critical Thinking: Comparison

Read *Silas Marner*. Perhaps you can obtain a copy of the movie *Silas Marner* from a video store, watch it, and discuss with your parents comparing the moving an the book.

Critical Thinking: Writing

Using the picture at right, write a 75-word eyewitness account of the sinking of the Titanic.

Ultimately, God is not calling us to be lawyers, doctors, educators etc., or even to do well on the SAT. He is calling us to be His children and to share His Good News with others. God is more interested in character than test scores. However, SAT preparation could be His instrument to build character in you!

TIP
The SAT Writing Section

- The SAT writing section lasts one hour and is scored on a scale of 200 to 800.

- The SAT writing section includes multiple-choice questions and an essay.

- You will have 35 minutes to answer 49 multiple-choice questions, which account for 70 percent of your writing score. These multiple-choice questions test your ability to improve sentences.

- You will have 25 minutes to write an essay, which accounts for 30 percent of your writing score.

- You are welcome to write whatever you wish but remember this: most of the SAT I essay graders are English teachers. They much prefer a relevant story or metaphor from literature to a story about your last Thanksgiving dinner.

Joseph said to the people, "Now I have bought you and your land for the king. So I will give you seed. And you can plant your fields." —Genesis 47:23 (NCV)

Scripture: *Genesis 47*

    Treasure Island by Robert Louis Stevenson is one of the books most loved by American youth. It is a marvelous tale of buried treasure, sword fights, and angry pirates. But it is also the story of a young man—named Jim Hawkins—who takes a stand for truth. I like Stevenson's novels because they have a moral vision—the main characters always manifest Judeo-Christian values, and the bad guys always lose! In our Bible story today, Joseph, betrayed by his brothers, has forgiven all. He is a man who overcomes substantial obstacles to take a stand for God. He has a moral vision that saves his family and all of Egypt!

Analyze your moral vision. What is most important to you? Money? Fame? Good grades? Glorifying the Lord? Think about it.

Devotional Journal

Read/Vocabulary Cards

Vocabulary

Define italicized words from context:
A. I would see him in a thousand forms, and with a thousand *diabolical* expressions.
B. And altogether I paid pretty dear for my monthly fourpenny piece, in the shape of these *abominable* fancies. (from *Treasure Island* by Robert Louis Stevenson)

Solve

A. According to the line at right, identify the statements as true or false.
1. A = G
2. A > C
3. C > B
4. C + E = 0
5. F > C
6. A > G

-3	-2	-1	0	1	2	3
A	B	C	D	E	F	G

B. Write 8.75 X 105 without exponents.

At the very moment when American culture is clearly not providing the emotional, intellectual, and spiritual support that people need, and not making sense out of life, will you retreat? Or will you show our nation that Christ is the answer? Doing your best on the SAT is one avenue God has before you to prepare to be the kind of Christian who will change your world no matter what the obstacles!

Taking a Stand II

He said, "Look! I see heaven open. And I see the Son of Man standing at God's right side!"
—Acts 7:56 (NCV)

Scripture: Acts 7:54-60

In a time when it is easy to be a Christian, it is helpful to remember that at one time it was not easy at all. Christians were slaughtered by the thousands in early Church history. And thousands of others throughout history have joined them. A helpful resource on this topic is *Foxe's Book of Martyrs* by John Foxe. I highly recommend it! One of the earliest martyrs was Stephen. Stephen, full of the Holy Spirit, took a stand for Christ that he knew would one day end his life. He did it anyway.

How far are you willing to go to obey God? Is there a limit to your obedience? Would you die for Him?

Devotional Journal

Read/Vocabulary Cards

Vocabulary

Define italicized words from context:
  A. He lingered all day, breathing loudly like the old buccaneer at home in his *apoplectic* fit.
  B. …the little patch of sand inside the *palisade* ablaze with midday sun, I began to get another thought into my head. (from *Treasure Island* by Robert Louis Stevenson)

Grammar

Which sentence is better?
  A. The five-foot tall boy in the center of the field skillfully kicked the black and white soccer ball.
  B. In the center of the field, the five-foot-tall boy with much skill kicked the soccer ball that was black and white.

Solve

  A. Mary put $10,000 in the bank for 2.5 years at 8% simple interest. How much money did she get when she withdrew the money?
  B. Complete the table at right.

Fraction	Decimal	Percent
¾		
	.37	
		66⅔%

The SAT verbal exam is essentially a vocabulary exam. I want to tell you as plainly and forcefully as I can: If you do not consciously, deliberately increase your vocabulary base, you will not do well on the SAT I verbal exam.

Forgive the sins we have done, just as we have forgiven those who did wrong to us.
—Matthew 6:12 (NCV)

Scripture: Matthew 6:9-13

One of the most powerful books I have read is *Words by Heart* by Ouida Sebestyen. It is a metaphor for Matthew 6. This is the story of Lena and her father. Lena is a young, bright African-American who lived in the South at the turn of the century. Lena's precocious manners cause her to lose everything she loves…but will she forgive?

What is racism? Have you ever shown prejudice toward others?

Devotional Journal

Read/Vocabulary Cards

Critical Thinking: Main Idea

A. In two or three sentences, give the main idea of the following passage.
B. In one sentence give the main idea of the passage.

> The deceased theologian Henri Nouwen in his work *The Wounded Healer* makes some bold assertions: He argues that being wounded is not a sign of weakness. "We live in a society in which loneliness has become one of the most painful human wounds," he argues. "The growing competition and rivalry which pervade our lives…have created in us an acute awareness of our isolation." Therefore, we Christians, should not be afraid of brokenness. It makes us useful for the kingdom. It helps us speak with legitimacy to the deep loneliness and pain so prevalent in our world. Nouwen continues by suggesting that we are called upon to recognize the sufferings of our time in our own hearts and make that recognition the starting point of our service. This leads to great risk that the Emmaus Road travelers—as well as you and I—find quite threatening. We must learn to live with the same wounds and sufferings as others, and nobody likes that. Having to do without food and sleeping on the ground, as well as being persecuted by the Pharisees, was one thing with Christ alive; facing the same things now that He was dead was another thing altogether. The thought was unthinkable.

The main idea of a paragraph is a summary of what the paragraph is saying.

C. For each question following this section, select the best answer from the choices given.

> Dear Son: I have ever had pleasure in obtaining any little anecdotes of my ancestors. You may remember the inquiries I made among the remains of my relations when you were with me in England, and the journey I undertook for that purpose. Imagining it may be equally agreeable to you to know the circumstances of my life, many of which you are yet unacquainted with, and expecting the enjoyment of a week's uninterrupted leisure in my present country retirement, I sit down to write them for you. To which I have besides some other inducements. Having emerged from the poverty and obscurity in which I was born and bred, to a state of affluence and some degree of reputation in the world, and having gone so far

Lesson continues on the next page.

through life with a considerable share of felicity, the conducing means I made use of, which with the blessing of God so well succeeded, my posterity may like to know, as they may find some of them suitable to their own situations, and therefore fit to be imitated. That felicity, when I reflected on it, has induced me sometimes to say, that were it offered to my choice, I should have no objection to a repetition of the same life from its beginning, only asking the advantages authors have in a second edition to correct some faults of the first. So I might, besides correcting the faults, change some sinister accidents and events of it for others more favorable. But though this were denied, I should still accept the offer. Since such a repetition is not to be expected, the next thing most like living one's life over again seems to be a recollection of that life, and to make that recollection as durable as possible by putting it down in writing. Hereby, too, I shall indulge the inclination so natural in old men, to be talking of themselves and their own past actions; and I shall indulge it without being tiresome to others, who, through respect to age, might conceive themselves obliged to give me a hearing, since this may be read or not as any one pleases. And, lastly (I may as well confess it, since my denial of it will be believed by nobody), perhaps I shall a good deal gratify my own vanity. Indeed, I scarce ever heard or saw the introductory words, "Without vanity I may say," but some vain thing immediately followed. Most people dislike vanity in others, whatever share they have of it themselves; but I give it fair quarter wherever I meet with it, being persuaded that it is often productive of good to the possessor, and to others that are within his sphere of action; and therefore, in many cases, it would not be altogether absurd if a man were to thank God for his vanity among the other comforts of life (*The Autobiography of Ben Franklin*, Benjamin Franklin).

I. Franklin is telling his son details about his life
   A. because Franklin feels that it would interest him and Franklin wanted to use his own life as an example of how a person could rise from poverty to riches.
   B. because Franklin will soon die and he wants to leave a written legacy with his son.
   C. Franklin wants to feel the pleasure of remembering his relatives.

II. How does Franklin use the word felicity?
   A. loyalty
   B. courage
   C. happiness
   D. dissatisfaction

III. This passage implies that Franklin's life has a paradox. What is it?
   A. The humble Franklin is forced in his old age to admit that he made many mistakes.
   B. Franklin notes that honest appraisal of life's events coupled with humility is not vanity; but if it is, it is appropriate in this case.
   C. Franklin was unable to accomplish as much in his life as he wished to accomplish.
   D. Franklin was nothing like what people thought he was.

Solve

Which is larger?
   A. ⅔ or 65%
   B. 0.02 or 0.008

Then he asked Jesse, "Are these all the sons you have?" Jesse answered, "I still have the youngest son. He is out taking care of the sheep." —1 Samuel 16:11 (NCV)

Scripture: *1 Samuel 16:7-13*

Samuel is in search of a king. He examines all of Jesse's boys. What an impressive group! But not God's anointed...so he asks if there are any more sons. There is—David, the little shepherd boy. Folklore and tradition tell us that David was a very short, handsome boy. He was a young man of God who knew how to pray, how to sing praises unto God. A faithful, trustworthy young man. A boy who obeyed God. It was more than enough to commend David to the Lord!

How are you in the area of obedience? A place to begin is in the area of obedience to your parents or guardians. Do you willingly, gladly, obey them? Why or why not? God commands you to do so. Think about it.

Devotional Journal

Read/Vocabulary Cards

Vocabulary

Kim by Rudyard Kipling is the story of a small boy, an unlikely hero who, like David, is called to a great task. Raised by an Indian woman, Kim is an orphaned Irish boy who becomes a secret agent. You will love the story!

Define italicized words in context:

> The old lady explained to Kim, in a tense, indignant whisper, precisely what manner and fashion of *malignant* liar he was. Had Kim hinted this when she was a girl, he would have been *pommelled* to death that same evening by an elephant. (from *Kim* by Rudyard Kipling)

Lesson continues on the next page.

Critical Thinking: Summary

Summarize the following passage.

A branch cut off from the adjacent branch must of necessity be cut off from the whole tree also. So too a man when he is separated from another man has fallen off from the whole social community. Now as to a branch, another cuts it off, but a man by his own act separates himself from his neighbor when he hates him and turns away from him, and he does not know that he has at the same time cut himself off from the whole social system. Yet he has this privilege certainly from Zeus who framed society, for it is in our power to grow again to that which is near to us, and again to become a part which helps to make up the whole. However, if it often happens, this kind of separation, it makes it difficult for that which detaches itself to be brought to unity and to be restored to its former condition. Finally, the branch, which from the first grew together with the tree, and has continued to have one life with it, is not like that which after being cut off is then ingrafted, for this is something like what the gardeners mean when they say that it grows with the rest of the tree, but that it has not the same mind with it (*Meditations*, Marcus Aurelius).

Solve

Find x

    A. 4x = 12
    B. 5x - 2 = 13
    C. 7x - 0 = 14

So Mephibosheth ate at David's table like one of the king's sons. —2 Samuel 9:11

Scripture: *2 Samuel 9*

The Miracle Worker by William Gibson is one of the most beautiful and profound dramas of our time. This is the inspiring story of physically challenged Helen Keller and her teacher, Anne Sullivan—the miracle worker. A physically challenged person we meet in Scripture is Mephibosheth, the grandson of King Saul. When Mephibosheth was young, his nurse dropped him and he was permanently crippled (2 Samuel 4). Later, when David discovered his existence, Mephibosheth was honored as if he were a son of David.

Helen Keller

Are you, or do you know anyone, physically or mentally challenged? Do you treat them as children of God?

Devotional Journal

Read/Vocabulary Cards

Review your vocabulary cards with your parents or guardian.

Critical Thinking: Comparison

Science gone awry is a common theme in modern literature. Compare the way Mary Shelley in *Frankenstein* develops this theme with the way Robert L. Stevenson does in *Dr. Jekyll and Mr. Hyde.*

Solve

A. ab^2c^3 if a = 3, b = 4, c = 2
B. Write 4,500,000 in scientific notation.

Long reading-comprehension passages are common on the SAT.

An American Hero

Fight the good fight of the faith. Take hold of the eternal life to which you were called when you made your confession in the presence of many witnesses. —1 Timothy 6:12

Scripture: I Timothy 6:11-16

Recently, young people were asked to rate the most important people in the world. Only one true hero—Billy Graham—appeared in the top ten. Really! Popular singers were perceived as being more important than a man who has led millions to Christ! Where have all the heroes gone? A genuine hero is the apostle Paul. Full of courage, strong, a man of integrity, Paul was a man who walked his talk. Now, in this passage of Scripture, he is giving some departing advice to the young pastor Timothy.

On a piece of paper, list the top ten most important people you know. I do not necessarily mean the people you see in the headlines—I mean the top ten people God has used to influence your life.

Devotional Journal

Read/Vocabulary Cards

Vocabulary

Before there was a Davy Crockett or an Annie Oakley, there was Hawkeye. James Fenimore Cooper, in *The Last of the Mohicans*, continues the story of the memorable frontier scout Hawkeye. Honorable, honest, hard-working, unpretentious Hawkeye was considerably different from many of today's "heroes."

Define italicized words:

> When they rejoined the expecting and anxious females, he briefly acquainted them with the conditions of their new guide, and with the necessity that existed for their hushing every *apprehension*, in instant and serious *exertions*. (from *The Last of the Mohicans* by James Fenimore Cooper)

Critical Thinking: Summary

Restate the above paragraph taken from The Last of the Mohicans in your own words.

Grammar

Correct the following sentence.
> The house has been made a national landmark where Abraham Lincoln was born.

Solve

$3w - 4 = 5w + 7$

Do you know that you are penalized for incorrect answers on the SAT? For every correct answer, you receive one point. For a blank answer, you receive zero points. For an incorrect answer, however, you lose a fraction of a point—either $1/4$ or $1/3$ of a point depending on the number of answer choices. Therefore, it is best not to guess unless you can eliminate one or two of the answer choices.

Deliver Us

And lead us not into temptation, but deliver us from the evil one. —Matthew 6:13

Scripture: Matthew 6:9-13

If you asked me, when I was an eight-year-old, what my favorite holiday was, I would have enthusiastically proclaimed: "Halloween!" Haunted houses, costumes, candy—it all captured my imagination. Since I gave my heart to Christ—twenty-five years ago—I have grown increasingly uncomfortable with Halloween. It is anything but Christian. In fact, Halloween is a celebration of death.

The origins and traditions of Halloween can be traced back thousands of years to the Druids, a pagan tribe in the British Isles who regularly practiced human sacrifice. The eve of October 31 marked the transition from summer into the darkness of winter. They believed that on this night, the spirits of the dead rose up. Demons, fairies, and ghouls roamed about the town. They destroyed crops, killed cattle, soured milk, and generally made life miserable, unless an appropriate appeasement was offered—a human sacrifice. So, anticipating these goblins, on October 31, Druid towns chose young maidens and sacrificed them in honor of the pagan gods. I hate to be such a killjoy, but Halloween is not funny, it is not harmless. This is not the same as having a Christmas tree, or believing in the Easter Bunny—Halloween is a celebration of death, destruction, and hell. Matthew invites us to pray from deliverance for the evil one. Jesus Christ is the way, the truth, and the life. He is hope and mercy and love—not death, destruction, and murder.

Do you agree? Why or why not?

Devotional Journal

Read/Vocabulary Cards

Critical Thinking: Analysis

Delineate the arguments I offer in the previous paragraph. Analyze these arguments, and offer a counter-argument.

Critical Reading

In this part of our journey I had many thoughts on the different circumstances of Friends [Quakers] who inhabit Pennsylvania and Jersey from those who dwell in Maryland, Virginia, and Carolina. Pennsylvania and New Jersey were settled by Friends who were convinced of our principles in England in times of suffering; these, coming over, bought lands of the natives, and applied to husbandry in a peaceable way, and many of their children were taught to labor for their living. Few of these, I believe, settled in any of the southern provinces; but by the faithful labors of traveling Friends in early times there was considerable convincement among the inhabitants of these parts. I also remembered having read of the warlike disposition of many of the first settlers in those provinces, and of their

The SAT I does not measure motivation, creativity, or special talents (even though these qualities will contribute to your success in college and throughout life). Nor does it measure spiritual maturity. The SAT most certainly does not measure your worth or potential as a human being. It can help you and colleges better understand how you compare with other students preparing for college. It is a fairly accurate predictor of college performance.

Lesson continues on the next page.

numerous engagements with the natives in which much blood was shed even in the infancy of the colonies. Some of the people inhabiting those places, being grounded in customs contrary to the pure truth, were affected with the powerful preaching of the Word of Life and joined in fellowship with our Society, and in so doing they had a great work to go through. In the history of the reformation from Popery [Roman Catholicism] it is observable that the progress was gradual from age to age. The uprightness of the first reformers in attending to the light and understanding given to them opened the way for sincere-hearted people to proceed further afterwards; and thus each one truly fearing God and laboring in the works of righteousness appointed for him in his day findeth acceptance with Him. Through the darkness of the times and the corruption of manners and customs, some upright men may have had little more for their day's work than to attend to the righteous principle in their minds as it related to their own conduct in life without pointing out to others the whole extent of that into which the same principle would lead succeeding ages. Thus, for instance, among an imperious, warlike people, supported by oppressed slaves, some of these masters, I suppose, are awakened to feel and to see their error, and through sincere repentance cease from oppression and become like fathers to their servants, showing by their example a pattern of humility in living, and moderation in governing, for the instruction and admonition of their oppressing neighbors; these, without carrying the reformation further, have, I believe, found acceptance with the Lord. Such was the beginning; and those who succeeded them, and who faithfully attended to the nature and spirit of the reformation, have seen the necessity of proceeding forward, and have not only to instruct others by their own example in governing well, but have also to use means to prevent their successors from having so much power to oppress others (*The Journal of John Woolman*, John Woolman).

John Woolman, an eighteenth century Quaker, argues that Carolina Quakers were poor laborers because

    A. the warmer climate encouraged laziness.

    B. the religious persecution of Quakers encouraged unhealthy intolerance.

    C. they had participated in anti-Quaker activities such as warfare and slavery and, as a result, had weakened the very heart of Reformation Quakerism.

    D. they were mostly Roman Catholic.

Solve

    A. $3w + 2 - w + 4 = -5 - w - 4$

    B. How far can a car drive in 4 hours if it is moving at 65 mph?

Jesus answered, "I am the way and the truth and the life. No one comes to the Father except through me." —John 14:6

Scripture: John 14:1-14

The Christian teacher Tony Campolo argues that we confuse the spiritual with the material. He argues that there is a tendency to satisfy our spiritual needs by materialistic means. But it cannot be. Although product advertisements promise us happiness and fulfillment, they will not deliver. Coca Cola may have promoted itself as the "real thing" and wanted to teach the world to sing in perfect harmony, but it won't happen until the world learns to trust Jesus Christ as its Savior and live accordingly.

Is Jesus Christ your Lord and Savior?

Devotional Journal

Read/Vocabulary Cards

Sentence Completion

If you liked *Ben-Hur* the movie, you will love *Ben-Hur* the book (by Lew Wallace). Set in the time of Christ, this is the inimitable and powerful story of a man whose unquenchable desire for vengeance on the man (and the Empire) who caused the destruction of his home, the disappearance of his mother and sister, and his own enslavement, eventually propels him to the foot of the Cross.

Choose the best words for this sentence taken from Ben-Hur:

These thoughts, as they passed, in nowise _____ the growing respect for the merchant of which he was each instant more and more conscious. A(n) _____ of our admiration for another is that it is always looking for circumstances to justify itself.

A. militated…assurance
B. disturbed…peculiarity
C. soothed…oddity

> Sentence completions are sentences from which one or two key words have been removed. You are asked to choose the best word(s) for the sentence.

Solve

A. 0.50 of 86 is what number?
B. What fraction of 90 is 30?
C. 0.25 of what number is 50?
D. What is the area of this figure?

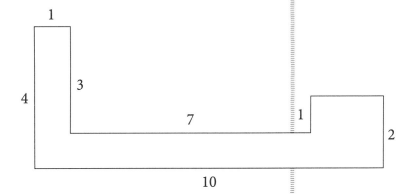

Measurements are in feet.

Lesson continues on the next page.

Critical Thinking: Essay

Cause and Effect Essay

Cause and effect essays will the causes of some event that you always took for granted or chronicle the effects of some phenomenon in society or nature. The writer should consider whether you will explore causes or effects or both and what is the order of the causes or effects you will pursue—from least to most important or vice versa.

You will have to determine which causes or effects you write about. If there are too many causes for you to deal with in your essay, you must decide what are the main causes and then suggest to your reader that there are other, relatively minor, causes.

To conclude your essay, it might be enough to point out causes or effects that people might not have thought of before, or to present them with fresh insight or in a newly organized fashion. On the other hand, your essay might lead to action based on patterns of cause and effect that you have presented.

Write an essay discussing the effect of the automobile on American society.

Sentence completions are sentences from which one or two key words have been removed. You are asked to choose the best word(s) for the sentence.

The Sacrifice

For God so loved the world that he gave his one and only son, that whoever believes in him shall not perish but have eternal life. —John 3:16

Scripture: John 3:16

The pastor/professor John Killinger tells a story about a movie he saw entitled *The Bridge,* about a loving father who has a son. We see the father going off to his job as the switchman for a railroad line. Part of the line lies over a river, and must be kept back most of the time for the boats to pass. It is his job to wait until the last moment, and then pull the switch that will swing the bridge into place before the thundering approach of the train. We, the viewers of the film, see what the father does not see: His little son has followed him down to the river and is coming across the bridge. As the train whistle blows to signal its speeding approach, the father sees his son standing on the bridge! If he closes the track the boy will die. We watch the agony on his face. He loves his son more than anything in his life. But finally he pulls the lever and the bridge locks into place. We see the people on the train laughing and having a good time as the train races across the bridge. They do not know how narrowly they have avoided disaster—or what it has cost the switchman. That is what God has done for us on the cross. And so we continue laughing in the night.

List several things for which you are grateful.

Devotional Journal

Read/Vocabulary Cards

Sentence Completion

Choose the best word to complete this sentence taken from Charles Dickens' *A Tale of Two Cities*—a story of unselfish sacrifice:

> Every living creature there [in Saint Antoine Prison] held life as of no account and was _____ with a passionate readiness to sacrifice it.

A. subdued
B. uncomfortable
C. unhappy
D. demented

When you fill in sentence completion test items use contextual and structural clues.

Lesson continues on the next page.

Critical Thinking: Analysis

The following are charts examining European and other immigration from 1861-1930 (U.S. Bureau of the Census). What can you conclude from these charts?

Period	Total Immigrants Admitted	Northern and Western Europe		Southern and Eastern Europe	
1861-70	2,314,824	2,031,624	87.4%	33,628	1.4%
1871-80	2,812,191	2,070,373	73.6%	201,889	7.2%
1881-90	5,246,613	3,778,633	72.0%	958,413	18.3%
1891-1900	3,687,564	1,643,492	44.6%	1,915,486	51.9%
1901-10	8,795,386	1,910,035	21.7%	6,225,486	51.9%
1911-20	5,735,811	997,438	17.4%	3,379,126	58.9%
1920-30	4,107,209	1,284,023	31.3%	1,193,830	29.0%

A. The same percentage of northern and western Europeans immigrated 1861-70 as southern and eastern Europeans immigrated 1911-20.

B. More northern and western Europeans immigrated 1861-1930 than southern and eastern Europeans in the same period.

C. Immigration from southern and eastern Europe was never more than 50% of total immigration.

D. All of the above.

E. None of the above.

F. A and B

G. A and C

Solve

The sum of twice a number and 14 is 76. What is the number?

This is how God showed his love among us: He sent his one and only Son into the world that we might live through him. —1 John 4:9

Scripture: *1 John 4:9-10*

Sir Thomas More, the Bishop of Canterbury, once defied a king to stake his hope in a God of love and mercy. King Henry VIII of England tried—in vain—to destroy Sir Thomas' loyalty to God. So, he killed him. But he could not kill his spirit. Robert Bolt, in his famous play *A Man for All Seasons*, explores the faith of Sir Thomas. At one point in the play Margaret, More's wife, argues with him about giving into the king's demands to follow the king rather than his faith. She knows that if More refuses, he will surely die. "But in reason," Margaret pleads, "haven't you done as much as God can reasonably want?" "Well," More gently responds, "finally, it isn't a matter of reason; finally it's a matter of love."

Can you think of any cause for which you would die?

Devotional Journal

Read/Vocabulary Cards

Critical Reading

A. Read the following passage from Augustine's Confession and answer the following question.

> I would lay open before my God that nine-and-twentieth year of mine age. There had then come to Carthage a certain Bishop of the Manichees, Faustus by name, a great snare of the Devil, and many were entangled by him through that lure of his smooth language: which though I did not commend, yet could I separate from the truth of the things which I was earnest to learn: nor do I so much regard the service of oratory as the science which this Faustus, so praised among them, set before me to feed upon. Fame had before be-spoken him most knowing in all valuable learning, and exquisitely skilled in the liberal sciences. And since I had read and well remembered much of the philosophers, I compared some things of theirs with those long fables of the Manichees, and found the former the more probable; even although they could only prevail so far as to make judgment of this lower world, the Lord of it they could by no means find out. For Thou art great, O Lord, and has respect unto the humble, but the proud Thou beholdest afar off. Nor dost thou *draw near*, but to the contrite in heart, nor art found by the proud, no, not though by curious skill they could number the stars and the sand, and measure the starry heavens, and track the courses of the planets (*Confessions*, Augustine).

The only way to be foolishly happy in this world is to be young enough, well enough, and have money enough—and not give a care about other people. But as soon as you don't have any of the first three, or if you have compassion for the weeping world around you, then it is impossible to have the foolish kind of happiness that I believe some Christians present as Christianity.
—Francis Schaeffer

Lesson continues on the next page.

The best thesis for this passage would be:
   A. Faustus, a snare of Satan to many, made an instrument of deliverance to St. Augustine.
   B. The faith of a mother drives Augustine to God.
   C. The conversion of Augustine comes so quickly.
   D. The heresy of the Manichees causes Augustine to reject his faith.

   B. George Marsden in his book *The Soul of the American University* seeks to explain why American academic life excludes religion. He argues that because the reasons for this exclusion are not valid, there should be more room for the free exercise of religion in higher learning. Initially, the relegation of religion to the periphery of American universities was justified on enlightenment grounds. Today, however, few believe in pure scientific objectivity and understand that all intellectual inquiry takes place in a framework of presuppositions and moral commitments. We find today the university in a moral crisis. Tolerance and diversity are the prevailing values, but there is no longer any standard by which limits can be placed on tolerance.

In your own words summarize Dr. Marsden's argument.

Grammar

Correct the following sentence.

   The <u>boys or Jane are</u> going to the store.

   A. boys or Jane is
   B. boy nor Jane are
   C. boys and Jane is
   D. boy and Jane is
   E. No error.

Solve

Four times a number decreased by 8 equals 92. Find the number.

Love's Choices

I lay it down of my own accord. —John 10:18

Scripture: *John 10*

A train pulls into Auschwitz concentration camp during World War II. Even before the steam has ceased hissing from the engine, the hapless victims are being unloaded. An SS captain stands erect with two ominous police dogs at his side. A motion with his right hand to the right means life in the work camp nearby, called Birkenau. A motion with his left hand means instant death in the gas chambers. The Jews knew what was up—no one could ignore the ominous smoke billowing from the stacks of the crematorium, and the awful stench of flesh burning was unavoidable. Yet, no one could move. Everyone hoped to be motioned to the right—the effort of escape should at least be postponed until one saw to which side he would be sent. The line moved ever so slowly. Right, right, and then a whole series of people were sent left. A couple was perceivably nervous as the line moved closer to the captain. The persons ahead of them were sent to the right. They felt hope! And, then, the horror of hopelessness hit them. The woman was sent to the right and the man to the left. Suddenly a man, a prisoner, approached the captain. He interjected, "Excuse me, Herr Captain, but may I take the place of the young man you are sending to the left? I am a broken, unhealthy, man. He is strong. Wouldn't it be better if he lived and I died?" The young man was spared. The prisoner was gassed. Recently, the man and his bride, now old people, attended a ceremony where the prisoner, a priest, was honored.

Create a list of people who regularly sacrifice themselves to make sure you are safe, warm, and healthy.

Devotional Journal

Read/Vocabulary Cards

Vocabulary

Billy Budd by Herman Melville is a disturbing story of a young man who dies unjustly yet somehow is able to forgive his captors before his death. Define these words:

    A. auspicious
    B. innate
    C. felonious

Solve

    A. Twice a number is 42 less than -102. What is it?
    B. Five times a number is 21 less than twice the opposite of the number. What is the number?

> To solve word problems, look for statements in the problems that describe equal quantities. Then use algebraic phrases to write equations to express the problem.

20 To Love or to Hate

I lay down my life for the sheep....No one takes it from me, but I lay it down of my own accord. —John 10:15,18

Scripture: John 10

A sixteen-year-old boy who lives in West-bury, Long Island, was picked up by the police several years ago for defacing a synagogue. It seems that the boy went on a Halloween spree with some friends. They sprayed obscenities on the front door of the synagogue. The young man, a Christian, was caught. He was fined $150 and ordered to give one hundred hours of service to his hometown church. His parents publically deplored what their son had done. Their pain drew letters of understanding support from people near and far. But most touching of all was a letter that had to do with court costs and expenses of legal counsel. The family incurred a debt of $1000 to defend their son. They were finding it hard to come up with the money. One day a letter arrived. It contained a check for $1000. It was from a Jewish lawyer in Manhattan. We consciously, deliberately, choose to love or to hate; love is not something that we unconsciously wander into.

Purpose this week to love someone who has harmed or offended you.

Devotional Journal

Read/Vocabulary Cards

Critical Thinking: Comparison

The Killer Angels by Michael Shaara and *The Red Badge of Courage* by Stephen Crane are both fictional accounts of the Civil War. Shaara's book, however, is historical fiction—a fictional account of a real event—the Battle of Gettysburg. Stephen's book is merely a fictional account of one imaginary battle whose main purpose is to describe his vision of life.

Take an incident from your life and write about it. Then write it again as a fictionalized account. This would be historical fiction—a fictionalized account of an actual event. How are they different?

Critical Thinking: Essay

Write a cause and effect essay about global warming.

I will come back. Then I will take you to be with me so that you may be where I am.
—John 14:3 (NCV)

Scripture: John 14:1-5

Thomas has an obsession to know. But the simple truth is, Jesus never offers knowledge. He offers a revelation of truth. Instead of offering an advanced briefing, Jesus says, "I will come back...." Your hope, then, is never in knowledge, or performance, but rather in the promise of divine companionship. Your hope is not based upon control, but on relationship with the One who controls. On the faithful basis of God's past faithfulness you are able to rest assured that what you need in the future will be there just like it was yesterday. During this course you will concentrate on preparing for the SAT. But never forget that true worth comes not by *what* you know—or how well you do on the SAT—but *Who* you know!

Of what are you most proud? What makes you feel secure?

Devotional Journal

Read/Vocabulary Cards

Critical Thinking: Analysis

From the data presented in the graph, what is true?

- A. The largest number of states choosing electors was in 1800.
- B. The smallest number of states choosing electors was in 1824.
- C. If the present percent of decline continued, no electors were chosen by 1860.
- D. All of above
- E. None of above
- F. A and C
- G. A and B
- H. C and B

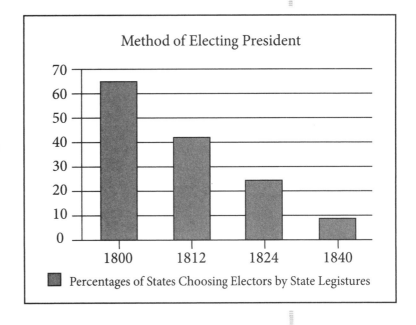

Method of Electing President

Percentages of States Choosing Electors by State Legistures

Solve

- A. The odometer of a new automobile functions improperly and registers only 2 miles for every 3 miles driven. If the odometer indicates 48 miles, how many miles has the automobile actually been driven?
- B. If a man is driving 60 miles/hour for 2 days, 8 hours/day, how far did he go?

I purposely use challenging vocabulary words in the devotion. Will you look up the words that you do not know?

TIP
The Math Section

Over the last 30 years I perceive two trends in the SAT I Math Section:

1. The number of word problems is increasing.

2. The computation, generally speaking, has gotten easier.

To that end I have discovered that students who read well, generally score high. For example, I have observed that debate students in particular do well on the math section. Why? I conclude that debate students are better readers.

SAT includes general mathematics, geometry, and algebra. Calculus and trigonometry are not tested on the math section. Topics include probability, statistics, exponential growth, absolute value, and functional notation. It also places emphasis on geometric problems (but no proofs and formulas are provided). Important skills such as estimation and number sense are standard fare.

You may use a four-function, scientific, or graphing calculator, although it's still possible to solve every question without a calculator. I recommend that you use a calculator sparingly. Calculations generated by calculators take precious time. Besides surely you know the product of five and four without a calculator's help!

Test-taking tips:

1. Watch your time. Do not spend too much time on one question. Answer the easy questions first. Come back later and answer more difficult questions.
2. Remember: questions are arranged from easy to difficult. I would like to see you get the first ten correct.
3. Look for obvious clues. For example, you know that the answer is between 10 and 15. Eliminate all other answers.
4. Write in the test booklet! This is your only scrap paper.
5. Initially skip questions with multiple answers like this: I only, II only, III only, I and II only, I, II, and III. Only answer these questions if you have time.
6. As a last resort, if you have time, use backsolving--try each answer choice in the problem and see if it works.

Jesus answered, "I am the way. And I am the truth and the life. The only way to the Father is through me." —John 14:6 (NCV)

Scripture: John 14:6

One of the most basic human needs we have is the need to know the future. We spend billions trying to predict it and then to control it. But that, of course, is not possible. Thomas said to Christ, "Lord, we do not know where you are going; so how can we know the way to get there?" (John 14:5). We all would have been very pleased if Christ had answered that question. We like to know what we face. That is the genius in the McDonald Corporation—however we might feel about the Big Mac, we prefer the known and predictable over the unknown and unpredictable. The Holiday Inns lure travelers to their motels with the promise, "No surprises." Jesus never told Thomas his future…or did He? "…I am the Way, the Truth, and the Life.…"

Write a one sentence goal for your life. How will you attain this goal?

Devotional Journal

Read/Vocabulary Cards

Vocabulary

"Although I am not *disposed* to maintain that being born in a workhouse is in itself the most fortunate and *enviable* circumstance that can possibly befall a human being…" (from *Oliver Twist* by Charles Dickens, a story of a boy struggling with poverty and despair in Victorian England).

Do you know what the words enviable and disposed mean? Use each of them in another sentence.
Define them. Check your definition against the dictionary definition. If you do not know them, add them to your vocabulary cards.

Grammar

Choose the sentence(s) that are incorrect.
1. It's me!
2. I am running, dancing, and praising God!
3. Who were you speaking to?
4. Running the gauntlet, the tepee was in front of the brave warrior.
   A. All
   B. None
   C. 1, 3, 4
   D. 2 and 4

SAT vocabulary words are not part of most speaking vocabularies. Therefore, you must consciously make them part of your repertoire. Include them in your dinner conversation.

Solve

What is a five-letter word in which you take away two letters and have one?

Dare to Be Daniel

Every time the king asked them about something important, they showed much wisdom and understanding. —Daniel 1:20 (NCV)

Scripture: *Daniel 1:17-20*

Daniel is a prisoner. He also gives the king advice. He is in Babylon—but he is no Babylonian. God is using Babylon to make Daniel more effective for Him. For you, preparation for the SAT represents a time of "training in Babylon." The SAT is not a "Christian" test. It is no measure of your worth. Yet, to bring glory to God, to be all that you can be, you want to do your very best. Like Daniel.

How can you prosper in Babylon without becoming Babylonian?

Devotional Journal

Read/Vocabulary Cards

Solve

Art had $2, but he needed $3 for his cab fare home. Undaunted, he went to a pawn shop and pawned his $2 for $1.50. Art saw Duncan and told him that he would sell him his $2 pawn ticket for $1.50. Duncan agreed. Because Art started out with $2, and he ended up with $3, who lost money? (MindTrap®)

Critical Reading

G. Campbell Morgan was riding with Dwight L. Moody, when suddenly Moody asked, "What is character anyway?" Moody answered his own question. "Character," Moody said, "is what a person does in the dark."

Answer a question on the following passage.

He had also a very good and noble appearance; his beard was well grown, his forehead large, and his nose aquiline, giving him altogether a bold, masculine look, that reminded people of the faces of Hercules in paintings and sculptures. It was, moreover, an ancient tradition, that the Antonys were descended from Hercules, by a son of his called Anton; and this opinion he thought to give credit to, by the similarity of his person just mentioned, and also by the fashion of his dress. For, whenever he had to appear before large numbers, he wore his tunic girt low about the hips, a broadsword on his side, and over all a large, coarse mantle. What might seem to some very insupportable, his vaunting, his raillery, his drinking in public, sitting down by the men as they were taking their food, and eating, as he stood, off the common soldiers' tables, made him the delight and pleasure of the army. In love affairs, also, he was very agreeable; he gained many friends by the assistance he gave them in theirs, and took other people's raillery upon his own with good-humor. And his generous ways, his open and lavish hand in gifts and favors to his friends and fellow-soldiers, did a great deal for him in his first advance to power, and, after he had become great, long maintained his fortunes, when a thousand follies were hastening their overthrow. One instance of his liberality I must relate. He had ordered payment to one of his friends of twenty-five myriads of money, or *decies*, as the Romans call it, and his steward, wondering at the extravagance of the sum, laid all the silver in a heap, as he should pass by. Antony, seeing the heap, asked what it meant; his steward replied, "The money you have ordered to be given to your friend." So, perceiving the man's malice, said he, "I thought the *decies* had been much more; 'tis too little; let it be doubled." This, however, was at a later time (*Lives*, Plutarch).

Plutarch would characterize Antony as a man
    A. who was flawed, even surly at times, but his generous nature caused many to forgive his excesses.
    B. who was a ruthless, hateful man who held grudges.
    C. who was a complicated man, both dishonest and honest, depending on the circumstance.
    D. who was a noble Roman, without guile or evil.

The Mountain Called Obedience

Take your only son, Isaac, the son you love. Go to the land of Moriah.
—Genesis 22:2 (NCV)

Scripture: Genesis 22:1-14

Abraham was called by God into the Promised Land. And he went. It was not as nice a place as Ur, but he went. He was promised many descendants. Then he waited—even into his nineties. And God gave him a son…but then he was sent to Mt. Moriah, the place of sacrifice. God asks for everything from us, and when we think we've given all, He asks for more. This year of SAT preparation is a real challenge. But I am asking you, child of God, to come to Mt. Moriah and to meet a God who demands everything.

How much does your God demand of you? What is your bottom line? Is there anything He might ask of you that you would be hesitant to give?

Devotional Journal

Read/Vocabulary Cards

Solve

A. Six is ⅓ of what number?
B. What is 25% of 24?
C. At 65 mph how far will the car travel in 6 hours?
D. $(-7) - (-9) =$

Critical Thinking: Essay

Pretend that your brother is borrowing your toothbrush. In 75 words, discuss the problem and the solution to this problem.

Memorize

Preparing for college and the SAT is more than learning facts and test-taking tips. It is about preparing for life. Learning and memorizing the Word of God will help on the SAT in the same ways that God's Word brings comfort, joy, peace, etc. in other areas of your life.

Find two verses that inspire you and memorize them.

Suggested Scripture verses include: Galatians 6:7-8; Philippians 1:11, 2:13, 3:12-14; Ephesians 1:13-14; 2 Corinthians 5:17, 9:10; Romans 5:1-5; Romans 8; Luke 8:15. See also Appendix E.

Reading good books is the single best preparation for the SAT.

How to Solve a Problem

1. Stop the action, pray.
2. What does the question ask?
3. Restate the problem.
4. What do I know? What do I need to know?
5. Eliminate the wrong answers. Choose an answer.

They traded the truth of God for a lie. —Romans 1:25 (NCV)

Scripture: *Romans 1:18-25*

Western culture has been influenced greatly by a philosopher named Hegel. Among other things, Hegel argued a notion called "dialecticism." Dialecticism advances a thesis (a position put forward for argument) that truth is fluid. Dialecticism rejects all absolute truth—except the "truth" that there is no absolute truth! Truth is always open to interpretation. Truth lies in the "search" for the truth. Hegelian dialecticism assumes that ultimate truth will never be known. Thus, dialecticism invites compromise. Compromise and dialecticism are not all bad in some issues but in others they can be devastating. Concerning abortion, for instance, there is no room for compromise. Abortion is murder.

Are you willing to stand for what is right even if no one else stands with you?

Devotional Journal

Read/Vocabulary Cards

Meet with your parents or guardians one evening this week. Suggested agenda: prayer, vocabulary check-up, and other sharing. Make this a time to celebrate another week of preparation for the SAT.

Solve

A. A one-foot measuring stick can be divided into how many 1½-inch portions?
B. If ⅜ of a class voted to watch Lassie and ⅜ of the class voted to watch Star Trek, what part of the class did not vote?
C. State the degree of this equation:

$$4X^6 - 27X\_ + 9 =$$

SAT I Practice Test

This weekend, take a practice SAT. Allow about four hours.

…because you did not know the time…. —Luke 19:44 (NCV)

Scripture: *Luke 19:41-44*

Jesus is weeping over Jerusalem. Their time has come—and gone—and they never knew it. The Greeks have a word for this, kairos, which means, "window of opportunity or a decisive moment." We must recognize that these are special times. Jerusalem did not recognize the unique kairos when Jesus came to save it (Luke 19:44), and there was to be no second chance for many in that generation. Young people, God has given you this special moment, this sacred time.

Will you make the most of your time? Name three obstacles to your SAT preparation.

1.

2.

3.

What are you doing about them?

Devotional Journal

Read/Vocabulary Cards

Vocabulary

Define the italicized words in your own words, use them in a sentence, check your definitions, and use these three words in a sentence sometime today.

> Elizabeth-Jane, having now changed her *orbit* from one of gay independence to *laborious* self-help, thought the weather good enough for such declined glory as hers…she went to the boot-room where her patterns had hung ever since her *apotheosis*… (from *The Mayor of Casterbridge* by Thomas Hardy)

Grammar

Where is the grammatical problem?

<u>The disagreement</u> <u>between</u> <u>Mary and she</u> <u>was easily settled.</u>
     (A)   (B)   (C)   (D)
[No error.]
  (E)

The Mayor of Casterbridge is a beautiful book about bad choices being made and penalties being exacted. But, in the end, a repentant soul triumphs.

Be thou my Vision, O Lord of my heart! Nought be all else to me, save that thou art! Thou my best thought, by day or by night, Waking or sleeping, Thy presence my light.
—from the hymn "Be Thou My Vision."

You can throw us into the blazing furnace. The God we serve is able to save us from the furnace and your power....But even if God does not save us, we want you, our king, to know this: We will not serve your gods. —Daniel 3:17,18 (NCV)

Scripture: *Daniel 3:1-30*

It seems that Shadrach, Meshach, and Abednego—three teenage Jewish captives in Babylon—have two choices: either bow down and worship great King Nebuchadnezzar or burn. But there is another choice: to obey God. Now comes one of the most powerful challenges in Scripture, an affirmation so radical, so anti-modern, so brave it defies explanation: "Whether it feels good or not, whether it is convenient, or profitable, or easy to do, we will still obey God. At all costs. Come what may." Wow! The moment you take a stand like this there will be trouble—the Nebuchadnezzars, the Ahabs, the Herods will make it their business to give you trouble.

I know most of you have Jesus Christ as your Savior, but have you purposed in your heart to obey Him at all costs? If you have, what evidence can you offer?

Devotional Journal

Read/Vocabulary Cards

Sentence Completion

Agnostic George Gaylord Simpson, in his book *The Meaning of Evolution* argues that egotistical humankind, created and sustained by human ingenuity and acumen, is the result of a _____ and _____ process that did not have him in mind. We were not planned...the workings of the universe cannot provide any automatic, universal, eternal, or absolute criteria of right and wrong.

    A. positive...negative
    B. purposeless...materialistic
    C. good...bad
    D. laudatory...acclamatory
    E. accidental...deliberate

Solving Sentence Completions

1. Carefully read the sentence.
2. Review the definitions of your choices.
3. Remove obviously wrong answers.
4. What sounds right?
5. Choose the right answer.

Lesson continues on the next page.

Critical Reading

These are the most memorable circumstances recorded in history of Demosthenes and Cicero which have come to our knowledge. But omitting an exact comparison of their respective faculties in speaking, yet thus much seems fit to be said; that Demosthenes, to make himself a master in rhetoric, applied all the faculties he had, natural or acquired, wholly that way; that he far surpassed in force and strength of eloquence all his contemporaries in political and judicial speaking, in grandeur and majesty all the panegyrical orators, and in accuracy and science all the logicians and rhetoricians of his day; that Cicero was highly educated, and by his diligent study became a most accomplished general scholar in all these branches, having left behind him numerous philosophical treatises of his own on Academic principles; as, indeed, even in his written speeches, both political and judicial, we see him continually trying to show his learning by the way. And one may discover the different temper of each of them in their speeches. For Demosthenes' oratory was without all embellishment and jesting, wholly composed for real effect and seriousness; not smelling of the lamp, as Pytheas scoffingly said, but of the temperance, thoughtfulness, austerity, and grave earnestness of his temper. Whereas Cicero's love of mockery often ran him into scurrility; and in his love of laughing away serious arguments in judicial cases by jests and facetious remarks, with a view to the advantage of his clients, he paid too little regard to what was decent; saying, for example, in his defence of Caelius, that he had done no absurd thing in such plenty and affluence to indulge himself in pleasures, it being a kind of madness not to enjoy the things we possess, especially since the most eminent philosophers have asserted pleasure to be the chiefest good (*Lives*, Plutarch).

In the above passage Plutarch compares Demosthenes and Cicero. What conclusions does he advance?

    A. Both Demosthenes and Cicero were fervent soldiers.

    B. Demosthenes, whose speeches were never sarcastic, was a master of rhetoric while Cicero, whose speeches were often full of sardonic humor, was more the scholar.

    C. Demosthenes participated in a plot to overthrow Caesar; Cicero declined to participate.

    D. All of the above

Solve

    A. Round $6.6666 to the nearest cent.

    B. The perimeter of a square is 4 meters. How many centimeters long is each side?

    C. ¼ - ½ =

...to serve as a sign among you. In the future, when your children ask you,"What do these stones mean?" tell them that the flow of the Jordan was cut off....These stones are to be a memorial... —Joshua 4:6,7

Scripture: Joshua 4:1-7

The forty-year wilderness experience is finally over. The children of Israel are going home. It is time to celebrate...and to remember. To that end, the nation piles high its stones. Each stone, twelve in all, represents God's faithfulness to the twelve tribes of Israel. They are to remember. To tell their children. In this society, where there are no televisions or tape recorders, the oral tradition is vitally important. They are to tell their children of God's faithfulness. Mark well these days, young people, when God is so faithful to you. Pile high the stones. Remember.

Devotional Journal

Read/Vocabulary Cards

Solve

A. What is the average of 5.6, 6.2, and 6.3?
B. Of the 30 students in class, 5 scored 100%. This was what percent of the class?
C. 2¾ divided by 4 =
D. $(0.5 \times 4) + (4 \times 0.5) =$
E. $2x - 19 = 37$

Critical Reading

Paul Johnson, in his book *Modern Times*, states that the decline and ultimately the collapse of the religious impulse will leave a huge vacuum. The history of modern times is in great part the history of how that vacuum is filled.

A. What is this so-called "huge vacuum"?
B. What causes it to exist?
C. As a Christian, what do you suppose will fill it?
D. Give a one-sentence summary of what Paul Johnson is arguing.

Critical Thinking: Writing

Write a letter to the editor that advances a particular point of view on a topic of your choice.

Math Test-Taking Tips Review

1. The math portion of the SAT is essentially an arithmetic exam. Theorems and formulas are given. Critical reading skills are helpful.
2. Do not guess unless you can eliminate one or more choices.
3. Bring a calculator.
4. Be careful not to miss the first ten problems of each section.
5. Pace yourself. Leave time to check your answers.

29
The Death Cycle

...the Israelites once again did evil in the eyes of the Lord. —Judges 4:1

Scripture: *Judges 4:1*

The Book of Judges covers the period in Israel's history between Joshua's death and the rise of Samuel. This was a time of transition from nomadic existence to the beginning of permanent settlements. An endless cycle is repeated: Israel deserts God for the heathen gods. Repents. And sins again. As a consequence God allows the nation to suffer at the hands of the Canaanites. Israel cries to God for help. God sends a deliverer. Then the old pattern of infidelity reasserts itself. Israel is in a death cycle.

Are you, or have you been, in a cycle of failure? Can you trust God to give you victory?

Devotional Journal

Read/Vocabulary Cards

Critical Reading

Critical Reading Questions

1. Reading well is critical to a high SAT score.
2. Read the questions first.
3. Read the passage slowly one time. Do not give into the impulse to skip portions!
4. Most important information in paragraphs occurs in the first and last sentences.
5. Answer the questions.

Every year His parents went to Jerusalem to the feast of the Passover. When He was twelve years old, they went up according to custom; when the feast was ended, they left but the boy stayed behind in Jerusalem. His parents did not know it, but supposing Him to be in the company they went a day's journey, and when they did not find Him, they returned to Jerusalem seeking Him. After three days they found Him in the temple, sitting among the teachers, listening to them, and asking them questions; and all who heard Him were amazed at His understanding. And when they saw Him they were astonished; and His mother said to Him, "Son, why have you treated us like this? Your father and I have been anxiously searching for you." (Luke 2:41-50)

1) What would be a good title for this passage?
   A. A Boy and His Bible
   B. A Mom Worries about Her Boy
   C. Jesus Stays Behind in the Temple
   D. The Feast of the Passover

2) Luke believes that:
A. Jesus was a bad boy   .
B. the Pharisees were awful people.
C. the Torah is useless.
D. Jesus was an extraordinary child.

Solve

A. What is ½ raised to the third power?
B. What is the square root of ¹⁄₆₄?
C. $(-25X)^0 + 4(800)^0 =$

So the Lord sold them into the hands of Jabin, a king of Canaan.... —Judges 4:2

Scripture: Judges 4:1-24

The first strophe of William Butler Yeats' poem "The Second Coming" begins:

> *Turning and turning in the widening gyre,*
> *The falcon cannot hear the falconer.*
> *Things fall apart; the centre cannot hold;*
> *Mere anarchy is loosed upon the world,*
> *The blood-dimmed tide is loosed, and everywhere*
> *The ceremony of innocence is drowned;*
> *The best lack all conviction, while the worst*
> *Are full of passionate intensity.*

Deborah's society had lost its way. It was in a cycle of death. In many ways, today, America is at the same place. "The best lack all conviction, while the worst/Are full of passionate intensity."

I believe that the next generation—that is you!—may be America's greatest hope to turn the tide of moral depravity. Will you be ready? Doing your best on the SAT is a starting point.

Devotional Journal

Read/Vocabulary Cards

Review your vocabulary cards tonight.

Grammar

Choose the right answer.

The facts in one book (have, has) never been confirmed.

Solve

Six glasses are in a row. The first three are filled with pineapple juice, and the last three are empty. By moving only one glass, can you arrange them so that the full and empty glasses alternate? (MindTrap®)

We must learn to pass through situations like a fish, rather than carrying them with us like a snail. We should certainly emerge with a little bit more experience of life, but there is no need to carry with us more than we have to—each situation carries quite enough trouble with it by itself!
—from *Prayer* by Simon Tugwell

…of which I, Paul, have become a servant….to present to you the word of God in its fullness…which is Christ in you, the hope of glory. —Colossians 1:23,25,27

Scripture: *Colossians 1:23-27*

In his book *The Holocaust*, Martin Gilbert describes a man named Michalowski. Michalowski, a Polish Jew, escaped from the Nazis shortly before he was to be executed. He fled to the home of a widow he knew. "Let me in!" he pleaded. She slammed the door in his face. In desperation he knocked again. "I am your Lord, Jesus Christ," he cried. "I came down from the cross. Look at me! The blood, the pain, the suffering of the innocent. Let me in." In our diversity, the Church is nothing more than an anemic version of other social organizations. But in our unity, based on Truth, we are the body of Jesus Christ—literally the hope for all creation.

Name four ways you can be Jesus Christ to your friends:

1.

2.

3.

4.

Devotional Journal

Read/Vocabulary Cards

You must not miss any of the first ten questions on each portion. Remember: each question counts the same and the last questions are usually more difficult. The corpus of knowledge on which the SAT I is based is rather basic. That is not the problem. The problem is that you must think critically and logically and be able to problem solve.

Critical Reading

We are born believing. A man bears beliefs, as a tree bears apples. A self-poise belongs to every particle; and a rectitude to every mind, and is the Nemesis and protector of every society. I and my neighbors have been bred in the notion, that, unless we came soon to some good church,—Calvinism, or Bohmenism, or Romanism, or Mormonism,—there would be a universal thaw and dissolution. No Isaiah or Jeremy has arrived. Nothing can exceed the anarchy that has followed in our skies. The stern old faiths have all pulverized. 'Tis a whole population of gentlemen and ladies out in search of religions. 'Tis as flat anarchy in our ecclesiastic realms, as that which existed in Massachusetts, in the Revolution, or which prevails now on the slope of the Rocky Mountains or Pike's Peak. Yet we make shift to live. Men are loyal. Nature has self-poise in all her works; certain proportions in which oxygen and azote combine, and, not less a harmony in faculties, a fitness in the spring and the regulator (*Worship*, Ralph Waldo Emerson).

The central argument that Emerson makes is
- A. that everyone should belong to a good church.
- B. that nature is fine and good, but no substitute for a Calvinist liturgy.
- C. that everyone is born believing in what we are participating and everyone is a part of nature.
- D. that orthodox religion is inadequate.

Solve

Give the area and perimeter of this figure.

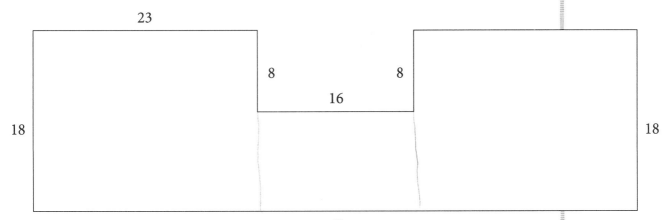

32
Rejoicing in Suffering

Now I rejoice in what was suffered for you... —Colossians 1:24

Scripture: *Colossians 1:24-27*

Say what? I rejoice in suffering? Paul intentionally uses a strong Greek word for *rejoice*. He is not mildly happy, or gently smiling—no—he is *thrilled* to suffer for the Colossian Church. Thrilled! I agree with the Christian psychologist Scott Peck who says that accepting necessary suffering is a key to Christian maturity.

How has necessary suffering helped you to grow in Christ?

Devotional Journal

Read/Vocabulary Cards

The Thinking Game

Think of a problem you are having and use the following outline to solve it.
   A. State the problem or issue in five sentences, then in two sentences, and, finally, in one sentence.
   B. Name three or more subtopics of the problem.
   C. Name three or more subtopics of the subtopics.
   D. What information must be known?
   E. State the answer to the question/problem in five, three, two, and one sentence(s).
   F. Once the problem is solved, what are one or two new problems that may arise?

Both the verbal and mathematic portions of the SAT are thinking games—clear thinking is more important than any one single learned corpus of information.

God is love. Love is the deepest depth...Love is the essence of His character...the love that forsees creation is itself the power to create.
—George MacDonald

...to present to you the word of God...the mystery that has been kept hidden for ages and generations, but is now disclosed to the saints. —Colossians 1:25,26

> ## Scripture: *Colossians 1:24-27*

My father is on my mind a lot these days—he died on Father's Day, 1982. My dad made me go to church. No matter how often we hunted or fished on Sunday morning—and we often did—we always managed to return before Sunday school. On many of my childhood Sunday mornings I had to exorcise huge black bass from my mind and to rub sleep from my eyes. But I went. And it was by watching my father that I learned that God was in control. That some things were more important than my agenda. It did not come easily. I remember one infamous Sunday morning when I mistakenly deposited some leftover bass entrails from an early Sunday morning fishing trip on Mrs. Higginbotham's expensive fox fur during the assurance of pardon. Although her quiet scream was interpreted by most of the congregation as an exuberant expression of gratefulness for God's forgiveness, my father, at least, knew that I had improperly washed my hands earlier in the morning. My admiration for my dad's dedication to church attendance was somewhat compromised when I realized that there were limits to his tolerance of childhood improprieties! But I fell in love with the man's God. I knew that if God was half as considerate, consistent, fair, and loving as my dad...well, then, He was the kind of God to whom I wanted to trust my life. So, when I was seventeen years old I gave my life to God. And I have never regretted my decision.

What does the Church mean to you? Is it part of your life? Have you made Christ your savior? Write your testimony.

Devotional Journal

Read/Vocabulary Cards

Solve

A. 80 people had been employed for 30 years and averaged $40,000/year. 60 people had been employed for 20 years and averaged $30,000/year. What was their overall average salary?

B. $3^0 + 2^0 =$

Sentence Completion

The notion that children have _____ rights, that they have ipso facto value, is a relatively late phenomenon to develop within social welfare circles.

      A. human   B. inalienable   C. unborn   D. intrinsic

Critical Thinking: Essay

Write a 500-word essay describing your father or another significant adult in your life. Use at least ten new vocabulary words.

Remember: the purpose of reading is not merely to increase your knowledge of literature. It is also to increase your reading speed, comprehension level, and vocabulary.

34
Holy Ground

...but the Lord appeared to Abram and said, "To your offspring I will give this land."
—Genesis 12:7

Scripture: *Genesis 12:1-7*

Seven years of my life were spent in the East Liberty area of Pittsburgh. My old church is right around the corner. To many people East Liberty is an inhospitable, dangerous place. And it is foreboding. Drug dealing is probably the most prosperous business in the area. Prostitution is openly practiced, and gangs flaunt their colors on street corners—at Shaky Frank's corner. Once upon a time a friend of mine, a homeless man named Frank (no one on the street had a last name), tried to make a living at Penn and Negley. Alcoholism had permanently damaged Frank's nervous system, so he constantly shook. Therefore, Shaky Frank was his appellation. Day after day, rain or shine, Frank stood on that corner, sold *Pittsburgh Gazettes*, and finally died there one cloudy spring day—but not before Frank visited my former church's drop-in center for the homeless and heard the Gospel. He was my friend until he died. Palestine, surely, is not the Garden of Eden. But, like East Liberty was to me, it was Abraham's promised land. It was the place he met God. And that made it a Holy Land.

It is my prayer that you will find God in this SAT preparation. Mark well these days. And may this be a Holy Place for you.

Devotional Journal

Read/Vocabulary Cards

Grammar

Is the following sentence correct or incorrect?

Everyone is finished with his homework.

Solve

A. Scheming Suzie and her younger brother were fighting. Their mother, who had had enough, decided to punish them by making them stand on the same piece of newspaper in such a way that they couldn't touch each other. How could this be done? (MindTrap®)

The rules for the order of operations are as follows:
—Simplify inside out beginning with the parentheses.
—Then proceed from left to right.

B. $5x - \{4[3x - (45 + 3x)]\} + 2(3x-6) = 38$

C. $7x - (4x - 10x) = 728$

Just as I am, without one plea, But that thy blood was shed for me, And that thou bidst me come to thee, O lamb of God, I come, I come!
—Charlotte Elliott

So they cried to the Lord for help...we need a mother! —Judges 4:3,4 (author paraphrase)

Scripture: *Judges 4:3-24*

The nation was crying out for help. The Lord called a woman, or mother (in Hebrew the words are similar). This mother's name was Deborah. *The Cotton Patch Gospel* interprets Judges 4:4 as "Things were bad until a woman arose...we needed a mother!" Deborah, an unlikely heroine, assisted by her military aide, Barak, rallied the tribes of Israel to unite in an attack on Sisera and the Canaanites, who had been raiding the tribes for several years. In the great battle at Kishon, a violent storm helped the Israelites defeat the Canaanites. Deborah and Barak immortalized the victory in a famous song in Judges 5.

What unlikely hero have you known in your life? Can you be an unlikely hero for others?

Devotional Journal

Read/Vocabulary Cards

Meet with your parents or guardians to review your vocabulary cards and pray together.

Matching

Match the following words with their meanings:

_____ hideous	A.	artistic
_____ adapt	B.	modify
_____ adversary	C.	ugly
_____ perforate	D.	attacker
_____ aesthetic	E.	opponent
_____ aggressor	F.	pierce

Critical Reading

A. Because the speed of sound is constant through a given material at a given temperature and density, the frequency of the waves varies with the length of the wave, resulting in high frequency or high pitch for short wavelengths and low pitch or low frequency for long wavelengths.

   1. In what sort of science textbook would this paragraph be found?

     A. Chemistry

     B. Botany

     C. Earth Science

     D. Zoology

   2. If a scientist observes that a wavelength suddenly changes, he/she can deduce that

     A. time as a variable is changing.

     B. the material through which the wave is moving has changed.

     C. the elements outside the material through which the wave is moving have changed.

     D. he/she is unable to deduce anything.

Lesson continues on the next page.

B. A man that is young in years may be old in hours, if he have lost no time. But that happeneth rarely. Generally, youth is like the first cogitations, not so wise as the second. For there is a youth in thoughts, as well as in ages. And yet the invention of young men is more lively than that of old; and imaginations stream into their minds better, and as it were more divinely. Natures that have much heat and great and violent desires and perturbations are not ripe for action till they have passed the meridian of their years…. Young men are fitter to invent than to judge; fitter for execution than for counsel; and fitter for new projects than for settled business. For the experience of age, in things that fall within the compass of it, directeth them; but in new things, abuseth them. The errors of young men are the ruin of business; but the errors of aged men amount but to this, that more might have been done, or sooner. Young men, in the conduct and manage of actions, embrace more than they can hold; stir more than they can quiet; fly to the end, without consideration of the means and degrees; pursue some few principles which they have chanced upon absurdly; care not to innovate, which draws unknown inconveniences; use extreme remedies at first; and that which doubleth all errors will not acknowledge or retract them; like an unready horse, that will neither stop nor turn. Men of age object too much, consult too long, adventure too little, repent too soon, and seldom drive business home to the full period, but content themselves with a mediocrity of success. Certainly it is good to compound employments of both; for that will be good for the present, because the virtues of either age may correct the defects of both; and good for succession, that young men may be learners, while men in age are actors; and, lastly, good for extern accidents, because authority followeth old men, and favor and popularity youth (*Essays: Civil and Moral*, Francis Bacon).

A fair summary of Bacon's argument is:
  A. Both old and young men have weaknesses and the best strategy is to combine characteristics from both.
  B. Young men are too precipitous in their actions.
  C. Old men are too cautious in their initiation of innovative solutions to problems.
  D. Young and old men are better than any woman.

Solve

When n is divided by 5, the remainder is 3. What is the remainder when 2n is divided by 5?
  A. 0
  B. 1
  C. 2
  D. 3
  E. 4

On that day Deborah…sang… "Praise the Lord! Hear this, you kings! Listen you rulers! I will sing to the Lord, I will sing;…to the Lord, the God of Israel." —Judges 5:1–4

Scripture: *Judges 5*

Deborah was more than a military genius. She was a woman who remembered Israel's past. She was a songwriter. Deborah called her nation to remember the God of their mothers and fathers. Deborah the mother was a singer, a culture creator. But she also was a woman who understood power. Understanding that true power arises from God, not humankind, she led her anemic nation to victory. She was not to be deterred. Deborah encouraged her community to defy Baal. To stand against the forces of darkness and to win. "Souls are like athletes," Thomas Merton writes. "And they need opponents worthy of them." Deborah challenged her people to reach beyond themselves and to find the strength to be and to do all that God wanted them to be and to do.

Can you sing songs of victory in a foreign land? Will you stand against the tide?

Devotional Journal

Read/Vocabulary Cards

Vocabulary

Define italicized words from context:

> "Atticus Finch went to Montgomery to read law and his younger brother went to Boston to study medicine. Their sister Alexandra was the Finch who remained at the Landing: she married a *taciturn* man who spent most of his time lying in a hammock by the river wondering if his trot-lines were full." (from *To Kill A Mockingbird* by Harper Lee)

Solve

A. $7\frac{1}{8} - 4\frac{3}{16} =$

B. $8\frac{1}{8} - 5\frac{3}{24} =$

C. $\frac{3}{4} - \frac{1}{2} =$

D. Express $\frac{1}{4}$ as a percentage

E. Express $\frac{2}{25}$ as a percentage

F. Express $\frac{9}{10}$ as a percentage

To Kill a Mockingbird is a classic but timely story of how one man can make a courageous stand in the face of injustice.

Suggestion: Use unabridged audio book recordings. Audio recordings are no substitute for an English assignment, but work well for vocabulary development.

Lesson continues on the next page.

Critical Thinking: Essay

Persuasive Essay

A persuasive essay, also known as an argument essay, attempts to convince the reader to embrace a particular course of action or point of view. Its sole purpose is to persuade. The writer must develop a limited topic that is well defined and debatable and that has more than one side. The writer must choose one side of an issue, clearly state a thesis, and offer convincing date that utilizes logic and reason to show that one idea is more legitimate than another. Remember to be aware of the arguments for the other side and reasonable address them rather than ignoring them completely.

Write an essay persuading your parents to let you borrow their new Jaguar.

Abram lived in the land of Canaan, while Lot lived among the cities of the plain and pitched his tents near Sodom. —Genesis 13:12

Scripture: Genesis 13:1-12

Scripture implies that Lot, like his uncle Abram, was a good man. He did not set out to sin. But he did. Before long he found himself in the center of one of the most notoriously bad cities in Palestine. And it all began by pitching his tent toward Sodom....

Are there areas in your life that are too close to the edge? Are you rationalizing away your bad behavior? List at least three areas that you will ask God to change in the next year.

1.

2.

3.

Devotional Journal

Read/Vocabulary Cards

Review Your Target Scriptures

Solve

A. The game and fish commission stocked 4521 pheasants. 1200 were shot by hunters. What percentage remains?

B. The radius of a circle is 6 inches. What is its circumference and its area?

C. Shadow turned and walked into the Secret Service Building. He got into the elevator, inserted his security card, pressed the button for floor 36, and dropped to government intelligence headquarters. Shadow got off the elevator and strolled to the window while he waited for his next assignment. Shadow stared out the window watching the little ant-like pedestrians and cars crawl along the streets below. He was enjoying the day; the sky was royal blue and not a cloud was in sight. Suddenly there was a flash of brilliant light. Shadow jumped quickly as he realized what had happened. What was so strange about the window? (MindTrap®)

One of the greatest challenges to American youth today is to be different in meaningful ways.

38
Delaying Pleasure

So Abram said to Lot, "Let's not have any quarreling between you and me…you go to the left, I'll go to the right"…Lot…pitched his tents near Sodom. —Genesis 13:8,12

Scripture: *Genesis 13:1-12*

Abram had every right to the beautiful land in the plain of Jordan. God had given it to him. But his nephew Lot wanted the plain of Jordan, so Abram allowed Lot to choose first. The Jordan plains held rich pasture and beautiful streams, but they also held Sodom. Sodom was to be Lot's undoing. Since Sigmund Freud's philosophies freed Americans from guilt (or what the Christian calls "conviction of sin") at the beginning of this century, it felt like we were on the plains of Jordan. But there was also a Sodom of sorts we had to face. Our sin. Freud's philosophies invited Americans to pursue their pleasure without any consequences. We became the center of our universe. We entered Sodom.…

A mature Christian is able to delay pleasure. Are you?

Devotional Journal

Read/Vocabulary Cards

Grammar

Is the following sentence correct?

Twenty-nine soldiers or one prisoner is to take the witness stand.

Solve

A. 16¼ divided by 4⅔ =
B. 4⅔ divided by 7 =
C. A jacket costs $125. That price represents a 40% discount. What was the original price?
D. It took a man 4 hours to travel 280 miles. How fast was he traveling?
E. What is the average of 45, 78, 49, and 88?

Critical Thinking: Paraphrase

Rewrite Luke 4:18-19 in your own words.

39

Back to the Future

Climb to the top of Mount Pisgah. Look west, north, south and east. You can look at the land. But you will not cross the Jordan River. —Deuteronomy 3:27 (NCV)

Scripture: *Deuteronomy 3:23-28*

Moses walked along across the plain to the foot of Mount Pisgah. Slowly he climbed up the steep rocky mass, higher and higher, until he finally reached the summit. Looking back, he could see his people camped far below him on the plain. The sun had begun to set, and the evening fires flickered among the tents. His eyes finally rested on the sacred encampment. Smoke was rising from the altar, where the priests were sacrificing a lamb. Reluctantly he turned away and looked westward, out over the far side of the mountain. There in the light of the setting sun lay the land of Canaan. Directly below he could see the fertile green valley of the Jordan River and, just beyond, the Canaanite town of Jericho. To the south he saw the waters of the Dead Sea, glimmering red and gold in the sunset, and the purple Judean hills rising steeply westward toward Jerusalem (not yet so named). His eyes followed the winding course over the rough, rocky hills of central Canaan. This was the land that was soon to belong to the young nation of Israel…but not Moses. Except from distant Mt. Pisgah and later Mt. Nebo, Moses was not to enjoy the Promised Land. Even after Moses pleaded with God whom he had loved so long and served so well, God responded "That is enough—do not speak to me anymore about this matter" (Deuteronomy 3:26).

Are you willing to work hard during this preparation course knowing that you still may not go to the Promised Land? That your score may not be what you wished? What might be God's purposes for your life?

Devotional Journal

Read/Vocabulary Cards

Solve

There were 3 times as many girls as boys in the class. There were 8 times as many dogs as boys. If there were 15 boys, how many boys, girls, and dogs were there in all?

Matching

Match the following words with their meanings

_____ surrender	A.	friendly
_____ agreement	B.	calibrate
_____ adjust	C.	concord
_____ amiable	D.	unchanging
_____ congruous	E.	ready to yield

Reminder: The verbal SAT is essentially a reading comprehension and vocabulary exam.

Lesson continues on the next page.

Critical Reading

A.

Marxist history is a process. Marxism argues that one person is free—and then a few people are free—and then everyone feels that they are free. Self-consciousness arises and increases in each case. Tension of opposites drives the whole process. For example, in France the tyranny of Louis XIV leads to the anarchy of the French Revolution that ultimately leads to the tyranny of Napoleon Bonaparte. Karl Marx believed that it was materialism—industry—power that really drove history. Therefore, Marxism understood that a leader had to control ideals if he wanted a revolution.

Based on this passage, a Marxist would argue that the American Civil War was caused by
  A. the Southern proletariat rebelling against Northern capitalists
  B. slavery
  C. the blockade of the Southern coast
  D. European interference

B.

If under changing conditions of life organic beings present individual differences in almost every part of their structure, and this cannot be disputed; if there be, owing to their geometrical rate of increase, a severe struggle for life at some age, season, or year, and this certainly cannot be disputed; then, considering the infinite complexity of the relations of all organic beings to each other and to their conditions of life, causing an infinite diversity in structure, constitution, and habits, to be advantageous to them, it would be a most extraordinary fact if no variations had ever occurred useful to each being's own welfare, in the same manner as so many variations have occurred useful to man. But if variations useful to any organic being ever do occur, assuredly individuals thus characterized will have the best chance of being preserved in the struggle for life; and from the strong principle of inheritance, these will tend to produce offspring similarly characterized. This principle of preservation, or the survival of the fittest, I have called Natural Selection. It leads to the improvement of each creature in relation to its organic and inorganic conditions of life, and consequently, in most cases, to what must be regarded as an advance in organisation. Nevertheless, low and simple forms will long endure if well fitted for their simple conditions of life (*Origin of the Species*, Charles Darwin).

The best title for this passage would be:
  A. The End of Creationism
  B. The Infinite Complexity of the Relations of All Organic Beings
  C. Natural Selection: Survival of the Fittest
  D. The Strong Principle of Inheritance

40

Remember and Obey

Now, Israel, listen to the laws and commands I will teach you. Obey them so that you will live. Then you will go over and take the land. The Lord, the God of your ancestors, is giving it to you. —Deuteronomy 4:1 (NCV)

Scripture: Deuteronomy 4:1-4

This text grows out of Moses' profound and sad realization that he could not go with his people to their destination. So what could he leave with them? What could he tell them that would summarize his own life? Obey. "Follow these commands so that you may live and may go in and take possession of the land that the Lord, the God of your fathers is giving you" (4:1). Remember. Remember what the Lord did to Israel because of their idolatry. In case you've forgotten, God killed 24,000 Israelites who had been seduced by the Moabite god Baal of Peor (Numbers 25). Remember. Remember God's faithfulness day by day. Remember and obey are two quintessential elements of the Christian faith.

Identify areas of disobedience in your life that need some attention.

Devotional Journal

Read/Vocabulary Cards

Vocabulary

Define italicized words from context:

> Wang Lung nodded and left her and did not see her again until the guests came crowding in, his uncle jovial and sly and hungry, his uncle's son an *impudent* lad of fifteen, and the farmers clumsy and grinning with shyness. Two were men from the village with whom Wang Lung exchanged seed and labor at harvest time, and one was his next door neighbor, Ching, a small, quiet man, ever unwilling to speak unless he were *compelled* to it. (from *The Good Earth* by Pearl S. Buck)

The Good Earth is deeply moving story of a poor Chinese farmer who finally becomes wealthy but loses much in the process.

Solve

A. Mary sold 40 bushels of apples for $640. How much money would she get for 100 bushels?

B. Express the perimeter of this figure in centimeters. All angles are right angles.

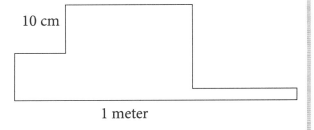

10 cm

10 cm

1 meter

Just do it! Just do it! Read! Read! Read! Nothing will improve your SAT scores more than reading. Just do it!

Critical Thinking: Essay

Write a 75-word persuasive essay discussing the importance of forgiveness.

41
Iron Chariots

...though the Canaanites have iron chariots and though they are strong, you can drive them out. —Joshua 17:18

Scripture: Joshua 17:1-18

The tribe of Joseph needed more land. No problem. For most of the Book of Joshua God miraculously gave the nation of Israel most everything they needed. At least from Shittim to Gilgal. But, then, there was hesitation. The hill country people had iron chariots. Egad! You see, the Israelites had no iron. They were still a bronze-age people and their fragile bronze weapons broke against the iron weapons of their enemies. So, suddenly, they were afraid. But nothing really changed. They were the same people. They served the same God. He had faithfully delivered them for years. Why would He stop?

What is the bottom line for you? What problem do you have that you do not think God can help you overcome?

Devotional Journal

Read/Vocabulary Cards

Remember to review your vocabulary cards.

Sentence Completion

During the seventies a _____ development occurred in the drug and supermarket businesses: generic pricing. Removing all frills, expunging expensively adorned packing, and thereby lowering advertising costs, drugstores and grocery stores were able to offer a profitable alternative to name brand products.

    A. fortuitous
    B. unlucky
    C. intentional
    D. serendipitous

Solve

    A. $4\frac{1}{12}$ divided by $2\frac{1}{3}$ times $3\frac{1}{2}$ divided by $1\frac{1}{24}$
    B. Use words to write 7267186.8
    C. Suppose you are delivering pizza to a church youth group. You leave the youth group room and walk up four floors, down seven, and up nine to the pastor's office on the top floor. Then you go down six, up two, and down eight to the water fountain on the first floor. On what floor is the youth group?

Sentence Completion Tips

1. Put the sentence in your own words.
2. See how each choice fits.
3. What if you do not know what each answer means? Look for roots. Many books tell you to narrow your choices to two and then guess—it is up to you.
4. Watch for contrasts, negative words, and causation.

This is a good time to use your target Scripture!

Then Moses led Israel from the Red Sea and they went into the Desert of Shur. For three days they traveled in the desert without finding water. —Exodus 15:22

Scripture: *Exodus 15:22-27*

In general, the Jewish exiles, recently freed from Egyptian captivity, did not like the wilderness. They always thought of it as harsh and unnerving. Their references to it were usually uncomplimentary. But the pilgrimage of the Israelites through the wilderness of Sinai figured as one of their most cherished motifs. They remembered it with pride and fondness. It was their years in the wilderness that forged them as a nation that had developed their character and marked them as the people of God. The theologian Walter Brueggemann reminds us that the wilderness is a place of diminished resources but increased possibilities. Yet, even in the midst of hard times, the Israelites sensed God's presence. And that made the hard times worthwhile.

We have all entered some sort of wilderness in our lives. We have been in places where it was really hard. Can you describe such a place in your life? Where was God?

Devotional Journal

Read/Vocabulary Cards

Grammar

Choose the right answer.

Every man, woman, and child (was, were) asked to take a stand for Christ.

Sentence Completion

1. A good idea in the consumer marketplace, generic strategies fare very poorly in church work. Too many of us have tried with perfectly pure intentions to _____ Christianity to its noncontroversial if unexciting basics.
    A. make
    B. exact
    C. claim
    D. distill
2. What does this _____ toward a noncontroversial Christianity mean to us?
    A. dislike
    B. propensity
    C. penchant
    D. disinclination

Too often we have sacrificed theological efficacy for mass appeal.

More on Critical Reading
1. Check your answers.
2. Critical reading questions are the only ones to which you can find the right answers on the test—if you have enough time to find them.
3. As you read, look for key words.
4. I have never seen a 1200+ SAT score that did not have almost a perfect reading comprehension score!

43
Entering the Wilderness II

Then they came to Elim, where there were twelve springs and seventy palm trees, and they camped there near the water. —Exodus 15:27

Scripture: *Exodus 15:22-27*

I entered a wilderness one fall day in 1975 when I had an auto accident while traveling to seminary. As I recovered in my windowless hospital room, I encountered a side of life that I did not know existed. For seven months I lay in traction and then in a full body cast. But as my body healed my soul languished. The same God who had saved me and called me to the ministry now seemed to be destroying me. Surely I was in darkness—and in spite of the fact that I had known only light for more than five years! Where was the God of my salvation? Today, I look back at September 11, 1975, as a watershed day in my life. Oh, I still feel the pain of my accident. And I have had, and may yet again face even worse catastrophes in my life. But that time of sitting in darkness, that long day's journey into night, taught me a very important fact: God will never forsake or abandon me. He will deliver me. And He does even more. When I mess up my life, figuratively and literally, He will always be there to help me sort it out. Sure, I walk with a limp. But He gave me the courage and strength to go on when I did not want to do so. And He took what should have been a disaster and made it a good thing in my life. It is not that I grew accustomed to the darkness. It is that I found a light that shines into every darkness I can experience or imagine. This wilderness experience is special to me because it is where I found a God who can do all things.

Are you willing to go wherever God leads you?

Devotional Journal

Read/Vocabulary Cards

Critical Reading

The word value it is to be observed, has two different meanings, and sometimes expresses the utility of some particular object, and sometimes the power of purchasing other goods which the possession of that object conveys. The one may be called "value in use;" the other, "value in exchange." The things which have the greatest value in use have frequently little or no value in exchange; and on the contrary, those which have the greatest value in exchange have frequently little or no value in use. Nothing is more useful than water: but it will purchase scarce any thing; scarce any thing can be had in exchange for it. A diamond, on the contrary, has scarce any value in use; but a very great quantity of other goods may frequently be had in exchange for it (*The Wealth of Nations*, Adam Smith).

Adam Smith argues that
   A. value and scarcity are connected.
   B. value is a static entity.
   C. nothing increases in value without a concomitant increase in price.
   D. value in use has very little connection to value in exchange.

Matching

Match the following words with their meanings

_____ combination	A.	scorn
_____ contempt	B.	resistance
_____ pugnacious	C.	mysterious
_____ credible	D.	condemn
_____ cryptic	E.	reduce
_____ diminish	F.	skeptic
_____ cynic	G.	mixture
_____ loaf	H.	quarrelsome
_____ defiance	I.	believable
_____ denounce	J.	waste time

Critical Thinking: Perspective

Rewrite today's devotion from the perspective of a person who does not believe in God's miraculous intervention in human history.

44
Entering the Wilderness III

He said, "If you listen carefully to the voice of the Lord your God and do what is right in his eyes, if you pay attention to his commands and keep all his decrees, I will not bring on you any of the diseases I brought on the Egyptians…."—Exodus 15:26

Scripture: *Exodus 15:22-27*

In the black slave community a frequent part of family life was telling stories. The folktale was an especially important way in which older slaves could express hostility toward their masters and impart wisdom to the young. One favorite story was "The Tar Baby Tricks Brer Rabbit." Brer Rabbit slyly convinces his arch enemies—Fox and Bear—to throw him into the briar patch rather than into the well. "Please, sir, don't throw me in the briar patch. Those briars will tear up my hide, pull out my hair, and scratch out my eyes. That'll be an awful way to die!" Of course that is exactly what Bear and Fox did and exactly what Brer Rabbit wanted them to do. Because, now, Brer Rabbit could escape and no one could follow! Likewise, Satan thinks that we will fail, that we will not make it in the wilderness. But we are thrown into the briar patch only to find ourselves safe and secure in the arms of God! The wilderness is not what we expected. The wilderness is the place where we find our way to the Cross.

Can you remember a time when you thought all was lost but God turned things around?

Devotional Journal

Read/Vocabulary Cards

Vocabulary

Define italicized words from context:

> Mademoiselle Bourienne was the first to recover herself after this *apparition*…. Natasha and Princess Marya gazed dumbly at one another, and the longer they gazed dumbly at one another without saying what they wanted to say, the more unfavourably each felt *disposed* to the other…. When the count returned, Natasha showed a *discourteous relief* at seeing him, and made haste to get away…. Natasha's expression as she looked at Princess Marya was *ironical*, though she did not know why. (from *War and Peace* by Leo Tolstoy)

Solve

16 bike tires can be bought for $96. How much would 4 tires cost?

Critical Thinking: Essay

Write a persuasive essay on the topic of courtship.

In Leo Tolstoy's classic, *War and Peace*, we meet Pierre. "Shy, observant and natural looking," Pierre was distinguished by no particular gift of intelligence, good looks, or moral courage. And, while his physical appearance never changed, his character did. And he became a hero of epic proportions. He selfishly put himself in harm's way numerous times and eventually married the beautiful and equally heroic Natasha. Somehow the love between Natasha and Pierre mitigated all the horrible pain that the Napoleonic invasion of Russia had wreaked on their generation.

Get wisdom, get understanding… —Proverbs 4:5

Scripture: *Proverbs 4:4-10*

"There are two kinds of people," Mr. Merrill Lynch announced at lunch in the Harvard Club on my last day as a Harvard University Merrill Fellow, "those who went to Harvard and those who did not." At these words, I nearly choked on my overpriced, overdone filet mignon and wiped my mouth with my embroidered, white linen napkin. I was certainly glad to hear that—especially because I was wearing my best suit—and my worst suit—both at the same time. By mistake I had put on the jacket from one and the pants from another. They looked good to me in the pre-dawn morning when I boarded my plane in Pittsburgh to travel to Boston. But by lunch the crystal chandeliers in the Harvard Faculty Club painfully accentuated my error! I was so embarrassed! Everything about this place reeked of pretention and I was glad to get out of there and to fly home! Aren't we humans silly! We think that life-changing wisdom can be the exclusive property of one perspective, one institution. Wisdom, as Solomon understood it, can be found only in living a life centered on the Word of God. Jesus Christ is the Way and the Truth and the Life.

Are you seeking the Lord in the right places? If you are spending private time with the Lord every day, you are looking in the right place!

Devotional Journal

Read/Vocabulary Cards

Critical Thinking: Classification

Using these words, find two general topics in each group:

A.
bat	oyster	net	snail
lobster	clam	scallop	crab
racket	skates	ball	

B.
socks	mumps	slacks	dress
jacket	measles	mittens	chickenpox
pneumonia	shirt	strep throat	

Solve

A. 23 - {3 + (28 - x)} - [45 + 6{8(6 - 3x) - 4}] = 0
B. A sand box is 8 yards longer than it is wide. The surface area of the sand box is 20 square yards. What is the length? x = width.

46

God as Mystery

May my cry come before you, O Lord; give me understanding according to your word.
May my supplication come before you; deliver me according to your promise.
—Psalm 119:169,170

Scripture: Psalm 119:126-170

The Catholic scholar Sean Caufield says, "I've come to know that God is not a 'thing.' He is not of the things and bits of His own creation, one more objective thing out there, something amongst other things. He is not even the supreme thing, the first or best or greatest in a series. He is not relative to anything. He is the Mystery that cannot be contained or boxed in by any symbol or concept." Have you found that mystery? We must reach beyond ourselves and our troubles and find a God who is in control. Many of us don't pray until we are driven to our knees by the circumstances of life. Fair enough. But, young person, know that a loving God is waiting for you. He is not waiting with platitudes and empty promises. He meets you with action. Daily in our prayer lives and most especially when we gather with our Christian friends we should acknowledge our new life together. This newness is not simply a matter of time, new as opposed to old. It has a quality of difference. It is fresh, not tired. It is not somehow better than the old—it is infinitely different from the old.

Give an example from your life of when God was there for you but you did not know it.

Devotional Journal

Read/Vocabulary Cards

Vocabulary

Define italicized words from context:

> There passed some fifteen years of seeming prosperity. But beneath the deceptive surface a hideous depth of infamy lay concealed. The gods could no longer brook in silence the affront of Oedipus's unwitting sins. Pestilence and famine brought Thebes once more to the verge of utter extinction. (from *The Theban Plays* by Sophocles)

Grammar

Choose the correct answer.

> Six months on the road (seem, seems) like a hard way to make a living.

Critical Thinking: Précis

A précis seeks to capture the essence, the meaning of a passage in as cogent a way as possible. It differs from a summary, which is simply an abbreviated re-statement of the whole passage. A précis is written in your own words and is a great way to prepare for the SAT I verbal portion. A précis must not include more than a few words appearing in the passage. Read this passage and write a précis of it:

> The Church of Jesus Christ must be unambivalent in its confession that "there is neither Jew or Greek, there is neither slave or free person, there is neither male or female: for you are all one in Christ Jesus" (Galatians 3:28). In the areas of social justice, equality between the sexes and races, ministry to the poor, and to the homeless, peacemaking, the church must be prophetic. "For in as much as you helped the least of these, you helped me."

Read a short story of your choice and write a précis of it. If you have time, do the same thing with a newspaper article. Now work on your first copy and make it even more concise!

47
Losses and Gains

But whatever was to my profit I now considered loss for the sake of Christ…. I want to know Christ and the power of his resurrection and the fellowship of sharing in his sufferings. —Philippians 3:7,10

Scripture: *Philippians 3:1-10*

While in a Roman prison, Paul was assessing all the reasons he had to boast—great education, privileged birth, and advantageous citizenship—and he decided it was all meaningless when compared to the value that salvation had brought to his life. It is difficult to communicate to your friends with twentieth-century understanding that establishing a relationship with Jesus Christ is the most important thing that can happen to them in their lives. Paul is speaking of ultimate things. What really matters. This is a critical question for the Philippian community (who were undergoing persecution and other threats) and ourselves (who are constantly fighting against assimilation and compromise with the world). Nothing I am or have compares with knowing Christ. Wow! Do you see how incredibly threatening this statement is? Because if Paul really means it, his jailers, his accusers, his world has no control over him. Only God. And Paul is privileged to live under the wing of Romans 8: Nothing can separate me from the love of Christ Jesus. This knowledge takes Paul to where he wants to go: to a new understanding of his value as a person to God and to others.

Life is a series of gains and losses. What have you lost since you gave your heart to Christ? What have you gained? Has it been worthwhile?

Devotional Journal

Read/Vocabulary Cards

Critical Reading

As to their other schemes of taxation, it is impossible to say anything of them with certainty; because they have not yet had their operation; but nobody is so sanguine as to imagine they will fill up any perceptible part of the wide gaping breach which their incapacity has made in their revenues. At present the state of their treasury sinks every day more and more in cash, and swells more and more in fictitious representation. When so little within or without is now found but paper, the representative not of opulence but of want, the creature not of credit but of power, they imagine that our flourishing state in England is owing to that bank-paper, and not the bank-paper to the flourishing condition of our commerce, to the solidity of our credit, and to the total exclusion of all idea of power from any part of the transaction (*Reflections on the French Revolution*, Edmund Burke).

The word "sanguine" in line 2 means
   A. worried
   B. skeptical
   C. confident
   D. pleased

Solve

   A. Karen is 8 years younger than David. 3 years from now David will be twice as old as Karen. How old are Karen and David?
   B. Mary drove 255 miles in 5 hours. What was her average rate of speed per hour?
   C. What is the average propane usage for the first six months? The last six months? What was the greatest increase? If propane cost $100/ton, how much did the business spend for the year?

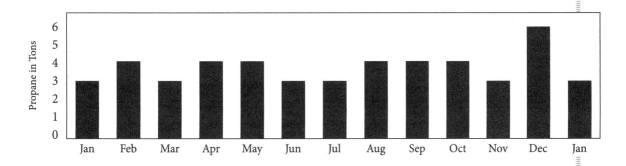

48 Ultimate Worth

What is more, I consider everything a loss compared to the surpassing greatness of knowing Christ Jesus my Lord, for whose sake I have lost all things. —Philippians 3:8

Scripture: *Philippians 3:1-13*

When is loss gain? It is gain when we surrender our control and our search for security in tangible things, and we discover that trusting in God and God's design is ultimately more satisfying. As a historian I understand and firmly believe that human history is always reconstructed; it is never created. History is always reconstructed from evidence. But Paul is telling us that salvation is out of history. That it is really something new. Something is created that was not here. A new birth. And that is worth more than all the knowledge, money, or prestige in the whole world.

What do you want more than anything else in the whole world? To win the World Cup? To be rich? Handsome? To receive a full academic scholarship to Harvard University? What does Paul tell you is of inestimable worth?

Devotional Journal

Read/Vocabulary Cards

Matching

Match the following words with their meanings:

_____ deny   A. removed
_____ contempt   B. hindrance
_____ derivative   C. contradict
_____ detached   D. extraction
_____ obstacle   E. ridicule

Critical Thinking: Précis

Take a research paper or some other assignment you have recently written and write a one-page précis on it. Write a one-paragraph précis on the same paper. Finally, write a one-sentence précis on the same paper.

In spite of all the talk about the SAT I being a "reasoning test" it still is, as I have said before, essentially a vocabulary test. If you do not know the words in the questions, a Sentence Completion, or Critical Reading passage, how can you answer it correctly? Cramming does not work with vocabulary development. So get to work now!

Critical Reading

The Idea of the University, by Jaroslave Pelikan, argues that the true crisis of the university lies not in financial exigencies, political assaults from the left or right, or the myopia of modern life; it lies in the crisis of confidence within the university itself about its abiding nature/purpose. George Marsden, in his book The Soul of the American University would entirely agree; however, he knows exactly where the trouble lies—in the loss of the university's Judeo-Christian roots. Pelikan is sure that the university has lost something, but like the main character in Kafka's The Stranger, it has lost its way, lost its identity, but it does not quite know where it has come from, where it is, or where it is to go from here. In any event, it is a quest for an existential goal—not a Judeo-Christian one. Pelikan's university is King Belshazzar's feast (Daniel 7). Marsden's university is a time on Mt. Horeb, humbling bowing before Almighty God, freely admitting our own limits and extolling His omnipotence (Exodus 3).

1. Based on this passage, theorize what Pelikan and Marsden would say on the following topics:
    A. Increased substance abuse on university campuses
    B. The absence of courses on creation offered in university science curricula
    C. Most college juniors have no idea who John Milton was
    D. 80 percent of college graduates admit that they cheated in college

2. Compare Daniel 7 to Exodus 3. What is meant by the last sentence of the above passage?

Critical Thinking: Essay

Comparison/Contrast Essay

A comparison/contrast essay involves comparing and contrasting two subjects—either comparing how two subjects are alike or contrasting how two subjects differ. When choosing a topic, you must not choose totally unrelated subjects but rather two subjects that have some basic similarities. For example, you could choose to compare/contrast two movies, two authors, or two modes of transportation, but you would not compare airplane travel with Ernest Hemingway.

When writing, first think of everything you know about each subject and look for connections that show similarities and differences. The introduction of your essay should mention both subjects and clearly define your thesis statement.

Then write your essay in one of two ways. Give all the supporting details for one subject and then all the supporting details for the other subject, or alternate between the subjects, giving details from each as you compare or contrast.

> Write an essay in which you compare life before and after you learned to drive a car.

For it is we who are the circumcision, we who worship by the Spirit of God, who glory in Christ Jesus, and who put no confidence in the flesh. —Philippians 3:3

Scripture: *Philippians 3:1-10*

From the first moment I saw my daughter's generous brown eyes, they beckoned me toward unexplored lands. Those eyes belonged to an attractive, six-month-old, chocolate brown, curly haired transracial (i.e., black/white) baby girl: my new soon-to-be adopted daughter. Rachel clung to her new mother as she suspiciously surveyed her new father. I—the new father—was uncomfortably Caucasian. Although my wife's family had several adopted siblings of sundry nationalities and racial mixtures, I had never known anyone who was adopted—of any race—until I met Karen's family two years previously. And now I was adopting a child who looked very much like a group of people whom I had been taught to dislike and to mistrust! I was still, I fear, too much a product of my past, my land, my family, my time. That land was southern Arkansas. That time was the 1960s. That family was a deeply rooted Southern genus. Of course I had changed in the last few years—God had saved me during my senior year in high school six years before, and no doubt He had begun to smooth many of my rough edges. But, I must confess, as I stood and looked at my daughter for the very first time, I was worried that all my old prejudice was still there. But however I felt, in fact, I was a new creation. Reborn. I had given my life to the Lord and had asked Him to be my personal Savior. This was not good intentions or sentimentality. I had willfully invited Jesus Christ to be Lord of my life. And when I invited my daughter Rachel to join our family, it was from a place of new birth.

Do you sometimes feel as if you are not saved? That this Christianity stuff is not really worth it? Talk about it with a special person and then with God.

Devotional Journal

Read/Vocabulary Cards

Vocabulary

Define italicized words from context:

> The *ingot* seemed almost a living thing; it did not want to run this mad course, but it was in the grip of fate…a great red snake escaped from *purgatory*; and then, as it slid through the rollers, you would have sworn it was alive—it *writhed* and squirmed, and wriggles and shudders passed out through its tail…Jarvis became *indifferent*. (from *The Jungle* by Upton Sinclair)

Solve

A. A baseball team played 125 games and won 100. What is the ratio of games lost to the number of games won?

B. Solve this equation: $2x^2 - 5x - 3 = 0$

The Jungle by Upton Sinclair is a creative book that is more a social history than a piece of literature. It is part of the stream of naturalism (i.e., nature and an impersonal god rule) that was so strong at the end of the last century. Sinclair's description of the Chicago meat factories will make eating a hot dog an adventure!

Not that I have already obtained all this, or have already been made perfect, but I press on to take hold of that for which Christ Jesus took hold of me. —Philippians 3:12

Scripture: *Philippians 3:1-12*

My wife, Karen, and I deliberately chose to tie our lives to our daughter's life. And so it is with God. Christians were chosen by God before time had any meaning. He chose us! We responded to His love—as Rachel responded to ours. But we chose her—she did not initially choose us. We adopted her. We did not ask her advice. It was an act of our volition. Likewise God willingly sent His only begotten Son to die for our sins (John 3:16). He did this so that we could be adopted into His family. Baby girl Jane Doe, a female infant with no name, no past, no future, is suddenly, inextricably, permanently drawn into our lives. In the eyes of God and the United States of America, Rachel is reborn as our daughter. We even have a new birth certificate! Now think about how extraordinary adoption is: At the moment we adopted Rachel, our parents became her grandparents, her children our grandchildren. Her pain is our pain; her victories, our victories. How extraordinary, and incomprehensible it is that a white boy from the heart of Dixie, who once was himself prejudiced, is connected forever with a perfect stranger of another race! Something is created that was not here. A new birth. And that is worth more than all the knowledge, money, or prestige in the whole world.

If Jesus Christ is your Lord and Savior, then you are born again. A new creation. Adopted into the family of God. Congratulations! Christ has laid hold of you—now will you lay hold of Him? Spend some time today in prayer and writing in your prayer journal, expressing how it feels to be in this special family.

Devotional Journal

Read/Vocabulary Cards

Review your vocabulary cards with your parents or guardians tonight. Pray together, too!

Grammar

Choose the correct answer.

The new soccer player, (who, whom) came from Equador, led the team to victory.

Solve

Find the area and perimeter of this figure.

There are two types of questions on the math portion of the SAT I: multiple choice questions and student-produced responses.

A New Past

Brothers, I do not consider myself yet to have taken hold of it. But one thing I do: Forgetting what is behind and straining toward what is ahead, I press on toward the goal.
—Philippians 3:13

Scripture: *Philippians 3:1-13*

Psychotherapy is almost exclusively interested in the past. Because Freud suggested to us that the future lies in the past, so to speak, we have spent our energies trying to understand the past. In therapy, through hypnosis, by drugs—we drag up the past, we study the past, we review the past, we discuss the past. *But* we do not *change* the past. We can change the future, remake the present, but nobody, nobody can change the past. That is, no one but God. Through adoption, He gives us a new past. Things that may have been meant for bad are made good for us, through the power of the Holy Spirit. This is heavy duty stuff! Let me explain. No doubt my great-great-grandparents were slaveholders—or at least they fought in the Civil War to preserve slavery. I myself was once prejudiced. But, now, my children, their great-great-great grandchildren through adoption, who once would have been slaves, are now their flesh and blood. They have a new life. And my past has been changed. When I committed my life to Christ, the past was rewritten. Not that I will not have problems. But now I am facing those problems as a son of the King.

How has God changed your past? What bad thing happened to you in the past that God has changed through your salvation?

Devotional Journal

Read/Vocabulary Cards

Critical Reading

A.

> By some curious chance one morning long ago in the quiet of the world, when there was less noise and more green, and the hobbits were still numerous and prosperous, and Bilbo Baggins was standing at his door after breakfast smoking an enormous long wooden pipe that reached nearly down to his wooly toes (neatly brushed)—Gandalf came by. Gandalf! If you had heard only a quarter of what I have heard about him, and I have only heard very little of all there is to hear, you would be prepared for any remarkable tale. Tale and adventures sprouted up all over the place wherever he went, in the most extraordinary fashion. He had not been down that way under the Hill for ages and ages, not since his friend the Old Took died, in fact, and the hobbits had almost forgotten what he looked like. (from *The Hobbit* by J.R.R. Tolkien)

What was the point of view of this section? Who is the protagonist? Who would be a foil?

B.

The time, it is to be hoped, is gone by when any defense would be necessary of the "liberty of the press" as one of the securities against corrupt or tyrannical government. No argument, we may suppose, can now be needed, against permitting a legislature or an executive, not identified in interest with the people, to prescribe opinions to them, and determine what doctrines or what arguments they shall be allowed to hear. This aspect of the question, besides, has been so often and so triumphantly enforced by preceding writers, that it needs not be specially insisted on in this place. . .Let us suppose, therefore, that the government is entirely at one with the people, and never thinks of exerting any power of coercion unless in agreement with what it conceives to be their voice. But I deny the right of the people to exercise such coercion, either by themselves or by their government. The power itself is illegitimate. The best government has no more title to it than the worst. It is as noxious, or more noxious, when exerted in accordance with public opinion, than when in opposition to it. If all mankind minus one, were of one opinion, and only one person were of the contrary opinion, mankind would be no more justified in silencing that one person, than he, if he had the power, would be justified in silencing mankind. Were an opinion a personal possession of no value except to the owner; if to be obstructed in the enjoyment of it were simply a private injury; it would make some difference whether the injury was inflicted only on a few persons or on many. But the peculiar evil of silencing the expression of an opinion is, that it is robbing the human race; posterity as well as the existing generation; those who dissent from the opinion, still more than those who hold it. If the opinion is right, they are deprived of the opportunity of exchanging error for truth: if wrong, they lose, what is almost as great a benefit, the clearer perception and livelier impression of truth, produced by its collision with error (*On Liberty*, John Stuart Mill).

The main point of this essay by Mill is that
A. freedom of the press is sacrosanct.
B. A fervent belief in freedom of the press is no excuse for the masses to bully others to accept its position and thereby sacrifice individuality.
C. the best government has no more or less right to rule than the worst government.
D. liberty is a gift that must be preserved at great cost by each new generation.

Solve

A. ⅓ [(2½ x ⅓) - (¾ x ½)] =
B. Find the perimeter of this figure in centimeters. Dimensions are in meters.

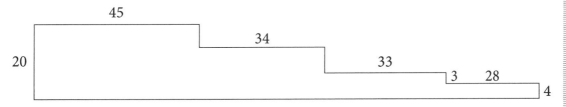

A Paradox I

…It was the law that put me to death. I died to the law so that I can now live for God. — Galatians 2:19 (NCV)

Scripture: *Galatians 2:17-21*

A powerful philosophical impulse of the twentieth century has been existentialism, which argues that there is no meaning to existence outside of human experience. The existential movement grew out of the cynicism of World War I engendered in writers like Sartre, Kafka, and Camus, who believed that idealism—including Christianity—was responsible for the carnage of that war. Thus, in your high school courses you read books like *The Sun Also Rises* and *For Whom the Bell Tolls*—both by Ernest Hemingway—which are full of sterile, lonely, broken people. People without hope. What a dreary view of life!

I thank God that I am His child. Redeemed by the blood of the Lamb. My salvation is no accident, and I am no "mere being." I am a child of the living God. Are you? When things get bad do you remind yourself of your destiny?

Devotional Journal

Read/Vocabulary Cards

Matching

Match following words with their meanings

____ disperse	A. spread
____ disseminate	B. odd
____ oppose	C. obedient
____ dissuade	D. scatter
____ eclectic	E. outdo
____ docile	F. emphatic
____ dogmatic	G. various
____ eccentric	H. advise against
____ surpass	I. support
____ sanction	J. disagree

Moby Dick by Herman Melville is one of the most exciting American classics. *Moby Dick* redefined the American novel. On the surface, *Moby Dick* appears to be an epic saga of a one-legged, vengeful, fanatic Ahab, pursuing a white whale. But, in fact, it is much more. It is an allegory of humankind's struggle with fate and nature.

Vocabulary

Define italicized words in context:

> As the sky grew less gloomy; indeed, began to grow a little genial, he [Ahab] became a little *genial*, he became less and less a *recluse*; as if, when the ship had sailed from home, nothing but the *bleakness* of the sea had then kept him so *secluded*…But the Pequod was…regularly cruising; nearly all whaling *preparatives* needing supervision the mates were fully *competent* to do…. (from *Moby Dick* by Herman Melville)

Solve

  A. Represent 4 consecutive integers beginning with 3x + 1 where x is an integer.
  B. Convert ½% to a decimal
  C. Convert 3½% to a decimal

Critical Thinking: Essay

Write an essay in which you show the difference between two computer games. Explain how the games are played, the different skills needed to play each game and why you prefer to play one of the games.

Friedrich Nietzsche

I was put to death on the cross with Christ, and I do not live anymore—it is Christ living in me. I still live in my body, but I live by faith in the Son of God. He loved me and gave himself to save me. —Galatians 2:19,20 (NCV)

Scripture: *Galatians 2:7-21*

The history of modern times is the history of how our culture has tried to replace its Judeo-Christian roots. The German philosopher Friedrich Nietzsche rightly perceived that the most likely candidate would be what he called the "Will to Power." In place of religious belief, there will be secular ideology. This "secular ideology" has been manifested in everything from commercials on televisions to the surrogate messiahs—like Stalin and Hitler—uninhibited by any religious sanctions and with an unappeasable appetite for controlling humankind. To a Christian, though, reality is Christ. We are not in free-fall—as Nietzsche concludes—we are held in the palm of His hand! I understand now why Galatians 2:20 has had such a strong pull on my life: for it is at the Cross where I find hope and new life. I am forever captured in this paradox.

What Scriptures mean a lot to your life?

Devotional Journal

Read/Vocabulary Cards

Critical Reading

Writing a Summary
1. Read the article carefully.
2. Take notes.
3. Write the summary. It should be shorter than the article but it should include the setting, main characters, plot—including the climax and denouement— and the theme.

My small Southern community was unprepared to face the present, much less the future. The Civil War hung like a heavy *shroud* on this declining railroad town. One hundred years ago Yankee soldiers had unceremoniously marched through our swamps to Vicksburg. To our eternal shame, no significant resistance was offered, except a brief unsuccessful *skirmish* at Boggy Bayou. A pastor *distinguished* only by his mediocrity, Palmer Green seemed committed to irrelevance. Despite the fact that desegregation was fracturing our fragile community and some of our neighbors and relatives were warring with the Army Reserve units at Central High School in Little Rock, Arkansas, Green was warning us of "immoral thoughts." Most of us had not had an "immoral thought" since Elvis Presley played in the old VA gym. We never liked Green's sensitivity. It seemed so *effeminate*—un-Christian, really. He seemed to be an *incorrigible* sentimentalist, and while Southern ethos was full of tradition and *veiled* sentimentalism, we fiercely hid our true feelings. Green was, however, a greater threat to our fragile equilibrium. Dwight Washington, a black high school scholar and track star, had a conversion experience at one of our revival services. He foolishly thought that since Jesus loved him, we would too. So, he tried to attend our Sunday morning worship service. But he was politely asked to leave during the assurance of pardon. Green saw everything and was obviously displeased. Not that he *castigated* us. We could handle that. We enjoyed pastors who scolded us for our sins. We tolerated, even enjoyed his *paternalistic diatribes*. No, Green did the intolerable: he wept. Right in the middle of morning worship, right where great preachers like Muzon Mann had labored, where our children were baptized, Green wept! Right in the middle of morning worship, as if it was part of the liturgy, he started crying! Not loud, uncontrollable sobs, but quiet, deep crying. Like a man who was overwhelmed by the *exigencies* of life. Old Man Hendrick, senile and almost deaf, remembering the last time he cried—when his wife died—started crying too. And then the children. We owe so much to Palmer Green. He taught us how to cry....(from "The Call," by Jim Stobaugh, *Leadership* Magazine)

A. Define italic words.
B. Find examples of irony.
C. Write a one-sentence précis of this passage.

Solve

A triangle whose area is 16 square inches has a base of 4 that is ½ the height. What is the height?

Causes Worth Winning

But the nurses feared God. So they did not do as the king told them. They let all the boy babies live. —Exodus 1:17 (NCV)

Scripture: *Exodus 1:8–22*

Governor Robert P. Casey, several years ago, at a national gathering, in his speech entitled "Causes Worth Winning," quoted a letter written by my daughter Jessica:

Dear Governor Casey,

Hi! My name is Jessica Stobaugh. I am ten. I was adopted. My birth mother chose life for me. I would stand up like you for life. I think what you are doing is right. I would do the same thing if I were governor…Thank you for fighting for unborn children, even when it's a hard thing to do.

From your fan and friend, Jessica

Casey took a very controversial stand on the abortion issue—pro-life—that was not embraced by his political party. His courageous stand, most agree, ruined Casey politically. His decision to take a stand on behalf of the unborn child was motivated by his faith—not by politics. But, because he took a stand of conscience, as the midwives did in Moses' time, even if it was unpopular, he found himself left out in the political cold.

There will be times, no doubt, when you will be unpopular, even persecuted for your faith. Has this ever happened? How did you react?

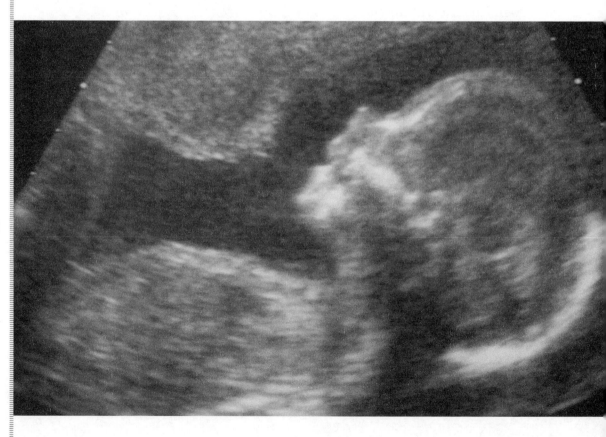

Using a Calculator

1. Have a fresh battery (or two) and practice replacing it.
2. Don't bring a calculator that tells you tomorrow's weather—keep it simple. One of the best calculators I've seen is a child's Mickey Mouse calculator with big numbers.
3. Your calculator must be quiet.
4. Use it if you need it but don't do every problem with a calculator.
5. Remember: enter numbers very carefully. Calculators do not leave a record of your entries.
6. Check your answers with it.

Devotional Journal

Read/Vocabulary Cards

Grammar

Choose the correct answer.

Did you work as hard as (they, them)?

Solve

A. The larger of 2 numbers is 24 more than the smaller. The sum of the numbers is 72. Find the numbers.

B. If one car costs x dollars, what is the cost of y of these cars?

Using a calculator, find a.

C. $\dfrac{30}{4a} = \dfrac{10}{24}$

D. $45a = 3825$

E. $\dfrac{2225}{25} = a$

F. $56(a - 74) = a$

G. $\dfrac{61,542}{78} = a$

H. $\dfrac{56,833,396}{4562} = a$

I. $32 + 89 - 67 + 34 \times 212 - 89 + 31 = a$

He fell on his knees and cried in a loud voice, "Lord, do not hold this sin against them!"
—Acts 7:60 (NCV)

Scripture: Acts 7:54-60

When my wife, Karen, and I started dating we were already in our middle twenties and firmly committed to our Lord. Separately, we had decided to serve the Lord no matter what. And, Karen, in a Christian college, and I, in a secular college, found the task equally challenging. We wanted to do what was right more than be safe. And, frankly, at times, very few folks encouraged us to stand firm. The American, Robert Frost, in his poem "West-Running Brook," writes:

> *What does it think it's doing running west*
> *When all the other country brooks flow east*
> *To reach the ocean? It must be the brook*
> *Can trust itself to go by contraries*
> *The way I can with you...*

I shared this poem with my wife, Karen, when we were dating. Then, and now, I feel that it is a prophetic word for all our lives—that God was calling us to be a west-running brook—it is the right direction to go—even if it is an east-running world. I am asking you to take a stand for Christ. Like Stephen. To show the world that you will not be intimidated, persuaded, or moved by what the "world" tells you is right—but you will only stand on the Word of God. I am asking you to take a stand in everything you say and do. No matter what the cost, no matter what the risk. Like Stephen.

Meditate on Acts 7. Can you be a Stephen to your world?

Devotional Journal

Read/Vocabulary Cards

Have your parents or guardians quiz you this evening.

Solve

A. If the first and third of three consecutive even integers are added, the result is 24 less than three times the second integer. Find the integers.

B. -36 divided by -9 =

Critical Reading

A. Write a one sentence précis of the following passage. Keep trying until you get one sentence. Give the passage a title.

I ran away and stayed away. Mother Theresa moved in and stayed. That is the difference.— Malcom Muggeridge

The Nepali man comes. Carrying his bloated, pale, obviously sick wife. Even though the young, emaciated man weighs barely 100 pounds, he carries his burden for two days through the treacherous Himalayan Mountains. But he is not to be deterred. He wants his wife to live. His limited knowledge, his own inadequacies are offset by his sheer stubbornness. He is not going to let anything stop him from reaching this hospital. He does not know this strange god the Christians served—after all he worships over a million Hindu gods. But, to him, this hospital and its doctors worship the God "Jesus Christ." And he means to have Him touch his wife and to heal her. Passing several government hospitals, this man puts himself at great risk and at great inconvenience to assure the healing of the one whom he loves.

B.

1   My own position at the threshold of Christianity was exactly the opposite of yours.
2   You wish it were true; I strongly hoped it was not. At least, that was my conscious
3   wish: you may suspect that I had unconscious wishes of quite a different sort and
4   that it was these which finally shoved me in. True: but then I may equally suspect
5   that under your conscious wish that it were true, there lurks a strong unconscious
6   wish that it were not. What this works out to is that all the modern thinking, however
7   useful it may be for explaining the origin of an error which you already know to be
8   an error, is perfectly useless in deciding which of two beliefs is the error and which is
9   the truth. For (a.) One never knows all one's wishes, and (b.) In very big questions,
10 such as this, even one's conscious wishes are nearly always engaged on both sides.
11 What I think one can say with certainty is this: the notion that everyone would like
12 Christianity to be true, and that therefore all atheists are brave men who have
13 accepted the defeat of all their deepest desires, is simply impudent nonsense. Do you
14 think people like Stalin, Hitler, Haldane, Stapledon (a corking good writer, by the
15 way) would be pleased on waking up one morning to find that they were not their
16 own masters, that they had a Master and a Judge, that there was nothing even in the
17 deepest recesses of their thoughts about which they [could] say to Him 'Keep out!
18 Private. This is my business'? Do you? Rats! Their first reaction would be (as mine
19 was) rage and terror. And I very much doubt whether even you would find it simply
20 pleasant. Isn't the truth this: that it would gratify some of our desires (ones we feel in
21 fact pretty seldom) and outrage a good many others? So let's wash out all the wish
22 business. It never helped anyone to solve any problem yet (*Letters*, C. S. Lewis).

What point is Lewis making in lines 12-18?
    A. He is making a point that neither Christianity or more evil positions seem
        inherently correct, nor are they particularly appealing on first glance, but
        only as they are embraced as a worldview do their true colors appear.
    B. Hitler, et al., are misguided people who could be Christians if the right
        argument was presented to them.
    C. Lewis is not anything like his friend—he fervently rejected Christianity until
        much later in life.

That if you confess with your mouth, "Jesus is Lord," and believe in your heart that God has raised him from the dead, you will be saved. —Romans 10:9

Scripture: Romans 10:1-13

In Romans 10:1-13 Paul is yearning for Israel's salvation. It is Paul's fervent desire! If only the law, if only the intellect, could bring salvation! But it cannot, Paul laments. Only a change of heart. In George MacDonald's (1824–1905) *The Curate's Awakening*, we meet a rather ordinary pastor in the Church of England named Thomas Wingfold. Wingfold's life "had not been particularly interesting…he had known from the first that he was intended for the church, and had not objected but accepted it as his destiny. Yet he had taken no great interest in the matter." He was a good man who "laid no claim to courage or devotion." He just dutifully did his job day after day…. But "could he in all honesty have said he believed there was a God? Or was this not all he really knew—that there was a Church of England which paid him for reading public prayers to a God in whom the congregation was assumed to believe?" The pastor, the religious man, was discouraged…. Indeed, we grow weary too, don't we? All this frenetic activity can weary our soul…and we wonder if God is, after all, real. As MacDonald explains, "To Wingfold, God had become an intellectual response…instead of a pursuit of the heart."

Is Jesus Christ in your heart as well as in your mind? Is He more than an intellectual exercise—is He your Lord?

Devotional Journal

Read/Vocabulary Cards

Critical Thinking: Classification

Using these words, find two general topics.

needle	piano	drum
guitar	thimble	pins
trombone	violin	trumpet
scissors	flute	

Should one guess? Some people guess if they can narrow the answers to two choices. You pray about it.

Grammar

Correct the following sentence.

It was nearly impossible for <u>John and I, sitting in the last row, to hear Margaret and he</u> speak their lines.

A. John and I, sitting in the last row, to hear Margaret and he
B. John and me, sitting in the last row, to hear Margaret and he
C. John and I, sitting in the last row, to hear Margaret and him
D. Margaret and he to be heard by John and me, sitting in the last row,
E. John and me, sitting in the last row, to hear Margaret and him

Solve

A. 8 + (7 x 3) 2 + 3 (12 - 3) =
B. Find the perimeter in centimeters.

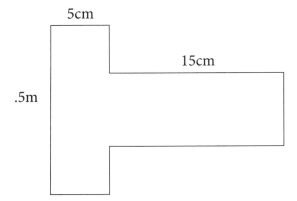

5cm

15cm

.5m

57

Woe Is Me!

"Woe is me," I cried. "I am ruined! For I am a man of unclean lips, and I live among a people of unclean lips, and my eyes have seen the King, the Lord Almighty!"
—Isaiah 6:5

Scripture: *Isaiah 6:1-6*

Some people claim that Isaiah was the greatest of the Old Testament prophets. His career spanned the turbulent period from King Uziah's death, about 740 b.c. to the fall of Jerusalem in 701 b.c. Judah's kings, especially timid and shaky Ahaz, persistently wanted to rely on political deals with foreign powers, usually Assyria or Egypt, to save the country. But Isaiah would not hear of it—"Tremble, you women who are at ease…" (32:11a). Isaiah's ministry began with the famous "call" in chapter 6 with which you are no doubt familiar. His call on Isaiah's life is specific, substantial, and spectacular. He never asks what Isaiah has—He wants much more! His call is specific—let us not look for excuses. And it is always spectacular!

What is God's call on your life? What excuses have you used in the past to miss God's best for your life?

Devotional Journal

Read/Vocabulary Cards

Vocabulary

Captains Courageous is one of many tales by Rudyard Kipling that have thrilled young people for over a century. Spoiled, good-for-nothing Harvey Cheyne is missed by no one but his mother when he falls over the side of an ocean liner. However, for the rest of the novel we watch Harvey's metamorphosis into a "captains courageous."

A. Define italicized words in context:

"Veer out the tiller-lines," cried Harvey, "and nail 'em to the bottom." That was a salt flavored jest he had been put up to by Tom Platt. Manuel leaned over the *stern* and yelled: "John Morgan play the organ! Ahaaa!" He *flourished* his broad thumb with a gesture of *derision*…. But the boys thought over the things that they might have said to the *discomfited* "Carrie." (from *Captains Courageous* by Rudyard Kipling)

B. Give synonyms for these words

1. amplify   6. misuse
2. ambitious   7. feasible
3. erratic   8. glib
4. esoteric   9. forthright
5. espouse   10. fortuitous

Solve

Factor this equation:

$8x^2 - 2x$

A. $2(2x^2 - x)$
B. $2x(4x - 1)$
C. $x(8x^2 - 2)$
D. None of these

When Our Terrors Cease

But the angel said to them, "Do not be afraid. I bring you good news of great joy that will be for all the people. Today in the town of David a Savior has been born to you...." — Luke 2:10,11

Scripture: *Luke 2:2-20*

Forty years ago beside a generous apple tree and a pink dogwood tree, Dad planted three pine trees. One died during our neighborhood football game. Our yard man accidently mowed down another the next summer. But one—the one now standing—grows and grows. The *interloper* overshadows the apple tree; it poisons the beautiful dogwood tree and gold-minnow hybrid fish with its toxic sap. And the darn thing continues to grow about a foot a year! That pine tree *intrudes* itself into my soul. Sticky, brown, ageless, untouched even by the coldest Arkansas winter, it still quietly stands, *smirking* at all of us dying human beings. *Flaunting* its immortality, the *venerable* tree postures itself in silent mockery at the rest of us who are struggling to deal with the many *vicissitudes* of life. I wish that pine was dead too. As it overshadows my old yard, robbing all other life of light and *sustenance*, so also it *overshadows* me. I see my poor dad, kneeling and gently placing that ungrateful pine tree into the Arkansas delta. Lovingly pouring water among its selfish, *grasping* roots, he squats in silent hope. He really expected to live to see that tree tower above our farmhouse. That tree gives me painful thoughts of what was and will never be again. What might have been but was not. As God or cancer or whatever it is that unmercifully, slowly, *torturously* stole life from Dad ...But...Jesus has come. Let the pine trees cover the sky! Let their arms reach beyond the world until they fill our souls, for, you see, we fear not. Our Savior has come.

Has a loved one died? How did it feel? How does it feel now?

Devotional Journal

Read/Vocabulary Cards

Vocabulary

Define the italic words in the paragraph above.

Grammar

Choose the correct answer. David and (myself, I) are cousins.

Critical Thinking: Summary

Write a one-sentence summary of this devotion.

Critical Thinking: Literary Devices

Give an example of figurative language in this passage.

For homeschoolers and students from small, unknown Christian schools, the SAT is extremely important. Especially if you need financial aid! While most students can get into college even with low SAT scores, financial aid will be more forthcoming for those students with high SAT scores. So, while the SAT is a flawed exam and has nothing to do with your value as a person, it remains the single most common resource on which colleges—both Christian and secular—base their offers of admission and financial aid.

Barnabas and Paul were sent out by the Holy Spirit. They went to the city of Seleucia. From there they sailed to the island of Cyprus. When they came to Salamis, they preached the Good News of God in the Jewish synagogues. John Mark was with them to help. —Acts 13:4 (NCV)

Scripture: Acts 13

Everything was going so well. Paul, his friend Barnabas, and his companion John Mark (John was his Jewish name, Mark his Gentile name) were leading many people to the Lord. This was the beginning of their missionary journey, and things couldn't have gone better. Acts 13:13 is a tribute to Barnabas—even though his name is not mentioned. It was Barnabas who had set out as the leader of this expedition, but then it became Paul and Barnabas. Paul had assumed the leadership of the expedition, and there was no evidence that Barnabas complained. Remember, Barnabas had first sponsored Paul in the Jerusalem Church—and then Barnabas was playing second fiddle to Paul!

Have you ever played "second fiddle" to someone else when you were once "first chair"? By all accounts, Paul could be a pretty difficult person to follow. But Barnabas never complains…. What about you?

Devotional Journal

Read/Vocabulary Cards

Critical Reading

"Christmas won't be Christmas without any presents," grumbled Jo, lying on the rug.

"It's so dreadful to be poor!" sighed Meg, looking down at her old dress.

"I don't think it's fair for some girls to have plenty of pretty things, and other girls nothing at all," added little Amy, with an injured sniff.

"We've got Father and Mother, and each other," said Beth contentedly from her corner.

The four young faces on which the firelight shone brightened at the cheerful words, but darkened again as Jo said sadly, "We haven't got Father, and shall not have him for a long time." She didn't say "perhaps never," but each silently added it, thinking of Father far away, where the fighting was.

Nobody spoke for a minute; then Meg said in an altered tone, "You know the reason Mother proposed not having any presents this Christmas was because it is going to be a hard winter for everyone; and she thinks we ought not to spend money for pleasure, when our men are suffering so in the army. We can't do much, but we can make our little sacrifices, and ought to do it gladly. But I am afraid I don't." And Meg shook her head, as she thought regretfully of all the pretty things she wanted (*Little Women*, Louisa May Alcott).

Slightly less than half of the math problems on the SAT I will involve your basic, run-of-the-mill, arithmetic. These include ratios, percentages, averages, and fractions. And, the fact is, most of you, by the time you take the SAT I, will not have had basic math since grade school! Added to that, the fact that most of you use calculators to figure out your allowances means that you need to pay close attention to these arithmetic exercises.

Lesson continues on the next page.

From the first, the reader knows that Jo is the assertive, vivacious sister and has no unspoken thought. Beth is clearly the sensible sister—she keeps the peace. Beth also speaks for her parents. Are these statements true or false?

Solve

A. There is a train one kilometer long, traveling at a rate of one kilometer per minute through a tunnel that is one kilometer long. How long will it take the train to pass completely through the tunnel? (MindTrap®)

B. Represent 20 times the number obtained when twice x is decreased by 10.

C. The perimeter of a field is 260 feet. Find its dimensions if the length is 5 feet less than twice the width.

D. Which word from Group B belongs with the words from Group A?
   A. BLAST, PAPER, BOX, BANK
   B. JUICE, BAG, CRADLE, CARPET
   (MindTrap®)

Barnabas wanted to take John, also called Mark, with them, but Paul did not think it wise to take him… —Acts 15:37,38

Scripture: Acts 15:36-41

But Barnabas really shined later—when we read Acts 15—because he was willing to give John Mark a second chance. Paul and Barnabas invited John Mark to join them on a new missionary journey—a great privilege. But, suddenly, for no apparent reason, John Mark abandoned his friends and returned home. We do not know why. Perhaps Mark resented the deposition of Barnabas from the leadership; perhaps he was afraid of the proposed journey up into the plateau where Antioch in Pisidia stood, for it was a dangerous road; perhaps he was homesick. In any event, he was a man who failed his God and his fellow Christians. Whatever the reason or combination of reasons for John Mark's failure, Paul thought Mark's failure was serious enough to disqualify him from accompanying them on the next missionary trip (15:38). Barnabas, though, wanted to take John Mark, and Paul and Barnabas went their separate ways over this issue.

Have you ever failed someone, I mean really blown it—like John Mark did? What did you do? What should you do?

Devotional Journal

Read/Vocabulary Cards

Remember! Go over cards with your parents tonight! Spend some time in prayer with them too!

Critical Reading

The sonata as a musical form dates back to the genesis of string instruments, especially the violin, in the baroque period (about 1580 to 1750). A popular baroque type was the trio sonata, with two violins over a bass part. An organist normally played the bass with his left hand, along with a cellist, and the harmony was filled in with his right hand. Famous baroque sonatas for solo violin were written by Arcangelo Corelli, Giuseppe Tartini, Jean-Marie Leclair, Johann Sebastian Bach, and George Frederick Handel. These were primarily sacred sonatas, written to glorify the Lord. Later, sonatas were written to entertain kings.

Lesson continues on the next page.

1. The best title for this passage would be:
   A. The Baroque Sonata
   B. The Music of George Handel
   C. An End to Serious Music
   D. To Glorify the Lord!
2. Which statement is false?
   A. The violin was important in the baroque sonata.
   B. A favorite type of baroque sonata was the trio sonata.
   C. Sonatas were written only for religious purposes.
   D. An organist normally played the bass part.
   E. None of the above are true.

Solve

Joe, Sam, and Bob have three adjacent reserved seats for the baseball game. How many different seating arrangements are possible?
   A. 3
   B. 4
   C. 5
   D. 6
   E. 8

Critical Thinking: Essay

Definition Essay

As the name implies, the definition essay defines or explains what a particular word or idea means. It often combines several essay styles to create a complete definition of a complex subject. It involves more than the typical dictionary definition of a word, and includes the meaning that a particular word has come to have in society, its history, and its various meanings.

Write an essay defining post-modernism.

A Second Chance

Barnabas wanted to take John, also called Mark, with them. —Acts 15:37

 Scripture: Acts 15:37-41

Then Mark vanished from history, although tradition says he went to Alexandria, Egypt, and founded the church there. When he re-emerges twenty years later he is the man who has redeemed himself. Paul, writing to the Colossians from prison in Rome, told them to receive Mark if he came to them. "Get Mark and bring him with you, for he is very useful in serving me" (2 Timothy 4:11). So, the man who was once a deserter became the writer of a Gospel and the person Paul wanted with him at the end of his life. The Christian community today has great need for individuals who will serve as encouragers of those who fail. John Mark needed to repent—confess his sin and change his direction—but then he needed to be forgiven and encouraged. Simple encouragement is not a difficult job. It is kindness shown at the right time when someone is in the grip of depression; it is talking with a friend who has problems at home. It is taking time to care. It is being Jesus Christ to someone in need. In Shakespeare's tragedies—like *Hamlet*—at the critical moment, the characters do not express self-giving, sacrificial, forgiving love. In the comedies—like *The Tempest*—love and forgiveness are present.

Can you take a tragedy in your own life and give it a happy ending? Can you give yourself a second chance? Will you find a friend who has failed and give him a second chance?

Devotional Journal

Read/Vocabulary Cards

Vocabulary

Define italicized words in context:

> Confused motions of rebellion stormed in him. He was too full of the sap of living, to submit so easily to the destruction of his hopes. Must he wear out of his years at the side of a bitter *querulous* woman? All the healthy instincts of self-defense rose up in him…. Under his cheek he felt a hard object with strange *protuberances*…why should he not leave with Mattie the next day, instead of letting her go alone? He would hide his *valise* under the seat of the sleigh…. (from *Ethan Frome* by Edith Wharton)

Solve

A. Using your calculator, find the square root of the following.
   1) .7744
   2) 338,724.
B. Express 178 in prime factored form.

Ethan Frome, by Edith Wharton, is one of my personal favorites. Disarmingly short, Wharton skillfully creates a story of love, betrayal, and tragedy. Jean Paul Sartre, in his play *No Exit* defines hell as "a place where one spends eternity with people one hates." Poor Ethan is in hell….

The Gospel of Mark is written to the Gentiles—those outside the promises of God. Surely John Mark, the one who failed, was preeminently qualified to write that Gospel. Take heart, those of you who need second chances!

62
Thanks for the Memories

For this reason, ever since I heard about your faith in the Lord Jesus and your love for all the saints, I have not stopped giving thanks for you, remembering you in my prayers.
—Ephesians 1:15,16

Scripture: *Ephesians 1:15-18*

I thank God for my little small town church. It was in this community of faith that I met the Lord. I thank God for gentle folk who loved me, who taught me to respect my elders, who gave me such an appreciation for history. For Mrs. Strout, my fourth grade Sunday school teacher, who taught me that all persons are equally valuable to God and should be to all of us. For Mrs. Emerson, my fifth-grade public school teacher, who recognized my academic gifts and did not let my learning disability hinder my development. Then I gave my whole life to Jesus Christ. I do not cease to give thanks for these special people, making mention of them in my prayers.

Make a list of all the people God has used to bring you to Him and then to mature you in Him.

Devotional Journal

Read/Vocabulary Cards

Grammar

Select the one underlined part that must be changed to make the sentence correct.

<u>Do you object</u>   to   <u>me</u>   being the   <u>master</u>   of ceremonies for the
    (A)   **(B)**   **(C)**

acceptance speeches   <u>after the election?</u>   <u>[No error.]</u>
                (D)   **(E)**

Critical Thinking: Classification

Using these words, find two general topics in each group:

A.
| shale | sandstone | marble | granite | quartz |
| fry | broil | steam | bake | saute |

B.
| buttons | brown | green | red | crimson |
| zippers | hooks | gray | snaps | velcro |

Vocabulary

Find a word with each of these prefixes and learn its meaning:

A. super (above)
B. ambi (both)
C. ante (before)
D. anthropo (man)

E. arch (main or principal)
F. aqua (water)
G. aster (star)
H. audi (hear)

Solve

A. Mr. Jones bought six new suits for $40 each. He made a 20% profit on each suit. What was the price he charged his customers?
B. What was Mr. Jones' total profit?
C. Mary was excited. She found a suit marked down 30%. It originally cost $80. What was the new price of the suit?

63
Responsibilities to Unbelievers I

Sir Walter Scott

Continue praying and keep alert. And when you pray, always thank God. Also pray for us. Pray that God will give us an opportunity to tell people his message.
—Colossians 4:2,3 (NCV)

Scripture: *Colossians 4:1-5*

During Vacation Bible School, one of our children misbehaved. As a result, my wife said something that made me think: "Do you really want to hinder the work of the Lord with your bad behavior and bad choices?" Of course, most of us would not. We can serve God in a pagan manner. The pagan performs acts in order to fulfill selfish ends.... But if we serve God in obedience, our objectives will always be secondary to what He wants. *Responsibility*. This is a key word to the growing Christian. We have responsibilities to our God and to one another and to outsiders. We are not here merely to feel good. As a matter of fact, in Colossians 4:1-6, Paul gives us a few responsibilities to outsiders, or non-believers. First of all, we must conduct ourselves with wisdom. That has to do with our way of life and lifestyle. We have a responsibility to make sure that our walk in life is in line with Scripture. Remember, nonbelievers are observing us. We are on display! Remember that when you go to the video store! Remember, when you consider shoplifting, that your non-Christian friends are looking! You are Christ's representative to your world!

List at least five persons in your life who need to know the Lord. Pray for them and look for opportunities to share the Gospel with them.

1.

2.

3.

4.

5.

Devotional Journal

Read/Vocabulary Cards

Critical Reading

Scott's career, of writing impromptu novels to buy farms with, was not of a kind to terminate voluntarily, but to accelerate itself more and more; and one sees not to what wise goal it could, in any case, have led him. Bookseller Constable's bankruptcy was not the ruin of Scott; his ruin was, that ambition, and even false ambition, had laid hold of him; that his way of life was not wise. Whither could it lead? Where could it stop? New farms there remained ever to be bought, while new novels could pay for them. More and more success but gave more and more appetite, more and more audacity. The impromptu writing must have waxed ever thinner; declined faster and faster into the questionable category, into the condemnable, into the generally condemned (*Sir Walter Scott*, Thomas Carlyle).

To what does Carlyle ascribe Scott's ultimate demise?
- A. to bad health
- B. to loss of talent
- C. to belonging to the wrong political party
- D. to his ambition

Sentence Completion

Chemistry is the science that deals with the composition, structure, and properties of substances. Understanding how materials can be changed is _____ to understanding chemistry.
- A. must
- B. superfluous
- C. essential
- D. helpful
- E. extreme

Solve

Pete bought two boats. He sold both boats for $6000 each. On one boat he realized a profit of 20% and on the other boat he lost 20%. Did Pete make money? (MindTrap®)

64

Responsibilities II

Be wise in the way you act with people who are not believers. Use your time in the best way you can. When you talk, you should always be kind and wise. Then you will be able to answer everyone in the way you should. —Colossians 4:5,6 (NCV)

Scripture: *Colossians 4:5,6*

The second responsibility that growing Christians have toward unbelievers is to make the most of every opportunity. That does not mean manipulation! Situations will present themselves in which we shall have an opportunity to share Him. We must be patient but alert. Opportunities cannot be recaptured once they are missed.

Have you ever missed an opportunity to share Christ with a friend? Purpose to do better next time.

Devotional Journal

Read/Vocabulary Cards

Critical Reading

Charles Darwin, Sigmund Freud, and Karl Marx have reshaped the modern mind. Darwin is an example of a gifted amateur who made a stunning contribution. He never held an academic post and never was a biologist. He came from an Anglican background, and once considered becoming a priest, but his interests led him in other directions. At the end of his life, Darwin died as an agnostic. Rumors of his deathbed conversion are false. And Darwin never repudiated his ideas. At best, his ideas of nature were deistic. Darwin was a cautious scholar who was careful in his assertions. His ideas were original, but they were a synthesis of ideas done in a way that made sense—they were commonsense deductions based on very little scientific evidence. The world was ripe for Darwin, because he provided a way to explain origins without the need for a deity to serve as a creator. What later generations discovered was that Darwin had repudiated the idea of divine design or teleology. Until Darwin wrote *Origin of the Species*, if a person saw an animal with specific characteristics (i.e., fur on a polar bear) he saw those characteristics as evidence of divine design. After Darwin, scientists began to look at the animal in relation to the environment, not God. Pandora had opened her box and it would never be closed again.

1. Write a one-paragraph précis of this article; write a one-sentence précis of this article; give this article a three-word title.
2. Why is the book Origin of the Species so threatening to Judeo-Christian culture?
3. Define the word teleological.
4. Before Charles Darwin wrote Origin of the Species, what explanation would a scientist offer for the fact that whales are mammals? How would a scientist (who rejected the creation story in the Bible) explain the same phenomenon?
5. In spite of the fact that Darwin was no scientist and had very little evidence for the theory of evolution and natural selection, his theories were almost universally embraced. Why?

Charles Darwin

6. What is your view of creation?
7. Explain the reference to Pandora in the last sentence.

Critical Thinking: Essay

Write an essay defining grace.

65
Responsibilities III

Let your conversation be always full of grace, seasoned with salt, so that you may know how to answer everyone. —Colossians 4:5,6

Scripture: *Colossians 4:5,6*

What about the chance we have to share the love of Jesus Christ in our social groups? By our social behavior? Our talk must be gracious and perceptive. Gracious talk is talk that is courteous, cordial, cheerful, controlled, compassionate, and Christlike. If we trash a teacher, or gossip about an enemy, the unbeliever will notice and think that all Christians act this way. And, unfortunately, many Christians love to talk about others—friends and foes alike—who have made mistakes or bad choices. Chuck Swindoll loves to remind us Christians that we are the only army in the world who shoots its wounded! Are we forgiving and Christlike toward others as Christ is with us? The world is watching! Think about it....

List five ways that your witness to unbelievers could be improved.

1.

2.

3.

4.

5.

Devotional Journal

Read/Vocabulary Cards

Be sure to meet with your parents or guardians for prayer and to go over your vocabulary cards!

Sentence Completion

The idea of land is very important in Mexican culture. The Mexican Revolution (1910–1916), for instance, had as its slogan, "Land and Liberty." One of the happy results of the revolution was that the government _____ some of the land, _____ many poorer peasants to own their own land.

A. sold...stopping
B. redistributed...enabling
C. retained...enabling
D. destroyed...prohibiting

Vocabulary

Give a synonym for each word:
1. nurture
2. feeble
3. hopeless
4. frustrate
5. heed
6. barrier
7. animosity
8. humble
9. deceptive
10. conjectural
11. immune
12. impair
13. impartial
14. unnoticed
15. implication

Solve

A. Give all the prime factors of 264.
B. A coin is tossed three times. What is the probability that heads will come up every time?
C. Answer A occurs four times straight on an SAT I exam. What is the probability that it will occur as the fifth answer?
D. $\dfrac{10y^4}{14} \times \dfrac{14y^2}{2y^3}$

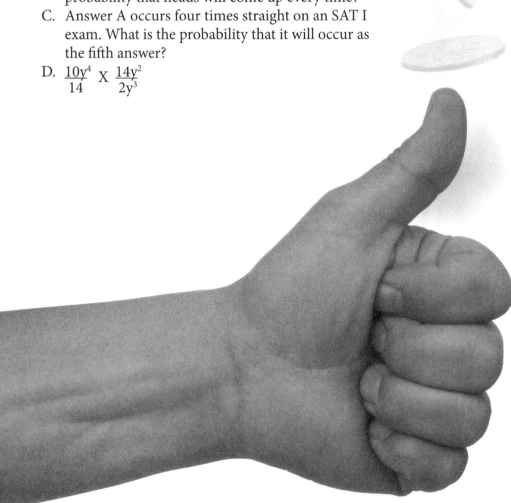

66
What Is Truth?

"What is truth?" Pilate asked.... —John 18:38

Scripture: *John 18:37-39*

Pilate was right to ask Jesus about truth. After all, Jesus Himself is the Way, the Truth, and the Life (John 3:16). Several years ago, as a seminary student at Harvard Divinity School, I can remember hurrying to chapel for the opening convocation. It was an inspiring day! All the professors were decked out in their finest and most impressive regalia. Being late again, I hurried across Divinity Avenue to my shortcut behind the Peabody Museum. Suddenly, though, I saw two professors hurrying in the opposite direction. Although I knew my shortcut was a good way to the yard, far be it from me to reject a better way. And these gentlemen, obviously smarter than I, going faster than I, more sure of themselves than I, were going to chapel. So, why not? I decided to follow them. Alas, we all were very late. My shortcut was the best way to go after all! I decided then that teachers are only fellow travelers in a discovery of truth. But no matter how you get there, the Bible is the only reliable basis for truth and really is the best way to go where you want to go. Along with research, the degree to which the university and its teachers helped me along on that journey is the degree to which that university and professors have done their job.

Write down at least three biblical truths (promises) given to you in the Bible. Memorize them!

1.

2.

3.

Devotional Journal

Read/Vocabulary Cards

Vocabulary

Learn these roots and make 3 by 5-inch cards for each root and include a word that contains it.

A. trans (across)
B. pro (before)
C. phila (love)
D. luna (moon)
E. scribo (write)
F. bi (two)
G. unus (one)
H. demos (people)
I. geo (earth)
J. photos (light)
K. megas (big)
L. graph (write)
M. logos (study)
N. video (see)
O. aqua (water)

Grammar

Choose the correct answer.

I will soon (lie, lay) down.

Solve

Give decimal answers for the following problems.

A. $\dfrac{4\frac{1}{3} \times 3\frac{1}{6}}{1\frac{1}{3} \times 2\frac{1}{4}}$

B. $\dfrac{\frac{7}{8} - \frac{1}{4}}{\frac{4}{32}}$

C. $\dfrac{2\frac{5}{6}}{\frac{6}{8} - \frac{2}{6}}$

67

Absolutely Murder

You shall not murder. —Exodus 20:13

Scripture: *Exodus 20:13*

Abortion in the U.S. is presently an industry producing $700 million a year. Over 500,000 babies are aborted every year in the United States. What this means is that each day an average of 1,369 unborn babies are murdered in the United States of America. In Washington, D.C., our nation's capital, abortions now outnumber live births. God is inviting His people, in Exodus 20, to embrace His laws. His laws bring life. Their violation brings death.

Pray for our nation. Pray for our leaders.

Devotional Journal

Read/Vocabulary Cards

Critical Thinking: Synthesis

From these Scriptures create a doctrine or synthesis (or composite view) of Christ:
  A. In the beginning was the Word, and the Word was with God, and the Word was God (John 1:1).
  B. And the Word became flesh and dwelt among us, and we beheld His glory, the glory as of the only begotten of the Father (John 1:14).
  C. And declared to be the Son of God with power according to the Spirit of holiness, by the resurrection from the dead (Romans 1:4).

Critical Reading

A. Answer a question on the reading.

Claude Monet was one of the founders of an art form known as impressionism. Impressionists used hundreds of small brushstrokes side by side, often in contrasting colors, to give an impression of solid forms. By placing unmixed colors side by side on his canvas, Monet showed how light splits into the colors of the prism. To show how light could completely change the appearance of a scene, he painted the Rouen Cathedral twenty times, in conditions varying from a colorful autumn day to a brilliant winter sunset.

By now you probably have concluded if there is an SAT I then there must be an SAT II. There is. The SAT II is what my generation called the old "Subject Area Achievement Tests." Some schools do not require the SAT II. Others require English and math. It is up to you, but I recommend that you take SAT II subject area tests in subjects in which you shine. For instance, in my case, I loved American history. I did very well on the subject area test. This looked good on my application. Other options could be French, German, any of the sciences, etc.

A title for this passage might be:
A. Monet Sets the Trend
B. Splitting Light
C. The Rouen Cathedral
D. Monet and the Genesis of Impressionism

B.

Gracious affections are attended with evangelical humiliation. Evangelical humiliation is a sense that a Christian has of his own utter insufficiency, despicableness, and odiousness, with an answerable frame of heart. There is a distinction to be made between a legal and evangelical humiliation. The former is what men may be the subjects of, while they are yet in a state of nature, and have no gracious affections; the latter is peculiar to true saints: the former is from the common influence of the Spirit of God, assisting natural principles, and especially natural conscience; the latter is from the special influences of the Spirit of God, implanting and exercising supernatural and divine principles: the former is from the mind's being assisted to a greater sense of the things of religion, as to their natural properties and qualities, and particularly of the natural perfections of God, such as his greatness, terrible majesty, which were manifested to the congregation of Israel, in giving the law at mount Sinai; the latter is from a sense of the transcendent beauty of divine things in their moral qualities: in the former, a sense of the awful greatness, and natural perfections of God, and of the strictness of his law, convinces men that they are exceeding sinful, and guilty, and exposed to the wrath of God, as it will wicked men and devils at the day of judgment; but they do not see their own odiousness on the account of sin; they do not see the hateful nature of sin; a sense of this is given in evangelical humiliation, by a discovery of the beauty of God's holiness and moral perfection. In a legal humiliation, men are made sensible that they are little and nothing before the great and terrible God, and that they are undone, and wholly insufficient to help themselves; as wicked men will be at the day of judgment: but they have not an answerable frame of heart, consisting in a disposition to abase themselves, and exalt God alone; this disposition is given only in evangelical humiliation, by overcoming the heart, and changing its inclination, by a discovery of God's holy beauty: In a legal humiliation, the conscience is convinced; as the consciences of all will be most perfectly at the day of judgment; but because there is no spiritual understanding, the will is not bowed, nor the inclination altered: this is done only in evangelical humiliation. In legal humiliation, men are brought to despair of helping themselves; in evangelical, they are brought voluntarily to deny and renounce themselves: in the former, they are subdued and forced to the ground; in the latter, they are brought sweetly to yield, and freely and with delight to prostrate themselves at the feet of God. Legal humiliation has in it no spiritual good, nothing of the nature of true virtue;

A great SAT II score might mitigate an average SAT I score. For instance, if you receive an average score on the Verbal SAT I, and you are pre-med, and you do well on the Biology SAT II, a college will be pleased. In any event, NEVER TAKE THE SAT II ON THE SAME DAY THAT YOU TAKE THE SAT I. To do so, while it might satisfy your need to get the whole thing over, would significantly reduce your SAT II scores. I recommend that you take the SAT I, May, junior year, and SAT II, June, junior year. Pray about it.

Lesson continues on the next page.

whereas evangelical humiliation is that wherein the excellent beauty of Christian grace does very much consist. Legal humiliation is useful, as a means in order to evangelical; as a common knowledge of the things of religion is a means requisite in order to spiritual knowledge. Men may be legally humbled and have no humility: as the wicked at the day of judgment will be thoroughly convinced that they have no righteousness, but are altogether sinful, and exceedingly guilty, and justly exposed to eternal damnation, and be fully sensible of their own helplessness, without the least mortification of the pride of their hearts: but the essence of evangelical humiliation consists in such humility, as becomes a creature, in itself exceeding sinful, under a dispensation of grace; consisting in a mean esteem of himself, as in himself nothing, and altogether contemptible and odious; attended with a mortification of a disposition to exalt himself, and a free renunciation of his own glory (*Religious Affections*, Jonathan Edwards).

Edwards would define humiliation as:
A. sadness
B. pride
C. stubbornness
D. contriteness

Jesus straightened up and asked her, "Woman, where are they? Has no one condemned you?" "No one, sir," she said. "Then neither do I condemn you," Jesus declared. "Go now and leave your life of sin." —John 8:10,11

Scripture: John 8:1-11

Ah, look at all the lonely people!
Ah, look at all the lonely people!

Eleanor Rigby
Picks up the rice in the church where a wedding has been,
Lives in a dream,
Waits at the window
Wearing the face that she keeps in a jar by the door.
Who is it for?

Father McKenzie,
Writing the words of a sermon that no one will hear,
No one comes near
Look at him working,
Darning his socks in the night when there's nobody there.

Eleanor Rigby
Died in the church and was buried along with her name.
Nobody came.
Father McKenzie,
Wiping the dirt from his hands as he walks from the grave,
No one was saved.

All the lonely people
Where do they all come from?
All the lonely people,
Where do they all belong?

—John Lennon and Paul McCartney

Read this song carefully. In an essay, give three reasons why the song is so depressing. Using the Scriptures, what would you say to Father McKenzie and Eleanor Rigby? Where do believers find their ultimate worth?

Devotional Journal

Read/Vocabulary Cards

Lesson continues on the next page.

Solve

A. "It's just my luck!" screamed Barney. "It was about 10:30 in the morning. I was driving along at the legal speed of 100 kilometers/hour. My car had just passed a safety inspection and my license plates, license, and insurance were all in order. I was wearing my seat belt, too. I pass a couple of cars, being certain, again, not to exceed 100 kilometers/hour. The next thing I know a policeman pulls me over and gives me a ticket." Why? (MindTrap®)

B. Answer the questions concerning this graph:

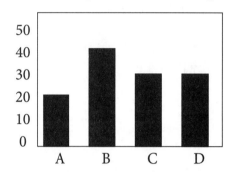

1. Estimate A+B+C+D
2. What is the average of A+B+C+D?
3. A = Average salary (in thousands) of 20 people. B = Average salary (in thousands) of 40 people. What is their overall average?
4. If there are 120 employees, C = D, A = 20 people, B = 40 people, what does C equal?

Critical Thinking: Essay

The SAT test often gives a student two quotes with an assignment for essay writing. This example is taken from a sample test on the College Board Web site. Please write an essay following these instructions.

ESSAY PROMPT: Think carefully about the issue presented in the following quotations and do the assignment below.

1   While secrecy can be destructive, some of it is indispensable in human lives. Some control over secrecy and openness is needed in order to protect identity. Such control may be needed to guard privacy, intimacy, and friendship. (Adapted from Sissela Bok, "The Need for Secrecy")

2   Secrecy and a free, democratic government, President Harry Truman once said, don't mix. An open exchange of information is vital to the kind of informed citizenry essential to healthy democracy. (Editorial, "Overzealous Secrecy Threatens Democracy")

Assignment: Do people need to keep secrets or is secrecy harmful? Plan and write an essay in which you develop your point of view on this issue. Support your position with reasoning and examples taken from your reading, studies, experience, or observations.

I the Lord do not change. —Malachi 3:6

Scripture: *The Book of Malachi*

John Knowles in his novel *A Separate Peace* describes several young men growing up during World War II. They can't wait to join the army! To fight the enemy! To die for their country, if necessary! World War II made such an impression on his life that he writes, "It is 1942 now, it was 1942 then, and it will be 1942 forever!" Malachi must have felt that way as he stared out into fifth-century Jerusalem. It is 575 b.c. now and it will be 575 b.c. forever! In his book, Malachi is lamenting, in contemporary language, how much things change to stay the same! Malachi's contemporaries were making the same mistakes as their moms and dads. Nothing seemed to have changed. It was as though he were looking in a five-hundred-year-old yearbook. With incredulity and some discouragement, Malachi must have blinked his eyes and thought that he was looking at an old yearbook with snapshots of his ancestors. Have you ever looked at an old yearbook with your first-grade picture? You know, that skinny little kid hiding in the corner? Malachi's generation seemed to be unstuck in time. Same old problems, same old mistakes…however, our world does change—even if it gets worse—but God never changes. He is the same yesterday, today, and forever. Malachi takes some comfort in that fact. God will not change—but we must change. We must.

Name at least three areas that need to be changed in your life.

1.

2.

3.

Devotional Journal

Read/Vocabulary Cards

Young people always ask me, "Do I concentrate on improving my weak areas, or do I make my strengths stronger?" I always respond, "Both!" For the first few months of SAT preparation, I want you to identify your weaknesses, and work to improve them. But, for the last few months, I want you to emphasize your strengths. Remember! All answers count the same! In my case, I never did well on analogies, but I rarely ever missed a reading comprehension question. Ergo, I concentrated on reading, and ultimately my strengths, not my weaknesses, gave me a decent score.

Lesson continues on the next page.

Critical Reading

The social welfare system is a runaway juggernaut. We have spent over $5 trillion since 1965 and we are worse off. If all this money had given us happy, healthy families, it would have been worth it. But the opposite is true. It has consigned untold millions of children to lives of bitterness and failure. In 1960 five of every 100 American births were illegitimate. By 1991 that figure was thirty of every 100, and the upward trend shows no sign of slowing. Government welfare programs dealing with the problem have also increased. But the cost of illegitimacy is not measured only in dollars. Crime, violence, unrest, disorder—most particularly the furious, unrestrained lashing out at the whole social structure—that is not only to be expected, it is very near to inevitable. By 1994 the figure of illegitimate births grew to 40 percent and, an even more alarming figure, 27 percent of pregnancies were aborted. Children who do not live with a mother and a father are more likely to be high-school dropouts, more likely to abuse drugs and alcohol, and more likely to be dependent on welfare than children who live with both parents. Psychologists point out that fathers are not simply substitute mothers. Boys are much less likely to develop good self-control when fathers are not present. A man, already suffering from his failure as a provider, is further demeaned by becoming dependent on the woman who gets the welfare check. I blame human depravity and the social welfare system for this problem.

1. Write a précis of this passage.
2. Create paragraphs. Find the topic sentence in each paragraph.
3. The last paragraph has an unnecessary sentence. What is it?
4. Identify and define any words that you do not know.
5. Write a title for this passage.
6. What is the article's main argument? Do you agree or disagree?

Solve

Answer this question: 89 = ?

   A. $89 + X^0$

   B. $89 + 0$

   C. $89 + X$

   D. All of the above

70

Empty Hands Reaching Through a Seam in the Crowd

And a woman…came up…and touched the fringe of his garment… —Luke 8:43 (RSV)

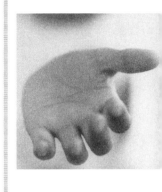

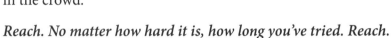
Scripture: 8:43-48

In our Scripture reading we saw a woman reaching out. She came to be healed. She risked everything—and she could not be stopped. She meant to be healed no matter how painful or costly the effort. Are you sick in your heart? In your body? Are you isolated by your problem? For twelve years God seemed to be silent. How long has He appeared to be absent from your life? Jesus is reaching to you. He wants to heal you. Whatever the problem—He cares. If you need help on this SAT preparation, if you need guidance for your future, seek Him. If your family situation is so-so, or you are struggling through a bad relationship, He is here. Ready to listen. And, you see, He really understands. I cannot really understand your problem. I have not walked in your shoes. But He has. He understands. And He will heal us…but only if we reach with our empty hands through a seam in the crowd.

Reach. No matter how hard it is, how long you've tried. Reach.

Devotional Journal

Read/Vocabulary Cards

Go over vocabulary cards with your parents or guardians. Are you memorizing a target Scripture?

Grammar

Choose the correct answer.

If I (would have thought, had thought) of it, I would have invited you.

Vocabulary

A. Define italicized words in context:

He was an angry, impatient, *sarcastic* teacher. I had had angry teachers before, but their anger had always been accompanied by a redeeming humor. There was nothing humorous about Rav Kalman. He rarely sat still behind his desk. He paced. I would watch him pace back and forth…. He smoked *incessantly*…. His classes left me *nerveless*, tense…. He did not answer my questions…. Textual *emendation* of Talmudic passages as practiced by those who studied Talmud in the modern, scientific manner was unheard of in

Chaim Potok

The Promise by Chaim Potok is a story of two Jewish boys struggling to gain an identity in a world both liberated and enslaved by tradition.

Lesson continues on the next page.

my school…. We had no way of knowing how Rav Kalman might react to any of our questions, and I had no desire to become the target of his *sarcasm*…. The annual college senior show, to which girls had always been invited, was called off because he waged a *vitriolic* campaign against girls sitting together with boys in the yeshiva auditorium…. [His speeches] were delivered with sarcasm and anger, and one is rarely *ennobled* by such *exhortations*. (from *The Promise* by Chaim Potok)

B. Give a synonym for each word:

1. incentive
2. incongruity
3. indict
4. nonchalant
5. induce
6. inept
7. destined
8. ingenious
9. innovation
10. complexity

Solve

A. Draw a graph to represent the scores of students on the SAT.
    Mary = 560 verbal, 610 math
    Susan = 690 verbal, 650 math
    David = 490 verbal, 510 math
    Steve = 500 verbal, 540 math

B. What is their combined average math score? Verbal score?

71

Generic Christianity

...you do not know the Scriptures or the power... —Mark 12:24

Scripture: Mark 12:13-24

During the seventies a fortuitous development occurred in the drug and supermarket businesses: generic products. Removing all frills, expunging expensively adorned packing, and thereby lowering advertising costs, stores were able to offer a profitable alternative to name-brand products. The results have been astounding: Food prices and drug prices have essentially stayed the same in the last ten years. But although a good idea in the marketplace, generic strategies fare very poorly in Christian youth culture. Too many young people have tried—with perfectly pure intentions—to distill Christianity to noncontroversial and unexciting basics. Many have reached for the least common denominator as they sought to find common ground with the world. We have sacrificed theological efficacy for mass appeal. What does this propensity, this overwhelming urge toward a digestible, noncontroversial Christianity mean to us? What it means is that some of us have transformed the most revolutionary message of all time into a ho-hum religion. No risk, no challenge. A faith that may keep us going around in circles, but not the kind of faith that will give us strength at a party when everyone else is drinking. The Pharisees in our passage today have a faith that couldn't cut the mustard when the rubber met the road and Jesus knew it. Think about it.

What areas of your life need to be "radicalized"?

Devotional Journal

Read/Vocabulary Cards

Critical Reading

A. Answer the questions following this passage on the basis of what is stated or implied.

> Anger, as a socially acceptable emotion, is a twentieth-century phenomenon. We have always been comfortable with guilt—the early Puritans who settled in the United States built their entire morality on guilt. But not until the middle of the twentieth century were we comfortable with anger. The study of race relations in America is essentially a study of anger. And anger is related to power: who has it, who does not, how it is gained, how it is lost, and how it is maintained. Powerlessness is inversely related to attempts of people to control the environmental factors in their life situations; that is, a low feeling of powerlessness is related to a high level of effort toward manipulating situations. To experience powerlessness usually leads to anger. Such has been the case in black America. The origins of racism lie in comparativism. To most of the early American thinkers it appears obvious that races are not equally gifted.

We all live with freedom and limits for one expressed call: to do His will.

Lesson continues on the next page.

1. What is an appropriate title for this passage? What is the cause of anger in the black community?
2. How are power and anger related?
3. Why did I mention the Puritans? Where do the origins of racism lie?
4. How long did it take you to read this passage and understand it?

B.

As he turned to go on, he spat speculatively. There was a sharp, explosive crackle that startled him. He spat again. And again, in the air, before it could fall to the snow, the spittle crackled. He knew that at fifty below spittle crackled on the snow, but this spittle had crackled in the air. Undoubtedly it was colder than fifty below—how much colder he did not know. But the temperature did not matter. He was bound for the old claim on the left fork of Henderson Creek, where the boys were already. They had come over across the divide from the Indian Creek country, while he had come the roundabout way to take a look at the possibilities of getting out logs in the spring from the islands in the Yukon. He would be in to camp by six o'clock; a bit after dark, it was true, but the boys would be there, a fire would be going, and a hot supper would be ready. As for lunch, he pressed his hand against the protruding bundle under his jacket. It was also under his shirt, wrapped up in a handkerchief and lying against the naked skin. It was the only way to keep the biscuits from freezing. He smiled agreeably to himself as he thought of those biscuits, each cut open and sopped in bacon grease, and each enclosing a generous slice of fried bacon ("The Blue Hotel," Stephen Crane).

The narrative technique in this passage is:
A. Limited Omniscient
B. Objective Third Person
C. Omniscient
D. First Person

Solve

If x ♣ y = $\sqrt{x + y}$ for all positive integers, what is the value of 6 ♣ 3?
A. 0
B. 1
C. 3
D. 6
E. 9

…People always serve the best wine first. Later, after the guests have been drinking a lot, they serve the cheaper wine. But you have saved the best wine until now!
—John 2:10 (NCV)

Scripture: John 2:1-11

It was the winter of 1976. Thirty below. A foot of snow. This meteorological turn of events was especially painful for me—I had seen snow only once or twice before 1976. I thought a cold day was when it was below 50 degrees! I was sitting in a drafty Harvard Yard building listening to Dr. Williams, lecturing on a miracle described by the Venerable Bede, one of the first British church historians. Williams was notorious for his criticism of miracles—supernatural hocus-pocus he called it. Miracles did not really happen didn't you know! But Professor Williams was sick and needed a miracle. He knew it, too. As he lectured on Venerable Bede he reached a point in his lecture where he paused and looked out the window at Widener Library. We all sat and waited. "You know," he finally said, still looking out the frosted window, "I used to laugh at people who believed in miracles." In good nature, we all laughed with him. "But, now, it is not funny. I need a miracle. And now, laugh at me too, but now I believe in them, too." It is the shortage of wine that causes Christ to perform a miracle—the recognition that there is a need. For most of us the greatest miracle was the day Christ came into our hearts.

Are you willing to admit to Him that you need a miracle?

Devotional Journal

Read/Vocabulary Cards

Solve

545 ÷ 1000 =
  A. 5.45
  B. .545
  C. 545
  D. $^{5.45}/_{10}$

Critical Thinking: Essay

Write an essay defining faith.

Is God intimately involved in the affairs of mankind or not? The answer to this question is more or less the battle that is raging on college campuses today.

73
It Is Finished!

When he had received the drink, Jesus said, "It is finished." With that, he bowed his head and gave up his spirit. —John 19:30

Scripture: John 19:25-30

Jesus died for your sins on the cross at Calvary. We say that so often without hearing what we say. Several years ago there was a fire in Chicago. Every person in one family died except a five-year-old boy. During the fire, a stranger ran into the fire and saved the little boy. The little boy suffered from smoke inhalation but the stranger's hands were badly burned. The boy and the man went to separate hospitals and never saw each other again. In fact, no one knew who the stranger was. Finally the child recovered and the courts tried to decide who could adopt him. Several relatives were contacted and none of them were interested. Finally, he was about to be turned over to the state. But, during the hearing to determine the future of the little boy, a man entered the court room. He proceeded to ask the judge politely if he could adopt the child. "Who are you?" the judge asked. "And what right do you have to adopt this child?" The man said nothing but he took his hands out of his pockets and showed the judge what was left of his severely burned hands. It was the man who had rushed in and saved the child's life. Likewise, Jesus died for our sins on a cross at Calvary. What He asks in return is that we give Him our hearts. Trust Him. Give Him everything.

Jesus died for you. Who else has ever done that for you? Have you invited Him into your heart and asked Him to be your Lord and Savior?

Devotional Journal

Read/Vocabulary Cards

Critical Thinking: Comparison

As I stared at Rachel I remember that I had seen those ubiquitous brown eyes before. I had seen them on fourteen-year-old Lamar who was hiding behind our junior high music building. He was trying to elude our white classmates who were intent upon enforcing their special form of segregation.... My wife turned, smiled, and handed me my new daughter, Rachel, and I felt such peace. "Now the Lord said unto Abram, get thee out of thy country, and from thy kindred, and from thy father's house, unto a land I will show thee." Abram was called to a new land, a new time, a new family, and to a new name. The risks were very great—all the time in fact. At any time the promise could be lost and the rewards were singularly obscure. But he trusted God more than he feared the wilderness.

Rachel was my promised land. She was my new time, my new land, my new chance. She was more than my daughter: She was God's invitation to me to experience wholeness and new life.

1. Read Genesis 12 and study the call of Abram. Is the comparison between adopting my interracial daughter Rachel and Abram's call accurate?
2. The Rachel story takes on epic proportions. Explain what I mean.
3. Discuss the essence of *risk* as it relates to this passage.
4. Give a title to this passage. Write a summary of it. And write a one-line précis about it. How effective is its emotional effect?

Old Solutions

Sense and Sensibility, by Jane Austen, is a poignant and insightful novel of upper class life in early 19th century England. Austen's works are to be rivaled only by those of the equally famous Alcott oeuvre, particularly *Little Women.* In fact, if you like *Little Women,* you will love *Sense and Sensibility*! Austen had an unerring ear for dialogue and a perceptive eye for the nuances of gesture and behavior that so affect the fortunes of men and women, and in the story of Elinor and Marianne Dashwood—sisters widely divergent in temperament and personality—we come to know and love two of Austen's most unforgettable heroines.

Then Jehoshaphat stood up in the assembly of Judah and Jerusalem at the temple of the Lord in front of the new courtyard and said: "O Lord…no one can withstand you."
—2 Chronicles 20:5,6

Scripture: 2 Chronicles 20

I once heard a story of a man who fell off a cliff. Fortunately he was able to grab a small limb that kept him from falling to his death. But this was a momentary respite: At any time he could tire, let go of the branch, and surely fall to his death. In great anguish he cried, "Help! Anyone! Help me! Please!" Unfortunately no one was near enough to answer his cries. Finally, in great frustration, he called, "God! If You are really up there, save me!" To the man's surprise a strong and clear voice responded, "I am God, son, let go of the branch and take My hand." After a few moments of strained silence, the poor man cried again, "Is there anyone else up there?"

As the sun teasingly nestled beneath the western horizon, King Jehoshaphat's short reign was also sinking. "God," he cried, "What am I to do?" God was going to tell Jehoshaphat to do some things he would rather not do. Time-honored solutions to problems of the past were not going to solve future problems. And I am sure that he wondered if there was anyone else up there! Young Jehoshaphat, a good king himself but the successor of evil Asa, shivered as he considered this new challenge: Earlier that day he had heard that the dreaded Moabites, Ammonites, and their allies were invading Judah. Any one of these dreaded Arabian tribes was a formidable enemy—and all of them were attacking tiny Judah! It was just too much for poor Jehoshaphat. At least, he had the good sense to know it. So, he did what we all naturally do when we face overwhelming obstacles: Jehoshaphat turned to time- honored ways to solve his problems.

The fact is, some of our problems will not be solved unless we look to God for help. Are you willing? Think of difficulties in your life that need God's miraculous intervention.

Devotional Journal

Read/Vocabulary Cards

Grammar

Choose the correct answer.

(Having been wrong, Being wrong) five times in a row, I now had no credibility with this audience.

Vocabulary

Define italicized words in context:

These words, which conveyed to Elinor a direct *avowal* of his love for her sister, *affected* her very much. She was not immediately able to say anything, and even when her spirits were uncovered, she *debated* for a short time on the answer it would be most proper to give…Elinor turned *involuntarily* to Marianne, to see whether it could be unobserved by her. At that moment… her whole *countenance* glowed. (from *Sense and Sensibility* by Jane Austen)

Seeking Answers to Life's Problems

After consulting the people, Jehoshaphat appointed men to sing to the Lord and to praise him for the splendor of his holiness as they went out to the head of the army, saying: "Give thanks to the Lord, for his love endures forever." —2 Chronicles 20:21

Scripture: 2 Chronicles 20

Like all previous generations Jehoshaphat naturally looked to old solutions to solve new problems. No doubt he asked the army: "Can you defeat these armies?" After all, Deborah and Gideon had lead the scrappy Hebrew army to victory once before—why not now? What they needed, Jehoshaphat clearly understood, was an old-time miracle. Perhaps the army could provide this miracle. But this time they could not. The Arabian hordes were too much—and probably would have been too much for Gideon, Deborah, and even Samson or King David. This time, traditional solutions would not work. Then, he must have asked the priests, "What can you do to help me?" Again, nothing—no known solution would bring salvation. Jehoshaphat was really in trouble this time, and he knew it.

Have you ever been in so much trouble that you could simply not talk your way out of it or had no known solution to solve it? Did you turn to the Lord for answers?

Devotional Journal

Read/Vocabulary Cards

Go over them with your parents or guardians this evening.

Critical Reading

None of them knew the color of the sky. Their eyes glanced level, and were fastened upon the waves that swept toward them. These waves were of the hue of slate, save for the tops, which were of foaming white, and all of the men knew the colors of the sea. The horizon narrowed and widened, and dipped and rose, and at all times its edge was jagged with waves that seemed thrust up in points like rocks (*"Open Boat,"* Stephen Crane).

The strongest literary element in this passage is:
A. Characterization
B. Plot
C. Theme
D. Setting

Solve

A. $\frac{4}{1} \times \frac{2}{16} =$

B. $35A = \frac{1 \times 38}{7}$

C. $56A + 3 = 9$

Never have I known a student with an exceptionally high critical reading score to do poorly on the exam. Therefore, you should pay particularly close attention to those parts of your preparation. Remember! Almost half of the verbal portion of the SAT I exam is related to reading passages. Similarly, a high score on the quantitative comparison section is critical. A high critical reading score and a high quantitative comparison score will almost automatically give you a high SAT I score.

Lesson continues on the next page.

D. In a jar full of dimes and nickels the ratio of dimes to nickels is 4 : 3. If the jar contains a total of 175 coins, how many of them are dimes? Nickels?

E. What is the value of the nickels in dollars? Of the dimes?

F. If two packages of cookies contain a total of 24 cookies, how many cookies are there in 6 packages?

Critical Thinking: Essay

ESSAY PROMPT: Think carefully about the issue presented in the following quotations and do the assignment below.

1. "Prosperity is the blessing of the Old Testament; adversity is the blessing of the New." Francis Bacon, "Of Adversity"

2. "You live longer once you realize that any time spent being unhappy is wasted." Ruth E. Renkl

Assignment: Is suffering or adversity beneficial to a Christians' life. Plan and write an essay in which you develop your point of view on this issue. Support your position with reasoning and examples taken from your reading, studies, experience, or observations.

76

A Piece of Bread to Hold

The Lord is my shepherd, I shall lack nothing. He makes me lie down in green pastures.
—Psalm 23:1,2

Scripture: *Psalm 23*

Charles Allen, pastor emeritus of First Methodist Church, Houston, Texas, in his book *God's Psychiatry* tells how the Allied armies gathered up homeless children and cared for them. But at night the children were restless and afraid. A psychologist hit upon a solution. He gave each child a slice of bread to hold, and the child would go to sleep immediately, knowing that there would be something to eat the next day. Likewise, in Psalm 23, we are given a slice of bread that we can hold through the night times of life. Faith that will carry us through. The attraction of Psalm 23 does not lie in its profound theology or its comforting lyrics. But comfort lies in the simple way we meet a loving Shepherd God face to face. When we say, "The Lord is my Shepherd"—and mean it—then, for sure, God is very real.

Is God your shepherd? Do you know His voice? How do you recognize His voice?

The SAT I, as contrasted with the old SAT, will have comparisons between two passages. This development demands that you read very carefully both passages before you answer the questions.

Lesson continues on the next page.

Devotional Journal

Read/Vocabulary Cards

Critical Thinking: Comparison

A. The New Testament is literally riddled with references to Christ's coming again. The matter is mentioned in over three hundred places. Obviously it was basic to early Christian doctrine. But, I must admit, a sermon on the Second Coming rarely enters my repertoire. Why is it that in the mainline churches one seldom hears the subject mentioned? Sects, the cults, conservative groups almost never stop mentioning it. They hammer on it night and day; they make films concerning it; they write books about it—many of which are bestsellers. They preach about it incessantly. But the rest of us stay away from it. While so much of the Christian world argues about being premillennialism versus post-millennialism, we are standing around yawning. What bothers us about the Second Coming of Christ?

B. We cannot live without hope. Walter Brueggemann, in his book *Hope Within History* explores the meaning of apocalyptic hope in history. Using Jeremiah as background, Brueggemann argues that real history makers are those who can invest in a dream. In spite of pretty bleak conditions—Jeremiah's nation was about to be conquered and taken in captivity—Jeremiah was still able to have great hope. He had apocalyptic hope. He understood who really had power. God told Jeremiah to buy a piece of land (Jeremiah 32:6; 29:4-9). He did. Even though Jeremiah was never to enjoy this land, he invested in it anyway. Hope causes us to invest in dreams we may never see consummated. People with apocalyptic hope assert the sovereign and omnipotent will of God in all circumstances no matter how bad things may be.

1. In one sentence, explain what each passage means.
2. Create a transitional sentence or phrase that could connect the paragraphs.
3. What does Dr. Brueggemann mean when he says, "We cannot live without hope"? And what does this have to do with the Second Coming? What is a history maker? What do history makers have to do with the Second Coming? Define "Apocalyptic hope."

Critical Thinking: Essay

Narrative Essay

A narrative essay tells a story and reflects the author's values told in story form. It is often written in the first person point of view and includes anecdotes to illustrate the writer's point in telling the story. It could use an experience from your own life to prove a point or illustrate an idea.

Write a personal story illustrating the importance of telling the truth.

Even though I walk through the valley of the shadow of death, I will fear no evil, for you are with me; your rod and your staff, they comfort me. —Psalm 23:4

 Scripture: *Psalm 23*

References to sheep in the Bible occur more than five hundred times. Sheep represented the chief wealth and the total livelihood of most Israelites. They provided food to eat (1 Samuel 14:32), milk to drink (Isaiah 7), wool for the weaving of cloth (Leviticus 13), and even rough clothing (Hebrews 11). Inevitably sheep became a medium of exchange (2 Kings 3) and figured centrally in the worship service (Exodus 20). However, in spite of the existence of several pastoral societies in antiquity, none of them referred to their deity(ies) as a shepherd. This is a uniquely Judeo-Christian phenomenon. For the last few years, my family has lived on a small farm. For a while, we raised Suffolk sheep. Sheep hate wind more than anything—more than rain, more than the cold, more than the dark. One stormy afternoon, while the wind was blowing horribly, I heard our sheep crying. So, I went outside to comfort them. I called to them. They had two options: Go to the barn or come to me. They chose to come to me. To my sheep, my presence was safer, my voice more comforting, than a dry barn.

Would you rather be safe with God or popular with your friends?

Devotional Journal

Read/Vocabulary Cards

Solve

A. The length of a lot is 10 yards more than its width. Its perimeter is 380 yards. What are its dimensions?

B. A building is 50 feet shorter than another one. The smaller one is 100 feet. Find the height of the taller one.

C. A man invests in the stock market and makes a 10% return. A second sum is invested and profits exceed the first by $500. He makes a 15% return on that money. What is his total profit if his original investment was $1000?

D. During a township basketball game, Mary sold 13% of 650 cups of regular coffee at $.65/cup. However, she ran out of small cups and was forced to sell the rest at $.90/cup because she had only large cups. How many were sold at each price?

E. In the equation a/b = c/d, this statement says that ad = bc. This is an example of:
  A. product of the extremes equals the product of the means
  B. prime factorization
  C. prime numbers
  D. relativity

Critical Thinking: Analysis

1. Rewrite Psalm 23 in modern youth-culture language. What is gained in your revision? Lost?

2. Analyze Psalm 23 in several different versions. Describe the stylistic differences. Are there differences in syntax? Word selection? Do these differences affect the meaning of the passage?

On exam day you should bring a snack—no candy—like a peanut butter sandwich. Eat the snack at or near 10:30 a.m. Most poor scores occur from 10:30-12:30. You should sleep well the night before an exam, eat well the morning of the exam, and arrive at the test site thirty minutes before the exam begins. No late nights before the exam!

You prepare a table before me in the presence of my enemies. You anoint my head with oil; my cup overflows. —Psalm 23:5

Scripture: *Psalm 23*

Among shepherds there is an appellation for recalcitrant sheep who refuse to stay inside the fence: fence crawlers. Fence crawlers love to walk along the fence looking for an escape. They eventually find a way through the broken fence: the weak link. And when they do they are in great danger. You see, the fence is there to keep the sheep in the field, but even more so, it is there to keep wild dogs and other predators out. Once a sheep leaves the safety of the fence he is an easy mark for an enemy. Sheep are almost defenseless, so they need the protection of a fence. Within the fence there is safety, food and water, and freedom. Outside the fence is destruction. (See W. Phillip Keller, *A Child's Look at the Twenty-Third Psalm.*)

Are you a fence crawler?

Here is the strategy to solve sentence completion problems: Identify the relationship between the parts of the sentence, eliminate wrong answers, and use the part of speech in each sentence.

Devotional Journal

Read/Vocabulary Cards

Grammar

Select the one underlined part that must be changed to make the sentence correct.

Margaret Elwood, the sensational and talented singer of the <u>1940s</u>,
(A)

became a recluse and <u>remained</u> isolated but <u>looking</u> <u>beautifully</u>
(B) (C) (D)

unto the day she died. <u>[No error.]</u>
(E)

Solve

A. 35 - {6[8(2a + 9) - 7] - 8} = a
B. 28a + 3 = 1571

Sentence Completion

1. Our forefathers and mothers were offered a handsome sum of money for their downtown church. The outrageously extravagant offer _____ some of the pain of leaving old memories behind and their church board accepted the offer and moved within a month!
   A. assuaged
   B. increased
   C. militated
   D. expanded

2. At this time, a new type of church emerged: the urban residential church. This church, as contrasted with the downtown cathedral church, drew an _____ congregation who lived around the church.
   A. expatriate
   B. suburban
   C. indigenous
   D. wealthy

3. As _____ as social action may be, and as _____ as it may be, it did not substitute for good preaching that was necessary to draw people into the life of the downtown church.
   A. pleasant…unnecessary
   B. laudatory…necessary
   C. difficult…consuming
   D. expensive…admirable

Fence Crawlers II

Surely goodness and love will follow me all the days of my life, and I will dwell in the house of the Lord forever. —Psalm 23:6

Scripture: *Psalm 23*

My friend Craig and I loved to go to the Saturday afternoon matinee. We would save our RC Cola tops all week (all you needed was six) and we would cash them in at the local cinema. If you did not have bottle caps you could always pay the outrageously large amount of $1.25! One Saturday afternoon, after an incredible serialized version of Flash Gordon, we played in a barn. Craig had an umbrella. We decided to parachute off the roof of the barn. But yours truly, with less faith than Craig, decided to stand and watch. Craig jumped off the barn and broke his arm. Now, Craig believed with all his might that he would float down like a feather. He was sincere. It seemed right. But he still broke his arm. Why? Because of the law of gravity. And while Craig thought he could break the law of gravity, in fact he could not. The law broke him.

We do not break God's laws, they break us. Respond with an example from your life.

Devotional Journal

Read/Vocabulary Cards

Vocabulary

Define italicized words from context:

> In between songs…tea in abundance…the table was heavy with every *mortal* thing that can be made by women who are anxious to please the stomachs of their guests, and their own *vanity*. Nothing pleased my mother more than to be told how good were her dishes…[Mr. Elias, a friend, scolds Huw's family for preparing a Sabbath meal]…You have forced your way into this house and you have been *abusive*, and you have chosen to take your *authority* from the Bible. There are too many of your sort walking the earth. (from *How Green Was My Valley* by Richard Llewellyn)

How Green Was My Valley, by Richard Llewellyn is a Walton-type story of a Welsh family whose love and courage overcome all obstacles.

Benchmark

1. Are you reading a good book?
2. Are you keeping 3 by 5-inch vocabulary cards and having your parents or guardians go over them with you?
3. Are you spending time with the Lord every day?
4. Are you working on your target Scripture(s)?
5. Are you completing all SAT daily activities?

Critical Reading

A.

American blacks have definitely moved primarily from southern agricultural settings to northern urban settings. And, inevitably, they ended up in ghettos. Although the ghetto served as a springboard for other ethnic groups, the blacks mostly never managed to escape it. The increase in residential segregation that accompanied black ghetto development was, again, dramatic in the twentieth century. Although there were black enclaves in many cities in the nineteenth century, in no case was the overwhelming majority of a city's black population concentrated in one neighborhood with densities of 75 to 90 percent. Instead, blacks inhabited several neighborhoods in modest numbers and shared territory with non-black groups. But in the twentieth century, while ethnics were enjoying residential dispersion, blacks were being funneled into Watts and other ghettos. For no other group in America has residential segregation increased so uniformly.

According to the passage, blacks
I. moved from southern farms to northern cities.
II. settled all over the city.
III. did not advance like other immigrants.
    A. I only
    B. II only
    C. I and II only
    D. I and III only
    E. I, II, and III

B.

Amuse not thy self therefore with the numerous Opinions of the World, nor value thy self upon verbal Orthodoxy, Philosophy, or thy Skill in Tongues, or Knowledge of the Fathers: (too much the Business and Vanity of the World). But in this rejoice, That thou knowest God, that is the Lord, who exerciseth loving Kindness, and Judgment, and Righteousness in the Earth (*Fruits of Solitude*, William Penn, seventeenth century punctuation and spelling maintained).

What advice is Penn offering to his listeners?
    A. Be concerned about things of God, not things of the world.
    B. Be careful what you say.
    C. Don't find your reference point in traditions, philosophy, or vainglorious comments; find your identity in the Loving God of Creation.
    D. Don't show off.
    E. None of the above

80
Next to the Shepherd

I am the good shepherd; I know my sheep and my sheep know me. —John 10:14

Scripture: *John 10:1-18*

Fence crawlers create problems for everyone. Others follow them. And, before you know it, the shepherd has to drop everything to go and search for them. The sad thing is, the wayward sheep usually end up on poor pasture, or worse, injured in a ravine. No, the best place to be if you are a sheep is right next to the shepherd. At times, a shepherd will break the legs of a particularly stubborn lamb. Because the lamb is so dependent on the shepherd during the recovery period, the lamb learns to obey its master.

God pursues us. Can you think of a time when you were lost, the Good Shepherd found you, and brought you back home?

Devotional Journal

Read/Vocabulary Cards

Critical Reading

Tony kicks the snow into the gutter at Friendship and Soup. It isn't apparent to the casual observer, but his right shoe is an air-cushioned Nike with an optimistic green horizontal racing stripe running along each side. His left shoe is a less spectacular Converse with faded baby blue spots— obviously two sizes too large. In spite of the fact that he has only one air-cushioned shoe—the other one was stolen at the local cooperative shelter last July—Tony is very proud of his Nike. The Nike is a *wistful* memory of a life he has had to abandon. It is the last vestige of a capitalistic economy that he *unceremoniously* abandoned—along with his wife and two children— ten years ago. Losing his Westinghouse electrical engineering job to an ambitious M.B.A., Tony proudly declined less *prestigious* and financially rewarding demotions and resigned from his job. His wife was worried… but the Commonwealth of Pennsylvania agreed that he was worthy of unemployment. So between unemployment and an IRA the family hardly suffered at all. And, for the next fifty-two weeks Tony with *rancorous* glee, with his Cross pen, signed his unemployment checks and hung around the house. Everyone was surprised when things *deteriorated* so rapidly. Tony was used to being in control. But now he was losing it. At first, as if he was designing a new electrical circuit, Tony read the want ads in the daily paper. Then, he played the lottery and began drinking Gallo Wild Rosé. It was surprising how little time it took Tony to lose all remaining vestiges of middle-class America. Then, he lost his 486 digital lap top, then he lost his home, then he lost his family.… At the beginning, Ellen, Tony's wife, had been only mildly concerned. After all, he more or less had been looking around for a new job. And Ellen was made of sensible stuff. The unemployment checks were humbling, but tolerable. Even when Tony began to drink a little she stood beside him. She got a job. And finally she had asked him to go. It was that awful look in his eyes. He was embarrassing Ellen. And Tony knew it and hated knowing it. A lost soul. Many times Ellen had seen Tony peer into the *surrealistic* late night *hue* of his lap top. With his *persevering* gaze and anxious tongue *protruding* from the right side of his mouth, Tony appeared *invulnerable*. Now, though, his eyes were dulled from all the broken places life had taken him.

A. What is the attitude of the author toward Tony? His wife Ellen?
B. Define the italicized words.
C. What was embarrassing to Ellen—the fact that Tony was unemployed or that his condition had deteriorated so badly or that he was not accepting help?

81

The Pet Lamb

I will feed them on the mountains of Israel, by the fountains…I will feed them with good pasture…there they shall lie down in good grazing land, and on fat pasture…I myself will be the shepherd. —Ezekiel 34:13–15 (RSV)

Scripture: *Ezekiel 34:11-16*

The two most extended biblical allegories of the shepherd in the Old Testament are found in Ezekiel 34. "I will feed them on the mountains of Israel, by the fountains…I will feed them with good pasture…; there they shall lie down in good grazing land, and on fat pasture…I will be their shepherd." Ezekiel 34 also castigates the Israelite priests for abusing their flocks. God is a good shepherd. He never abuses us. He is merciful. He never neglects us. The sheep in His care see that God loves them. He tenderly examines each one of us. He talks to us in low, gentle tones. He keeps us from poisonous plants. When we are tired and weak, He carries us. In a hundred little acts of tenderness He shows His mercy and love for His flock. But this is part of God's character. He will not be any other way. Some people think that the Good Shepherd is bad. No, He is good. We think that we are His pet lambs. I am amused by my children's discussions about who Karen and I love the most. "I was born first!" or "I was born last!" But, the fact is, we love all our children equally. It is our very nature to love our four children. To feel otherwise would be unnatural.

I know most of you are born again—but do you feel special? You are, you know. You are of inestimatible value to the Father. Remember! He sent His only begotten Son to die for you!

Devotional Journal

Read/Vocabulary Cards

Solve

To solve problems, always begin by asking these two simple questions: "What do I know?" and "What do I need to know?"

A. Charles was racing around in his new sports car when he noticed that his throat was parched. He stopped in front of a hotel, and nine police cars, which had been chasing him, slammed into the back of his car and each other's. How many bumpers will have been hit?

B. The tallow obtained by burning ten candles will yield one extra candle. If you burned 1000 candles, how many extra candles could you make? (MindTrap®)

C. Find a: $(a + 5)(a - 3) =$ $\qquad$ $ab - a = 2ab + a$ $\qquad$ $33a = 66$

D. What is a degree of polynomial?

Vocabulary

Give a synonym for each word:

1. obsessive	5. pervasive	9. inert	13. passive
2. opaque	6. pessimism	10. deception	14. prophetic
3. optimist	7. cantankerous	11. precedent	15. provocative
4. paradox	8. philanthropist	12. pretentious	16. amorous

And we know that in all things God works for the good of those who love him, who have been called according to his purposes.—Romans 8:28

Scripture: *Romans 8:28-30*

Arthur John Gossip, a famous English preacher, was preparing a sermon one Wednesday afternoon when he heard that his beloved wife had been killed in an accident. In spite of this great catastrophe, Gossip chose to preach the next week's sermon. He ended that famous sermon entitled "When Life Tumbles In," with these words:

"I don't think that you need be afraid of life. Our hearts are very frail; and there are places where the road is very steep and very lonely. But we have a wonderful God. And as Paul puts it, 'What can separate us from His love? Not death!' he says immediately, pushing that aside at once as the most obvious of all impossibilities. No, not death. For, standing in the roaring of the Jordan, cold to the heart with its dreadful chill, and very conscious of the terror of its rushing...I too, like Hopeful in John Bunyan's *Pilgrim Progress*, can call back to you...'Be of good cheer, my brother, for I feel the bottom, and it is sound.'"

No matter what life may bring us, however dangerous the river we cross may be, we can overcome, because "All things work for good...."

Have things ever been so bad that you doubted God's love for you?

Devotional Journal

Read/Vocabulary Cards

Grammar

Choose the correct answer.

The student felt (real badly, really bad) about the test score.

"I see myself now at the end of my journey, my toilsome days are ended. I am going now to see that Head that was crowned with Thorns, and that face that was spit upon for me. I have formerly lived by Hearsay and Faith, but now I go where I shall live by sight, and shall be with Him in whose company I delight myself."
—*The Pilgrim's Progress*, by John Bunyan

Lesson continues on the next page.

Solve

1. If C is the midpoint of AB, and F is the midpoint of DE, and FE > AC, then
   A. AC < DF
   B. DF > CB
   C. AB < DE
   D. AC + CB < DF + FE
   E. All of the above

2. If C is the midpoint of AB, and F is the midpoint of DE, and FE > AC, then
   A. AB > DE
   B. AB < DE
   C. AB = DE
   D. All of the above

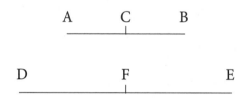

3. If x > y, y > z, z > w, then
   A. x > w
   B. x < w
   C. x < z
   D. z < w
   E. x < y

Hints for Math Problems

1. Know what the questions mean.
2. Answer the right question. If they are asking for the value of A do not give them the value of B!
3. Avoid lengthy math exercises. Remember! The test has a time limit! If it is taking too long, skip it and come back. Don't expect to answer every question.
4. Estimate your answer first.
5. If a formula is required be sure to apply it properly.
6. Write on the question paper if you need to do so. But do not mark the answer sheet with anything but answers!
7. Avoid "None of the Above" if you can. Be sure there is an answer "E" before you use it.
8. Don't panic!

83

In the Image of God

H. G. Wells

So God created man in his own image, in the image of God he created him; male and female he created them. God blessed them and said to them, "...Rule over the fish of the sea and the birds of the air and over every living creature that moves on the ground."
—Genesis 1:27, 28

Scripture: *Genesis 1:26-28*

There are several unique aspects of the Judeo-Christian faith. One of the most radical is the notion that we are all created in the image of God. Imagine! The omnipotent, omniscient Creator decided to create a people who looked like Himself. Wow! Genesis has further good news for us: We are a unique entity where the Spirit of God resides. In fact, our situation on earth replicates God's situation in heaven. Wow again!

Do you honor your Father God by living a holy life?

Devotional Journal

Read/Vocabulary Cards

Vocabulary

A. Define italicized words in context:

Under the railway bridge I found a group of soldiers...I saw one of the men standing *sentinel* there. I talked with these soldiers for a while...they discussed their fight with great *acuteness*...I was a little depressed with the *contagion* of my wife's fears... the air was full of sound, a *deafening* and confusing conflict of noises—the *clangorous din* of the Martians. (*The War of the Worlds* by H.G. Wells)

B. Create words with these prefixes and suffixes
in (into)
in (not)
inter (between)
ist (one who practices)
itiner (road)
ity (state or condition)

Books by H. G. Wells remain some of the most challenging literature for American readers. Wells' vocabulary is especially useful for SAT students. I recommend you read his short books (*The Time Machine, The Invisible Man, The War of the Worlds*, et al.) and then check out the movies from the video store—with your parents' permission, of course!

Lesson continues on the next page.

Critical Reading

1　The end then of learning is to repair the ruins of our first parents by regaining to
2　know God aright, and out of that knowledge to love him, to imitate him, to be like
3　him, as we may the nearest by possessing our souls of true virtue, which being united
4　to the heavenly grace of faith makes up the highest perfection. But because our
5　understanding can not in this body found itself but on sensible things, nor arrive so
6　clearly to the knowledge of God and things invisible, as by orderly conning over the
7　visible and inferior creature, the same method is necessarily to be followed in all dis-
8　creet teaching. And seeing every nation affords not experience and tradition enough
9　for all kind of learning, therefore we are chiefly taught the languages of those people
10　who have at any time been most industrious after wisdom; so that language is but the
11　instrument conveying to us things useful to be known. And though a linguist should
12　pride himself to have all the tongues that Babel cleft the world into, yet if he have not
13　studied the solid things in them as well as the words and lexicons, he were nothing
14　so much to be esteemed a learned man, as any yeoman or tradesman competently
15　wise in his mother dialect only. Hence appear the many mistakes which have made
16　learning generally so unpleasing and so unsuccessful; first we do amiss to spend
17　seven or eight years merely in scraping together so much miserable Latin and Greek,
18　as might be learned other wise easily and delightfully in one year. And that which
19　casts our proficiency therein so much behind, is our time lost partly in too oft idle
20　vacancies given both to schools and universities, partly in a preposterous exaction,
21　forcing the empty wits of children to compose themes, verses and orations, which are
22　the acts of ripest judgment and the final work of a head filled by long reading and
23　observing, with elegant maxims, and copious invention. These are not matters to be
24　wrung from poor striplings, like blood out of the nose, or the plucking of untimely
25　fruit: besides the ill habit which they get of wretched barbarizing against the Latin
26　and Greek *idiom*, with their untutored *Anglicisms*, odious to be read, yet not to be
27　avoided without a well continued and judicious conversing among pure authors
28　digested, which they scarce taste, whereas, if after some preparatory grounds of
29　speech by their certain forms got into memory, they were led to the praxis thereof in
30　some chosen short books lessoned throughly to them, they might then forthwith pro-
31　ceed to learn the substance of good things, and arts in due order, which would bring
32　the whole language quickly into their power. This I take to be the most rational and
33　most profitable way of learning languages, and whereby we may best hope to give
34　account to God of our youth spent herein: and for the usual method of teaching arts, I
35　deem it to be an old error of universities not yet well recovered from the scholastic
36　grossness of barbarous ages, that instead of beginning with arts most easy, and those
37　be such as are most obvious to the sense, they present their young unmatriculated
38　novices at first coming with the most intellective abstractions of logic and meta-
39　physics; so that they having but newly left those grammatic flats and shallows where
40　they stuck unreasonably to learn a few words with lamentable construction, and now
41　on the sudden transported under another climate to be tossed and turmoiled with
42　their unballasted wits in fathomless and unquiet deeps of controversy, do for the
43　most part grow into hatred and contempt of learning, mocked and deluded all this
44　while with ragged notions and babblements, while they expected worthy and delight-
45　ful knowledge, till poverty or youthful years call them importunately their several

Vague and insignificant forms of speech, and abuse of language, have so long passed for mysteries of science; and hard or misapplied words with little or no meaning have, by prescription, such a right to be mistaken for deep learning and height of speculation, that it will not be easy to persuade either those who speak or those who hear them, that they are but the covers of ignorance and hindrance of true knowledge.

—John Locke

46 ways, and hasten them with the sway of friends either to an ambitious and mercenary,
47 or ignorantly zealous divinity; some allured to the trade of law, grounding their pur-
48 poses not on the prudent and heavenly contemplation of justice and equity which
49 was never taught them, but on the promising and pleasing thoughts of litigious
50 terms, fat contentions and flowing fees; others betake them to State affairs, with souls
51 so unprincipled in virtue and true generous breeding, that flattery, and court shifts
52 and tyrannous aphorisms appear to them the highest points of wisdom; instilling
53 their barren hearts with a conscientious slavery, if, as I rather think, it be not feigned.
54 Others lastly of a more delicious and airy spirit, retire themselves knowing no better,
55 to the enjoyments of ease and luxury, living out their days in feast and jollity; which
56 indeed is the wisest and the safest course of all these, unless they were with more
57 integrity undertaken. And these are the fruits of misspending our prime youth at the
58 schools and universities as we do, either in learning mere words or such things
59 chiefly, as were better unlearned (*Of Education*, John Milton).

In what lines will the reader find the main point of this passage?
  A. Lines 1-11
  B. Lines 13-20
  C. Lines 22-34
  D. Lines 43-53

84
Bless the Children

"Let the little children come to me, and do not hinder them, for the kingdom of God belongs to such as these." —Mark 10:14

Scripture: Mark 10:13-16

She had done it again. Roshanna was never subtle. During morning worship Roshanna had an uncanny ability to find, sit next to, and irritate the most irascible congregants. This particular morning Roshanna was sitting next to Mrs. Musick—a vintage grouch (although I love her dearly!!!). She always timed her sneak attack during the silent prayers of confession, while her victim was most contrite and vulnerable. Before the assurance of pardon was pronounced, poor Mrs. Musick was snagged. At the end of the doxology—in celebration of the midpoint of our service—Roshanna deposited her used Bazooka bubble gum on Mrs. Musick's open red-letter Bible. The awful mess was placed between "He" and "multitudes" in Matthew 5:1. Poor Mrs. Musick's Bible would sport Bazooka bubble gum for generations to come. In our text today Jesus reminds us that the kingdom of God belongs to the Roshannas. Think about it.

Thinking of your younger brother or sister, or any younger friend, list three ways he or she is Christlike. Pray for that person this week.

1.

2.

3.

Devotional Journal

Read/Vocabulary Cards

Be sure to review your vocabulary cards.

Critical Thinking: Comparison

On many critical reading passages of the SAT I there will be questions about the attitude of the author. To figure out the tone or attitude of an author, examine the words he or she uses. Content will have very little to do with tone.

A. In *Men and Marriage* George Gilder examines, sentimentally, very nostalgically, the loss of the family and the well-defined sex roles that he extols. Poverty comes from the destruction of the family. Gilder's argument develops in this way: 1) Gilder critiques the sexual revolution. This revolution has profoundly changed all aspects of American society. Men—males—are by nature, predatory and philandering. They are, "sexual barbarians." Marriage induces men to redirect these destructive behaviors into constructive behavior and the result is civilization. 2) Finally, it is the religious community that will rescue us. But it could be the revivalistic, evangelical community we all love and admire—or Scientology—as long as they embrace Judeo-Christian morality as Gilder defines it. That is, one wife, one husband, wife stays at home and does not work, and so on. Gilder sees a mass movement coalescing. It includes conservatives of all types, sizes, and ideologies. It is religion—what Gilder calls ideology—that will save us. He, by the way, is less discriminating in this area, than you and I. He welcomes Moonies and Christian Evangelicals into his camp.

B. In *Men and Marriage* George Gilder examines the loss of the family and the unfortunate loss of well-defined sex roles. Poverty comes from the destruction of the family. Gilder's argument develops in this way: 1) The sexual revolution has profoundly changed all aspects of American society. Everyone knows that men are by nature predatory and philandering. Marriage induces men to redirect these destructive behaviors into constructive behavior and the result is civilization. 2) Finally, it is the religious community that will rescue us.

1. What is each author's tone?
2. Which author liked the book and why? Which author disliked the book and why?
3. Who is most convincing? Why?

Solve

A plant pathologist notices the growth of a new plant disease in his laboratory. On Tuesday he counted only 3 infected plants but by Saturday there are 375. If he takes no action to stop the spread of the disease, how many noninfected plants out of the original 2000 would he expect to find on Sunday?

    A. 500
    B. 1875
    C. 1625
    D. 125
    E. none

Critical Thinking: Essay

Give a personal story illustrating a problem the United States faces.

On coming to the house, they saw the child with his mother Mary, and they bowed down and worshiped him. Then they opened their treasures and presented him with gifts of gold and of incense and of myrrh. —Matthew 2:11

Scripture: Matthew 2:7-12

So we were not surprised when she came to the Christmas pageant. Roshanna was one of the Wise Men. And what a wise man she was! With her heavy make-up and red lipstick, dangling cheap gold earrings, high-heeled shoes, green stockings and red bath robe (in the spirit of the season), Roshanna looked like she had stepped off Times Square rather than the streets of Babylon. But she was to be the only Wise Man we had this evening and we meant to make the most of her. "We have come to give frankenstein (sic), myrrh, and gold," she confidently proclaimed, "although I bet you would prefer a puppy or something." Roshanna was never one to let the Word of God or anything else hold her back from a little redaction! Roshanna was an unlikely Wise Man, but she was probably closer to the real wise men than some of us.

Ask God what gift He would like to receive from you and then give it to Him.

Devotional Journal

Read/Vocabulary Cards

Pray with your parents or guardians and have them quiz you with your 3 by 5-inch vocabulary cards.

Vocabulary

Choose an antonym for each word.

1. abrogate:
   A. punish
   B. institute
   C. covenant
   D. commiserate
   E. launch

2. amity:
   A. hostility
   B. exhaustion
   C. verification
   D. orientation
   E. innovativeness

Solve

A. Find the area and perimeter of this figure.

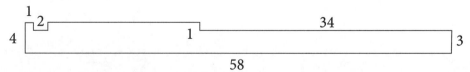

B. What are conjugates?

In my SAT coaching classes over the years, I have discovered two strange tendencies among students: 1. They do not like to answer with the same letter more than once or twice. So, if the right answer was A for two previous times, I know students who would never answer the third question A—even if it was right! Of course that is silly. I don't care if A is the right answer five times straight! 2. Students oftentimes think that the answer is always the longest word, hardest answer. Not so. Be careful.

A bruised reed he will not break, and a smoldering wick he will not snuff out.
—Isaiah 42:3

 Scripture: *Isaiah 42*

But God does not blow out the smoking wick. Or break the bruised twig. An old Hasidic rabbi, Levi Yitzhak of Berdichev in the Ukraine, used to say that he discovered the meaning of love from a drunken peasant. Entering a tavern in the Polish countryside, he saw two inebriated peasants at a table. Each was protesting how much he loved the other, when Ivan said to Peter: "Peter, tell me what hurts me." Bleary-eyed, Peter responded: "How do I know what hurts you?" Ivan's answer was: "If you don't know what hurts me, how can you say you love me?" God knows what hurts people. He showed us that He knows when He sent His only Son to die for our sins. The compassion we meet in Isaiah 42 is impossible to sentimentalize. The implication in Hebrew is that God feels so deeply our needs and our wants that His heart is torn, His gut wrenched, the most vulnerable part of His being laid bare. Many of your friends are hurting, lonely, depressed. Perhaps you are, too.

Can you trust Him to minister to your needs? Write these needs down and offer them to the Lord.

Devotional Journal

Read/Vocabulary Cards

Grammar

Select the one underlined part that must be changed to make the sentence correct.

I agree with George's thought that each person is in   <u>themselves</u>
                                                        (A)

a complicated puzzle and that all of us need to set   <u>aside</u>   time   <u>for</u>
                                                       (B)   (C)

trying   <u>to</u>   solve it.   [<u>No error.</u>]
(D)   (E)

Sentence Completion

1. By the 1930s and 1940s, the goods and services once provided by a neighbor were supplanted by mass retail outlets. This trend continued until 1970. In spite of affirmative action, federal job training programs, and _____ relationships with predominantly white unions, the number and proportion of black skilled workers continued to decline.
   A. ameliorated
   B. unhappy
   C. dangerous
   D. debilitated.

What's new in the verbal section of the SAT I? Critical reading, critical reading, critical reading! Passages will be longer, much longer, and, while they will be readable, don't expect them to be that interesting. I surveyed the readings from last year and many were boring, boring, boring. And—by the way—how will you handle a passage on evolution? Be ready! Answer the question according to the author's viewpoint. A correct answer does not mean you agree with the author! And, expect lots of questions: there may be over ten in some cases. So, if you do not understand a particular passage— just one passage— your verbal score could be severely compromised.

Lesson continues on the next page.

2. The December 1984 meeting of the American Medical Association issued a statement to the American public telling them that a person could, on the average, live eleven years longer if he _____ cigarettes and alcohol, _____ his consumption of fatty foods, and used a seat belt when riding in an automobile.
   A. smoked—increased
   B. removed—decreased
   C. avoided—reduced
   D. avert—lessen

Therefore, if anyone is in Christ, he is a new creation; the old has gone, the new has come!
—2 Corinthians 5:17

Scripture: *2 Corinthians 5:17*

She was my twenty-first client. An overall-clad toddler was attached to one hand, and a mini-cart was in the other. This middle-aged black woman seemed ordinary enough as she requested a bag of groceries from the East End Cooperative emergency food pantry. I was one of the afternoon volunteers entrusted with this *sacred* duty. "Hello," I offered without looking up from my work pad. "My name is Jim." Number twenty-one replied with a quiet, defeated "Viola." Unusual name, I thought. I once knew a Viola. Thirty years ago, in Arkansas, my family *subcontracted* most of our game cleaning to a thin, tobacco-chewing woman named Viola. Viola's claim to fame was her gift: She could clean, dress, and fillet black bass faster than any person alive. Her hands moved like wild birds. Her gift generally unappreciated, Viola lived in poverty. Her house was a plyboard shack, absent of indoor plumbing or electricity. She had never ridden in a car, never been ten miles from where she lived, and had no hope of doing either in her lifetime. She ate cornbread, mustard greens with a little lard, and Great Northern beans. She had never visited a dentist or a medical doctor, and she never would. And danger—her brother was one of the last victims of the Ku Klux Klan before Governor Faubus sent an aide to speak to Uncle George, the grand dragon of the KKK and a ruling elder in my church, and advised him to employ more "subtle ways to keep the n-----s in line." Viola had a shy, namesake granddaughter whom she affectionately called her "grandbaby." Every summer this child visited her grandmother and chopped Old Man Smith's cotton. With unmatched expertise and enthusiasm, young Viola single-handedly massacred whole acres of crabgrass. With her six-foot hoe, she effectively equalized the equation. Old Man Smith knew he owed his cotton-growing success to a *wiry* little chopper from Marianna, Arkansas.… "Viola. That's V-I-O-L-A," said the woman sitting in front of me. "Do you have any ground meat today?" I was lost in a remembered cotton field. This woman in front of me, number twenty-one, was my Old Man Smith's cotton chopper, the granddaughter of my old fish-cleaner. For the next twenty minutes, Viola, with great *reticence*, and I shared our stories. Once the county chopping queen, now Viola was just another unwed mother who would eat generic peanut butter until her new food stamps would arrive.… At times we will run headlong into people and circumstances we thought were gone and forgotten. And then we meet an old friend, face an old problem, encounter an unresolved habit. What Viola needed to know is that in Christ we can be a new creation. Old things have passed away.

Viola is a person from my past I had forgotten. An unresolved tension. Recall a situation, problem, or relationship that is still unresolved. Deal with it, and give it to the Lord.

Devotional Journal

Read/Vocabulary Cards

Lesson continues on the next page.

Critical Reading

1. Define the italicized words in the devotional passage.
2. This article is full of irony and sarcasm. Give an example of each.
3. In one sentence, what is the theme of this article?
4. What is the tone of this article? What is my attitude toward Viola?
5. How would Uncle George interpret Viola's situation?
6. This passage has several instances of "stream of consciousness." Define this term and give one example.

Critical Reading

Petrifaction is of two sorts. There is petrifaction of the understanding; and also of the sense of shame. This happens when a man obstinately refuses to acknowledge plain truths, and persists in maintaining what is self-contradictory. Most of us dread mortification of the body, and would spare no pains to escape anything of that kind. But of mortification of the soul we are utterly heedless. With regard, indeed, to the soul, if a man is in such a state as to be incapable of following or understanding anything, I grant you we do think him in a bad way. But mortification of the sense of shame and modesty we go so far as to dub strength of mind! (*Golden Sayings*, Epictetus).

What is the central point of this passage?
A. One should be careful to preserve meat well.
B. People as well as trees can become petrified.
C. Petrifaction of the soul is more dangerous than of the body.
D. There are two sorts of petrification.

Solve

If Set R contains only positive even numbers and Set T contains positive numbers divisible 3, how many positive 2-digit numbers less than 30 are in R ∩ T?
A. 3
B. 6
C. 10
D. 19
E. 20

For the Time Being

I, the Lord, have called you in righteousness; I will take hold of your hand. I will keep you and will make you to be a covenant for the people and a light for the Gentiles.
—Isaiah 42:6

Scripture: Isaiah 42:4-6

My teenage daughter recently stopped referring to me as Daddy. She insists on calling me "Dad." "It is the 90s thing, Dad," she says. "Okay, so what will you call me in the twenty-first century?" I ask. "Jim," she quickly responded. My daughter, the teenager! In the book Walking with the Wise—a book that I highly recommend—Benny and Sheree Phillips remind us that the term "teenager" did not exist until the 1960s. In the 1930s teenagers were called "young people" or "youth." "Teenager" was not a noun—in fact it was not in any dictionary until 1961. Only in modern history have we as a culture separated teens from the rest of us. There were laudable reasons. For example, teenagers do have special problems and opportunities. But, at the same time, separating teens from other age groups made this group vulnerable to exploitation—economic and otherwise. It also takes the heat off the rest of us parents for some of the lousy parenting decisions we have made. Let's just blame the teenagers and puberty and so forth for the rebellion. But whether we are fourteen or forty-four, if the Lord is our Savior, we are "called in righteousness" and we "have a covenant with God." He will keep us and make us a light for folks who need to know Him.

In your devotional journal list several challenges you and your parents both have. Consider things like unforgiveness for those who hurt you, problems finding enough time for a daily devotion, and so forth. Purpose to pray for your parents on a daily basis.

Devotional Journal

Read/Vocabulary Cards

Vocabulary

Define italicized words in context:

> About the year 1734 there arrived among us a young Presbyterian
> preacher, named Hemphill, who delivered with a good voice, and apparently
> *extempore*, most excellent *discourses*, which drew together considerable
> numbers of different persuasions, who joined in admiring them. Among
> the rest, I became one of his constant hearers, his sermons pleasing me, as
> they had little of the *dogmatical* kind, but *inculcated* strongly the practice of
> virtue…I became a *zealous partisan*…. (from *The Autobiography of Benjamin
> Franklin*)

The Autobiography of Benjamin Franklin is the first of its genre in American literature. It's an engaging account of the early years of an extraordinary figure from our history, and one that every college-bound student should read. Franklin's story is the American story: a poor youth who, through industry, assiduous self-education, and thrift, becomes prosperous, respected, and famous.

Lesson continues on the next page.

Solve

A. Mary leaves Boston at 8 p.m. driving 30 mph. At 10 p.m. Harry leaves Boston toward the same destination as Mary. At 3 a.m. Harry is 50 miles ahead of Mary. How fast is Harry traveling?

B. What is larger $^{45}/_{78}$ or .60?

Critical Thinking: Essay

Give a personal story illustrating the importance of friendship.

"The Spirit of the Lord is on me, because he has anointed me to preach good news to the poor. He has sent me to proclaim freedom for the prisoners and recovery of sight for the blind, to release the oppressed, to proclaim the year of the Lord's favor."
—Luke 4:18,19

Scripture: Luke 4:16-19

In Book VII of *The Republic*, by the Greek philosopher Plato (427-347 b.c.), is the Myth of the Cave. Plato illustrates the human tendency to accept darkness with too much ease. Inside a cave are several slaves. They have been there all of their lives—that is their world—they know no other. One day, a stranger joins them. He too is a slave, but he has seen the light. He knows that there is a better world. Finally, one day, the new slave manages to free himself. He escapes to the light. But he comes back. He tells his friends about the light. They are curious, but too scared to go with him. One day, though, several agree to go with him to the light. They break their chains and escape. When they reach the light, it is indeed, wonderful. Bright, warm, free. However, the light hurts their eyes…and freedom has some responsibility, too. So, ultimately they prefer to return to the shadows of the cave! Jesus stands in the midst of His community and speaks the truth. But the truth hurts. As Plato wrote: "When he approaches the light his eyes will be dazzled, and he will not be able to see anything at all of what are now called realities" (paragraph 5, chapter VII, *The Republic*).

Do you prefer the "safe familiar" over the "risky new"?

Devotional Journal

Read/Vocabulary Cards

Remember! Go over your cards with your parents or guardians this evening.

Solve

A. Miss Patience is babysitting 10 children. She has a jar with only 10 crackers in it. All the children want to have a cracker, but they also want Miss Patience to leave one cracker in the jar. How is Miss Patience able to give each child a cracker and still leave one in the jar? (MindTrap®)

B. A school bus holds 35 students. 173 members of the third grade are going on a field trip. How many buses will be needed?

C. Which of the following is a quadratic equation?
   A. $Ax^3 + Bx^2 + x = 0$, A is not = 0
   B. $Ax^2 + Bx + C = 0$, A is not = 0
   C. $Ax^2 + Bx + x = 0$, A is not = 0
   D. $Ax^2 + Bx + Bx = 0$, A is not = 0

Draw a floor plan of your dream house.

Draw everything to scale (for example, ¼ inch = one foot).

Plato was an original political science thinker. Most SAT I exams include a passage on Greek philosophy. Studying Plato's doctrine of ideas or Forms—the theory that beyond the forms of the physical world there exist ideal Forms or Verities—would be a good place to begin.

90
Fight the Good Fight

I have fought the good fight, I have finished the race, I have kept the faith.
—2 Timothy 4:7

Scripture: 2 Timothy 4:6-8

The Newsboys sing a song called "Somethin's Missing." "Do you know who you're gonna be today? Do you know what part you're gonna play? When you stare into the mirror yeah. Empty eyes speak more words than I can say." The Newsboys are singing about ultimate things. Things that matter, things that last. I know that being younger than twenty makes one feel immortal—I know I felt that way when I was your age—but things do end someday. And, if Christ is your Savior, you will be going to heaven when that day comes. But what about now? The Christian teacher Bill Gothard in his "Basic Life Principles" series reminds us that the decisions we make when we are eighteen will affect our lives at age forty. I'm sure Timothy found Paul's words hard to understand: Paul is speaking about the ultimate value of his own life. Paul is at the end of his life; Timothy is at the beginning. But, still, Timothy needed to hear these words. And so do you. Think about it.

What sorts of decisions should you make now that will positively affect your future? For instance, if God intends for you to be married, even if you do not know who the person will be, are you praying for your future spouse? Are you praying about your college choice? What is your ultimate goal? Money? Power? Or bringing glory to the Lord?

Devotional Journal

Read/Vocabulary Cards

Grammar

Which sentence is correct?
- A. She is more smarter than I.
- B. She is smarter than I.

Critical Thinking: Facts, Inferences, Opinions

—A *fact* can be proven by at least one other source.
—An *opinion* is a biased but sincerely held view of the author.
—An *inference* is a guess, really, by the author, based upon a known corpus of information.

Tell whether the following statements are facts, inferences, or opinions.
- A. German people are naturally neater than other kinds of people.
- B. Abortion is murder.
- C. Creation science is a religious myth.
- D. Human beings evolved from a lower primate.
- E. Harvard University was founded in 1636.
- F. Harvard University is the best college in the country.
- G. Based on statistical evidence, going to Harvard Business School will guarantee a high salary.
- H. O.J. Simpson kept a low profile for several weeks because he was tired of all the publicity.
- I. O.J. Simpson was acquitted of all charges because there were mostly black people on the jury.
- J. Jesus Christ is the Son of God.

91

Where Have All the Heroes Gone?

Now there is in store for me the crown of righteousness, which the Lord, the righteous Judge, will award to me on that day—and not to me only, but also to all who have longed for his appearing. —2 Timothy 4:8

Scripture: 2 Timothy 4:6-8

Mother Teresa

At the end of the 1980s an article in the magazine *U.S. News and World Report* gave a list of famous people Americans clearly wanted to emulate. This impressive list included such humanitarian giants as "Go ahead, make my day" Clint Eastwood (#1); actor, comedian, and diplomat Eddie Murphy (#2); and, thank God, Nobel Prize winner, the truly great Mother Teresa, founder of the Sisters of Charity, rated third! Fortunately, Billy Graham was a not-too-distant fourth. But, to use the theologian Walter Brueggemann's language, notwithstanding what most Americans think, people like Mother Teresa are the real history makers. They are the ones who really change the course of history. Although they may not drive fancy cars, they are the ones who really change the way the world looks at itself. History, as it were, belongs to those who are able to obey God no matter how long it takes, no matter how much it costs, no matter how painful it may be. Now, in 2 Timothy, we listen to Paul as he languishes in a Roman jail. Writing to the young pastor, Timothy, Paul is trying to make sense of his life, a life that will soon end. Within days, presumably, Paul will die. His head will be chopped off. And Paul knows it. "I have done my best in the race," Paul writes. "I have run the full distance, and I have kept the faith." God help us to have such a testimony when our lives end!

List three people whom you most admire. Three people whose lives you would most want your life to be like.

1.

2.

3.

Devotional Journal

Read/Vocabulary Cards

In critical reading passages, four main questions are usually asked:
1) Find the main idea;
2) Spot details;
3) Draw inferences;
4) Identify the mood or theme.
When comparing two articles, read the first one and answer specific questions. Then follow the same strategy with the second.

Lesson continues on the next page.

Critical Reading

It hath been observed by wise and considering men that wealth hath seldom been the portion, and never the mark to discover good people; but that Almighty God, who disposeth all things wisely, hath of his abundant goodness denied it—He only knows why—to many whose minds He hath enriched with the greater blessings of knowledge and virtue, as the fairer testimonies of his love to mankind: and this was the present condition of this man of so excellent erudition and endowments; whose necessary and daily expenses were hardly reconcilable with his uncertain and narrow estate. Which I mention, for that at this time there was a most generous offer made him for the moderating of his worldly cares; the declaration of which shall be the next employment of my pen (*The Life of Dr. Donne*, Izaak Walton).

The purpose of this paragraph mostly likely is to introduce:
  A. a passage explaining the ameliorating potentiality of poverty
  B. a scolding of John Donne for his servility
  C. an apology of sorts for the weak God whom Donne served
  D. a rendition of the lesson Donne remembered all his life

Solve

  A. If seven people meet each other and each shakes hands only once with each of the others, how many handshakes will there have been? (MindTrap®)
  B. When Sandy was 6 she hammered a nail into her favorite tree to mark her height. 10 years later, Sandy returned to see how much higher the nail was. If the tree grew by five centimeters each year, how much higher would the nail be? (MindTrap®)

Critical Thinking: Essay

Write an essay describing in great detail someone whom you admire and why. Include physical descriptions, character qualities, and actions. Find a scriptural character who is most like this person.

92

A New Car or a Life Saved?

For I am already being poured out like a drink offering, and the time has come for my departure. I have fought the good fight, I have finished the race, I have kept the faith. Now there is in store for me the crown of righteousness, which the Lord, the righteous Judge, will award to me on that day—and not to me only, but also to all who have longed for his appearing. —2 Timothy 4:6–8

Scripture: 2 Timothy 4:6-8

I have kept the faith…How will you be remembered? For buying a new car every year? Or, for leading a person to Christ? What has more eternal value? Those are the sorts of questions you will have to ask yourself someday, young people. Paul is trying to encourage Timothy to keep his priorities straight. Timothy was the child of a mixed marriage—his mother was Jewish, his father Greek. His grandmother converted him to Christianity. And for the most part, Timothy was just an average young man. He was not naturally brave, nor was he particularly strong. He needed constant encouragement. But Paul saw his potential and called him "my son in the faith." Paul rightly sought to invest his life in this young pastor.

If you had a million dollars, what would you do with it?

Devotional Journal

Read/Vocabulary Cards

Critical Thinking: Worldview

Take a number of publications and discern their worldview or slants on these topics: gun control, capital punishment, and/or abortion.

Compare for instance *World Magazine, U.S. News and World Report, Time, The National Rifleman, Christianity Today.* You can find these magazines in most libraries.

Solve

Answer these questions true or false.

```
 A      B      C      D      E      F      G      H      I
 +------+------+------+------+------+------+------+------+
-2    -1.5    -1    -.5     0     .5     1     1.5     2
```

1. A = I
2. D < 1
3. C > D
4. G > H
5. D > I
6. I > A
7. B + F = 2
8. A - C = -1
9. I - A = 0
10. C - G = - 2

Critical Thinking: Essay

Write a personal story illustrating the way to lose a sporting event.

How does one determine the slant of a passage?

(A) Look for phrases like "I prefer" or "in my opinion." In these cases, the author is telling what his slant will be.

(B) Identify sarcasm. Often an author will slant a view by making fun of his opponent.

(C) How much evidence is he giving? He often gives more evidence, better evidence for his own position—particularly if he is holding a strong position.

(D) Look for politically charged wording: liberals, right-wingers, pro-abortionists, rednecks and other vocabulary that may reveal the perspective of the writer.

167

93
Dreams of Damascus

I consider that our present sufferings are not worth comparing with the glory that will be revealed in us. —Romans 8:18

Scripture: *Romans 8*

This is Paul's last and most moving moment of his life. After a lifetime of service and suffering for Christ he is going to die. He is alone except for Luke. Yet there is no hint of self-pity; there are no regrets. His last word is one of encouragement to all who follow after. He is ready for death because he lived his life with no regrets. The race is over. He is ready for the reward. "For I am sure," Paul writes, "that neither death, nor life, nor angels, nor principalities, nor things present, nor things to come, nor powers, nor height, nor depth, nor anything else in all creation, will be able to separate us from the love of God in Christ Jesus our Lord!" (Romans 8) Wow! I have run the race… kept the faith. At the end of his life, memories must have flooded Paul's mind. What might have been. Memories of Damascus—the place his Christian faith journey began. What if Christ had not stopped him on the road to Damascus and turned him around? Endless trips with uncomfortably hard beds. Shipwrecked. Snake bitten. Beaten. And what did it get him in the end? An axe! Paul is saying it has been worth it.

Are you making your life have eternal meaning?

Devotional Journal

Read/Vocabulary Cards

Critical Thinking: Worldview

What is the slant of each viewpoint? Offer evidence for your position.
A. The necessity of the death of Christ on the cross is grounded on the fundamental moral fact that in the sight of God certain actions are inherently worthy of punishment. The moral scales of the universe must be righted. The concept of retributive justice is rooted in the very heart of God's character and the Gospel itself. The good news is not that God has disregarded standards of justice, but that He Himself has satisfied those standards for us and taken our rightful punishment upon Himself in the person of Jesus Christ His only Begotten Son. (from *Evangelical Ethics* by John Jefferson Davis)
B. An opponent of Dr. Davis would argue: Indeed, God demands justice. Life in prison, monetary fines, but not death. No man or woman is morally correct to take another person's life. This is not self-defense. Capital punishment is cold-blooded murder.

Solve

A. Represent algebraically:
1. If one puppy costs A dollars, and puppy B costs twice A, what is the cost of puppy B?
2. A is three more than five times B.
3. A is sixteen less than eight divided by B.

B. Which statement is true.
   A. A rate is a ratio of two variables with different units like 30 miles/2 hours.
   B. A rate is a ratio of two numbers with similar units like 30 miles/2 hours.
   C. A rate is a ratio of two variables with similar units like 40 miles/2 hours.
   D. A rate is a ratio of two numbers with different units like 30 miles/2 hours.

C. Which of the following graphs best depicts the absolute value equation
   $2y = 6\,|x + 1|$?

A.

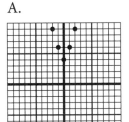

B.

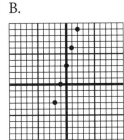

C.

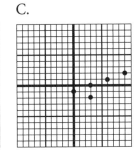

D.

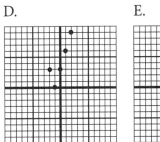

E.

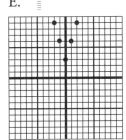

Is there no balm in Gilead? Is there no physician there? —Jeremiah 8:22

Scripture: Jeremiah 8:18–9:3

She visited our corner almost every day. *Harbinger* of hope, preserver of *continuity*. She lay neatly cut squares of white bread under the blue and white sign that warned would-be villains that there was a "Neighborhood Watch" *ubiquitously* watching over this community. Some said that this lady was crazy. We whose stories are so complete and well-rehearsed are *suspicious* of those with stories we do not know or cannot comprehend. But she had no story. At least she was not talking. She offered us very few hints—a frayed coat two sizes too large, her pockets stuffed with West Penn Hospital brochures entitled "Cancer—You can survive!" That was all we knew. The old woman who ruled our corner remained an *anonymous citadel.* She guarded her bread from *unscrupulous* ants, barking blue jays, and *mischievous* school children. Her face was all seriousness—no trace of a smile. For her work was sacred and important, even if no one else thought so. But I did. And even if I did not know who she was—she accepted my friendly "hellos" with a suspicious frown—I appreciated this *eccentric* lady who brought bird song to a community muted by hard luck. She stood alone at our corner next to two abandoned buildings *ravaged* and neglected by time. She brought beauty and hope to a community that desperately needed both. To me at least, the bag lady was the balm of Gilead. The balm of Gilead was a valuable oil found only in northern Israel that was thought to have medicinal value. Much of its value was that people thought it could heal.

Do you have a friend whose very presence brings joy and hope? Thank God for that friend!

Devotional Journal

Read/Vocabulary Cards

Review with your parents or guardians tonight!

Grammar

Choose the correct answer

Henry Ford (discovered, invented) the automobile.

Critical Reading

1. Define the italicized words in the above devotional.
2. What do "preserver of continuity" and "harbinger of hope" mean?
3. Give an example of an *opinion*, a *fact*, and an *inference*.
4. This passage about city ministry comes from an article I wrote for *Leadership Magazine*. Am I being critical of homeless people?

The Adventures of Tom Sawyer and *The Adventures of Huckleberry Finn*, by Mark Twain, are "must" reading for college-bound students. I know many of you read them when you were younger, but read them again. How are these novels an image of the American West circa 1835?

Vocabulary

Define italicized words in context:

At last the sleepy atmosphere was stirred—and *vigorously*: the murder trial came on in the court. It became the *absorbing* topic of village talk immediately. Tom could not get away from it. Every reference to the murder sent a *shudder* to his heart…. (from *The Adventures of Tom Sawyer* by Mark Twain)

Why not watch the latest Huck Finn/Tom Sawyer movie and compare it to the book(s)?

95
Written on Your Hearts

You yourselves are our letter, written on our hearts, known and read by everybody.
—2 Corinthians 3:2

Scripture: 2 Corinthians 3:1-3

Several years ago, in Chicago, Illinois, an elderly lady died. When she was discovered by her neighbors, no one seemed to know who she was. She was called "Sister Mary" because she was a nun and member of the Cenacle Sisters (Roman Catholic). But no one knew her last name. So, the police investigated. It was more difficult than they thought it would be. You see, Sister Mary owned almost nothing. She had no credit cards, no automobile, no television. People knew and loved her, though. She was well known at the local food bank. And almost every homeless person in the neighborhood knew her. But, the police could not identify her until they contacted the Cenacle Sisters and sent them a photograph. "I have no need of credentials," the Apostle Paul writes the Corinthian Church. "My life is written on your hearts." Paul owned almost nothing, but his value as a person was to be found in the persons with whom he had shared Jesus Christ. Those were the riches he carried with him to the Roman gallows.

This SAT preparation is about making decisions today that will affect tomorrow. Are you studying hard and preparing for the SAT so as to bring glory to God? To yourself? Or, are you just doing it to please your parents? Think about it.

Devotional Journal

Read/Vocabulary Cards

Critical Reading

A.

A man said to him, "I will follow you wherever you go." And Jesus said to him, "Foxes have holes, and birds of the air have nests, but the Son of Man has no place to lay his head." He said to another man, "Follow me." But the man replied, "Lord, first let me go and bury my father." Jesus said to him, "Let the dead bury their own dead, but you go and proclaim the kingdom of God." Still another said, "I will follow you, Lord; but first let me go back and say good-by to my family." Jesus replied, "No one who puts his hand to the plow and looks back is fit for service in the kingdom of God" (Luke 9:57-62).

Give a title to this passage. Based on the information in it, give an analysis of who Jesus is.

You must not miss any of the first ten questions on each portion of the SAT I. Remember: each question counts the same and the last questions are usually more difficult. The bottom line is that if you can get all the simple and average questions, you will make about 1250 (math plus verbal) on the exam. Getting a few hard ones will only put icing on the cake.

B.

   The death of Antony and Cleopatra is a subject which has been treated
by the greatest wits of our nation, after Shakespeare; and by all so variously,
that their example has given me the confidence to try myself in this bow of
Ulysses amongst the crowd of suitors, and, withal, to take my own measures,
in aiming at the mark. I doubt not but the same motive has prevailed with
all of us in this attempt; I mean the excellency of the moral: For the chief
persons represented were famous patterns of unlawful love; and their end
accordingly was unfortunate. All reasonable men have long since concluded,
that the hero of the poem ought not to be a character of perfect virtue, for
then he could not, without injustice, be made unhappy; nor yet altogether
wicked, because he could not then be pitied. I have therefore steered the
middle course; and have drawn the character of Antony as favorably as
Plutarch, Appian, and Dion Cassius would give me leave; the like I have
observed in Cleopatra. That which is wanting to work up the pity to a greater
height, was not afforded me by the story; for the crimes of love, which they
both committed, were not occasioned by any necessity, or fatal ignorance,
but were wholly voluntary; since our passions are, or ought to be, within our
power (*All For Love*, John Dryden).

This passage is primarily concerned with:
   A. Ulysses
   B. Plutarch
   C. Antony and Cleopatra
   D. Cassius

Solve

   A. What percent of 72 is 94.7?
   B. What percent of 63 is 9?
   C. Write $^{3419}\!/_7$ as a mixed number.

So we fix our eyes not on what is seen, but on what is unseen. For what is seen is temporary, but what is unseen is eternal. Now we know that if the earthly tent we live in is destroyed, we have a building from God... —2 Corinthians 4:18–5:1

Scripture: 2 Corinthians 4:16–5:1

What do people say about us? "He wears designer clothes." Or, "His front yard is beautiful." If we died tomorrow, what would people say about us? In America, unfortunately, we are most often known by what we own. By our job. Our success is determined by how much wealth we accumulate. You know the old joke—"Success is determined by how many toys we have accumulated at the end of our lives." Sister Mary owned very little, so she could not be identified by outsiders. But her life was written on the hearts of thousands of people. And you can bet that God knew her when she got to heaven!

Do you know someone who is very special to you (maybe this person shared Christ with you), but to others is unimportant? If so, thank that person today.

Devotional Journal

Read/Vocabulary Cards

Critical Thinking: Comparison

Compare and contrast these two prayers.
   A. Prayer of Adoration

   I love you, O Lord, my strength! The Lord is my rock, my fortress and my deliverer; my God is my rock, in whom I take refuge. He is my shield and the horn of my salvation, my stronghold. I will call to the Lord, who is worthy of praise, and I am saved from my enemies (Psalm 18:1).

   B. Prayers of Confession

   "Come now, let us reason together," says the Lord. "Though your sins are like scarlet, they shall be as white as snow; though they are red like crimson, they shall be like wool" (Isaiah 1:18).

Compare and contrast questions are best solved by highlighting similarities first and then identifying differences. Confusion results when contrast identification precedes similarity identification.

Solve

How long does it take your dad to drive 180 miles at 50 mph?

Critical Thinking: Essay

Create a dialogue between two four-year-olds discussing the prospect of attending nursery school.

So when the Midianite merchants came by, his brothers pulled Joseph up out of the cistern and sold him for twenty shekels of silver to the Ishmaelites, who took him to Egypt. — Genesis 37:28

Scripture: Genesis 37:18-36

The story of Joseph is a story of false perceptions of reality. His brothers incorrectly perceived Joseph as an enemy, and the reader, if he has never read the Joseph narratives, thinks that all is over for Joseph. Our perceptions and our understanding of reality are often incomplete. I remember just such a case in my own life. While I was a student at seminary, I visited a Christian friend who was spending the summer at Hampton Beach, New Hampshire, with other youths, sharing her faith with vacationers. Hampton Beach in 1976 was a loathsome commercialized stretch of pop machines and greasy hotdog stands. None of these diversions mitigated my joy at spending an afternoon with an old friend.

After I met the Lord in high school, I had chosen to avoid pairing off with girls. I had many female friends, but they were only that—friends. I did lots of things with girls—but usually in a group. My friend at Hampton Beach, I fear, had other plans. "Oh Lord," she began, as I poured sand out of my Converse tennis shoes, "Thank you that some day I will marry a minister." I did not share the same feelings about her as she felt about me. This friend of mine remained a friend for many years after this, but on this day she was operating from the wrong set of assumptions. All her sincerity, innocence, and good intentions—and they were legion—although they were praiseworthy, did not move her forward. What moves us forward is obedience and faith. This story reminds us that we need to keep our eyes on what He wants—not what we want. I heard my friend married a wonderful Christian man and is very happy today. The very weekend after I visited this young lady I met my future wife. In the big things as well as in the little things, God is in control.

Has anything sad ever happened to you that later turned out for the better? Did you give God the glory?

Devotional Journal

Read/Vocabulary Cards

Vocabulary

Give synonyms for these words:

1. contradiction
2. nonviolent
3. perjury
4. shyness
5. pervasive
6. pessimism
7. pugnacious
8. precedent
9. pretentious
10. prologue

I purposely use challenging vocabulary words in the devotion. Are you looking up the words that you do not know?

Every SAT I have examined includes this vocabulary word: pejorative. Know it!

Lesson continues on the next page.

11. oracle
12. recluse
13. refute
14. disgraceful
15. repudiate
16. bitterness
17. confinement
18. delectable

Solve

A. Joe begins a job at 11:00 a.m. He finishes five hours later. What time did he finish? Give the answer in military time.

B. London time is six hours ahead of New York time. New York time is three hours ahead of Los Angeles time. It is 3:00 a.m. London time. What time is it in Los Angeles?

C. Is ⅚ greater than 60%?

D. The multiplicative inverse of a number, X, is:

A. x

B. x - y

C. x/y

D. $1/x$

Joseph's master took him and put him in prison...the Lord was with him; he showed him kindness... —Genesis 39:20, 21

Scripture: Genesis 37–47

Joseph was part of a dysfunctional family, a blended family. Two moms in the same household! Jealousy. Favoritism. Violence. It is all there. Anger. Hurt. Differentiation. Triangulation. Strangulation! Joseph had a hundred reasons why he could have failed and, if he lived in modern day America he would not be blamed! Since Sigmund Freud enlightened us to the fact that we are not at fault—we should blame our moms—and since B. F. Skinner with his M&Ms and dog tricks showed us that we really are a product of our environment, it has been A-OK to blame all our problems on someone else. You don't see any of that stuff in the Joseph narratives. Joseph never whined, complained, or blamed anyone. Why? Because he knew that God was in control. No excuses. I am not making light of your bad family situation, if it exists, nor am I suggesting that our environment has no impact on us. What I am saying, though, is that God can overcome all obstacles. But He first likes us to take responsibility for our lives and our problems. No, you and I can't help where we were born, or that our parents are divorced, but we can now purpose to give our lives to Christ and obey Him every step of the way.

Is there a difficult situation in your life that you need to give to Him? Can you take responsibility for that problem and then ask Him to help you?

Devotional Journal

Read/Vocabulary Cards

Grammar

Choose the correct answer.

A number of changes were (effected, affected) by the new president.

Vocabulary

Define italicized words in context:

Such strange, *lingering* echoes of the old demon-worship might perhaps even now be caught by the diligent listener among the gray-haired *peasantry*; for the rude mind with difficulty associates the ideas of power and *benignity*. A *shadowy* conception of power that by much persuasion can be *induced* to refrain from inflicting harm.... To them...pain is all overgrown by *recollections* that are a *perpetual* pasture to fear.... Experience had bred no fancies in [Silas Marner] that could raise the *phantasm* of appetite. (from *Silas Marner* by George Eliot)

George Eliot, the nom de plume of Mary Ann Evans, was one of the finest English authors of the nineteenth century. In addition to *Silas Marner* (my personal favorite), she wrote *Middlemarch, Adam Bede,* and *The Mill on the Floss.* Silas Marner is an embittered recluse who raises an abandoned child who appears on his hearth one night. Through her, Silas learns to love, redicovers hope, and regains his trust in mankind. This is an unforgettable story, and you can bet it will be referenced in your freshman English course in college!

99

Lemonade from Lemons

And now do not be distressed…because you sold me here; for God sent me before you to preserve life. —Genesis 45:5 (RSV)

Scripture: *Genesis 45*

This is one of the most powerful verses of Scripture in the Bible. It flies in the face of modern thinking. God takes things that are bad and makes them good. There are no accidents. And Joseph does the unthinkable—he forgives his guilty brothers. Wow! When I was in college, twenty-five years ago, I put a poster above my desk, "When life gives you lemons, make lemonade." Pushing aside the bad theology here, the obvious existential prejudices, and the triteness of the whole expression, it still captures the essence of what God does: He takes something bad in our life and makes it good. I thank God that I saved myself for my wife. (And she did the same for me.) But if we make mistakes, and bad choices, and I mean big ones, God forgives them. They disappear. Like what happens when I mistakenly turn off my computer and lose my whole manuscript! It was once there—but now suddenly gone. Forever. Forgiveness, though, does not always take care of the matter. Old habits will take some time to change and sinning does have consequences. But God has forgiven us. No one will make a better offer to you on this day!

Be a Joseph today to someone you know.

Devotional Journal

Read/Vocabulary Cards

Review your vocabulary cards with your parents or guardians.

Critical Reading

The lamp must be replenish'd,
But even then
It will not burn so long as I must watch.
My slumbers—if I slumber—are not sleep,
But a continuance of enduring thought,
Which then I can resist not: in my heart
There is a vigil, and these eyes but close
To look within; and yet I live, and bear
The aspect and the form of breathing men.
But grief should be the instructor of the wise;
Sorrow is knowledge: they who know the most
Must mourn the deepest o'er the fatal truth,
The Tree of Knowledge is not that of Life.
Philosophy and science, and the springs
Of wonder, and the wisdom of the world,
I have [Critical Thinking:] essay'd, and in my mind there is
A power to make these subject to itself—
But they avail not: I have done men good,
And I have met with good even among men—
(*Manfred*, Lord Byron)

Several of the critical reading questions on the SAT I will refer to "point of view" or "opinion of the author." The questions will be something like this: "Compare these two viewpoints and answer the questions following." It is very important that you learn to suspend your own viewpoint and assume another.

What does Byron mean by this statement, "The Tree of Knowledge is not that of Life."?

- A. Mankind sinned and lost its way.
- B. Knowledge, science, and philosophy will neither solve all the problems of this age nor will they satisfy the human soul.
- C. Life is more than good feelings, altruistic intentions, or worthy actions.
- D. None of the above.

Critical Thinking: Writing

Write a diary entry for each point of view:

- A. You are a mother of three children. Your name is White Feather and you are a Lenape Indian. Your husband is an average Indian brave. You are watching these strange people in their big ships land at Jamestown. They have been there for more than ten years and still there is trouble. Describe your fears and hopes. It is 1619.
- B. You are a man named Ebenezer Davis. It is 1619. You are a settler in Jamestown. You have left your family behind in Yorkshire, England. You are tired, scared, and lonely. And you have never seen anything like America, much less a Lenape Indian! How does it feel? What are your fears and expectations?
- C. You are Joe Black (your English name) to your slave owners, but you know that your real name is Lomatata (your African name). You were captured and enslaved in West Africa two years ago. You have a wife and three children in Africa. But you have not seen them and doubt that you will ever see them again. You have spent two years working in the West Indies. Now you are being sold to new owners in Jamestown, Virginia. It is 1619.

Solve

Michael can paint a house by himself in 12 hours. When both John and Michael are painting they can complete the house in 8 hours. How long would it take John to paint the house by himself?

- A. 20 hours
- B. 24 hours
- C. 4 hours
- D. 12 hours
- E. 30 hours

100

Love that Outlives Our Griefs

Christ Jesus: Who being in very nature God, did not consider equality with God something to be grasped...and became obedient to death—even death on a cross!
—Philippians 2:6–8

Scripture: *Philippians 2*

I recently read an essay by Duke University Chaplain William Willimon entitled "Christus Victor," in which he offers a wrestling match as a metaphor for what happened on the first Easter morning—a flawed metaphor, I must admit, because God is certainly not in a wrestling match with Satan. Because if He were, Satan would be history! God is absolutely in control of everything! This essay, though, brought back so many good feelings.... By far, the most important social event in my hometown, in 1958, was the annual professional wrestling match held in the Veterans of Foreign Wars Hall. Of course there were more "*scandalous*" events held at the VFW Hall—like the time an unknown controversial singer from Mississippi, named Elvis Presley, held a dance. My parents refused to allow any of us to watch Elvis "shake his hips on stage." It turned out that almost no one bothered to go anyway and those who did said that he was no big deal and would never be famous. But there was no more well-attended event than the wrestling match. My grandfather was a leading citizen in my hometown and was also an *inveterate* wrestling fan. People of all shapes and sizes crowded in rows of bleachers surrounding a homemade canvas ring highlighted by a high-intensity light fastened to the ceiling by army-issue parachute cord. My grandfather and I carefully tiptoed to our seat, avoiding discarded chewing tobacco and snuff juice. To my five-year-old eyes it was an amazing sight. Everyone was screaming and shouting. The bad guys were clearly bad and really mean—three-hundred-fifty-pound overweight Big Bad Hans with his tight black trunks and equally small muscle-shirt, sporting chains and a swastika tattooed on his left arm. And our hero—two-hundred-twenty-pound *svelte* Gorgeous George—blond hair, blue-eyed, wearing a red, white, and blue silky outfit—was even more impressive. No one had to tell us that Big Bad Hans was evil incarnate and Gorgeous George was good.

We live in an age where bad is not always bad—or is it? We call it relativism. Memorize the Ten Commandments.

Devotional Journal

Read/Vocabulary Cards

Vocabulary

Define the italicized words in the above devotion.

Remember: writing always benefits from pre-writing disciplines like an outline and rough draft. Take time to write these before you do your final copy!

Solve

A linear equation
  A. in one variable can be written in the form AX = B, A is not equal to 0. A linear equation in two variables can be written in the form AX + BY = C.
  B. in one variable can be written in the form BX = A, B is not equal to 0. A linear equation in two variables can be written in the form AX + BY = C.
  C. in one variable can be written in the form AB =X, A is not equal to 0. A linear equation in two variables can be written in the form AX + BY = C.
  D. in one variable can be written in the form AX = B, A is not equal to 0. A linear equation in two variables can be written in the form A Y + BX = C.
  E. None of the above.

Critical Thinking: Essay

Create a dialogue between two high-schoolers discussing what their pastor preached on Sunday.

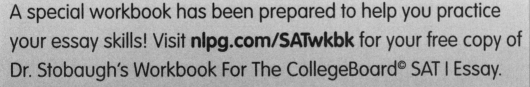

Ready to Practice?

A special workbook has been prepared to help you practice your essay skills! Visit **nlpg.com/SATwkbk** for your free copy of Dr. Stobaugh's Workbook For The CollegeBoard© SAT I Essay.

Gorgeous George Wins Again

Therefore God exalted him to the highest place...that at the name of Jesus every knee should bow...every tongue confess that Jesus Christ is Lord... —Philippians 2:9–11

Scripture: *Philippians 2*

Evil Hans walked around the ring growling at us, frowning, showing off. George, on the other hand, was suitably shy, smiling, and waving at the crowd. The fight began. Big Bad Hans had no intentions of fighting fairly. And, so, before long Gorgeous George was in big trouble. In fact, his head was bleeding profusely and it appeared that Big Bad Hans had won. The referee stood over the bloodied and unconscious Gorgeous George and began to count "one, two...." We were furious! The bad guy was going to win! And he had done it unfairly! But, before the referee counted "three," George managed to stand. Everyone cheered. And, as if to accent this new fortunate turn of events, the VFW loud speaker system—of dubious quality—cracked and encouraged us with something that sounded like the William Tell Overture (better known as the theme song from *The Lone Ranger*). We were ecstatic...good would yet prevail. And, of course, from there, it was no contest. Gorgeous George made short work of Big Bad Hans, and, within few a minutes, Hans was happily subdued and George was the new heavyweight wrestling champ of my small town. We all felt better for the experience. The Russians might bomb us tomorrow, cotton prices were at an all-time low, and polio was sweeping the nation, but tonight, in this place, right prevailed. At first it appeared that Big Bad Hans would win, but, to our delight, we discovered that Gorgeous George won after all! You will experience some rough days. Days that are so hard that you will be tempted to lose perspective, to forget about the mighty God we serve. You may go down for the count...but take heart! The righteous will yet overcome! Every knee will bow, every tongue confess!

Ask the Lord to help you overcome the greatest obstacle of your life. He will be there for you.

Devotional Journal

Read/Vocabulary Cards

Solve

A. Mary has a secret number. The sum of 4 times her number and 40 is equal to 120. What is it?
B. Twice the sum of 2 times a number and 50 is 137 greater than the opposite of the number. Find the number.
C. What fraction of 3 is ⅓?
D. Find the area in square inches.

48 inches

1 foot

Critical Thinking: Essay

Write a 300-word essay incorporating the italicized words that you defined in Lesson 100.

The SAT I has introduced a new phenomenon: the Grid-in Questions! You will have to answer some questions on your own. In other words, there will be no answers provided. The bad news is that for some reason my students are missing these problems more than ever. Why? I am not sure. The good news is that there are only a few on the exam and you will not be penalized for guessing. So if you have an answer that seems right—grid it in!

Deliver Us from the Evil One

And lead us not into temptation, but deliver us from the evil one. —Matthew 6:13

▌ Scripture: *Matthew 6:9-15*

Christian psychiatrists, Dr. Karl Menninger and Dr. Scott Peck, among others, have lamented the fact that Western society, especially American society, has lost a healthy respect for sin, and therefore, evil. In a world where everything goes, nothing is wrong, there is no sin—no real evil. However, there really is evil. Scott Peck says that evil is something that takes life away from someone (*evil* is *live* spelled backward). Jesus is urging His disciples to have a healthy respect for evil, to pray that we will be delivered from the evil one. The good news is that even though Satan is alive and well, he is nothing compared to our God. After all, God reigns in hell as well as in heaven and on earth!

Have you ever met or read about someone who did something that was evil? Why do we have such a hard time calling some act evil? Have you ever done something for which you need to repent? Deal with it today!

Devotional Journal

Read/Vocabulary Cards

Grammar

Choose the correct answer.

> There is no difference (between, among) Mary, Susan, and Betty.

Vocabulary

Define italicized words from context:

> I remember when I was at Lilliput, the *complexion* of those *diminutive* people appeared to me the fairest in the world; and talking upon this subject with a person of learning there, who was an *intimate* friend of mine, he said that my face appeared much fairer and smoother when he looked on me from the ground, than it did upon a nearer view.... He said he could discover great holes in my skin; that the stumps of my beard were ten times stronger than the *bristles* of a boar, and my complexion made up of several colours altogether disagreeable…they were a *comely* race of people. (from *Gulliver's Travels* by Jonathan Swift)

Solve

A. Twice a number is 46 less than -102. Find the number.
B. Five times a number is 84 more than the opposite of the number. Find the number.
C. If the sum of twice a number and -13 is multiplied by 3, the result is 24 greater than the opposite of the number. Find the number.
D. If the sum of twice a number and -15 is multiplied by 2, the answer is 10 greater than the opposite of the number. Find the number.

Jonathan Swift

Memorize Matthew 6:13-15 this week (if you have not already done so).

Gulliver's Travels by Jonathan Swift is much more than the Saturday morning comic book version that you have enjoyed. It is one of the most devastating satires in Western literature. It is the account of four voyages from Lilliput to Brobdingnag. I highly recommend the New American Library version, London, England, with a forward by Marcus Cunliffe. I have a 1960 paperback edition, but you may be able to find a more recent copy. Enjoy!

Reign in Hell

Your kingdom come, your will be done on earth as it is in heaven. —Matthew 6:10

Scripture: Matthew 6:9-14

In the distance I could hear an inspiring rendition of "America, the Beautiful." Over the horizon a glow of light kissed the horizon. The comforting light and inspiring melody were disarming. More comfortable with the drone of crickets and the *ubiquitous* hum of distant automobile traffic, my Suffolk sheep, however, obviously did not appreciate the *harmonious* offering from a short distance away.

The music came from a neighbor's farm where over two hundred members of the Ku Klux Klan were singing patriotic songs and the glow on the horizon was reflecting three burning crosses. To me it seemed like hell. In John Milton's description of hell in *Paradise Lost*, there is a brilliant image of both utter darkness and the burning fire of God's judgment juxtaposed in the same place—just as sin and love can coexist in one's heart. "In utter darkness, their portion set/As far removed from God and light of Heaven." Then, Milton lights the fires of hell with hatred, rebellion, and prejudice. "… the *unconquerable* will,/ And study of revenge, *immortal* hate,/And courage never to submit or yield." "Better to reign in hell than serve in heaven," Satan cries to God from the floor of hell. I felt and saw the *cosmological* battle between good and evil on the horizon of my property and in the center of my heart.

Respond to Milton's statement. Give examples of biblical characters who fit this description (e.g., Herod).

Devotional Journal

Read/Vocabulary Cards

Vocabulary

Give antonyms for the italicized words above.

Critical Reading

> How often have we not been told that the study of physical science is incompetent to confer culture; that it touches none of the higher problems of life; and, what is worse, that the continual devotion to scientific studies tends to generate a narrow and bigoted belief in the applicability of scientific methods to the search after truth of all kinds. How frequently one has reason to observe that no reply to a troublesome argument tells so well as calling its author a "mere scientific specialist." And, as I am afraid it is not permissible to speak of this form of opposition to scientific education in the past tense; may we not expect to be told that this, not only omission, but prohibition, of "mere literary instruction and education" is a patent example of scientific narrow-mindedness? (*Science and Culture*, Thomas Henry Huxley)

Develop a personal strategy before test day: Will you guess or not? How much time will you allow for checking the exams? Have you concentrated on your strong areas? Have you done the best you can with your weak ones?

What does Huxley mean by this statement, "How often have we not been told that the study of physical science is incompetent to confer culture?"

A. Huxley believes that physical science should be a hobby but never a serious educational endeavor.
B. Huxley is poking fun at literary critics who scornfully call a scientist "a mere scientific specialist."
C. Huxley believes that neither the discipline nor the subject matter of classical education is of such direct value to the student of physical science as to justify the expenditure of valuable time upon either and that for the purpose of attaining real culture, an exclusively scientific education is at least as effectual as an exclusively literary education.
D. Huxley believes that physical science education has been ruined by scientific narrow-mindedness.

Critical Thinking: Comparison

Below are two renditions of the Lord's Prayer. Matthew was writing primarily to a Jewish audience. Luke was writing primarily to a Gentile audience. How is this emphasis reflected in their versions of the Lord's Prayer?

"Our Father in heaven, hallowed be your name, your kingdom come, your will be done on earth as it is in heaven. Give us today our daily bread. Forgive us our debts, as we also have forgiven our debtors. And lead us not into temptation, but deliver us from the evil one." For if you forgive men when they sin against you, your heavenly Father will also forgive you. But if you do not forgive men their sins, your Father will not forgive your sins. Matthew 6:9–15

He said to them, "When you pray, say: 'Father, hallowed be your name, your kingdom come. Give us each day our daily bread. Forgive us our sins, for we also forgive everyone who sins against us. And lead us not into temptation.'" Luke 11:2–4

I think it is necessary to send back to you Epaphroditus…whom you sent to take care of my needs. —Philippians 2:25

Scripture: *Philippians 2:25-30*

My very first close friend was Craig Towles. The third of seven children, Craig, with his too-short crew cut and faded red football hand-me-down jacket, was somehow lost in the mob he euphemistically called "my family." Even when I stuffed "oak leaves" (or, more accurately, poison ivy) down his back, Craig was my friend. Craig is still my friend! A few years ago, when Karen and I went to my hometown, we visited Craig's business: a restaurant that sells catfish and hush puppies along with rich, greasy barbecue. A huge smile broke on his scarred mouth, and he gave me a great big "bear hug." Craig made it easy for me to go home. Good friends make it easy for us to go home—anytime, under any circumstances. Paul made it easy for his good friend Epaphroditus to go home. A few years earlier, when the Philippian Church heard that Paul was in prison, they sent a gift by the hand of Epaphroditus. Epaphroditus was instructed not only to deliver their gift but also to stay in Rome as Paul's personal servant. He did so with great joy. Paul refers to Epaphroditus as "my very close brother"—not an ordinary brother, but a "close" brother. While in Rome, Epaphroditus fell ill and very nearly died. Paul knew that jail life was not good for Epaphroditus. So it was time for Paul's good friend to leave him… never to see him again. Paul urged Epaphroditus to leave.

Do you have a really close friend? Praise God for him or her. Pray for your friend daily.

I have found that praying Scripture— that is, finding a verse that means a lot to me, meditating on it, and then actually praying it—is very effective. It has obvious value to you who are preparing for the SAT. Pray with me. *"Father, God, I love you. Who can understand my errors? You can! Cleanse me from my secret faults. Keep back Your servant also from presumptuous sins; let them have no dominion over me. Then, Oh, God, I shall be blameless, forgiven. And I shall finally be free!"* (from Psalm 19:12,13)

Devotional Journal

Read/Vocabulary Cards.

Have your parents or guardians go over your vocabulary cards.

Vocabulary

Give an antonym for each word:

1. reverence
2. satirize
3. serenity
4. shrewd
5. stagnant
6. suppress
7. taciturn
8. versatile
9. withhold
10. sarcasm
11. scrutinize
12. sever
13. skeptical
14. subdued
15. symmetrical
16. vigor
17. vivacious
18. vulnerable

Solve

$4^4 \times 4^6 =$

A. 4^2
B. 4^3
C. 8^4
D. 4^{10}

Critical Thinking: Essay

Create a dialogue between you and the person you will someday marry.

Is Anyone in Charge Here?

My flesh and my heart may fail, but God is the strength of my heart and my portion forever. —Psalm 73:26

| **Scripture: *Psalm 73*** |

Psalm 73 is the story of a religious person who has reconciled himself to the world in a negative sort of way. This affects his conception of God and of how God is running things. He is a good man, but this outlook upon the world and life has driven him into a sort of skepticism and doubt. He looks upon his world and what he sees shakes his soul: wicked persons, prospering and successful. On every hand, goodness is persecuted, inequality flaunted, fairness squashed. This man is ready to jettison his faith…He doubts the integrity of God and is skeptical regarding the dependability of humankind. He feels his grip on God breaking, and in a peevish bit of temper he is ready to write off the world. There are no rewards after all for goodness and the prizes inevitably go to scoundrels. Suddenly the psalmist cries, "Is there anyone in charge here?"

Many people are very upset when they see evil people prosper. Does a bad life always make a person unhappy? Yes and no. In the short run, maybe not. But, in the long run—absolutely. Pray for someone who you know needs to turn his or her life around.

Devotional Journal

Read/Vocabulary Cards

Solve

A. What is the value of one-half of two-thirds of three-quarters of four-fifths of five-sixths of six-sevenths of seven-eighths of eight-ninths of nine-tenths of one thousand? (MindTrap®)

Marbles

Style	Red	Blue	Green	Total
Big	5		3	14
Small	2	6		9
Total	7			23

B. The incomplete marble table above categorizes the color and types of marbles in a unit group.
   1. How many big blue marbles are there?
   2. How many small green marbles are there?
   3. How many blue marbles are there altogether? Green?

Critical Thinking: Writing

A. Write your own prayer based on Romans 5:1, 2.
B. Write a 300-word essay arguing from a perspective with which you disagree. For example, perhaps you believe abortion is wrong—if so, argue that it is right.

"The word of the Lord you have spoken is good," Hezekiah replied. For he thought, "There will be peace and security in my lifetime." —Isaiah 39:8

Scripture: *Isaiah 39:1-8*

The words of King Hezekiah—"there will be peace in my time"—are some of the most tragic words of the Old Testament. The king of Babylon sent a diplomatic mission to Jerusalem (verses 1-2), probably to establish an alliance in which Judah would be the subservient partner. Hezekiah was delighted to receive the ambassadors—what else could he do? He showed the representatives of Babylon everything: He exhibited the finances of his realm and his defense system. What a foolish man Hezekiah was! Showing his enemies his money and military potential! Enter the prophet Isaiah, the voice of uncompromising truth. Isaiah, in effect, told Hezekiah that he was one foolish king who had now given away the kingdom to the Babylonian conquerors. The king's response was pitiful and wimpish (verse 8a). He said quickly and agreeably to the prophet: "Thanks for the good word," and conceded the truth of the prophecy with the haunting addendum, "There will be peace and security in my days…." He was willing to sacrifice the future of his children for the pleasure of the moment. Some young people overlook the eternal consequences of their actions and compromise their future: AIDS. Drug overdose. Sexually transmitted diseases. Teen pregnancy.

Will you purpose to avoid foolish Hezekiah-like decisions that could put your entire future in jeopardy?

Devotional Journal

Read/Vocabulary Cards

Grammar

Choose the correct answer.

He could (have, of) finished his homework if he (would of, had) tried.

Internal conflict is conflict that arises within a character. For instance, a character may be experiencing internal conflict as he decides whether or not to lie or to tell the truth. External conflict is conflict between characters. For instance, typically a protagonist has conflict with an antagonist.

Lesson continues on the next page.

Critical Thinking: Analysis

The following statements exhibit internal conflict and external conflict. Identify which type of conflict the following is:

1. I decide to love my KKK enemies because Christ loves me.
2. I do not stay up at night with a gun and shoot my KKK enemies.
3. I think about staying up all night and shooting my enemies.
4. I phone the police.
5. I pray and ask God to deliver us.
6. I refuse to return insults to someone who insults my children.
7. I think of what I would like to do to them!
8. Several KKK members threaten to "take care of" my family. They drive around my property in an intimidating manner.

Solve

A. If x = 6 + y and 3x = 6 - 3y, what is the value of x?
B. In the previous equations, what is the value of y?
C. Find all the solutions to the equation $2\sqrt{x+3} - x = 3$

    A. -3

    B. 3

    C. 1, -3

    D. -1, 3

    E. 1

107

Forgiving the Unforgivable

"O my son Absalom! My son, my son Absalom! If only I had died instead of you..."
—2 Samuel 18:33

Scripture: *2 Samuel 18:31-33*

We must forgive those who harm us. Consider the story of David and his wayward son Absalom. Absalom rebelled against his father. David had every reason to hate Absalom. But he found the strength within himself to forgive Absalom. David forgave Absalom when he drove him from Jerusalem. And, what a poignant moment it was when David learned that one of his generals had killed his beloved son. "Absalom, Oh Absalom, Absalom, my son," David wept. "If only I had died instead of you" (2 Samuel 18:33). His tears were the tears of a father who had forgiven his unrepentant son. One of the awful, maybe unjust, aspects of unforgiveness is that if we do not forgive, we are strangely drawn into a web of bitterness. A tragic story of unforgiveness is reflected in the story of what happened to many concentration camp survivors. The Nazis killed over six million Jews during World War II. No one disagrees that the Jews were treated horribly during the war. They were unjustly brutalized, even exterminated by the Nazi regime. And, in a way, the survivors were left with an awful legacy. A psychologist did a survey of the survivors of the concentration camps and their Nazi captors. What did he find? Well, I wish that I could tell you that he found that the Nazis were doing very poorly. Not so. Their suicide rate, divorce rate, and early death rate was average. However, the death, divorce, and suicide rates for the concentration camp survivors were significantly higher than the general population! But what the psychologist concluded was interesting: The survivors had been unable to forgive their captors. And it had destroyed their lives. I truly feel sorry for men like Elie Wiesel, a concentration camp survivor who wrote, "I lost my faith in the fires of Birkenau" (a concentration camp).

Is there someone in your life whom you haven't forgiven? Forgive today!

Devotional Journal

Read/Vocabulary Cards

Vocabulary

Define italicized words in context:

> Now *faith*, in the sense in which I am here using the word, is the art of holding on to things your reason has once accepted, in spite of your changing moods. For moods will change, whatever view your reason takes.... Now that I am a Christian I do have moods in which the whole thing looks very *improbable*: but when I was an *atheist* I had moods in which Christianity looked terribly probable. This *rebellion* of your moods against your real self is going to come anyway. (from *Mere Christianity* by C.S. Lewis)

C. S. Lewis is a phenomenon. Read everything he has written! His vocabulary is exemplary, and his material is incredibly edifying. My favorite Lewis quote is in reference to why human beings enjoy sin so much: "We are half-hearted creatures, fooling around with drink and sex and ambition, when infinite joy is offered us. Like an ignorant child who wants to go on making mud pies in a slum because he cannot imagine what is meant by the offer of a holiday at the sea, we are far too easily pleased."

Lesson continues on the next page.

Critical Reading

In giving my views of the elevation of the laboring multitude, I wish that it may be understood that I shall often speak prospectively, or of changes and improvements which are not to be expected immediately, or soon; and this I say, that I may not be set down as a dreamer, expecting to regenerate the world in a day. I fear, however, that this explanation will not shield me from this and like reproaches. There are men who, in the face of all history, of the great changes wrought in men's condition, and of the new principles which are now acting on society, maintain that the future is to be a copy of the past, and probably a faded rather than bright copy. From such I differ, and did I not differ I would not stand here. Did I expect nothing better from human nature than I see, I should have no heart for the present effort, poor as it may be. I see the signs of a better futurity, and especially signs that the large class by whose toil we all live are rising from the dust; and this faith is my only motive to what I now offer (*On the Elevation of the Laboring Class*, William Ellery Channing).

One major concern Channing expresses in this passage is
- A. that things will move too slowly.
- B. that many will disagree with him.
- C. that his readers will think Channing does not realize that these changes will take a long time.
- D. that workers are not worthy individuals.

Solve

- A. Write 80% as a reduced common fraction.
- B. 4.6 - ¼ = (decimal answer)

Unforgiveness Bites Both Ways

Therefore, I tell you, her many sins have been forgiven—for she loved much. But he who has been forgiven little loves little. —Luke 7:47

Scripture: *Luke 7:36-50*

In the middle of the 1970s the Christian leader John Perkins made a decision that transformed the discussion about racial reconciliation forever. One evening, while in a Mississippi prison, African-American John Perkins was mercilessly beaten by his white captors. In the next few days he could have chosen to hate them. He decided to forgive them. This transformed John Perkins and the whole discussion about racial reconciliation. Today, Dr. Perkins is spreading a message of hope across America. And many are finding his message of forgiveness the road to racial reconciliation. If forgiveness gives life and hope, unforgiveness leads to death. Unforgiveness is like holding a rattlesnake: It bites both ways. We must forgive one another, even if the offending party does not wish to be forgiven. Even if we are in the right. As Francis B. Sayre suggests, "Christ depends upon us to show others what He is truly like. It is an awesome thought. But how better can the knowledge of Christ be gained in a world of men and women imprisoned in human bodies?"

Perhaps you are most Christlike when you are able to forgive those who are undeserving of forgiveness. But, of course, judgment is an arduous undertaking—perhaps it is best left up to God. Reflect on how much God has forgiven you through your life.

Devotional Journal

Read/Vocabulary Cards

Solve

A. Complete this graph.
B. Solve:
    1. X (2A - 3Y)
    2. 5 (2 - 4P)
    3. 3 (X - 2Y)
    4. 24x - 6 (3x - 7) = 24
    5. 14 (22 - x) + 34 = 8
    6. 46 = 67 - 3x
C. Write 290 as a product of prime numbers.

	.75	
		33⅓%
$^{89}/_{100}$		
	.17	

Critical Thinking: Essay

Create a dialogue between a homeless man and a Harvard professor.

The math section of the SAT I is now called the "math reasoning section"; critical reading and understanding is vital to math exercises. The math section will emphasize arithmetic, algebra, and geometry. The test, however, does not require you to know formulas—they will be provided for you. The brilliance of the SAT I is that it truly is an aptitude test—it measures how well you know how to use what you know.

Faith that Saves

The people sitting at the table began to think to themselves, "Who is this man? How can he forgive sins?" Jesus said to the woman, "Because you believed, you are saved from your sins. Go in peace." —Luke 7:49,50 (NCV)

Read *Luke 7:40-50*

Ethan Frome, a turn of the century novel written by Edith Wharton, is an *insightful* study of the *consequences* of sin, guilt, and unforgiveness. Ethan is a hardworking New England farmer with a *shrewish* wife named Zeena. Zeena is a selfish, unloving hypochondriac—in short, a *despicable* person. Because of her *perceived* poor health, she asks her cousin Mattie to live with her and help with the chores. Mattie is *predictably* young, good natured—everything Zeena is not. You have already guessed what happens: Mattie and Ethan become attracted to one another. Because they are convinced that they can never marry, they try to commit suicide together. The suicide attempt fails, but Mattie is permanently disabled. At the end of the novel, we see Ethan taking care of an even more hateful, unforgiving wife and a *debilitated* mistress. Their home has become a *nightmarish* citadel of unforgiveness. Jean Paul Sartre describes hell as a place where we spend eternity with people whom we hate. By Sartre's definition many of us are living in hell now. We live together in hatred and *compromise*. *Specters* of unrepentance *lurk* in our homes. In spite of an almost *intolerable* situation, we survive in our hellish environment by not feeling, but ignoring our emptiness.

The way this cycle is broken is by forgiving one another. Just do it!

Devotional Journal

Read/Vocabulary Cards

Review vocabulary cards with your parents this evening.

Vocabulary

Give a synonym for each italicized word above.

Every year my SAT students ask the same question: "How can we answer questions about material we do not believe?" No doubt there will be one or two questions on views that are antithetical to Judeo-Christian morality. Several notable examples are: pro-abortion article, pro-evolution article, pro-big bang theory of creation, pro-feminist, pro-same sex relationship. What do you do?

1. Pray!
2. Distance yourself from the material. Ascertain very carefully what the author is thinking.
3. Finally, state what the *author* thinks; not what you think.

Critical Reading

It was not until the Silurian time, some 350 million years ago, that the first pioneer of land life crept out on the shore. It was an arthropod, one of the great tribe that later produced crabs and lobsters and insects. (from *Silent Spring* by Rachel Carson)

1. Compare and contrast the view of creation in this excerpt from *Silent Spring* and Genesis 1 and 2.
2. Ms. Carson betrays a certain point of view. What is it?
3. How would you respond if you were to encounter a passage like this on the SAT?

Solve

A. What is the product of the sum of 12 and 6 and the difference of 12 and 8?
B. Factor $49x^2 + 81y^2$
   A. $(7x + 9y)(7x + 9y)$
   B. $xy(16)$
   C. $(7x)(7x)+(9y)(9y)$
   D. None of the above

When you encounter views that are different than yours, discuss them with a significant adult. Try to discriminate between what you think and what the other person thinks.

Those who sow in tears will reap with songs of joy. —Psalm 126:5

Scripture: *Psalm 126*

Psalm 126 is a psalm describing the struggles of being a Palestinian farmer. Farming in this arid climate was a precarious enterprise, to say the least. The key to success in arid farming is to grow enough to feed one's family, but, at the same time, to save enough seeds to begin a harvest next year. And that was the rub. All winter the farmer would require his family to sacrifice. They could eat everything—everything but the seed grain. Under no circumstance could they eat the seed grain. It was not unusual that one or two members of the family would die in the winter. But the seed grain must be preserved.... No wonder, then, the farmer sowed in tears. Remembering the sacrifice. Appreciating the sacrifice. But why would he do it? Because of the harvest. The ultimate, wonderful, life-sustaining harvest made it all worthwhile. Keep sowing good seeds. Be willing to sow in tears. Believe in the harvest.

Do you believe in the harvest? What is the "crop" you are cultivating in your life? A lot of friends? Good grades? Memorizing Scripture? Making a high SAT score?

Comparison

1. Make sure the comparison is based upon an essentially similar item or feature.
2. Notice details.
3. Identify the slant of the author: What view does the author prefer?
4. Compare meaningful differences, not irrelevant ones.

Devotional Journal

Read/Vocabulary Cards

Grammar

Choose the correct answer.

There were (fewer, less) players at the game today.

Critical Thinking: Comparison

Carefully read the following paragraphs and answer these questions.

1. What is (are) the issue(s) being argued? What are the major arguments offered by both sides? These arguments are from my dissertation. What do you think the title of my dissertation is?
2. What mutual criteria(ion) are (is) being considered by both sides? What does "marginality" mean?
3. Which argument is most persuasive?

View One: Race Is an Insignificant Category

Some scholars argue that race is an insignificant category. And, in the long run, worth ignoring. Particularly if one is an Evangelical Christian. Because, after all, the Gospel is the great equalizer. They argue that the only legitimate categories are "Christian" or "non-Christian." To judge or to evaluate worth or the efficacy of human relationships according to any other category—like race or class—is wrong.

View Two: Race Is a Significant Category

On the other side of the coin is a view that argues that race is the most important category for human identity. One major supporter of this view is Sang Hyun Lee, Professor of Systematic Theology and Director of the Asian American Program at Princeton Theological Seminary. He calls this racial/cultural separatism "marginality." The whole idea of marginality relates to all minority groups—ethnic and racial—who are experiencing some form of exclusion in a dominant culture. One's marginality is understood as resistance from a minority group in a hierarchical relationship with another dominant group toward this dominant group. Likewise the nonmarginal/dominant group seeks to resist the marginal group's entrance to the group and enjoyment of its privileges. Sang Lee sees this resistance as being inevitable.

Solve

Simplify $\left(\frac{4}{3}\right)^{-\frac{1}{2}}$

A. $\frac{-2}{3}$

B. $\frac{-16}{9}$

C. $\frac{2}{\sqrt{3}}$

D. $\frac{2}{3}$

E. $\frac{\sqrt{3}}{2}$

111

Don't Give Up

When the Lord brought back the captives to Zion, we were like men who dreamed. Our mouths were filled with laughter, our tongues with songs of joy. Then it was said among the nations, "The Lord has done great things for them." —Psalm 126:1,2

Scripture: Psalm 126

Many of you are sowing good seeds, solid, respectable seeds seeking to please and serve the Lord with your life. Times haven't always been easy and you have languished waiting for the harvest. But, it is coming. Do not weary in doing good works! God will bring a good harvest. Sowing and reaping, sadness and joy—life is sort of that way. Psalm 126 illustrates my point well, for it is a bittersweet psalm, a psalm of sadness and celebration. This psalm laments the sacrifices and afflictions of the painful Jewish exile in Babylon. But it also celebrates the great deliverance of finally returning to Zion. Babylon—a time of sowing, being God's chosen people, even when it seemed there was no God to choose—was a painful reality, a great tribulation. It was a time of being separated from God, or seemingly so. A time when the vision was in danger, when men and women were tempted to give up, to seek partial answers, answers that the world offered instead of God. But they persevered—for fifty years they waited, and hoped, and never forgot Zion. They never lost the vision. They were sorely tempted—the enticements of Babylon were quite persuasive, and, in fact, many Jews left their faith and settled in that land. But, by and large, most remained faithful and returned to Zion, to Jerusalem.

Have you gone through something that seemed never to end? Like your parents divorcing or a close friend dying? Have you struggled and struggled, waited and waited, cried and cried, waiting for God's faithfulness? If you haven't, you will. Let this time of SAT preparation be a time of God's faithfulness in your life.

Devotional Journal

Read/Vocabulary Cards

Solve

A. Hardy was bragging about his church's baseball team. He said, "Three of our players hit home runs and two of those home runs were hit with the bases loaded. Our guys won 9 to 0 and not a single man crossed home plate." How was this possible? (MindTrap®)

B. How many centimeters long is the line?

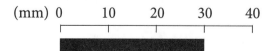

Critical Reading

I need scarcely observe that a poem deserves its title only inasmuch as it excites, by elevating the soul. The value of the poem is in the ratio of this elevating excitement. But all excitements are, through a psychal necessity, transient. That degree of excitement which would entitle a poem to be so called at all, cannot be sustained throughout a composition of any great length. After the lapse of half an hour, at the very utmost, it flags—fails—a revulsion ensues—and then the poem is, in effect, and in fact, no longer such (*The Poetic Principle*, Edgar Allan Poe).

What would be the best title for this passage?
  A. Poetry: Elevating the Soul with Brevity
  B. Poetry: The Art of Verbosity
  C. Poetry: Prose vs. Verse
  D. Poetry: Reading Verse as Drama

Critical Thinking: Values

All critical reading passages on the SAT will reflect certain values. It is important that you identify these values. Rank the following events according to their value to you, 5 = most; 1 = least.

_____ pleasing your friends
_____ pleasing your parents
_____ pleasing the Lord
_____ receiving a high score on the SAT
_____ going to college
_____ making a lot of money
_____ making good grades
_____ having a good time

Lord, remember your mercy and love. You have shown them since long ago. Do not remember the sins and wrong things I did when I was young. But remember to love me always because you are good, Lord. —Psalm 25:6,7 (NCV)

Scripture: *Psalm 25*

The family of God, at times, seems like a circus parade full of all sorts of unusual, diverse people. Indeed, at times the Christian community seems like a three-ring circus! Sick people, well people, spiritually mature, spiritually immature, saints—we have them all. We makes mistakes. We make absolutely terrible choices. But we keep going. Asking God, like the psalmist, not to remember the sins of our youth. Helping each other. Holding each other, we journey together. This is the Christian experience: journeying together, seeking God's best for our lives and our world, and asking forgiveness when we fail. Always separate but always together. And we do a lot of waiting. In Hebrew, waiting is not merely standing still—in fact, one waits on the Lord as one is continually moving in His will. Waiting is, indeed, like a parade, a strange, often uncomfortable combination of unperceived progress with painful, confusing waiting. We think of waiting as dry time, as a time of almost desperate nothingness. We feel as though we are caught in traffic. So many things to do. Places to go. We seem to be moving but going nowhere fast. We read Psalm 25 and we think of waiting in line for hours to attend a football game. Or we remember the last time we waited to eat at our favorite restaurant—we see this as wasted time. But it is not. We work so hard! And then we still sometimes fail… but we join the psalmist and ask God not to remember the sins of our youth. And then we wait again.

When I was young it seemed that time never moved—now it seems it goes too quickly! Does it seem that God is too slow? Why? Why not?

Devotional Journal

Read/Vocabulary Cards

Solve

A. Find three consecutive odd integers such that the sum of the first and third is 9 greater than the second decreased by 18.
B. Mary and Susan have 30 coins that are nickels and dimes. If the value of the coins is $2.10, how many coins of each type do they have?
C. I could finally afford a coat that was discounted 32% less than the original price. If the sale price was $215, what was the original price?
D. 4½ of 826 is what number?
E. What fraction of 60 is 30?
F. What is the average of 90, 85, 77, 44, and 89?
G. 3⅖ + .6 (fraction answer)
H. Round 6.666 to the nearest tenth

Critical Thinking: Essay

Create a dialogue between a Mormon and a Baptist discussing a doctrinal issue.

When solving word problems, it is important that you create a number picture. Never, I repeat, never skip a step! Spend the time to do it right!

A Time of Deliverance

Turn to me and be kind to me. I am lonely and hurting. —Psalm 25:16 (NCV)

 Scripture: *Psalm 25*

In the kingdom of God, though, waiting is not wasted time. It is a time of growth—though at times unrecognized growth. Oh sure, there are times of tremendous movement—a new spiritual revelation, a momentous happening, or a special blessing—but these moments, if we are honest, occur few and far between a whole lot of waiting. Theoretically we know that we should rejoice in these waiting times—most of our growth occurs during these times—but it is most difficult to do. There is always a time of deliverance. Psalm 25:1-12 is a psalm of thanksgiving for deliverance. But are the Israelites rejoicing over leaving the waiting period? Or are they rejoicing for what they learned in those dry times? The way a Christian handles deliverance is a good yardstick of his maturity. Nonetheless, a period of waiting has ended: The Israelite exiles were delivered from Babylonian captivity. The parade has rounded a corner, and genuine rejoicing is in order. There is, as it were, a crisis of celebration. Psychiatrists tell us that celebration can be as stressful as grieving. And waiting can be the most stressful human emotion. But do not be deceived: The waiting is not over. The stronghold of the enemy has momentarily been overthrown, but there will be new enemies. The Israelites were liberated from the Babylonians only to be given over in bondage to the Romans within a few short years. For a moment, though, in Psalm 25, we see that the immutable purposes of God are fulfilled—however long it took, God's will was vindicated.

Think about waiting. What has been the hardest thing for which you have had to wait in your life?

Devotional Journal

Read/Vocabulary Cards

Vocabulary

Define italicized words from context.

> He knew he was beaten now finally and without remedy and he went back to the *stern* and found the *jagged* end of the *tiller* would fit in the slot of the *rudder* well enough for him to steer. He settled the sack around his shoulders and put the *skiff* on her course. He sailed lightly now and he had no thoughts nor feelings of any kind. He was past everything now and he sailed the skiff to make his home port as well and intelligently as he could. (from *The Old Man and the Sea* by Ernest Hemingway)

Solve

Which are natural numbers:
(A) 5.1
(B) 8
(C) ½
(D) 3
(E) All of the above
(F) B and D

Ernest Hemingway is an enigma. On one hand, there is no denying that he is a major twentieth-century author. Everyone of you will read this great journalist-turned-writer who writes in a cogent, terse style. His worldview, though, is flawed. And, when you read his material be sure to place his life philosophy against Scripture. Why not begin with *The Old Man and the Sea*? This short novel is a metaphor for Hemingway's view of life. An old man fights all day and evening in the Caribbean with a giant fish. Read the novel to see the surprise ending....

A Severe Discipline

Lord, I give myself to you. My God, I trust you. Do not let me be disgraced.
—Psalm 25:1,2 (NCV)

Scripture: *Psalm 25*

Everyone at one time or another sings this song. We who have been through hard times, when we step out from the darkness of night into light, from pain to deliverance, from confusion to clarity, of course we sing, "Thou hast done wonderful things.…" The experience of suffering that so often walks hand in hand with waiting is never in vain if we are then able to see something of God's purpose in it, and can face life with new and deeper knowledge of his love. And, yet, until this dawn springs upon us, until we can know the inexpressible joy about which Isaiah speaks, we wait. God requires a severe discipline on our part. It is the discipline of waiting. It is the discipline of honesty about the human plight—injustice, unfulfilled hope, unanswered questions. It is the discipline of being willing to see faith as a now-but-not-yet sort of thing, the discipline of keeping close to those whose sad lives challenge our spiritual glibness. "Accept Jesus and your problems are over!" Don't we wish!

Give a few Christian clichés (e.g., God helps those who help themselves) and define them.

Devotional Journal

Read/Vocabulary Cards

Review cards this evening.

Grammar

Choose the correct answer.

Residents from poor countries often (immigrate, emigrate) from their own countries and move to more prosperous countries.

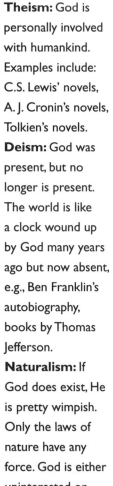

Worldviews
Christian Theism: God is personally involved with humankind. Examples include: C.S. Lewis' novels, A. J. Cronin's novels, Tolkien's novels. **Deism:** God was present, but no longer is present. The world is like a clock wound up by God many years ago but now absent, e.g., Ben Franklin's autobiography, books by Thomas Jefferson. **Naturalism:** If God does exist, He is pretty wimpish. Only the laws of nature have any force. God is either uninterested or downright mean, e.g., Stephen Crane, *The Red Badge of Courage.*

Critical Thinking: Worldview

Give the worldview of each passage.

1. Humans who bestow superior value on the lives of all human beings solely because they are members of our own species are judging along lines strikingly similar to those used by white racists who bestow superior value on the lives of other whites, merely because they are members of their own race. (P. Singer)
2. So God created man in His own image, in the image of God.
3. Gatsby believed…tomorrow we will run faster, stretch out our arms farther.… And one fine morning—So we beat on, boats against the current, borne back ceaselessly into the past. (from *The Great Gatsby* by F. Scott Fitzgerald)
4. For mere improvement is not redemption…God became man to turn creatures into sons: not simply to produce better men of the old kind but to produce a new kind of man. (from *Mere Christianity* by C.S. Lewis)
5. I don't see's there's much difference between the Fromes up at the farm and the Fromes down in the graveyard; 'cept that down there they're all quiet, and the women have got to hold their tongues. (from *Ethan Frome* by Edith Wharton)
6. If it feels good, do it!
7. The world is totally insane, out of control, stupid!

Solve

A. Write the median for these numbers:
   12, 19, 32, 36, 44, 88, 79
B. The volume of a gas varies inversely with its pressure when the temperature is held constant. If 4 liters of argon gas at 8 lb/in2 has its pressure increased to 24 lb/in2, what will its volume become?
   A. 12
   B. ¾
   C. 48
   D. 4/3
   E. 64

Absurdism: A modern movement where there is no god, nor any reason to have one. Everything is disorganized, anarchy rules, e.g., John Barth, *Floating Opera* and Kurt Vonnegut, Jr., *Cat's Cradle* and *God Bless You Mr. Rosewater*. **Existentialism:** Truth is open to debate. Everything is relative. A very pessimistic view, e.g., Albert Camus, *The Plague*, Franz Kafka, *The Stranger*, and Jean Paul Sartre, *No Exit*.

But the people who trust the Lord will become strong again. They will rise up as an eagle in the sky. They will run without needing rest. They will walk without becoming tired.
—Isaiah 40:31 (NCV)

Scripture: Isaiah 40:27-31

The most worthwhile lessons of life come slowly, are bought with a great price, require a great deal of patience. On the old television program *All in the Family* (one of my favorites!), Archie Bunker's agnostic son-in-law, Michael, asks him, "Archie, if there's a God, why is there so much suffering in this world?" There is only awkward silence, so Archie yells, "Edith, would you get in here and help? I'm having to defend God all by myself." In mock embarrassment we look sheepishly at the world, to the teenager abused by his parents, to the child born addicted to crack, and we shrug our shoulders as if to say that we do not know where God is and why He is not answering our prayers. But, if we feel as if we have to defend God, then we are simply not understanding the purpose of these times. Only a person who does not offer partial answers to complex problems—only these Christians can hope to march one day to the end of the parade. "Americans are always looking for love in forms it can never be," Kurt Vonnegut, Jr., quips, "in places it can never be." After we have done the work we have been called to do, it is our duty to painfully say, with broken hearts, "Wait." Wait until there will be justice, until there will be freedom. We deal with questions that defy ready answers—sin, injustice, evil, suffering, the demoniac power of poverty, and the social nightmare of unemployment.

Respond to Kurt Vonnegut, Jr.'s quote.

Devotional Journal

Read/Vocabulary Cards

Critical Reading

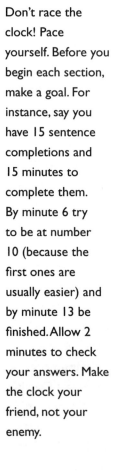

Don't race the clock! Pace yourself. Before you begin each section, make a goal. For instance, say you have 15 sentence completions and 15 minutes to complete them. By minute 6 try to be at number 10 (because the first ones are usually easier) and by minute 13 be finished. Allow 2 minutes to check your answers. Make the clock your friend, not your enemy.

A true classic, as I should like to hear it defined, is an author who has enriched the human mind, increased its treasure, and caused it to advance a step; who has discovered some moral and not equivocal truth, or revealed some eternal passion in that heart where all seemed known and discovered; who has expressed his thought, observation, or invention, in no matter what form, only provided it be broad and great, refined and sensible, sane and beautiful in itself; who has spoken to all in his own peculiar style, a style which is found to be also that of the whole world, a style new without neologism, new and old, easily contemporary with all time (*What is a Classic?* Charles Augustin Sainte-Beuve).

A true classic
  A. should be read several times.
  B. is contemporary with all time.
  C. is always long.
  D. is written in Greek or Roman times.

Solve

A rectangular solid has two faces the same size and shape as figure II below and four faces the same size and shape as figure I below. What is its volume?

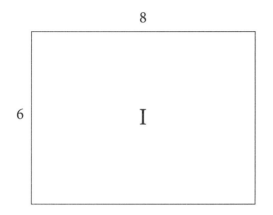

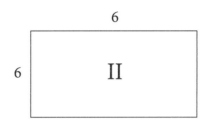

116

Costly Grace

"Repent, for the kingdom of heaven is near." —Matthew 3:1

Scripture: Matthew 3:1-12

In the summer of 1939, Dietrich Bonhoeffer, a German Lutheran pastor and lecturer in theology, was on a lecture tour in America. Already he was known as an enemy of the Nazi regime. To his certain peril, in 1933 Bonhoeffer had openly denounced Adolf Hitler on public radio. He had spent two years in London urging the German congregation there to oppose the Nazis. He had also written two influential books— *The Cost of Discipleship* and *Living Together*—which violently attacked compromise and false Christianity. Nonetheless, Bonhoeffer felt compelled to return to Germany. He never left Germany again. Bonhoeffer wrote in The *Cost of Discipleship*: "Cheap grace is the deadly enemy of our church.… Cheap grace is the preaching of forgiveness without repentance.… Costly grace is costly because it cost a man his life, and it is grace because it gives a man the only true life.…"

Give an example of a difficult decision facing you that could be categorized as "costly grace."

Devotional Journal

Read/Vocabulary Cards

Critical Thinking: Literary Devices

A rhetorical question is a question asked merely for effect with no answer expected. For example, in today's Scripture lesson John the Baptist asks "Who warned you to flee from the coming wrath?" (Matthew 3:7). Paul also loved to use rhetorical questions. Find a few examples from Romans 8, such as: "Who shall separate us from the love of God?" Write a few examples of your own.

Solve

A. A cube has how many more edges than it has vertices?
B. $\frac{5}{8} + \frac{1}{2} =$

Critical Reading

India is the mother of all major eastern-oriented religions: Hinduism, Buddhism, and Jainism. With regard to missions, India is more of a continent than a country. It is not unified culturally, historically, or linguistically. By early in the twenty-first century, India will be the most populated country in the world. Out of the current population of 900 million, about 3 percent claim to be Christian. In terms of world evangelism, India should be near the top of our list.

1. The author of this passage is a(n):
   A. Christian
   B. Existentialist
   C. Hindu
   D. Deist
2. India should be on the top of our mission priorities because:
   A. Hinduism is so harmful.
   B. Jesus is coming back soon.
   C. It is so densely populated with non-Christians.
   D. It may become Communist.
3. Why is India more a continent than a country?
   A. It is so large.
   B. It has so many different people groups.
   C. It is in South Asia.
   D. It has so many people.

Critical Thinking: Essay

Write a persuasive essay on the topic of your choice.

117

Simple Answers to Complex Problems

Can you compare God to anything? Can you compare him to an image of anything?
—Isaiah 40:18 (NCV)

> **Scripture: Isaiah 40:18-20**

God is not an idol, He is all-knowing. This should give us strength as we journey. God is not engaging us in a kind of hit-and-run game, always disappearing in the crunch. He is with us for the long run; and He demands no less from us. We are here to stay. We are here, right here to stay. We will not prostitute the Gospel by offering superficial answers to complex problems. As H. Lowe Crosby in Kurt Vonnegut, Jr.'s *Cat's Cradle*, we are tempted to offer simple quick answers to complex problems. No one enjoys waiting for justice to dawn. H. Lowe Crosby calmly describes the solution to thievery: "String up a few teen-age car thieves on lampposts in front of their houses with signs around their necks saying, 'Mama, here's your boy.' Do that a few times and I think that ignition locks would go the way of the rumble seat and the running board!" Like Crosby, we all are tempted to offer incomplete, unjust solutions to complex problems. When we look at them more closely we see how bizarre our solutions are. The problems we face in our lives defy superficial answers: They demand the Gospel, and the Gospel says that we must wait.

What big challenge looms in front of you that requires you to maintain a clear perspective of who God is and who you are?

Devotional Journal

Read/Vocabulary Cards

Solve

    A. $\dfrac{(-5 - 3) + (-3 - 2)}{-3 - (-2)}$

    B. $-3\frac{1}{4} + 2\frac{3}{11}$

    C. $-ab - a(a - b)$ if $a = -4$ and $b = -1$

    D. $-2 [-3 (-2 - 6)(3)]$

    E. Two of the following numbers are equal. Which is not equal? 0.4, $\frac{2}{5}$, 4%?

    F. A man is 13 times as old as his dog. In 10 years he will be 3 times as old as his dog will be. How old are they now?

Sentence Completion

For years many conservative Christians have vigorously opposed transracial marriages and, by _____ , transracial adoption.

    A. implication
    B. association
    C. insinuation
    D. suggestion

Surely you know. Surely you have heard. Surely in the beginning someone told you. Surely you understand how the earth was created. God sits on his throne above the circle of the earth… He makes powerful rulers unimportant. —Isaiah 40:21–23 (NCV)

Scripture: *Isaiah 40:21-26*

The modern American author John Barth describes a world that is all too real to many people. He compares the world to a showboat. This showboat with just one big flat open deck on it has a play going continuously. The boat is drifting up and down a river, and we, the audience, are sitting along both banks. We catch whatever part of the plot that happens to unfold as the boat floats past, and then we have to wait until the boat floats back again to catch another snatch of it. To fill the gaps we have to use our imaginations, or ask more attentive neighbors, or hear the word passed along from upriver or downriver. Most times we do not understand what is going on at all, or we think we know when we really don't. Lots of times we see the actors, but we do not hear them. It seems that is how much of life seems to work: our friends float past; the spiritual poverty surrounding us seems to float past as in a dream. We go to college, say good-bye to old friends and make new ones, and so on. We become involved with them for awhile, but we lose interest when there are no results. They float on, and we must rely on hearsay or lose track of them completely. They float back again and we either renew our friendship—catch up—or we find that they and we do not need each other anymore or we do not comprehend each other. But of course, Barth's analogy is flawed. It is flawed because God is personally involved in our lives. And, as Isaiah reminds us, God is very much in control.

In a prayerful way, share with God a problem you have.

Devotional Journal

Read/Vocabulary Cards

Grammar

Locate the error in this sentence.

My parents told <u>me</u>, <u>to finish</u> the chores <u>after</u>   <u>I finished eating</u>. <u>[No error.]</u>
         (A)   (B)   (C)   (D)   (E)

Try using five new words every day. If the vocabulary words that you are memorizing become part of your spoken vocabulary, they will never be forgotten.

Lesson continues on the next page.

Vocabulary

Give examples of words using these suffixes and roots, then define those words.

ity (state or condition)
ize (subject to an action)
jec (throw)
jur (law)
labor (hardship)
leg (law)
logy (study of)

Critical Thinking: Worldview

1. In his book *The Floating Opera*, John Barth puts forth the notion that the world is a floating opera. What sort of worldview does Barth project?
2. In Franz Kafka's haunting book *The Stranger* the characters remain anonymous! They have no intrinsic value. What worldview does Kafka portray?
3. There is an alternative view suggested. What is it?
4. Every person has a worldview. Based on a synthesis of your views, state your worldview. It should include things like: What is your value structure? On what is it based? The Bible? The Golden Rule?

Test-Taking Strategies

Now is a good to time to study the test-taking strategies in Appendix F.

And the Lord said to Joshua, "See, I have delivered Jericho into your hand, along with its king and its fighting men." —Joshua 6:2

Scripture: Joshua 6:1-21

Jericho was one of the most beautiful cities in the ancient Middle East. Barely four acres, it nonetheless was one of the most important border fortifications of the loosely governed Canaanite confederation. Besides that, the "city of palms" was a magnificently beautiful oasis in a desert of inhospitable terrain. This city-state was located a few miles inland, west of the Jordan River and somewhat north of the Salt Sea (what we today call the Dead Sea). Nestled in the arms of a spectacular valley between two formidable mountain ranges, the city oozed tranquility. But appearances can be deceiving: In fact, Jericho was an awesome citadel. It was probably not going to be taken by the greatest armies in the world—much less the ragtag nomadic Hebrew army. Surrounded by massive six-foot walls, it must have been a most discouraging sight indeed to Joshua and his people. Looming ahead of the Israelites was not a rest stop or an oasis but a despicable, overwhelming obstacle. This city was not going to fall to any trickery or good intentions or extra effort. No, Jericho was just too strong. But it fell anyway, though only after much faith and a week of dusty walks around the city doing crazy things.

What are your Jerichos? What are the problems you cannot overcome? A bad temper? Lying? Ask God to help you.

Devotional Journal

Read/Vocabulary Cards

Review cards with your parents or guardians this evening.

Vocabulary

Define italicized words in context:

> The *subsequent encounter* in the Captain's cabin was an odd one, and less *conclusive* than either Bennett or Lockhart had expected. Erickson listened while Bennett put his case—fairly enough, since he was on *impregnable* ground…. (from *The Cruel Sea* by Nicholas Monsarrat)

Solve

Arrange in order from least to greatest: -6, -7, 8, 0, 3, -3

Perhaps more than any book that I read in high school, Nicholas Monsarrat's *The Cruel Sea* indelibly changed my reading habits. Before Monsarrat, I thought that a "well-written" and "interesting" book was an oxymoron. After Monsarrat, I realized that one could, after all, read challenging books and still be interested. And, since then, I have found hundreds more! *The Cruel Sea* is an unpretentious World War II novel full of action.

When God Disappoints Us

But we had hoped that he was the one who was going to redeem Israel. —Luke 24:21

Scripture: *Luke 24:13-35*

Two of Jesus' disappointed followers were on the road to Emmaus. These travelers had a real crisis on their hands: The one whom they loved and by whom they were loved had deeply disappointed them. Thus, they did not see Him even when He was right before their eyes. In effect, their theology has failed them. Based on their own sacred journeys, based on their experiences, they drew conclusions. They found a way, as it were, to justify a belief in a dead Savior. And incredibly they were not able to see the live one right in front of them! A crisis moment for most of us is when God disappoints us. And He will, you know. Some rain has to fall into everyone's life! But there will be some downpours, too, and you will be disappointed. Does it have to be so hard?

What do you do when God disappoints you?

Devotional Journal

Read/Vocabulary Cards

Critical Thinking: Writing

Write 75 words that analyze the way one should eat a piece of pie.

There is nothing wrong with wanting to know more—as long as we understand that knowledge is not power. Power comes from Whom we know, not what we know.

Practice Makes Perfect Scores!

Then Jesus said to them, "You are foolish and slow to realize what is true. You should believe everything the prophets said. They said that the Christ must suffer these things before he enters his glory." —Luke 24:25 (NCV)

Scripture: Luke 24:13-35

What sort of theologies do we have? Are we walking around with our own maudlin theories of God based on years and years of the unmiraculous? The theology of the Emmaus travelers was divorced from the Word because their experience contradicted the Word of God. Jesus had told them all this stuff was going to happen. But they never believed Him. Their high views of Scripture ended on Good Friday afternoon. From that point on they sort of made things up as they went along. How many of us found truth in Sunday school as a child and rejected it later? Life was so hard on us that we simply gave up believing. I met such a man at seminary. Although he was a brilliant man he had no faith. He had Bible knowledge, but he did not believe that the Bible was the Word of God. He stopped believing in God's Word when his retarded younger brother was born. As he watched his brother struggle, and finally die, this professor—in spite of his great knowledge of the Bible—had no Sacred Word. The Bible as the Word of God ceased to exist the day they put his brother in that cold grave. Likewise, these disciples' faith died when they saw Jesus die on a cross. And, in spite of Jesus' skillful explanation of Scripture, they still did not recognize Him. True, their hearts were on fire, Luke says, and they had knowledge. But enthusiasm and knowledge is not enough. You need the Spirit! No, the heart has its reasons, which reason does not know (Pascal). They did not recognize Christ until they had a meal with Him—were reacquainted with Him on a personal basis.

Renew your mind daily with the Word (Romans 12:1,2).

Devotional Journal

Read/Vocabulary Cards

Critical Thinking: Analysis

A frequent question in critical reading exercises concerns assigning cause. While assigning cause is a matter of individual opinion, it is critical that you are able to discern that opinion. There are several kinds of causes. For example, Brown vs. the Board of Education has an immediate cause of outlawing racial segregation. But it took twenty or more years for the ultimate cause of racism to be overcome (and some think it is still not overcome!). You must also be able to distinguish between the necessary and sufficient cause of an event. For instance, cancer kills people and in that sense cancer is a sufficient cause of death. But, not everyone who has cancer dies of this disease. So it is not a necessary cause. Read the selection below and answer the questions.

It is true that geometric theorems will be provided for you on the exam (except for simple information, like the area of a rectangle). However, it still would be helpful to familiarize yourself with a few theorems. Also, more important, memorize the directions for each section. You will be able to save yourself a great deal of time. And more time will give you a better score!

Lesson continues on the next page.

The sociologist Peter Berger argues that one of the features of our modern day has been the loss of mediating institutions. Therefore, we now have increasingly atomistic individuals and a powerful state, with no buffers in between. We talk about community so much because we experience it so little in our life. As culture disintegrated in Roman times, the Church became a mediating institution. Likewise, as Western culture ceases to sustain its participants, the Church needs to reclaim its central role. Christianity in the 1990s will be credible as we demonstrate community that is "countercultural."

1. What is one cause of our fascination with community?
2. What is one major cause of the Church's irrelevance to Western society? Is it a necessary or sufficient cause?
3. What is an opinion and what is a fact in this reading?
4. What will be the true test of the Church's relevancy at the end of the twentieth century?

Solve

A. $2 + 3 (2 \times 4) =$
B. $45 - 18(34 + 3) =$
C. There are seven coins that look identical. One of the seven coins weighs slightly less than the other six. Using a balance scale, how could you determine which is the light coin in just two weighings? (MindTrap®)
D. $\dfrac{-3\frac{1}{5}}{2\frac{1}{3}} =$
E. $-3\frac{1}{8} + 1\frac{3}{5} =$
F. Compare .56 and $\frac{3}{5}$
G. $(x - \frac{2}{5})^2 = 4$

> Distributive Property:
> For any real numbers a, b, c,
> $a(b+c) = ab + ac$

"You have made your way around this hill country long enough..." —Deuteronomy 2:2

Scripture: *Deuteronomy 1:5-8; 2:1-8*

The Christian thinker and theologian Walter Brueggemann points out that the sense of lostness is pervasive in contemporary culture—we have everything but possess nothing. When we have God as our Abba Father then we have everything. There is a basic need for human beings to be "named." We need to be known, to be loved, to have an identity—to lose what Brueggemann calls "lostness" and Karl Barth calls "otherness." And what Paul Simon (Simon and Garfunkel) calls "the sound of silence:" "And in the naked light I saw/Ten thousand people maybe more,/People talking without speaking,/People hearing without listening,/People writing songs that voices never shared/And no one dared disturb the sound of silence." One of the great ironies of American culture is that, though shaped by a great emphasis on our vast physical environment, we are not encouraged to put down roots into that environment. Deep in all our hearts is a sense of wandering. It is time, now, though, that we stop wandering around the mountain...and come home to the Lord.

Are you wandering around not knowing who you are or where you are going? Come home.

Devotional Journal

Read/Vocabulary Cards

Grammar

Choose the correct answer:

> Mr. Smith faithfully took the doctor's advice, (and, but) his health did not improve.

Solve

A. At the Italian Flame Restaurant, the sales tax on a $45.00 dinner is $2.70. How much would a $65.00 dinner cost?
B. At Pizza Supreme, Larry thought that he had ordered $38.00 worth of food. But his bill was $43.70! He was told that the tip was included in the bill. What percentage of the bill was the tip!
C. Meanwhile, parsimonious Larry tried to recover the tip he had already left on the table. He had left $5.70. But he was too late! What percentage, overall, did he end up leaving as a tip?

Review of Mathematical Test-Taking Strategies

1. Know what types of questions you will have. Be familiar with the probable theorems you will be given. Memorize the instructions for each type of question.
2. Do not guess. If you do not know how to solve an equation, look at the answers. What do they imply? If you want to try all the choices (that is, if you have time) start with choice C. You want to do this because the answers are usually presented in ascending order and C will be in the middle. Work backwards and forwards from there.
3. Don't worry if you leave a few blank. Better that than a wrong answer.
4. Don't use the calculator if you can do things faster without it. But, if you do, watch what you punch!
5. Be careful with drawings. If they are not drawn to scale, they may not be what you think.
6. Be sure to get the first ten correct!!!

123

Pursued by God

"Go. Stand in front of me on the mountain. I will pass by you." —1 Kings 19:11 (NCV)

Scripture: 1 Kings 19:9-18

Verses 9-18 are some of the most extraordinary verses in the Bible. True, Elijah is pursued by Jezebel—but he is pursued even more by God! Elijah discovers that God loves him more than he imagines and God has no intention of letting Jezebel or anyone else destroy him. No, God has plans for Elijah. But we have to have a purpose, a ministry (verse 9). We will find God's love everywhere; but deliverance and health come to those who are willing to obey Him no matter what the cost. In verses 11-13a, God graciously makes Himself available to this one whose life has been "wasted." God comes in a whisper. In this moment Elijah is reminded that God is after all God and there is no other. Paul captures the same thought in Romans 8: "Who can condemn us? Only Christ… and He came to die for us!" After all is said and done, all we have to fear is the one who must be obeyed: God. And He loves us so much! Finally, this encounter with God—this confrontation with one's own fears and one's relationship with God—this plumbing the depths as it were of one's willingness to obey God, no matter what the cost—moves us from our own shortcomings and failures to God's dreams for our lives and for the world. At the end, the one who was wanted by the kingdom, then wanted more urgently by God, now wants to get on with it.

Describe a time when God used circumstances or persons to pursue you when you really needed Him.

Devotional Journal

Read/Vocabulary Cards

Vocabulary

Define italicized words in context:

> There is no confusion like the confusion of a simple mind, and as we drove away Tom was feeling the hot whips of panic. His wife and his mistress, until an hour ago secure and *inviolate*, were slipping *precipitately* from his control…. (from *The Great Gatsby* by F. Scott Fitzgerald)

Critical Reading

The 18th day of May, our General [Drake] thought it needful to have a care of such ships as were absent; and therefore endeavouring to seek the fly-boat wherein Master *Doughty* was, we espied her again the next day. And whereas certain of our ships were sent to discover the coast and to search an harbour, the *Marigold* and the *canter* being employed in that business, came unto us and gave us understanding of a safe harbour that they had found. Wherewith all our ships bare, and entered it; where we watered and made new provision of victuals, as by seals, whereof we slew to the number of 200 or 300 in the space of an hour. Here our General in

The Great Gatsby by F. Scott Fitzgerald is an extraordinary novel. Fitzgerald, an able spokesperson for the twenties, was one of America's most talented writers. In the figure of Jay Gatsby we meet the American dream, the American hero. And we all weep when this naive man, with so much promise, fails. This book is full of opportunity for theological reflection. Let me also recommend, for more mature readers, *Tender is the Night* and *This Side of Paradise*. Fitzgerald's vocabulary will be challenging for SAT students and therefore very helpful.

the *Admiral . . .* took out of her all the provision of victuals and what else was in her, and hauling her to the land, set fire to her, and so burnt her to save the iron work. Which being a-doing, there came down of the country certain of the people naked, saving only about their waist the skin of some beast, with the fur or hair on, and something also wreathed on their heads. Their faces were painted with divers colors, and some of them had on their heads the similitude of horns, every man his bow, which was an ell in length, and a couple of arrows. They were very agile people and quick to deliver, and seemed not to be ignorant in the feats of wars, as by their order of ranging a few men might appear. These people would not of a long time receive anything at our hands; yet at length our General being ashore, and they dancing after their accustomed manner about him, and he once turning his back towards them, one leaped suddenly to him, and took his cap with his gold band off his head, and ran a little distance from him, and shared it with his fellow, the cap to the one, and the band to the other. Having despatched all our business in this place, we departed and set sail. And immediately upon our setting forth we lost our canter, which was absent three of four days; but when our General had her again, he took out the necessaries, and so gave her over, near to the *Cape of Good Hope*. The next day after, being the 20th of June, we harbored ourselves again in a very good harborough, called by *Magellan, Port St. Julian*, where we found a gibbet standing upon the main; which we supposed to be the place where *Magellan* did execution upon some of his disobedient and rebellious company (*Sir Francis Drake's Famous Voyage Round the World*, Francis Pretty).

Pretty is writing what would best be described as a
- A. travel journal
- B. diatribe against natives
- C. polemic against Spain
- D. teaching on the South Seas

Solve

A. The sum of x and x + 2 is greater than 10 but less than 18. If x is an integer, what is one possible value of x?

B. f(x) = 2x - 3 and g(x) = x^3, find f(g(5))
- A. 343
- B. 247
- C. 125
- D. 27
- E. 21

124

A Modern Couple

"...I am the only prophet left..." —1 Kings 19:14 (NCV)

Scripture: *1 Kings 19:1-18*

After Elijah had the prophets of Baal put to death (see chapter 18), Jezebel, wife of Israel's King Ahab, threatened him with a similar fate. Elijah understandably was afraid. He fled for his life, going to Beersheba where he left his servant. Then, to escape Jezebel's vengeance, he entered the wilderness. There in the desert Elijah sat in the shade of a broom shrub, which has a delicate white flower with a maroon center. God, as always, would not be thwarted by discouragement and He delivered Elijah. He was to return to face King Ahab. King Ahab, Elijah's adversary, was not a bad man. He was in fact a good king and decent Jew. And so was Jezebel. But the problem was that they also were followers of Baal and any other gods or goddesses who served their purposes. They had no problem with Elijah's faith—only his parochialism. They objected to Elijah's claim that there was one God and only one. Thus, Ahab and Jezebel represent the modern urge to "let anything go." Elijah, indeed, in his enthusiasm—what some called obstinacy—was a definite threat to the eclecticism that Ahab and Jezebel espoused. And, likewise, the greatest threat to American society in general, is not atheism, nor agnosticism, nor even apathy: It is polytheism. I fear that most young people—and people my age, too—fall on their knees at many and sundry altars—they worship at the altars of money, power, sex, education, and so on. So, the problems that Elijah faced are modern problems.

Who is Lord of your life?

Devotional Journal

Read/Vocabulary Cards

Have your parents or guardians review vocabulary cards with you.

Critical Thinking: Analysis

What is the meaning of the following poem? What experience does it create in you? How does it feel? Does it evoke images of growing up with your mom or dad reading nursery rhymes to you? Or do you feel sadness because you never had a mom or dad read it to you? Have you heard an apocryphal version of the poem?

> Little Jack Horner
> Sat in a corner
> Eating a Christmas pie.
> He stuck in his thumb,
> And pulled out a plum
> And said, "What a good boy am I!"—Anonymous

The meaning of a reading passage is ultimately the experience it creates in your life. You need to be able to interpret that experience. In some cases the experience will be revolting—for example, if the passage was the description of an abortion. In other cases the experience will be wonderful—for example if the passage describes a man winning the million dollar lottery. I know what I am saying is abstract, but under the pressure of a timed exam, like the SAT I, you need to be in touch with these feelings.

Critical Thinking: Writing

Write an analysis on the causes of a man's baldness.

Solve

Consider the function of $\dfrac{3}{x^2 - 4}$ Which of the following statements are true?

I.   The range is always positive.
II. The domain is all real numbers except 2 or -2.
III. The domain must always be a positive number.

    A. I only
    B. II only
    C. III only
    D. I and II
    E. I and III

125

Called to Such a Time As This

But Esther had kept secret her family background and nationality. —Esther 2:20

Scripture: *Esther Chapters 1-4*

Notwithstanding that Esther is revered throughout the Jewish/Christian world as a godly, heroic woman, she in fact was very human, and, I suppose, a lot like many of us. In fact, Esther was a beautiful girl and clever, but self-seeking, and with little thought of God. It was a strange series of events that finally revealed the "heroine" in her soul. Ahasuerus (Xerxes), king of Persia, which held most of the Eastern world in its grasp, had staged a beauty contest. According to the published rules, every girl who was accepted as a participant would be received into the king's harem. The winner would become his queen. One of the girls who entered this contest (with her uncle's consent) was Esther. She knew that she would be dropped if it were known that she was Jewish, so she kept her identity a carefully guarded secret. For one whole year she remained at the royal court, undergoing the elaborate regimen recommended by the beauty experts. During this time, no one suspected her Jewish identity. Under somewhat similar circumstances, Daniel purposed that he would not defile himself (Daniel 1:18). But not Esther. She was unwilling to let her religion interfere with her worldly hopes.

Do you remain conveniently anonymous when you face obstacles and challenges? Do you let people know that you are a Christian?

Devotional Journal

Read/Vocabulary Cards

Solve

A. Two numbers form a "couple" if the sum of their reciprocals equals 2. For example, 9 and $\frac{9}{17}$ form a couple because $\frac{1}{9} + \frac{17}{9} = 2$. If a and b form a couple and $a = \frac{5}{2}$, what is the value of b?

B. $0.ABC + 0.BAC = 0.AAC$. In this correctly worked addition problem, A, B, and C are digits. $B = C$. What must the digit B be?

C. $4(x -12)= 2(-x)- 90$

Critical Thinking: Writing

Be as specific and concrete as you can and construct an imaginary dream, such as might come to the following:

1. A soldier about to die on the battlefield.
2. A camper sleeping next to a waterfall.
3. A baby sleeping next to a motorcar raceway.

PAY ATTENTION TO DETAILS!

Under stress from too little time, or too little sleep the night before, you will be tempted to ignore details. Especially after the 10:30 break. Spend a few minutes in prayer, eat a peanut butter sandwich (no candy please!), and then meditate on your target Scripture. When critical reading questions that occur late in the morning—PAY ATTENTION TO DETAILS!

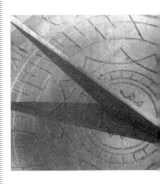

"And who knows but that you have come to royal position for such a time as this?"
—Esther 4:14

Scripture: *Esther 3 and 4*

In the end, Esther realized her ambition, won the beauty contest, and became the king's queen. Evidently she observed none of the peculiar rites of Judaism and if she prayed to God, no one was aware of it (cf. Daniel 6:10). She remained anonymous. One of the high officials of the court, Haman, who insisted that everyone pay him the proper respect, became enraged at Mordecai, Esther's uncle, because he refused to make the required obeisance. He transferred his dislike of an individual to the group that he represented. Haman arranged for a pogrom (stressing its economic advantage) devised to exterminate every Jew in the land (just as Adolf Hitler did at another time in history). When news of this came to Mordecai, he informed Esther that she must now reveal her faith and thus save her people. Esther, though, was thinking only of herself. She reminded her uncle that to approach the king without invitation would endanger her life. Mordecai warned her, "Think not that in the king's palace you will escape any more than all the other Jews. For if you keep silence at such a time as this, relief and deliverance will rise for the Jews from another quarter, but you and your father's house will perish." (Perhaps this was a threat that under such circumstances he would betray her identity.) Then, perhaps as an after-thought, Mordecai added, "And who knows but that you have come to the royal position for such a time as this?" (4:14)

In Greek there are two words for time: chronos or ordinary time and kairos or special time. Everyday, run-of-the-mill, ho-hum time is chronos time. Kairos time, on the other hand, is special time when things are happening. When the spirit is moving. Kairos is like a door opening that will soon be closed again. In a way this SAT preparation time is a kairos moment in your life. Will you walk through this door and make the most of what God is doing in your life?

Devotional Journal

Read/Vocabulary Cards

Remember! This evening have your parents or guardians review your 3 by 5-inch cards with you.

Vocabulary

Define the italic words in the above passage.

So we fix our eyes not on what is seen, but on what is unseen. For what is seen is temporary, but what is unseen is eternal. (2 Corinthians 4:18)

Lesson continues on the next page.

Grammar

Locate the problem in this sentence.

While attending college in Maui, Hawaii, his family suffered
          (A)   (B)

during the winter months in the Pennsylvania cold. [No error.]
     (C)   (D)   (E)

Solve

Fraction	Decimal	Percent
$^{13}/_{20}$		
	.7	
		125%

Critical Thinking: Paraphrase

Paraphrase the following passage.

> George Gaylord Simpson, in his book *The Meaning of Evolution*, argues: Charles Darwin believed that man is the result of a purposeless and materialistic act…. He was not planned…. Creation lacked any purpose or plan. This has the inevitable corollary that the workings of the universe cannot provide any automatic, universal, eternal, or absolute criteria of right and wrong.

"Who of you is left who saw this house in its former glory? How does it look to you now? Does it not seem like nothing?" —Haggai 2:3

Scripture: *Haggai 2:1-10*

Early in 1932, my grandmother, Helen Stobaugh, applied for a home mortgage. Although her financial resources were adequate, the location of her potential house was not. It was to be built on the "other side of the tracks" so to speak—in the "bad" part of town (which in 1930 Arkansas was where African-Americans lived). Her request was denied. But she was a woman with vision. When her energies flagged, when obstacles appeared, her untiring vision kept her moving. She was able to get a personal loan from a wealthy farmer. But once she had the money, she then needed to build her magnificent house. She had to bring her dream into reality. The bricks for the fireplace were from the streets of New Orleans; the house itself had only the finest building material. And gracing almost every room with priceless antiques, she lovingly, persistently brought her dream into reality. Nothing could stop her!

Haggai was a man of vision. His small book urges the people to rebuild the temple. It would be hard work—probably take longer than some of Haggai's contemporaries would live. But it was worth it.

Name a project or task that you are undertaking that might take the rest of your life to complete.

Devotional Journal

Read/Vocabulary Cards

Critical Reading

Norris Magnuson in his book *Salvation in the Slums: Evangelical Social Work 1865-1920* advances an ambitious thesis: The *pietistic*, *revivalistic*, and *holiness* (as contrasted with later evangelical and Fundamentalist movements) Christian movements of the latter part of the 19th century were actively involving themselves in evangelical social work that was critical to the lives of thousands of average urban Americans. Christian urban missionaries/pioneers involved themselves in a wide range of social concerns (food, shelter, recreation, health, unemployment, and so forth). And this was before there was a positive liberal state (that is where the government is funding most social welfare interventions). Magnuson points out that revivalist movements like the Salvation Army, the Volunteers of America, the Christian and Missionary Alliance, and the "Rescue Movement" attempted some of the most ambitious and *innovative* urban *redevelopment* projects that America knew in the Gilded Age. Revivalistic social reformers were able to reinforce the already natural link between revivalism and social reform. The revivalists saw soul-salvation as the only hope for society, to be sure. But obedience to biblical injunctions to preach the Gospel to all people, in

Lesson continues on the next page.

the evangelical revivalist mind, also required a *profound empathic* identity with the poor. This movement was, and Magnuson does not point this out, an aberration in the American religious scene. Remember that the famous Philadelphia Baptist preacher Russell Conwell was preaching his famous sermon "Acres of Diamonds" to millions of people. Religious giants like Andrew Carnegie expressed the ethic most clearly in an article entitled, "The Gospel of Wealth" (1889). In general, mainline Christianity praised wealth and *unabashedly* used it as a yardstick for spirituality. Riches were a sure sign of godliness and they stressed the power of money to do good. This attitude is in direct contrast to men like D. L. Moody who never made a general appeal for money. And, although the revivalists did not extol poverty, they saw the poor as victims of *systemic evil* more than *congenitally*, lazy people.

A. What is the main argument of this passage?
B. What evidence does the author use to support his argument?
C. From context, define the term revivalism.
D. In what ways were the revivalists different from the mainline church leaders?
E. Does the author really believe that Andrew Carnegie was a spiritual giant?
F. Explain what this quote means, "Revivalistic social reformers were able to reinforce the already natural link between revivalism and social reform."
G. Define "evangelical revivalist mind."

Vocabulary

Define the italicized words above.

Solve

The graph of two linear functions shows two lines which meet at 90° angles. One of the lines is formed by the equation $y = -\frac{1}{2}x + 3\frac{1}{2}$. Which of the following statements is false?

A. The other line has a y-intercept.
B. The other line has a positive slope.
C. Because they intersect they must have a common y-intercept.
D. The lines have slopes which are negative reciprocals.
E. The line with equation $y = -\frac{1}{2}x + 3\frac{1}{2}$ lies entirely above the origin.

No Guts, No Gain

Think about this from now on! Think about how it was before you started piling stones on top of stones. Think about how it was before you started building the Temple of the Lord. A person used to come to a pile of grain expecting to find 20 basketfuls. But there were only 10….from now on I will bless you! —Haggai 2:15–19 (NCV)

Scripture: *Haggai 2:15-19*

Most worthwhile projects begin with vision and then require hard work and fortitude. Like most great men, Haggai was at once a man of vision and a man with a sensible bent. His vision was rooted in his faith. He desired to see Jerusalem's temple restored to something of its former glory, so that God's presence among his people could be clearly proclaimed. But his vision was welded to practical realities. Unless he could persuade the people as a whole, and their rulers in particular, to set about the hard work of restoration, his vision would remain the stuff of dreams. He was a visionary, as it were, who was trying to persuade his community to catch the vision. Haggai's book provides a glimpse into some of the turning points from apathy to action. The Bible does not, in itself, tell the complete story of the temple's restoration, but it gives an extraordinary insight into the will and vision of one man who contributed to the realization of his own vision.

When it is all said and done, it comes right down to whether or not you have the fortitude, the guts, the courage to be all that God wants you to be. That may or may not mean that you get a great SAT score. How much are you ready to risk? More than help you attain a high SAT score, I pray that God will use this material to challenge you, to convict you, to urge you to be even more committed to Him.

Devotional Journal

Read/Vocabulary Cards

Critical Thinking: Argument

Many scholars mark the beginning of the modern world as May 29, 1919. This is the day when photographs of a solar eclipse proved Einstein's theory of relativity. Einstein argued, and then proved, that space and time are relative. To Einstein's horror, however, in the 1920s, the theory of relativity became the basis of a theory in the social sciences called relativism. In the theory of relativism, still popular today, there are no absolutes of time and space, of good and evil, of knowledge, and above all, of value. Murder, adultery, and stealing are at times permissible under certain circumstances. Relativism has become even more dangerous when it has been coupled with Freudianism, which is the single most influential psychological movement of the twentieth century. Suddenly, in the 1920s, the Judeo-Christian conscience was replaced by the ego, the id, and the alter-ego. Feelings of guilt were thus a sign not of vice, but of virtue. Repentance was no longer in vogue. Personal responsibility for sin was lost, too, though most scholars

On the SAT you will be asked to evaluate the validity of a particular passage that advances an argument.

1. Clearly state the argument,
2. Identify an alternate position,
3. Identify fallacious arguments; for example, advancing false analogy, false statistics, wrong causation connections.

Lesson continues on the next page.

blame Immanuel Kant for most of the confusion today. Kant set the tone for modern culture with his famous phrase "dare to know"—as if knowledge is some sort of salvation reality. He suggested that if there was a God—and that is doubtful—He is unknowable and perhaps is pernicious. Why would one want to listen to, much less obey, such a God? But what Joseph understood is that the Gospel is public truth, not simply one private truth among others. It is *the* truth and must overshadow all other facts.

1. What is the central argument?
2. Does the author employ any fallacious arguing techniques?
3. What is the alternative position?
4. Do you agree with the author? Why? Why not?

Critical Thinking: Essay

Write an essay that analyzes one of your pastor's sermons.

I scattered them like a hurricane to other countries. These were countries they did not know. This good land was left so ruined… —Zechariah 7:14 (NCV)

Scripture: Zechariah 7:1-14

Have you ever failed? I mean really failed—failed in ways you would probably never tell anyone; failures that are so painful that you hate to think of them? Although most of us are committed to denying this fact, I believe that we all have known failure at one time or another. In fact, failure may be the one common thread all humankind shares. Big failures. Small failures. They are a given of the human condition. Zechariah knew and understood failure well. A contemporary of Haggai, Zechariah was trying to encourage a community that had failed miserably. Miserably! The nation of Judah had foolishly, ungratefully disobeyed God and He sent them into exile. But Babylon was conquered by Persia, and King Darius had decided to allow the people of God to return to Jerusalem.

And they were returning home, but the question before Zechariah, and the question before us today, is "How do we return from failure?"

Devotional Journal

Read/Vocabulary Cards

Solve

A. A car traveling at an average rate of 60 kilometers per hour made a trip in 6 hours. How far did the car travel?

B. On the next leg of the trip, the car had a flat tire and it was able to travel only 300 kilometers in 6 hours. What was the car's average speed?

C. On the last leg of the trip the car traveled 450 kilometers at 50 kilometers per hour. How long did it travel? How many minutes more did this part of the trip take than the first part?

D. $(-\frac{1}{2})^2$

Word Problems Tips

1. Read the word problem carefully.
2. What do you know? What do you need to know?
3. What is the best mathematical path to follow?
4. Convert the word problem into a math equation.
5. Answer the question and double check your results.

130

How Do We Return from Failure?

Old men and old women will again sit along Jerusalem's streets.…And the streets will be filled with boys and girls playing. —Zechariah 8:4,5 (NCV)

Scripture: Zechariah 8

To admit failure is one of the greatest threats we will ever face. To admit one has failed is to admit one is fallible, that one is vulnerable. We find the risk excruciatingly painful…and with some justification. How many of us have risked vulnerability only to be rejected by those whom we love? But it is the first step we must face if we hope to experience healing. Upon entering a relationship, from the moment we begin to trust another human being with our lives, our greatest fear is always that the one who loves us will forsake and forget us. We are afraid that the one who loves us, if he or she truly discovers how bad, frail, and imperfect we really are, will reject us. To be rejected by one who loves us is to be lost, to be abandoned. It really is not true that it is "better to have loved and lost, than not to have loved at all." There is simply nothing more painful than to lose love, to lose a meaningful relationship. Inevitably, we secretly fear, our failures will surely terminate these meaningful relationships. Like Adam and Eve in the Garden, when we make bad choices, we always hide from those we love.

Other than God, is there anyone else in your life who will love you no matter what? If so, thank God for that person. What an irreplaceable gift!

Devotional Journal

Read/Vocabulary cards

Vocabulary

Define italicized words from context:

> She was absent such a while that Joseph proposed we should wait no longer. He *cunningly conjectured* they were staying away in order to avoid hearing his *protracted* blessing…. (from *Wuthering Heights* by Emily Brontë)

Grammar

Choose the phrase that best completes the sentence. Choice A repeats the original; the other four are different.

> Lewis and Clark made the dangerous journey during winter, <u>but no Native Americans were encountered</u>.

A. but no Native Americans were encountered.
B. but no Native Americans were overtaken.
C. but Native Americans had not been seen.
D. but encountered no Native Americans.
E. but no Native Americans had been seen.

Wuthering Heights by Emily Brontë is the literary opposite of *The Cruel Sea*. Romance, intrigue, revenge, mystery—it is all there. It's a haunting vision of life. Reading such classics instead of modern-day romances will help you on your SAT and interest you, too!

In Somerset Maugham's *Of Human Bondage* we meet a young man overcome with shame because he feels like such a failure! Read this great book and find out why!

Solve

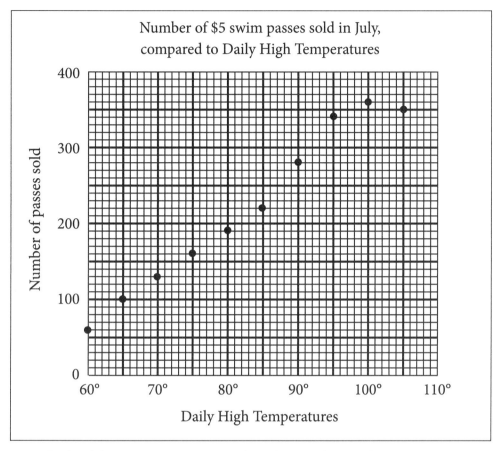

Number of $5 swim passes sold in July, compared to Daily High Temperatures

Which of these statements is true based upon the graph:

I. The most passes are sold when the high temperature is 100°.
II. Higher temperatures always produced greater sales.
III. The high temperature will probably need to be 80° to sell over $1000 worth of passes.
IV. The highest summer temperature never exceeds 110°.

    A. I and III
    B. IV only
    C. II and III
    D. III and IV
    E. II only

131

The Pain of Living

"What do you want with us, Jesus of Nazareth?" —Mark 1:24

Scripture: Mark 1:21-28

Many Saturday afternoons while I was growing up, Dad, my two brothers, and I would drive a few miles to the nearest rabbit Shangri-la and spend the rest of the afternoon pursuing wiry hares. I particularly remember those chilly, foreboding February afternoons when it was almost 32 degrees (a veritable cold wave for southern Arkansas!). All through the interminably long afternoon, we followed the descending sun from brush pile to brush pile. As we listened to the beagles chase the rabbits, we alternately rubbed our hands and stomped our feet, like ballet dancers warming up for a performance, to keep our extremities from freezing. Finally, we returned home to the inevitable hot beef stew steaming in our unpretentious kitchen. However, before my mother allowed us to enjoy the rewards of our labors—hot corn bread, homemade garlic pickles, and rat-trap cheese—she always insisted upon one very painful, preliminary ritual, a rite of passage, so to speak, before we committed gluttony: We had to wash our hands. Until this day, I still remember the excruciating pain of placing my cold, aching hands underneath tepid water that felt like steam. My hands turned purple, then red, and then white—as if to voice a protest of their own. Pins and needles—you know the feeling! I would have much preferred to face diphtheria, dysentery, or a whole host of other dirty hand diseases rather than face that warm water! The prophet brings fire to our cold spiritual lives! There comes a stage in the freezing process when it would be more comfortable to sink further into fatal numbness, where death seems to represent peace. But pain is the sign of returning life. At the approach of Jesus, a man with an unclean spirit cried, "Let us alone; what have we to do with you, Jesus of Nazareth?" Deliverance was an unwelcome possibility, because the prophetic voice of Jesus demanded a response—oftentimes an uncomfortable response!

In what ways does the Christian life make you uncomfortable?

Devotional Journal

Read/Vocabulary Cards

Review cards with parents or guardians.

Critical Reading

A.

"Thirty-nine and she is more beautiful than ever," I thought.

Karen, my wife for almost fifteen years, was carefully unpacking her 1960 Barbie dolls. While taking a break from my nervous Saturday night sermon review, I discovered my wife holding an archaic, but still beautiful, silver Barbie doll dress up to our dull attic light.

"Lord," she hopefully sighed, "please don't let Jessica think these clothes are corny."

Some of these 1950ish out-of-style clothes would be part of one of my daughter's Christmases. With four children to buy for, Karen, and I find

Harvard Divinity School professor Dr. Harvey Cox: "We once had dreams and no technology to bring them to pass. Now we have technology but no dreams!"

Christmas shopping to be a painful experience. My Scottish wife never hesitated to explore creative alternatives to huge post-Christmas Visa bills.

Karen is the sort of woman who looks better at thirty-nine than she did at twenty-four. Oh she was beautiful—but her cherubic face, looking somewhat juvenile at 24, was suddenly strikingly attractive at 39. I remember well the smile of my bride as she walked down the aisle—her generous smile dominating her face. But, although most of us find that the vicissitudes of life assault our outward vitality, Karen seemed to have grown stronger and more attractive in the fight. As Karen's grandmother from Glasgow, Scotland, would say: "Thirty-nine suited her."

SAT reading passages demand thoughtful reading of all material. You must be able to discern nuances and to pick out details.
1. What is the author's occupation?
2. Who is Karen?
3. What is the event being described?
4. Does this reading seem sentimental?
5. Give a title for the story.
6. What is the setting?
7. Is there any conflict?
8. Define "vicissitudes of life."

B.

That mixture in the English Government, that harmony between King, Lords, and Commons, did not always subsist. England was enslaved for a long series of years by the Romans, the Saxons, the Danes, and the French successively. William the Conqueror particularly, ruled them with a rod of iron. He disposed as absolutely of the lives and fortunes of his conquered subjects as an eastern monarch; and forbade, upon pain of death, the English either fire or candle in their houses after eight o'clock; whether he did this to prevent their nocturnal meetings, or only to try, by this odd and whimsical prohibition, how far it was possible for one man to extend his power over his fellow-creatures. It is true, indeed, that the English had Parliaments before and after William the Conqueror, and they boast of them, as though these assemblies then called Parliaments, composed of ecclesiastical tyrants and of plunderers entitled barons, had been the guardians of the public liberty and happiness (*Letters on the English*, Voltaire).

British constitutional democracy is not all that it appears to be. Why?
A. Historically it is a new phenomenon and, besides, excesses still exist (e.g., ecclesiastical tyrants).
B. It never really existed.
C. William the Conqueror destroyed it.
D. It may be somewhat ameliorating, but it does not hold a candle to the French Republic.

Saturday Night

I am the Lord. I do not change.... —Malachi 3:6 (NCV)

Scripture: *Malachi 3:1-12*

Usually time moves so slowly that we hardly notice its soft hand on our shoulders. A few isolated gray hairs, sags where there used to be muscles—time never stops moving. At times, though, it not only seems to move with us, it seems to pass us by! Subtle reminders are replaced by painful intrusions of a world that is much different from our world. For instance, a few weeks ago pre-Sunday excitement had evaporated any hopes that I could fall asleep before midnight. So, in desperation, I turned on a late night comedy. Across my screen wiggled bizarre Star Wars creatures with orange mohawks, dangling earrings, tattered clothing, and agonizingly loud songs, vulgar language, and a script that could have been written by my ten-year-old. Oh Beatles, Jefferson Airplane, the Monkees—where are you? Anyway, after that depressing violation of my post-midnight senses—which at best are dull, but were now stimulated beyond safe nocturnal limits—I gave up all hope of sleeping before 3:00 a.m., turned off the TV, and mused the next few hours about Malachi, of all people, and about some of the folks in the Bible and how they must have felt when they saw their world crumble. The world I once knew is gone and it has been replaced by something that is strangely alien. The fact is, somewhere in the last ten years or so, time passed me by. While the rest of the world watches CD-ROMs and drinks Diet Pepsi, I prefer a bottle of RC and a Moon Pie. While the rest of the world is talking about megabytes, I just recently learned how to format a disk. I was—am—experiencing cognitive dissonance, or culture confusion. At times, I cannot understand a world that is changing faster than I can keep up. Malachi felt the same way.

Only God (and perhaps your grandmother!) never changes, but the rest of us are forced to change. In what ways have you changed since you gave the Lord your life?

Devotional Journal

Read/Vocabulary Cards

Solve

A. $\frac{4}{3} \times \frac{7}{2} \times \frac{9}{5}$

B. $45 \times .00031$

C. Find w

$w - \frac{2}{3} = 3\frac{1}{3}$

D. Find a

$3\frac{1}{2}a + 2 = 9$

Critical Thinking: Essay

Analysis: Analyze the way your mother handles stress.

More on Problem Solving

1. Stop the action, focus, pray.
2. What is the question asked? What is the problem?
3. Restate the problem.
4. What do I know? What do I need to know?
5. Eliminate wrong answers. Choose an answer.
6. Do not guess unless you are choosing one of two answers.

Elijah will help fathers love their children. And he will help children love their fathers.... — Malachi 4:6 (NCV)

Scripture: *Malachi 4:1-5*

This is the final word Malachi gives us. In the end, it really does not matter why we sinned, why we missed His perfect will for our lives; why disaster struck us—whether we had anything to do with it or not. In the end, all that remains is a compassionate God, a God ever ready to forgive and to love. God will forgive "the remnant of His inheritance," and every man shall sit "under his own vine and under his own fig tree, and no one will make them afraid." How do we answer this God whom we shall at some time or another fail? How do we answer this God who demands so much from us? How do we accept and bear the anger of God? Life is larger than my shadow, and my world will change faster than I can follow. We will sin, in spite of our best efforts, and we must face the consequences of our actions. "Answer me!" God calls time and time again, and we must shake in despair... or repent and hold tightly to His Son. For, you see, He loved us so much that He sent His only begotten son. Through His Son's death on the cross God answers His own questions. "Answer me!" our Righteous Father asks. "Why should I forgive your iniquities?" The answer for two thousand years has been and remains, "No reason—I certainly do not deserve your compassion—except you loved me enough to die for me." Thank You, Father.

Stand firm in the next few years in the shadow of the Almighty.

Devotional Journal

Read/Vocabulary Cards

Critical Thinking: Comparison

One of the new parts of the SAT I is a comparison between passages—not only comparisons between internal parts of the reading passages, but actual comparisons between the passages.

Compare these two visions of God:

Praise be to the name of God forever and ever, wisdom and might are his. He changes times and seasons; He sets up kings and desposes them. <div align="right">(Daniel 2:20)</div>	O Lord, you deceived me, and I was deceived; you overpowered me and prevailed. <div align="right">(Jeremiah 20:7)</div>

1. Identify categories of comparison: power, judgment, altruism, and purpose, are only a few suggestions. Given these categories, how do the visions of Jeremiah and Daniel contrast? Intersect? Analyze their views.
2. Based on these two views of God, create a theology.
3. What tone or style does Jeremiah employ? Daniel? What is the purpose of their vision? Who are the speakers? What do their passages tell us about them?

Solve

Use your calculator.

$$\frac{5 \times 10^4}{88.514 \times 10^{-3}}$$

More on Comparison

1. Read the passages carefully—there is no way you can skip this step. Read the passage! Don't just skim it.
2. Next, reread the first and last sentences of each paragraph. That is where most of the questions come from.
3. Now, and only now, look at the questions quickly.
4. Now you are ready to read the passage with an eye to answering the questions.
5. Answer the questions. Do not contrive similarities between passages or ignore similarities. Ditto for contrasts.
6. Be careful. Style and tone will no doubt differ with each writer. Often a different view is offered on the same topic. Be sure to discern this view and mark it well.
7. Finally, remember this: Critical reading questions are the only questions whose answers are right in front of you. You could, if you had enough time, presumably, obtain a perfect score. Since critical reading is so critical to the entire SAT I exam, good reading habits will have an obviously laudatory effect. Let a top critical reading score carry you to the goal you have set before yourself! I have never seen a high SAT score with a low critical reading score.

Standing on Mt. Carmel

Elijah went before the people and said, "How long will you waver between two opinions? If the Lord is God, follow him; but if Baal is God, follow him." —1 Kings 18:21

Scripture: 1 Kings 18:17-40

And, so, in a sense we stand upon Mt. Carmel at the beginning of the twenty-first century, new Elijahs, challenging the Baals of this world. As unfriendly winds whirl around us, we boldly, prophetically proclaim: "No! Our Lord is the only God!" In Elijah's time, the Baals were the local fertility gods, worshiped at every village shrine. Canaanite in origin, the Baals had infiltrated into all parts of Hebrew life. The Baals controlled the weather; they gave or withheld fertility. King Ahab, and his despicable wife, Jezebel, as well as most Israelites, chose to serve the Baals, and, when convenient, the Lord God. They were afraid to forget God altogether, but they also saw advantages in serving Baal. They wanted to be covered no matter what! Syncretism is deadly because God and the Baals are not guests to be entertained. They are masters to be obeyed. "No servant can serve two masters" (Luke 16:13). The throne in the human heart is only big enough for one. We share that message without any equivocation, without any ambivalence. We speak this message with boldness tempered with compassion. We have earned the right to be prophetic, so let's prophesy! Let us ask our world, let us query our world. "How long will you halt between two opinions? If the Lord be God, follow him. But if Baal, then follow him."

How sold out are you to our Lord? Are you limping between two opinions?

Devotional Journal

Read/Vocabulary Cards

Grammar

Rewrite this passage using better grammar where appropriate.

John Knowles, who loved to write in big, fancy words, was a master at creating internal struggles with his characters. Knowles, like Gene, was never able to fight in World War II. In *A Separate Peace Gene*, the protagonist and perfect student, struggles with his feelings about his best friend Finny and Gene's alter-ego/ antagonist. Who knows, maybe Knowles had a friend like Finny. Knowles skillfully shows how Gene feels both love and hatred toward Finny.

Critical Thinking: Comparison

Synthesis is a high-level, critical-thinking process. It is the putting together of parts to form a whole. Using the following passages concerning the Holy Spirit, create a synthesis. In other words, from the passages, give characteristics of the Holy Spirit: who He is, how He works, and so on.

A. Where can I go from your Spirit? Where can I flee from your presence? (Psalm 139:7)

B. Flesh gives birth to flesh, but the Spirit gives birth to spirit. (John 3:6)

C. For we were all baptized by one Spirit into one body. (1 Corinthians 12:13)

D. Do not get drunk on wine, which leads to debauchery. Instead, be filled with the Spirit. (Ephesians 5:18)

E. There are different kinds of gifts, but the same Spirit. All these are the work of one and the same Spirit, and he gives them to each man, just as he determines. (1 Corinthians 12:4,11)

F. Having believed, you were marked in him with a seal, the promised Holy Spirit, who is a deposit guaranteeing our inheritance until the redemption of those who are God's possession. (Ephesians 1:13,14)

135

Frogs in Warm Water

Elijah started making fun of them. "Perhaps they are asleep! Or perhaps they've gone on a trip! Wake them up!" —1 Kings 18:27 (adapted from NCV)

Scripture: 1 Kings 18

Many of you are familiar with the story of a frog who mistakenly jumped into a pot of warm water. Even though the frog could have jumped out at any moment, he finally burned up because he loved the warmth more than safety. We may be captured in sinful life patterns, but it is a comfortable existence, even if it does bring inevitable destruction. Elijah tries to get the frogs out of the warm water. He challenges the prophets of Baal to a duel. The rules are simple: They were to build an altar and call down the fire of their gods. Elijah would do the same. The Baal prophets cried out to their gods but there was no response. Next, they mutilated themselves. The Baal worshipers were genuinely surprised. And so we also are sincerely surprised when our gods do not deliver: the instant happiness that expensive brand-name shoes seem to have brought others but did nothing for us or the pre-marital sex that was so glamorous on TV but brought only heartache to us.… Elijah mocked the priests. "Where is your god? Asleep? On a trip?" The silence must have been unnerving. Elijah, always with a flair for the dramatic, slowly, methodically built an altar. And with one last flourish soaked the whole altar with water. "This thing will never light," the people thought. But, Elijah prayed a very undramatic, simple prayer…and the fire came down!

Identify five gods of this age. Are they your gods?

Devotional Journal

Read/Vocabulary Cards

Critical Reading

A.   Read the first section as quickly as possible and answer the questions.

Nothing bothers Americans more than race mixing. Most Americans do not want to live next to, have their children go to school with, or attend church with people of another race. Fear and anger, in America at least, are particularly pronounced between whites and African-Americans. Fears of race mixing—held by both races—have clearly exacerbated an already difficult situation and have added fuel to black anger. African-American anger is essentially an American—not African—phenomenon. Black anger is caused most directly by racism (whose most obvious manifestation is opposition to race mixing). Chattel slavery has ended but its residual effect still angers contemporary black Americans. Again, the net result is that there is much unforgiveness in the black community. More than slavery, the Great Migration was an even greater disappointment to black Americans and has had a profound impact on race relations today. Most black Americans live in the city.

True or False:
1. The purpose of this passage is to explore white reactions to black civil rights movements.
2. Blacks are not naturally angry people.
3. The Great Migration brought laudatory results to the Black community.
4. At the root of black/white problems in the U.S. is a fear of race mixing.
5. To state that most blacks live in cities is a statement of fact and to state that the city was not good to African-Americans is opinion.

B.

An Englishman endeavoring sometime to write of our attire, made sundry platforms for his purpose, supposing by some of them to find out one steadfast ground whereon to build the sum of his discourse. But in the end (like an orator long without exercise), when he saw what a difficult piece of work he had taken in hand, he gave over his travel, and only drew the picture of a naked man, unto whom he gave a pair of shears in the one hand and a piece of cloth in the other, to the end he should shape his apparel after such fashion as himself liked, sith he could find no kind of garment that could please him any while together; and this he called an Englishman. Certes this writer (otherwise being a lewd popish hypocrite and ungracious priest) shewed himself herein not to be altogether void of judgment, sith the phantastical folly of our nation (even from the courtier to the carter) is such that no form of apparel liketh us longer than the first garment is in the wearing, if it continue so long, and be not laid aside to receive some other trinket newly devised by the fickle-headed tailors, who covet to have several tricks in cutting, thereby to draw fond customers to more expense of money. For my part, I can tell better how to inveigh against this enormity than describe any certainty of our attire; sithence such is our mutability that to-day there is none to the Spanish guise, to-morrow the French toys are most fine and delectable, ere long no such apparel as that which is after the high Almaine fashion, by-and-by the Turkish manner is generally best liked of, otherwise the Morisco gowns, the Barbarian fleeces, the mandilion worn to Colley-Weston ward, and the short French breeches make such a comely vesture that, except it were a dog in a doublet, you shall not see any so disguised as are my countrymen of England. And as these fashions are diverse, so likewise it is a world to see the costliness and the curiosity, the excess and the vanity, the pomp and the bravery, the change and the variety, and finally the fickleness and the folly, that is in all degrees, insomuch that nothing is more constant in England than inconstancy of attire. Oh, how much cost is bestowed nowadays upon our bodies, and how little upon our souls! How many suits of apparel hath the one, and how little furniture hath the other! How long time is asked in decking up of the first, and how little space left wherein to feed the latter! How curious, how nice also, are a number of men and women, and how hardly can the tailor please them in making it fit for their bodies! How many times must it be sent back again to

Lesson continues on the next page.

him that made it! What chafing, what fretting, what reproachful language, doth the poor workman bear away! And many times when he doth nothing to it at all, yet when it is brought home again it is very fit and handsome; then must we put it on, then must the long seams of our hose be set by a plumb-line, then we puff, then we blow, and finally sweat till we drop, that our clothes may stand well upon us. I will say nothing of our heads, which sometimes are polled, sometimes curled, or suffered to grow at length like woman's locks, many times cut off, above or under the ears, round as by a wooden dish. Neither will I meddle with our variety of beards, of which some are shaven from the chin like those of Turks, not a few cut short like to the beard of Marquess Otto, some made round like a rubbing brush, others with a pique de vant (O! fine fashion!), or now and then suffered to grow long, the barbers being grown to be so cunning in this behalf as the tailors. And therefore if a man have a lean and straight face, a Marquess Otton's cut will make it broad and large; if it be platter-like, a long, slender beard will make it seem the narrower; if he be weasel-becked, then much hair left on the cheeks will make the owner look big like a bowdled hen, and as grim as a goose, if Cornelis of Chelmersford say true. Many old men do wear no beards at all. Some lusty courtiers also and gentlemen of courage do wear either rings of gold, stones, or pearl, in their ears, whereby they imagine the workmanship of God not to be a little amended. But herein they rather disgrace than adorn their persons, as by their niceness in apparel, for which I say most nations do not unjustly deride us, as also for that we do seem to imitate all nations round about us, wherein we be like to the polypus or chameleon; and thereunto bestow most cost upon our —, and much more than upon all the rest of our bodies, as women do likewise upon their heads and shoulders, In women also, it is most to be lamented, that they do now far exceed the lightness of our men (who nevertheless are transformed from the cap even to the very shoe), and such staring attire as in time past was supposed meet for none but light housewives only is now become a habit for chaste and sober matrons. What should I say of their doublets with pendant codpieces on the breast full of jags and cuts, and sleeves of sundry colors? Their galligascons to bear out their bums and make their attire to fit plum round (as they term it) about them. Their fardingals, and diversely colored nether stocks of silk, jersey, and such like, whereby their bodies are rather deformed than commended? I have met with some of these trulls in London so disguised that it hath passed my skill to discern whether they were men or women (*A Description of Elizabethan England*, William Harrison).

How would the reader summarize Harrison's opinion of Elizabethan attire?
  A. It is attractive and appropriate.
  B. It is a offensive to one's morality.
  C. It is ostentatious and impracticable.
  D. None of the above.

Then fire from the Lord came down. It burned the sacrifice, the wood, the stones, and the ground around the altar.... When all the people saw this,...they cried, "The Lord is God! The Lord is God!" —1 Kings 18:38,39 (NCV)

Scripture: 1 Kings 18

I saw the glory of the Lord several weeks ago. As I waited for my children to finish their Friday afternoon swim at the YMCA, I noticed that several physically and emotionally challenged youngsters were entering the lobby of the Y. What extraordinary children they were! Many were without limbs and one was an autistic child. "Welcome, Joey!" one screamed with unabashed joy. "I missed you so much!" I was experiencing—in their unrehearsed joy—the glory of the Lord. To cement our connection and to make the afternoon even more special, one child gave me a peppermint candy—he could have given me a million dollars and it would have meant less....And then, whoosh! Fire descended from heaven and literally consumed the altar. We serve the same God, and we are called to be prophets, to be Elijahs. We may be called to sound silly, to do the unthinkable, to prophesy. We are called to stand on Mt. Carmel, in colleges and universities across America, and proclaim without any ambivalence that Christ is the answer to the ills of the world. Period. Where are all the Elijahs? We are right here, brothers and sisters, we are again calling down the fire of God on the idols of this world!

You should already be praying for the college where God will send you. Be a prophet there and everywhere you go for the rest of your life!

Devotional Journal

Read/Vocabulary Cards

Have your parents or guardians review your vocabulary words with you. Pray together too!

Vocabulary

Define italicized words from context:

> We could not *resolve* to leave the place. Our eyes still sought to pierce the night. Sometimes a glimmer...trembled on the surface of the lake. Then it vanished, and with it the foolish hope that it had *roused*. We thought we saw a shadow outlined against the dark, the *silhouette* of an approaching boat. Yet again, some *eddies* would swirl up at our feet, as if the Creek had been stirred within its depths. These *vain* imaginings were *dissipated* one after the other. They were but the illusions raised by our *strained fancies*. (from *Master of the World* by Jules Verne)

Kurt Vonnegut, Jr., once commented that he did not write science fiction: He wrote non-fiction, but the truth is so strange that it seemed like fiction! Indeed! I do not personally like science fiction as a genre; however, H. G. Wells, Arthur C. Clarke, and most assuredly Jules Verne, are exceptions. You are all familiar with Verne—but he is far more complicated than Disney portrays. I have highlighted *Master of the World*, but all his novels are extraordinary. *Master* is the story of a remarkable genius, mad though he may be, who seeks to take over the world. Verne is truly one of the first futurists.

Lesson continues on the next page.

Solve

A. What is the slope of a line that passes through the point (0,0) and (-3, -1)?

B. The length of a rectangle is 2 times the width. If the perimeter is 30, what is the width?

Critical Thinking: Essay

Literary Analysis Essay

A literary analysis essay critiques, compares, and judges a work of literature. The writer will interpret a piece of literature and try to convince the reader of a particular way of understanding it. The essay focuses on elements such as structure, character, theme, style, and tone to discover how and why it is put together the way it is. It may be your own interpretation, based only on your reading of the piece, or it may also include other's opinions. Literary analysis is often called "literary criticism" but this does not necessarily mean that the writer finds fault with the literature.

Write a literary analysis of your favorite novel.

Light in the Darkness

The Light shines in the darkness. And the darkness has not overpowered the Light!
—John 1:5 (NCV)

Scripture: John 1

The writer Unamuno creates a character, Augusto Perez, in his book *Mist*, who turns to his maker (e.g., Unamuno) and cries: "Am I to die as a creature of fiction?" Such is the cry of modern humankind. The Christian author and Harvard professor Robert Coles laments that "we have the right to think of ourselves, so rich in today's America, as in jeopardy *sub specie aeternitatis*, no matter the size and diversification of his stock portfolio." In spite of our hedonistic bravado, I find many young people to be desperately unhappy. And no wonder. This world does not provide what we need—not by a long shot. My Harvard classmate, Dr. Forrest Church, now pastor in a Unitarian church in New York City, was fond of saying, "In our faith God is not a given, God is a question…God is defined by us. Our views are shaped and changed by our experiences. We create a faith in which we can live and struggle to live up to it…compared to love a distant God had no allure"(Forrest Church, *Born Again Unitarian*). Indeed. This thought has gotten us into quite a mess. Now, we are reminded, the light has come. The light shines in the darkness and the darkness has not overpowered it! Wow! This is good news to our world!

Have you ever felt like Perez? Give an example.

Devotional Journal

Read/Vocabulary Cards

Critical Reading

Read this passage as quickly as possible and answer the questions following.

> While revolution may at times become a tragic and justifiable course for a people, the Christian should have no illusions concerning its dangers and limitations. Secular revolutionists such as Karl Marx… have had messianic expectations of revolutionary action, seeing in it the hope of heaven on earth…The Christian may be driven by the compelling demands of fundamental justice to support…a revolution, but at the same time the believer will never expect from any course of political or military action what only the Holy Spirit of God can accomplish: a renewed heart. (This passage is part of a larger section called "The Limits of What Revolution Can Achieve" from *Evangelical Ethics* by John Jefferson Davis.)

1. Dr. Davis says that revolution is OK but only . . .
   A. when everything else fails
   B. when people are getting hurt
   C. when a majority want it
   D. when fundamental justice demands this course of action

More on Speed Reading

One common mistake we make when we read is that we read word by word. A fast reader trains his eyes to read five words at a time. He trains himself to focus on groups of words—not on one word. If you practice this technique, often your rate will increase significantly. But how to increase comprehension? Practice reading a newspaper article. Key in on the title, the topic sentence (usually at the beginning). Remember! A fast reader is a smart reader! He knows how to read fast and where to find pertinent information.

Lesson continues on the next page.

2. Dr. Davis warns Christians that people have put too much stock in revolutions—what he calls "messianic expectations of revolutionary actions." Why?

   A. Revolutions will not renew one heart—only Jesus will.

   B. Revolutions can kill people.

   C. Good intentions are not as important as obedience to the Lord.

   D. Women and children can be hurt.

Solve

A. A composite number is a number

   A. that can be broken down into two or more factors.

   B. that includes a fraction.

   C. that includes a negative number.

   D. that includes a quadratic equation.

B. $\triangle$ ABC is similar to $\triangle$ GIH. $\overline{BC}$ is 4 cm. $\overline{GH}$ is 6 cm. $\overline{IH}$ is 3 cm. Which of the following statements is true.

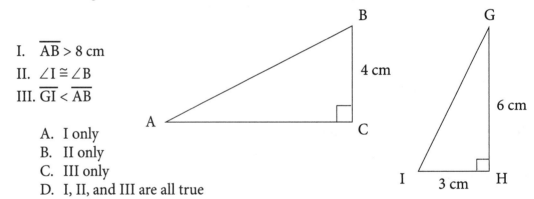

I. $\overline{AB} > 8$ cm

II. $\angle I \cong \angle B$

III. $\overline{GI} < \overline{AB}$

   A. I only

   B. II only

   C. III only

   D. I, II, and III are all true

   E. II and III only

Jesus answered, "I tell you the truth. Unless one is born again, he cannot be in God's kingdom." —John 3:3 (NCV)

Scripture: John 3:1-13

I know Jesus Christ. He is my Savior. I have known Him as my Lord for more than twenty-five years. I try to serve Him daily. But I know, too, that it is awfully hard at times to see Him…to know that He is alive. As T. S. Eliot in his poem "The Rock" observes: "All our knowledge brings us nearer to our ignorance." So, I, the religious man, struggle. How about you? Do you struggle? I remember visiting my Uncle Bobby who is a professor at Harvard Business School. His lecture was entitled "Managing in the 1990s" and he was discussing labor relations. The longer he spoke, the more I realized that the basic questions asked in the business world are essentially the same ones I was hearing in divinity school: How can success be achieved? How can we experience fulfillment? Business, while it appeared to be very concrete, was in fact very much an existential exercise, dealing with basic issues of being and doing. Yes, we all are dealing with basic questions in our life.

Are you wondering if it all matters? How far have you wandered from your faith?

Devotional Journal

Read/Vocabulary Cards

Grammar

Choose the correct answer:

I know (Gus', Gus's) hat when I see it.

Solve

1. In what month(s) did the company make its greatest profits?
2. Between which two consecutive months did the company show its greatest increase in profits?
3. What is the average profit for the first six months? The next six months?

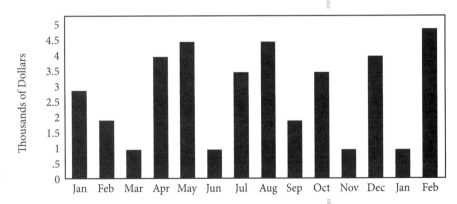

Critical Thinking: Worldview

Identify the worldview of these TV commercials:
   A. You deserve the very best!
   B. You can have it all!

Faith Commitment to Christ

But Jesus answered, "I tell you the truth. Unless one is born from water and the Spirit, he cannot enter God's kingdom." —John 3:5 (NCV)

Scripture *John 3:1-13*

I hope that our faith will offer a few answers. I was not born a Christian. No, we are not automatically Christians because our parents are Christians. Not any more than standing in a garage makes us a car. I had to make a faith commitment to Christ. Oh, I went to church every Sunday. I was a leader in the youth group. I went through communicant's class and joined the Church. But, still, I had not given Him everything. I did not have Jesus Christ in my heart. I was not reborn until senior year in high school when I confessed my sins and accepted Jesus Christ as my Lord and Savior. And then I was born again! Oh, I know, it sounds strange—being reborn. An old friend of mine chided me for being too parochial and closeminded in my insistence that a person needed a personal relationship with Christ. His unitarianism/universalism worships plurality—which is a religion centered around the notion "that anything goes as long as it does not hurt another person." Or, as he put it, "the allure of a God who loves versus one who judges is too great." Indeed. As if God cannot love us yet also judge us? That is OK, though. I guess I do seem a little silly when I talk about the need for a personal relationship with a man who died on a cross…but the foolishness of man is the wisdom of God.

Describe your born again experience.

Devotional Journal

Read/Vocabulary Words

Critical Reading

A.

> This, you must think, all things considered, was *tempting*; for the pilgrims already began to be *foiled* with the badness of the way; but there was not one of them that made so much as a motion to stop there…. I saw then in my dream, that they came to a place at which a man is apt to lose his way. Now, though, when it was light, their guide could well enough tell how to miss those ways that led wrong…. (from *The Pilgrim's Progress* by John Bunyan)

1. What is Bunyan's worldview? Give evidence for your answer.
2. *Pilgrim's Progress* is an allegory. What is an allegory? What advantages does an allegory offer Bunyan as he writes *Pilgrim's Progress*?
3. The theme of a pilgrimage is a common biblical theme. Give one example from the Bible.
4. Create an allegory for your faith journey.

The Puritan John Bunyan's classic, *The Pilgrim's Progress*, should be read by all college-bound students. No extra-biblical work—other than the works of John Milton—has had such an impact on Western Civilization. If you can work through the language style barriers, you are in for a literary and spiritual treat.

B.

   To His Most Christian Majesty, Francis, King of the French, and his
Sovereign, John Calvin wisheth peace and salvation in Christ. When I
began this work, Sire, nothing was further from my thoughts than writing
a book which would afterwards be presented to your Majesty. My intention
was only to lay down some elementary principles, by which inquirers on
the subject of religion might be instructed in the nature of true piety and
this labour I undertook chiefly for my countrymen, the French, of whom I
apprehended multitudes to be hungering and thirsting after Christ, but saw
very few possessing any real knowledge of him. That this was my design, the
book itself proves by its simple method and unadorned composition. But
when I perceived that the fury of certain wicked men in your kingdom had
grown to such a height, as to leave no room in the land for sound doctrine,
I thought I should be usefully employed, if in the same work I delivered
my instructions to them, and exhibited my confession to you, that you may
know the nature of that doctrine, which is the object of such unbounded rage
to those madmen who are now disturbing the country with fire and sword
(*The Institutes of Christian Religion*, John Calvin).

The purpose of this passage is to:
   A. warn the King of France that he was going to hell.
   B. encourage people, especially wicked people, of which there was an
       abundance in France, to commit their lives to Christ.
   C. vilify the English.
   D. None of the above.

Vocabulary

Define the italicized words in passage A.

Solve

   A. Through how many degrees does the minute hand of a clock turn from 4:20 a.m.
       to 5:05 a.m. of the same day?
   B. Is ⅚ equal to, greater than, or less than .8333?

Winston Churchill

...and she will name him Immanuel. —Isaiah 7:14 (NCV)

Scripture: *Isaiah 7:1-16*

It is difficult for us to understand how close the Allies came to losing World War II. I gained some appreciation for the sacrifice of my parents and grandparents when I listened to Grandma Miller (my wife's grandmother) discuss how it was to live in World War II Scotland. She and her friends were genuinely afraid in early 1940 that Germany would defeat Britain. And Grandma had reason to worry. By August 1940 Hitler had conquered all of continental Europe and most of North Africa. In fact, the only obstacle that remained between Hitler and total world conquest was the little island nation of Great Britain. By 1940, England and her Commonwealth had been defeated on all fronts. German U-Boats ruled the seas. The German air force controlled the skies. Outnumbered and outgunned, England would surely surrender before Christmas. But England's prime minister, Winston Churchill, had other plans. He had no intentions of surrendering. "We will fight on the beaches, in the hills…we will not give up." It was as if, Grandma explained, Churchill gave her nation the strength to go on. And, in fact, Great Britain persevered and eventually won the war (with the Allies' help!). The point I want to make is that Churchill saw things differently. He was not going to be discouraged. He was not going to be defeated. Even though his circumstances were desperate, his rhetoric became the reality. Because his rhetoric was based on determination: the determination that he and his little nation. His indomitable spirit saved England. His deep longing for victory was more profound than the very real threat he faced on his borders. And so King Ahaz found himself in a similar situation in 733 b.c. Jerusalem, and he found his way to victory through a promise of Immanuel, "God with us."

What overwhelming obstacle do you face that only God can overcome? Ask God for His perspective.

Devotional Journal

Read/Vocabulary Cards

Solve

1. 50% of 24 is equivalent to ½ of what number?
2. A car averaged 60 mph for ten hours. How far did it travel?
3. In a sequence that has each term 3 more than the previous one, which of the following could not be a term in the sequence?
    A. 999
    B. 145
    C. 111
    D. 453
    E. 270

Arithmetic Required for the SAT

1. Number lines
2. Ratios and proportions
3. Odd and even numbers, multiples
4. Simple addition, subtraction, multiplication, and division
5. Word problems including rate/time/distance, percentages, averages
6. Averages
7. Fractions

4. A delivery company charges $1.00 for the first pound, $.50 per pound or part thereof for the next 6 pounds, and $.25 per pound or part thereof for each additional pound. If the charge is $10.00, what is the weight in pounds of the package?

5. If $\overline{DC} \cong \overline{CB}$ and m $\angle$ ABD = 15° find the length of DC.
   A. 6 cm
   B. 2 cm
   C. 8 cm
   D. 4 cm
   E. Not enough information is provided.

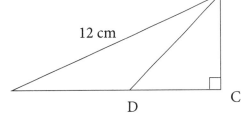

Critical Thinking: Essay

Write a literary analysis of your favorite poem.

A Heritage of Longing

"If you do not stand firm in your faith, you will not stand at all." —Isaiah 7:9

Scripture: Isaiah 7

The historical setting of Isaiah 7 is the crisis in which Judah found itself in 735-733 b.c. During this time the nations of Ephriam, Syria, and Judah were feeling the growing threat of Assyria, a mighty and terrible Middle East empire. Assyria was about to completely annihilate these three nations. In defense, Rezin, king of Syria, and Pekah, King of Ephraim (i.e., Israel) formed a military alliance against Assyria. They tried to force Ahaz, king of Judah, to join them in this alliance. And it was tempting for Ahaz to do so. It was no fun standing alone against the Assyrian onslaught. But the prophet Isaiah warned, "Do not join them…let the king have faith, for if you refuse to trust in the Lord, your nation will not stand." In fact, what Isaiah is saying is: "If you will not be firm, you will not be affirmed."

This Hebrew play on words makes an important point: We cannot keep our feet in both camps. Either we trust Rezin or we trust God. We must choose. From whom do you take your marching orders? Whom do you trust?

Devotional Journal

Read/Vocabulary Cards

Have your parents or guardians review your vocabulary cards.

Solve

There is much debate about whether the SAT is an accurate predictor of college performance. In my opinion it is. Combined with the GPA, the SAT I score seems to be a pretty fair forecast of college performance.

A. Answer questions based on the graph.
1. How long is line A? B? C? D? What is their average length?
2. How long is line C in feet? What is their total length in feet?
3. Line C is how much longer than the shortest line?

B. The distributive property is
A. ab + c = a + b
B. a + b + c = a + b + c
C. a(b + c) = ab + ac
D. a + b + c = d

Holy, holy, holy is the Lord Almighty; the whole earth is full of his glory. —Isaiah 6:3

Scripture: Isaiah 6:1-8

Did you ever have an identity crisis? You know: "Who am I? Why am I here?" I blame my father for my inability to have an identity crisis. He constantly was there to identify me! I "found myself," as it were, while Dad and I looked for an elusive dove hunting paradise—a desolate milo maze field or late autumn corn field—good for nothing at that point except to feed an anemic game animal or two. But we looked anyway. But we looked for a lot of things we never found—for instance we never saw a bluebird and we looked for twenty years. Ironically, every year I see bluebirds on my farm and my dad is not here to see them. I had no time for identity crises—I was busy getting my line untangled from ungracious cypress knees. I learned that there were more important things than my own desires—like what God wanted me to do and what I would be willing to sacrifice to catch that prize-winning goal. This text is one of the well-known calls of Isaiah, specifically, the fetal calling (cf., Jeremiah 1:5) to announce God's salvation to the whole world. Unlike Isaiah 42:1-7, here Isaiah is the speaker—not God. And he is having a real identity crisis.

Who are you? Why are you here? What are you called to do?

Devotional Journal

Read/Vocabulary Cards

Grammar

Choose the correct answer.

Franklin Roosevelt wrote his speech on (stationary, stationery).

Critical Thinking: Argument

The city is in trouble. The city church is in trouble. Cities all over America are approaching fiscal insolvency. Even in the midst of wealth, cities are failing. In June, for instance, the city of Bridgeport, located in Connecticut's wealthiest county, became the nation's first major city to file for bankruptcy. American cities are bled dry and abandoned by suburbia and the federal government, and I doubt the situation will improve in the next twenty years. City churches are dying—all denominations. They are being resurrected as condominiums and restaurants.

1. What is the proposition?
2. What are the assumptions? For instance, there is an unproven assumption that city churches and cities are connected. What would be a counter-assumption?
3. Is Bridgeport, Connecticut, a fair representation of American cities?

I believe that your best scores will occur in May or June of your junior year. If you do not obtain the score you wish, you can always retake the exam during the next fall.

Then I heard the voice of the Lord saying, "Whom shall I send? And who will go for us?" And I said, "Here am I. Send me!" —Isaiah 6:8

Scripture: *Isaiah 6*

Isaiah is articulating his own sense of call—his perception of what God wants him to be. We meet the one who is called—Isaiah—and we discover that he is in so close a relationship with God that he is "hidden" in the Lord's quiver. Anonymous, as it were, to other arrows, perhaps, but very much on the mind of the Lord. The Hebrew word for hidden implies specialness. Likewise, God called us into His kingdom and into a special work even before we were born. A Christian's calling does not begin nor end when a person accepts or rejects the very same calling. The more bold we are in our obedience to His Word, the more He reveals Himself to us. And, at the same time, we are ourselves a divine secret, slowly being revealed, marveling at how we grow into the person God has called us to be. To a large degree, our success at being revealed is determined by our ability to be used by Him.

What is God slowly revealing in your life?

Devotional Journal

Read/Vocabulary Cards

Critical Thinking: Argument

The early explorers who came to America in the late 15th and early 16th centuries thought that they were exploring a land populated by savages and barbarians. Not so. At the time Europeans were participating in the Crusades, North American Native Americans, called the Mississippians, were building mound cities. While Europeans were slaughtering one another in the Thirty Years War, the Iroquois Nation was being formed to guarantee peace and harmony in one-third of what would later be the United States. By and large, the Native Americans who inhabited the eastern United States were peaceful, civilized people who did not particularly wish to fight anyone. So, when John Smith and his English friends set foot in Virginia there was already an advanced civilization staring them in the face.

A. What is the crucial argument advanced by this author? How does he develop his argument?

B. Let's pretend you were one of the Virginia settlers who survived the 1622 Indian War. Would your views differ from those of this author?

C. The author compares the Thirty Years War to the formation of the Iroquois Nation. Is that a fair comparison?

D. The author used broad generalizations to support his case. How can you attack his argument?

Arguments

Throughout your life you will need to determine the veracity of arguments. From deciding whether or not to use drugs, to choosing your future spouse, to choosing a college, you will be making hundreds of decisions based on information provided, indeed, argued by partisan sides. How does one evaluate these arguments? Certainly this is a critical question to be asked before you take the SAT. Find helpful hints on page 251.

Critical Reading

In examining the character of these Princedoms, another circumstance has to be considered, namely, whether the Prince is strong enough, if occasion demands, to stand alone, or whether he needs continual help from others. To make the matter clearer, I pronounce those to be able to stand alone who, with the men and money at their disposal, can get together an army fit to take the field against any assailant; and, conversely, I judge those to be in constant need of help who cannot take the field against their enemies, but are obliged to retire behind their walls, and to defend themselves there. Of the former I have already spoken, and shall speak again as occasion may require. As to the latter there is nothing to be said, except to exhort such Princes to strengthen and fortify the towns in which they dwell, and take no heed of the country outside. For whoever has thoroughly fortified his town, and put himself on such a footing with his subjects as I have already indicated and shall hereafter speak of, will always be attacked with much circumspection; for men are always averse to enterprises that are attended with difficulty, and it is impossible not to foresee difficulties in attacking a Prince whose town is strongly fortified and who is not hated by his subjects (*The Prince*, Machiavelli).

What two admonitions does Machiavelli offer aspiring princes?
  A. Fortify cities and try not to alienate your subjects.
  B. Be ruthless.
  C. Be peaceful and fair.
  D. Form a council to advise you.

Evaluating Arguments

1. First clearly determine the point at issue, or the proposition. The proposition offers a simple truth that the author will argue for the remainder of the reading.
2. What assumptions is he making to begin his argument? Are these assumptions correct? One can, for instance, assume the sun will rise in the east, but it is wrong to assume that pre-marital sex has no consequences.
3. Each side of an issue advances its own proposition. Are the assumptions accurate? Are the comparisons fair? For instance, the comparison of the gay-rights position with the civil rights movement is a fallacious comparison.
4. Each side has a crucial argument. If each side can ascertain the other's argument, and then refute it, the argument will be killed. For instance, the pro-choice abortion group argued for years (and still does) that a three-month-old fetus is not a human being. Increasingly, the scientific community is proving that a three-month-old fetus feels pain, has movement—is indeed a person. That crucial argument has been refuted.
5. If one's crucial argument is refuted, one has to find another crucial argument. Thus, some pro-choice supporters concede that a three-month-old fetus is a person but a woman's right to choose is still paramount over the rights of the unborn child.
6. Finally, each side claims a certain authority. If the credentials of one side can be destroyed, that argument also loses credibility.

He is able to deal gently... —Hebrew 5:2

Scripture: *Hebrew 5:2-5*

Four Mile Creek. About ten miles outside my Arkansas hometown and about thirty years back in my memory. Four Mile Creek was more of a ditch than a creek as we would imagine a creek. There were no freshwater ripples dancing through smooth sandstones—no, it was only a slow, meandering mass of sediment, tadpoles, and water snakes. It was an indigenous creek going nowhere and meaning nothing except to an occasional crawdad—even the deer preferred to find fresher water elsewhere. But it meant everything to me. Some of my earliest and fondest memories include brilliant sunrises along its leaf-covered banks. Before I was barely a decade old, my unshaven father silently deposited me next to a moss-covered pecan (that is puh-con not pee-can!) tree with its scarecrow arms teasingly holding back the dawn. With my 410 calibre shotgun I waited for, prayed for, the dawn to come quickly. I waited, too, for any luckless furry phalange-type creature. I was just sure that a bear or giant rattler would kill me and leave me for my father to find later. There was an immutability about Four Mile Creek. I learned to trust things that I could not see. One particularly terrifying morning, I remember seeing my father standing behind a large oak tree. All this time I thought Dad had left me alone but he was there watching, caring for me. The author of Hebrews reminds us that God deals with us gently. He really cares for you. He is watching over you. Before the world was created He knew about you. And all creation rejoiced at your birth!

What is your earliest impression of God?

Devotional Journal

Read/Vocabulary Cards

Critical Thinking: Analysis

Occasionally a reflective essay will appear on the SAT I. A reflective essay is a rendition of the author's feelings and views. It may simply be a story, or it may be arguable. But it assumes a sympathetic audience and therefore has a more relaxed tone. Be careful with reflective essays. They appear deceptively easy and inevitably generate "what does the author think" questions.

> Observation: We have lost the prophetic edge. Everyone looks for therapy. The one who sins, the one on whom the sin is committed, and the one who observes the sin but does nothing. We all watch and hurt and do nothing. We talk. We examine the problem. We hope that time will heal. But it does not. Because no one says "No, don't do that!" or, "The Bible teaches something else." We just talk about how we feel, how we hurt, and what is wrong with the other person. We watch; we wait; and then we watch the Church become ineffectual. Nothing is really wrong. Nothing is really right. As T. S. Eliot observed, "The world will end with a whimper" (from my diary).

Sleep well the night before an exam, eat well the morning of the exam, and arrive at the test site thirty minutes before the exam begins.

How is this reflective essay different from an argument?

Solve

A. A————————————B————C

   AB is 8⅔ inches. AC is 9¾ inches. Find BC.

B. $\overline{CB}$ is tangent to the circle at point D. Diameter $\overline{AOD}$ bisects $\overline{CB}$ and right angle A. How long is $\overline{DB}$? The radius is 6 inches.

   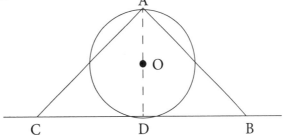

   A. 6
   B. $6\sqrt{2}$
   C. $6\sqrt{3}$
   D. 9
   E. 12

C. Line $\overline{AB}$ is bisected by $\overline{CD}$ at its midpoint. Point A is at (0,5) and point V is at (4,9). Which of these points could be on $\overline{CD}$?

   A. (3,6)
   B. (2,6)
   C. (1,8)
   D. (0,8)
   E. (7,2)

Critical Thinking: Essay

Write a literary analysis of your favorite short story.

Bless the Beasts and the Children I

Let the little children come to me…I tell you the truth, anyone who will not receive the kingdom of God like a little child will never enter it. —Luke 18:16,17

Scripture: *Luke 18:15-17*

This Bible story is one of the most shocking in the Bible. Think about it. In a society where power and prestige dominate, Christ is suggesting in Luke 18 that children—defenseless children—are the greatest in the kingdom. And, furthermore, we who claim to be His disciples had better become like little children or we shall have nothing to do with the kingdom! Radical. Not only do first-century Jewish children have no rights whatsoever, they had no status either. They were not considered to be persons until they were age twelve, and only then if they were males (women were always "property" to be bought and sold by husbands and fathers). Remember—and this is true in third-world countries—the infant mortality rate is very high, as it was in the first century. In Nepal, for instance, less than half of the children live to age five. Therefore, oftentimes parents do not even name children until age twelve, when they have a reasonable chance of survival. Of such is the kingdom of God!

How well do you get along with your younger brothers or sisters? Do you pray for them? Are you kind to them?

Devotional Journal

Read/Vocabulary Cards

Solve

A. Green lettuce weighed 16 ounces and cost 80 cents. Red lettuce weighed 12 ounces and cost 72 cents. What was the best buy?

B. $|-2| =$

C. Which of these functions could cross the x-axis three times when graphed?
   A. $y = |x + 4|$
   B. $y = x^2 - 3x + 2$
   C. $y = 3x$
   D. $y = (3x - 1)(3x + 1)$
   E. $y = x^3 + 3x^2 - x - 3$

Bring a good calculator and an extra battery. No need to have a calculator that can figure out the GNP. Just a basic calculator. Preferably one with big numbers. Use one with which you are familiar. Practice putting in a new battery with your eyes closed. It wouldn't hurt to have an extra calculator with you.

Bless the Beasts and the Children II

…the Kingdom of God belongs to people who are like these children.
—Luke 18:16 (NCV)

Scripture: *Luke 18:15-17*

Based on my experience as a high school English teacher, I can tell you that *Bless the Beasts and the Children* by Glendon Swarthout was one of the most popular books I assigned. Who can forget the nail-biters, thumb suckers, and teeth grinders at the Box Canyon Boy's Camp? Losers! Offspring of wealthy parents busy traveling, being divorced, and gathering fortunes. They were nothing until Cotton came. Cotton pulled them together… until one day they rode out to stop park rangers from killing buffaloes…. Read the book to see what else happened! One criticism I have of Swarthout's book is that he has a tendency to sentimentalize children. They always seem to be a little bit too good. But, the Gospel of Luke does not sentimentalize children. What you see is what you get. I like that. But, even though children in biblical times were of very little value to many people, they were of inestimatible value to our Lord.

Purpose to model Christian behavior to your younger brother or sister—or to another small child. Remember! He or she is watching you!

Devotional Journal

Read/Vocabulary Cards

Vocabulary

Define italicized word in context:

> Wheaties had a lockerful of vices and a gizzardful of *platitudes*. (from *Bless the Beasts and the Children* by Glendon Swarthout)

Grammar

Choose the correct answer.

I like football<u>, however,</u> I love soccer.

A. Place at beginning of sentence.
B. : However,
C. ; however,
D. Omit

Solve

What is the perimeter of the following figure?

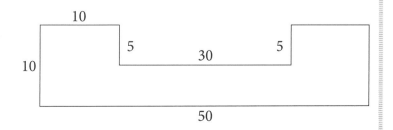

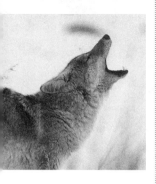

Remain in me, and I will remain in you. No branch can bear fruit by itself; it must remain in the vine. Neither can you bear fruit unless you remain in me. I am the vine; you are the branches. If a man remains in me and I in him, he will bear much fruit; apart from me you can do nothing. —John 15:4,5

Scripture: John 15:4,5

I learned to anticipate good things. The sound of my father whistling in the foreboding forest. The joy of seeing desirable game moving in my direction. The anticipation of home. William Faulkner's short story "The Bear" captures the essence of my early experience. A young boy named Ike, growing up in the Delta, as I did, was brought along on his first hunting trip. "It seemed to him that at the age of ten he was witnessing his own birth," William Faulkner wrote. It was in these woods, at this age, at Four Mile Creek, that I began to ponder the paradox of action and contemplation. It was with great sorrow that I heard recently that Four Mile Creek had been destroyed. Farmers had finally managed to harness its rich antediluvian soil for their purposes. But, as I reflect on this unfortunate turn of events, I realize that it is gone for my mother, for my friends, because they live next to it. But, for me, I fortunately will never lose Four Mile Creek: It will always be in my memory. Even though I am grown up, moved away, and my father is dead, Four Mile Creek is very much alive. I have worked hard to recover that memory. It reminds me of my roots, my genesis. He is the vine, we are the branches. Cut off from Him we can do nothing. Sometimes in my quiet time, God floods my memory with images of His goodness—His presence when I did not even know it. He is indeed the vine!

Find in your memory a "Four Mile Creek" and thank God for it! Then describe it in a 300-word essay.

Devotional Journal

Read/Vocabulary Cards

Vocabulary

Define italicized words in context:

> A few miles south of Soledad, the Salinas River drops in close to the hillside bank and runs deep and green. The water is warm too, for it has slipped twinkling over the yellow sands…willows fresh and green with every spring, carrying in their lower leaf *junctures* the *debris* of the winter's flooding; and sycamores with *mottled*, white, *recumbent* limbs…a lizard makes a great *skittering*. (*Of Mice and Men* by John Steinbeck)

Of Mice and Men by John Steinbeck is one of the best of the Steinbeck oeuvre. More mature readers will enjoy *Grapes of Wrath* and *East of Eden*, but a great place to begin is with *Of Mice and Men*. This small book carries a powerful punch. It is a story of the desperate longing of two men for a home—any home—and, in this case, of how the innocuous search leads to disaster.

Critical Reading

Buck was older than the days he had seen and the breaths he had drawn. He linked the past with the present, and the eternity behind him throbbed through him in a mighty rhythm to which he swayed as the tides and seasons swayed. He sat by John Thornton's fire, a broad-breasted dog, white-fanged and long-furred; but behind him were the shades of all manner of dogs, half wolves and wild wolves, urgent and prompting, tasting the savor of the meat he ate, thirsting for the water he drank, scenting the wind with him, listening with him and telling him the sounds made by the wild life in the forest; dictating his moods, directing his actions, lying down to sleep with him when he lay down, and dreaming with him and beyond him and becoming themselves the stuff of his dreams (*Call of the Wild*, Jack London).

Who is the protagonist in this novel?
   A. Buck
   B. Thornton
   C. the wolves
   D. nature

Solve

   A. .090045 divided by 5.06 =
   B. The radius of a circle is 6 inches. What is the circumference of the circle?
   C. 1.004 x 0.00015 =
   D. 9⅓ divided by 3½ =
   E. $^{48}/_3$ x $^{12}/_{24}$ x $^{60}/_{54}$ =

Song of the Redeemed

He will come and save you. Then the blind people will see again. Then the deaf will hear. Crippled people will jump like deer. And those who can't talk now will shout with joy. — Isaiah 35:4–6 (NCV)

Scripture: *Isaiah 35*

The task ahead of us is to live and evoke the spirit of Isaiah in our community. As the theologian Walter Brueggemann, and others like him, argue, our task is to nurture, nourish, and evoke a consciousness and perception alternative to the consciousness and perception of the dominant culture around us. And increasingly that culture has become inimical to the Gospel. Either way, a community rooted in the Lordship of Jesus Christ is a curiosity and a threat in such a culture. No wonder Isaiah's argument that one should rely on a faithful, historical God was such a threatening message to his generation—and to ours. Our world does not understand, much less believe in, our history. God is not to be trusted because He cannot be quantified. He cannot to be controlled. This God makes self-proclaimed kings of the earth uncomfortable. And this God of ours, therefore, has been making kings like Herod, Ahab, and Nero uncomfortable for ages. I remember a simple, powerful Gospel song that all of us in our 1966 Southern church sang. This was the song of the redeemed. But we scarcely knew it. "Jesus loves the little children…red and yellow, black and white, they are precious in His sight…." Because I was still too young to doubt the veracity of my parents and teachers, I actually believed that song. And, when I started living that song it changed my world. And when enough people live that message we will change our world. Our cause will become holy, our witness worthy of the Gospel. There will be opposition. But our song brings hope, life, and salvation. So it is worth it.

Be bold and courageous, young people, and sing a new song. Do your best on the SAT to bring glory to Him. And become a light to this new generation!

Devotional Journal

Read/Vocabulary Cards

Continue this practice for the rest of your life and your vocabulary will continue to expand exponentially!

Solve

A. Light travels at 186,000 miles per second and sound travels about one mile every five seconds. Thus, if you see lightning and are able to count to twenty before you hear the thunder, about how far away is the lightning?

B. How many ounces are in 8½ pounds?

C. (-6) - (-9)

Critical Thinking: Essay

Write a literary analysis of your favorite movie.

SAT I Mock Exam

Take your last practice SAT I exam.

Forget cramming. It will not help you. Period. Better to relax and to pray. In fact, I recommend that you do not look at your preparation material the last two nights before the exam.

"He told me everything I ever did." —John 4:39

Scripture: John 4

Dr. James Dobson, Christian psychologist, tells about a television documentary that he saw on elephants and their behavioral characteristics. The program was videotaped in India, where the magnificent pachyderms are trained to serve their human masters. Of course, if elephants knew how strong they were, they would never yield to the domination of anything, but they are subjected to a stressful form of brainwashing, which takes the fight out of them. The process begins with three days of total isolation from man and beast. Female elephants and their young are surprisingly social animals, and they react to loneliness in the same way that humans do. They grieve and fret and long for companionship. At that precise moment of vulnerability, they are brought to a nighttime ceremony of fire. Then for many hours in the flickering light, they are screamed at, intimidated, stroked, and ordered back and forth. By morning, half-crazed, the elephants have yielded. Their wills have been broken. You too are social creatures, born with irrepressible needs to be loved and accepted by family and friends. In fact, to deprive you of this emotional support during early childhood is to risk crippling you for life. The woman at the well knows only rejection, grief, and despair. She is traumatized by life. But, in this man Jesus Christ, she is healed. She learns to love again. To trust again. He told her everything she had done. And He still loved her.

Tell the Lord about something you have never told Him. Watch Him love you anyway!

Devotional Journal

Read/Vocabulary Cards

Critical Thinking: Comparison

During the last month before the SAT take as many mock tests as you can.

Joseph Stephens, an old and respected citizen of East Wheatfield Township, Indiana County, died last Friday about 4 o'clock…. Mr. Stephens leaves but 2 children…. He was a member of the Baptist Church for many years and believed with firm conviction in the rewards promised to those who are faithful Christians…. He had a large acquaintance and was universally respected by all who knew him (from an 1889 obituary).

Donald Charles, 59, formerly of Johnstown, died January 20,1996, at Lee Hospital…was a local musician for many years. Air Force veteran… Arrangements by Geisel Funeral Home (from 1996 obituary).

1. Compare and contrast these two obituaries.

Lesson continues on the next page.

2. What do the differences tell us about these two societies? What do the similarities tell us? What does the first article tell us about 1889 values and cultural preferences?
3. Which obituary portrays the most bias?
4. Write your own pretend obituary. For what do you most want to be remembered?

Solve

A. When graphed, the function f(x) has a maximum on the y-axis at y = 6. The function f(x-4) when graphed would show which of these changes:
   A. shifted up to y = 10
   B. shifted left 4 units
   C. shifted right 4 units
   D. shifted down to y = 2 on the y-axis
   E. shifted to x = 4 when y = 6

B. Consider the matrices A and B

$$A = \begin{bmatrix} 2 & 3 \\ 5 & 1 \\ 4 & 0 \end{bmatrix} \qquad B = \begin{bmatrix} 1 & 2 & 3 \\ -1 & 5 & 4 \end{bmatrix}$$

Which of these numbers would not be an element in the product A•B?
   A. 19
   B. 8
   C. 4
   D. -1
   E. 0

I am not pure. And I live among people who are not pure. But I have seen the King, the Lord, of heaven's armies. —Isaiah 6:5 (NCV)

Scripture: *Isaiah 6:1-5*

Theologian Sean Caulfield believes that God is not a "thing." He is not of the things and bits of His own creation, one more objective thing out there, something among other things. He is not even the supreme thing, the first or best or greatest in a series. He is not relative to anything. He is the altogether Other, the Mystery that cannot be contained or boxed in by any symbol or concept. Never has a culture spent so much time and money studying itself, talking about itself, as modern Americans have. As a result, our therapeutic society has created a therapeutic God. We have lost our way. But the God we meet in Isaiah 6 is much different.

You must release your troubles and find a God who is in control.

Devotional Journal

Read/Vocabulary Cards

Grammar

Choose the correct answer.

My grandparents travel to the (South, south) for the winter.

Critical Thinking: Comparison

The theologian and writer Fred Buechner, taking substantial liberty with Scripture, paraphrases Isaiah's call (in chapter 6) this way:

> There were banks of candles flickering in the distance and clouds of incense thickening the air with holiness and stinging his eyes, and high above [Isaiah], as if it had always been there but was only now seen for what it was (like a face in the leaves of a tree or a bear among the stars), there was the Mystery Itself whose gown was the incense and the candles a dusting of gold at the hem. There were winged creatures shouting back and forth… and Isaiah responding, "O God, I am done for! I am foul of mouth and the member of a foul-mouthed race…. I am a goner…." And God said, "Go give the deaf Hell till you're blue in the face and go show the blind Heaven till you drop in your tracks because they'd sooner eat ground glass than swallow the bitter pill that puts roses in the cheeks and a gleam in the eye. Go do it." (from *Peculiar Treasures*)

Analyze Buechner's view and then compare it to Caulfield's view.

The Last Few Days Before Your SAT

1. First, do not spend a lot of time studying material. If you have faithfully prepared, you will be ready.

2. Review your target Scriptures.

3. Rest, rest, rest. Eat a big breakfast the day of the exam.

4. On the night before, leave everything alone. Just rest and pray. I suggest that parents and students go out to eat dinner— and celebrate. If you do anything, just look over the directions.

5. Arrive at the test site early so that you will not have to add extra stress to yourself by rushing.

Lesson continues on the next page.

Solve

A. Which of these numbers is divisible by 2? By 5? By 10? By 3?

   A. 6

   B. 32

   C. 3020

   D. 99

B. A square has been inscribed in a circle as shown in this illustration. What is the probability that a point selected at random from inside the circle will fall inside of the shaded area if the radius of the circle is 5?

   A. 25π

   B. 5

   C. $25\pi - 50$ or $25(\pi - 2)$

   D. $\dfrac{25\pi - 50}{25\pi}$ or $\dfrac{\pi - 2}{\pi}$

   E. 10π

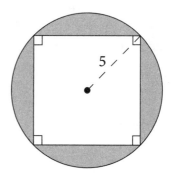

Lesson 1

Solve

WWW, WLWLW, WLLWW, WWLW, WLWW, LWWW, LLWWW, WWLLW= 9 different ways and counting!

Lesson 2

Grammar

Swimming is a gerund functioning as a subject/noun.

Vocabulary

Precocious means exceptionally early in development. Deprecation is disapproval.

Solve

1,451,500 ml x 1 liter/1000 ml = 1451.5 liters

Lesson 3

Read/Vocabulary Cards

A. apex (pinnacle)
B. gusto (enthusiasm)
C. phlegmatic (easy-going)
D. avaricious (greedy)
E. pertinacious (persistent)
F. voluminous (immense)
G. idiosyncrasies (unusual mannerisms)
H. sardonic (bitter or scornful)
I. inveigle (beguile)
J. impresario (director)
K. expostulate (to reason earnestly)
L. wizened (aged)
M. apoplexy (a stroke caused by a broken blood vessel in the brain)
N. astute (clever)
O. suavely (charmingly)

Solve

A. 30 cubic meters x 100cm/m x 100cm/m x 100cm/m =
   30(100)(100)(100) =
   30,000,000 cubic centimeters
B. Go from m^3 to cm^3 to liters.
   1200 m^3 x 100cm/m x 100cm/m x 100cm/m x 1 liter/1000cm^3 =
   1200(100)(100)(100)/1000 liters =
   1,200,000 liters

Critical Reading

I. Answer: D
   A. Pearl is indeed the daughter of an illicit love affair between Hester Prynne and Arthur Dimmesdale but this is not stated in the passage.
   B. On the contrary, Pearl is a gift of God.
   C. Pearl is a result of an adulterous affair; however, the passage does not state directly that it was a bad choice. This would be the second best answer.
   D. This is the best answer. From this passage the reader can only know for sure that Pearl is the

daughter of Hester Prynne. There is no identification of her father stated or implied.

II. Answer: D
  A. Chillingsworth is the antagonist.
  B. Hester Prynne is the protagonist.
  C. There is no narrator—Hawthorne tells the story using omniscient narration. The correct answer is
  D. foil. Pearl's only purpose is to develop her mother, Hester Prynne, the protagonist. Pearl is used to make Prynne into a rounded, well-developed character.

Lesson 4

Critical Thinking: Analysis

This is an analysis level question, which means that you are asked to examine, analyze data, and form a conclusion. In this case you could argue that Heyerdahl must find evidence, for instance, of Peruvian culture in Polynesia. Also, when looking for a solution to a scientific problem, you normally choose the easiest pathway. In this case, it makes a lot more sense for Asians to migrate to Pacific Islands—island by island—rather than traveling thousands of miles across an ocean.

Vocabulary
  A. myriad (abundance)
  B. coquettishly (flirtingly)

Solve
  A. 6.285
  B. 6.197
  C. 261.648

Critical Thinking: Essay

Answer: Here is an example of an effective descriptive paragraph:

> Whoever has made a voyage up the Hudson must remember the Catskill mountains. They are a dismembered branch of the great Appalachian family, and are seen away to the west of the river, swelling up to a noble height, and lording it over the surrounding country. Every change of season, every change of weather, indeed, every hour of the day, produces some change in the magical hues and shapes of these mountains, and they are regarded by all the good wives, far and near, as perfect barometers. When the weather is fair and settled, they are clothed in blue and purple, and print their bold outlines on the clear evening sky; but, sometimes, when the rest of the landscape is cloudless, they will gather a hood of gray vapors about their summits, which, in the last rays of the setting sun, will glow and light up like a crown of glory (*Rip Van Winkle*, Washington Irving).

Notice the very effective use of figurative language (e.g., "swelling up to a noble height…").

Lesson 5

Vocabulary
  A. gratuitously (freely)
  B. voracious (famished)

Critical Thinking: Evaluation
Answer: F

Solve
  A. 0.03142
  B. 0.1723125
  C. 19.454205

Lesson 6

Solve

A. 42 x Number of buses = 1264

N = 30 r 4

Therefore, the answer is 31 because another bus is necessary to take the remaining students. Or, 30 buses could be taken if 26 buses have 42 students and 4 buses have 43.

B. 3 x 12 = 36 inches; 4 x 12 = 48 inches

36 x 48 = 1728 sq. in.; therefore, it would take 1728 tiles

Grammar

Answer: A

A. It is better to use the active voice rather than the passive voice.

B. Normally a comma does not appear between an adjective and its object.

C. Replacement of the preposition "of" by "with" is unnecessary.

D. The replacement of "was" with "were" is wrong. The singular subject "game" requires a singular verb form.

Lesson 7

Solve

A. Boys/Girls = Boys/Girls

13/2 = 26/G

13G = 26 x 2

G = 26 x 2 divided by 13

G = 4

B. One pound of beans cost $12/60 or $0.20/pound

Critical Reading

Answer: C. William Bradford clearly sees all history to be controlled by God. The punishment of this young man, for instance, is providential.

Lesson 9

Vocabulary

A. diabolical (demonic)

B. abominable (dreadful)

Solve

A.

1. False
2. False
3. True
4. True
5. True
6. False

B. 875,000

Lesson 10

Vocabulary

A. apoplectic (out-of-control)

B. palisade (fortress)

Grammar

Answer: A

"The five-foot tall boy in the center of the field skillfully kicked the black and white soccer ball" is better. An author normally should use as few words as possible—especially as few prepositional phrases as possible—while giving all necessary, relevant details.

Solve

A. 10,00 x .08 = 800 for 1 year
    800 x 2.5 years = 2,000 interest
    Mary withdrew $12,000.

B.

Fraction	Decimal	Percent
¾	.75	75%
³⁷/₁₀₀	.37	37%
⅔	.667	66⅔%

Lesson 11

Critical Thinking: Main Idea

A. Nouwen argues that being wounded is not a sign of weakness. In fact, Nouwen argues, we can find ourselves growing stronger through weakness.

B. Being wounded is not a sign of weakness.

C.
    I.   Answer: A
    II. Answer: C
    III. Answer: B

Solve

A. ⅔ = 66%; therefore, ⅔ is larger than 65%

B. 0.02 is larger than 0.008

Lesson 12

Vocabulary

indignant (angry)
malignant (malicious)
pommelled (stomped)

Critical Thinking: Summary

Example: Using the metaphor of a branch being cut off a tree limb, Aurelius argues that a thoughtless act of hatred that causes a person to be separated from his community does irreparable damage to the person and to his community.

Solve

A. $4x = 12$
    $x = 3$

B. $5x - 2 = 13$
    $5x = 15$
    $x = 3$

C. $7x - 0 = 14$
    $7x = 14$
    $x = 2$

Lesson 13

Solve

    A. $3 \times (4)(4) \times (2)(2)(2) =$
        $3 \times 16 \times 8 = 384$

    B. Answer: 4.5×10^6

Lesson 14

Vocabulary

    apprehension (anxiety)
    exertions (energetic activity)

Critical Thinking: Summary

    Answers will vary. An example is:
    When they joined the nervous ladies, he briefly gave them the news about their new guide, and the necessity for them to stay calm in everything that they did.

Grammar

    "The house where Abraham Lincoln was born has been made a national landmark" is correct because the modifier "where Lincoln was born" must be placed closer to the word it modifies.

Solve

    $3w - 4 = 5w + 7$
    $-5w + 4 = -5w + 4$
    $-2w = +11$
    $w = -11\frac{1}{2}$

Lesson 15

Critical Thinking: Analysis

    Answers will vary, but the general idea is as follows: Halloween is anti-Christian, dangerous, and generally harmful. I think it is wrong to put it in the same category as the pagan celebrations of Christmas and Easter.

Critical Reading

    Answer: C

Solve

    A. $3w + 2 - w + 4 = -5 - w - 4$
        $2w + 6 = -9 - w$
        $3w = -15$
        $w = -5$

    B. rate x time =
        $65 \times 4 = 260$ miles

Lesson 16

Sentence Completion

    B. disturbed…peculiarity

Solve

    A. $.5 \times 86 = 43$

    B. $\frac{30}{90} = \frac{1}{3}$

    C. $.25 \times 50 = 200$

D. area of section a = 4 x 1 = 4
area of section b = 7 x 1 = 7
area of section c = 2 x 2 = 4
a + b + c = 15 feet

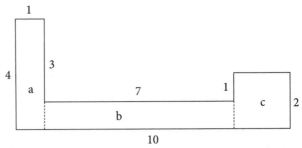

Critical Thinking: Essay
Example:

Angels Beware

Los Angeles conjures up a rainbow of images, many associated with the lifestyle and glitter of Southern California's good life. Today, however, the "City of Angels" is mired in too many people, too many cars and too much smog.

Granted, on a good day, you can see forever in the sprawling metropolitan area. You also can enjoy the excitement of watching the Dodgers play baseball, of attending a Broadway-type theater performance, of viewing some of the world's greatest art or taking rides in a theme park. The list of attractions seems endless.

To reside in L.A., you must cope with hordes of people, scurrying to and from work, to and from play on hundreds of miles of streets and highways.

You also must contend with the crush of vehicles, running bumper to bumper four to six abreast. Don't forget gridlock, blessed gridlock.

Haze, an euphemism for smog, often hangs like a blanket over the area. This should be no surprise, however, considering the soft prevailing winds off the Pacific that conspire with temperature inversions to trap pollutants generated by the nation's second largest city located in a basin surrounded by mountains.

In the beginning, the region was a chamber of commerce paradise. Even today, flowers, shrubs, trees and birds of exotic origin grace the area. Gardens flourish during the winter, and citrus trees bear fruit year round. Unfortunately, hordes of people invaded Los Angeles and in the ensuing years tarnished the image of this promised land of the West, the "City of Angels."

Lesson 17

Sentence Completion
D. demented

Critical Thinking: Analysis
Answer: B

Solve
2x + 14 = 76
2x = 62
x = 31

Lesson 18

Critical Reading
A. A
B. This is an extremely difficult passage to summarize, and answers will vary. But the general idea is: Marsden is discussing the departure of religion from the university. He blames a false reading of the enlightenment as one major cause. One unfortunate outcome, he concludes, is the demise of intolerance.

Grammar
Answer: A. When compound subjects are connected by "or" or "nor" the subject closest to the verb determines its number.

Solve

    $4x - 8 = 92$

    $4x = 100$

    $x = 25$

Lesson 19

Vocabulary

    A. auspicious (favorable)

    B. innate (inherent)

    C. felonious (criminal)

Solve

    A. $2x + 42 = -102$

        $x = -72$

    B. $5x + 21 = 2(-x)$

        $7x = -21$

        $x = -3$

Lesson 21

Critical Thinking: Analysis

    Answer: F

Solve

    A. $2/3 = 48/x$

        $2x = 3 \times 48$

        $2x = 144$

        $x = 72$

    B. $60 \times 8 = 480 \times 2 = 960$ miles

Lesson 22

Vocabulary

    disposed (inclined)

        example sentence: My neighbor is disposed to keeping his lawn well-maintained.

    enviable (highly desirable or coveted)

        example sentence: Their trip to France was enviable.

Grammar

    Answer: C

    1. Incorrect. It's I! Use nominative case after linking verb.

    2. Correct.

    3. Incorrect. To whom were you speaking? "Whom" is object of preposition "to."

    4. Incorrect. Running the gauntlet, the brave warrior ran to the tepee in front of him. Modifiers must be close to the words that they modify.

Solve

    stone, phone, etc.

Lesson 23

Solve

    Because Art started out with $2, and he ended up with $3, who is out the extra dollar and why? Duncan is out the extra dollar. Before the pawn broker will return the $2 to the ticket holder, he will want the $1.50, which he advanced, returned to him. Duncan will give the pawn broker the ticket and the $1.50, and the pawn broker will then return the $2. Duncan now has $2 for which he paid $3.

Critical Reading
Answer: A

Lesson 24

Solve
A. $\frac{1}{3} x = 6$
$x/_3 = {}^6/_1$
$1x = 6 \times 3$
$x = 18$
B. $24 \times .25 = 6$
C. $65 \times 6 = 390$ miles
D. $(-7) - (-9) = -7 + 9 = +2$

Lesson 25

Solve
A. 12 divided by $1.5 = 8$ portions
B. $\frac{3}{8} + \frac{3}{8} = \frac{6}{8}$
$\frac{8}{8}$ (the whole) $- \frac{6}{8} = \frac{2}{8} = \frac{1}{4}$ did not vote
C. Answer: 6th degree

Lesson 26

Vocabulary
orbit (course or path)
laborious (tedious)
apotheosis (idealization or deification)

Grammar
Answer: C. Use objective pronouns after the preposition "between"—Mary and her.

Lesson 27

Sentence Completion
B. purposeless…materialistic
As is so often the case with sentence completion questions, the answer to the question is implied in the sentences. For instance, because it says that Simpson is agnostic we know that he believes we were not planned, there are no absolutes. Thus, B clearly would be the right answer. Simpson makes no value judgment (so scratch A and C). D also implies purpose. E is the closest second answer and would work but "deliberate" implies "intentionality," which Simpson rejects. Simpson's view is an example of an atheistic worldview. Besides, the article "a" is a dead giveaway that the answer is a word that begins with a consonant!

Critical Reading
Answer: B

Solve
A. $6.67
B. Each side is 1 meter or 100 centimeters long.

C. ¼ - ½ = - ¼

Lesson 28

Solve
- A. 5.6 + 6.2 + 6.3 divided by 3 = 6.033
- B. $^5/_{30}$ = ⅙ = 16.67%
- C. 1¼ divided by 4 =
   1¼ x ¼ = $^{11}/_{16}$
- D. 2.0 + 2.0 = 4
- E. 2x - 19 = 37
   2x - 19 (+19) = 37 + 19
   2x = 56
   x = 28

Critical Reading

Answers will vary. The following are examples:
- A. The demise of religion (vs. politics, economics, etc.) as an institution in world society.
- B. The absence of a clearly defined, absolute corpus of truth (i.e., the Word of God! The Bible!).
- C. Anyone with the strength of will to fill it will fill it. In fact, as Nietzsche predicted, dictators like Adolph Hitler and Joseph Stalin filled the gap.
- D. Mr. Johnson is concerned about the void that the decline of religion has caused in world society. Obviously Mr. Johnson feels that the future of Western culture is tied to the preservation of Judeo-Christian morality and teachings.

Critical Thinking: Writing

Example:

Dear Editor:

I read your article on "China's One Child Policy" and I found it very disconcerting. Your editorial manifests bad morality and bad science!

For one thing, forced sterilization and infanticide (both practiced in China to maintain the one-child policy) are clearly against Scripture. From the very beginning mankind was given the mandate to be fruitful and to multiply and to fulfill the earth and to subdue it (Genesis 1:28). The commandment was repeated to Noah and his sons after the flood, which shows how important it was (Genesis 9:1). The promise of fruitfulness in procreation is an important feature of the Abrahamic covenant (Genesis 12:2). Therefore, if you are supporting China's policy of one child per family, you are supporting a policy that invites people to disobey the Word of God.

With married couples, birth control is acceptable (however not with unwed teens) and can even be encouraged by the state. In China, as documented by many different sources, married couples are required to have one child and only one child. If they become pregnant again, many times the child is aborted and the woman is sterilized. Abortion is murder; abortion is wrong. Therefore, again, the one child policy is wrong.

As is very common in the Marxist/Leninist worldview, man is often making his own decisions and relying on his own "wisdom" to choose for the "good" (or what is thought to be good). Dr. David Noebel, in *Understanding the Times*, states, "Because social and economic status are by Karl Marx's definition always changing according to the law of the dialectic mankind's ideas about morality must also be in a state of change." Obviously, making a decision based upon what seems right, what advances the Communist agenda, does not have the moral imperative to murder unborn children and to sterilize unwilling mothers.

Furthermore, Dr. John Jefferson Davis in his book *Evangelical Ethics* correctly argues that the population explosion is a hoax. In fact, there is no evidence to support that the world will be over populated any time soon. There is much evidence that the opposite is true. Most population theories of the 1960s have proven to be absolutely false. There is no reason to doubt that future agricultural advances will be able to meet the nutritional needs of a growing population. So, China is misguided in its pursuit of population decline.

Therefore, because the one-child policy violates the Word of God, I oppose it. At the same time, the policy betrays bad science—there is no evidence that the world will be overpopulated any time soon.

Sincerely, Jessy Stobaugh (*Skills for Rhetoric*, James P. Stobaugh).

Lesson 29

Critical Reading
1. C. Jesus Stays Behind in the Temple
2. D. Jesus was an extraordinary child.

Solve
A. ½ x ½ x ½ = ⅛
B. ⅛ x ⅛ = ¹⁄₆₄; answer = ⅛.
C. $(-25X)^0 + 4(800)^0 = 1 + 4(1) = 5$

Lesson 30

Grammar
Answer: have

Solve
Pour the pineapple juice from the second glass into the fifth glass.

Lesson 31

Critical Reading
Answer: C

Solve
Perimeter = 18 + 62 + 8 + 8 + 18 + 62 = 176
The area of this figure = A + B + C
Area of a = 23 x 18 = 414
Area of b = 16 x 10 = 160
Area of c = Area of A = 414
Therefore, the area of this figure is 414 + 160 + 414 = 988;
Area = 988

Lesson 33

Solve
A. $ 35,714.29. Be careful! This is one of the most often missed test items on the SAT I. This is called an "overall average." The average of the averages is seldom the overall average. The average is always the sum of the numbers divided by the number of numbers. Thus, in this problem you need to find the overall average of 140 people, not the average of the average of 80 people and 60 people. There is a difference.
B. $3^0 + 2^0 = 1 + 1 = 2$

Sentence Completion
D. intrinsic
The best answer is D, intrinsic, which is the same word as *ipso facto*. A is not specific enough. B and C do not mean the same as *ipso facto*. This sentence completion illustrates a common SAT strategy:

define the answer later in the sentence. In fact, this type of question is most common on the SAT. Again, therefore, we see why the name of the game in verbal SAT preparation is VOCABULARY! VOCABULARY! VOCABULARY!

Lesson 34

Grammar

Correct

Solve

A. Suzie's mother slid a newspaper under a door and made Suzie stand on one side of the door and her brother on the other.

B. $5x - \{4[3x - (45 + 3x)]\} + 2(3x - 6) = 38$

$5x - \{4[3x - 45 - 3x]\} + 6x - 12 = 38$

$5x - \{12x - 180 - 12x\} + 6x - 12 = 38$

$5x + 180 + 6x - 12 = 38$

$11x + 168 = 38$

$11x = -130$

$x = -\frac{130}{11}$

$x = -11\frac{9}{11}$

C. $7x - (4x - 10x) = 728$

$7x + 6x = 728$

$13x = 728$

$x = 56$

Lesson 35

Matching

C hideous

B adapt

E adversary

F perforate

A aesthetic

D aggressor

Critical Reading

A.

1. C. Earth Science

Sound waves are not connected to the other disciplines.

2. B. the material through which the wave is moving has changed.

Answer C is implied by the paragraph, but it is untrue. This illustrates an important point—avoid answers that are untrue even if you think they are implied by the paragraph.

B. Answer: A

Solve

Answer: B.

Lesson 36

Vocabulary

taciturn (quiet, shy)

Solve

A. $7\frac{1}{8} - 4\frac{3}{16} =$

$5\frac{7}{8}$ - $^{67}/_{16}$ =

$^{114}/_{16}$ - $^{67}/_{16}$ =

$^{47}/_{16}$ = $2^{15}/_{16}$

B. $8\frac{1}{8}$ - $5^{3}/_{24}$ =

$8^{3}/_{24}$ - $5^{3}/_{24}$ = 3

C. $\frac{3}{4}$ - $\frac{1}{2}$ =

$\frac{3}{4}$ - $^{2}/_{4}$ = $\frac{1}{4}$

D. $\frac{1}{4}$ = .25 = 25%

E. $^{2}/_{25}$ = .08 = 8%

F. $^{9}/_{10}$ = .90 = 90%

Critical Thinking: Essay

A good example of a persuasive essay is *Walking* by H. David Thoreau:

> I wish to speak a word for Nature, for absolute freedom and wildness, as contrasted with a freedom and culture merely civil—to regard man as an inhabitant, or a part and parcel of Nature, rather than a member of society. I wish to make an extreme statement, if so I may make an emphatic one, for there are enough champions of civilization: the minister and the school committee and every one of you will take care of that. I have met with but one or two persons in the course of my life who understood the art of Walking, that is, of taking walks, who had a genius, so to speak, for *sauntering*: which word is beautifully derived from "idle people who roved about the country, in the Middle Ages, and asked charity, under pretence of going *à la Sainte Terre*," to the Holy Land, till the children exclaimed, "There goes a Sainte-Terrer," a Saunterer, a Holy-Lander. They who never go to the Holy Land in their walks, as they pretend, are indeed mere idlers and vagabonds; but they who do go there are saunterers in the good sense, such as I mean. Some, however, would derive the word form sans terre, without land or a home, which, therefore, in the good sense, will mean, having no particular home, but equally at home everywhere. For this is the secret of successful sauntering. He who sits still in a house all the time may be the greatest vagrant of all; but the saunterer, in the good sense, is no more vagrant than the meandering river, which is all the while sedulously seeking the shortest course to the sea. But I prefer the first, which, indeed, is the most probable derivation. For every walk is a sort of crusade, preached by some Peter the Hermit in us, to go forth and reconquer this Holy Land from the hands of the Infidels. It is true, we are but faint-hearted crusaders, even the walkers, nowadays, who undertake no persevering, never-ending enterprises. Our expeditions are but tours, and come round again at evening to the old hearth-side from which we set out. Half the walk is but retracing our steps. We should go forth on the shortest walk, perchance, in the spirit of undying adventure, never to return—prepared to send back our embalmed hearts only as relics to our desolate kingdoms. If you are ready to leave father and mother, and brother and sister, and wife and child and friends, and never see them again—if you have paid your debts, and made your will, and settled all your affairs, and are a free man, then you are ready for a walk (*Walking*, Henry D. Thoreau).

Lesson 37

Solve

A. 4521 - 1200 / 4521 = 3321 / 4521 = 73.46%

B. The formulas for all geometric figures will be provided on the SAT but it is a good idea to memorize the most common ones. Circumference = πd and Area = πr2.

Circumference is 3.14 x 12 = 37.68 inches

Area is 3.14 x 36 = 113.04 sq. inches

C. It wasn't a window but rather a film screen. Shadow walked in from the street, inserted his card, pressed the button marked 36, and dropped down to intelligence headquarters. Because he was below ground level, he could not have been looking down at the antlike pedestrians. What he saw was a film of a clear day taken from a great height. When the projector ran out of film, the screen flashed white.

Lesson 38

Grammar

Answer: Correct.

Solve

A. 16¼ divided by 4⅔ = $^{65}/_4$ x $^3/_{14}$ = $^{195}/_{56}$ = 3.482

B. $^{14}/_3$ times ½ = $^{14}/_{21}$ = ⅔

C. x = original price

$125 = 60%x

$125 = .60x

$208.33 = x

D. Distance/Time = Rate, so, 280/4 = 70mph

E. 45 + 78 + 49 + 88 = 260/4 = 65

Lesson 39

Solve

a = girls, b = boys, c = dogs, T = total number

b = 15, a = 3 x 15 = 45, c = 8 x 15 = 120

T = 15 + 45 + 120 = 180

Matching

E surrender

C agreement

B adjust

A amiable

D congruous

Critical Reading

A. Answer: A. To a Marxist, slavery could lead to a war, but only if it develops a self-consciousness that motivates a class. A blockade is a military/political act, never a cause for a war to occur. Ditto for European influence. The rise of a Southern proletariat—a class consciousness—affects history.

B. Answer: C

Lesson 40

Vocabulary

impudent (arrogant)

compelled (coerced)

Solve

A. 40/640 = 100/x = 1/16 = 100/x = $1600 = x.

B. The perimeter = 10 cm + 10 cm + 100 cm + 100 cm + 20 cm = 240 cm

Lesson 41

Sentence Completion

A. fortuitous

Solve
- A. $^{49}/_{12} \times \,^{3}/_{7} \times \,^{7}/_{2} \times \,^{24}/_{25} = \,^{147}/_{25}$
- B. seven million, two hundred sixty-seven thousand, one hundred eighty-six and eight-tenths.
- C. 7th floor

Lesson 42

Grammar

Answer: was. "Every" and "many a" before a word or series of words is followed by a singular verb.

Sentence Completion
1. D. distill
   Distill means "to condense to its basic components."
2. C. penchant
   Propensity is close, but implies quantity rather than quality. C is the best answer because it implies a quality or style of attraction.

Lesson 43

Critical Reading

Answer: D

Matching

G combination
A contempt
H pugnacious
I credible
C cryptic
E diminish
F cynic
J loaf
B defiance
D denounce

Critical Thinking: Perspective

Answers will vary. Here is an example: If one did not believe in God, one would see the event as a catastrophic happening—rather than a growth experience leading to development of character.

Lesson 44

Vocabulary

apparition (a sudden, strange appearance)
disposed (inclined)
discourteous relief (impolite expression)
ironical (incongruous)

Solve

x = what 4 tires cost
4/x = 16/96
16x = 96(4)
16x = 384
x = 24

Lesson 45

Critical Thinking: Classification
    A. sports equipment and sea creatures
    B. diseases and clothes

Solve
    A. $23 - \{3 + (28 - x)\} - [45 + 6\{8(6 - 3x) - 4\}] = 0$
        $23 - 31 + x - [45 + 6\{48 - 24x - 4\}] = 0$
        $23 - 31 + x - [45 + 6\{44 - 24x\}] = 0$
        $-8 + x - [45 + 264 - 144x] = 0$
        $-8 + x - 309 + 144x = 0$
        $145x = 317$
        $x = {}^{317}\!/_{145}$
    B. Answer: W = 2; L = 10
        $x (x + 8) = 20$
        $x2 + 8x - 20 = 0$
        $(x-2) (x + 10) = 0$
        $x - 2 = 0$
        $x = 2$
        $L = x + 8 = 10$

Lesson 46

Vocabulary
    prosperity (abundance)
    deceptive (fraudulent)
    infamy (evil reputation)
    affront (humiliation)
    unwitting (unintentional)
    extinction (desolation)

Grammar
    Answer: seems. "Six months" functions as one unit so it needs a singular verb form.

Critical Thinking: Précis
    Answers will vary. Here is an example:
    Regardless of gender, age, or race, the Church must clearly embrace all people.

Lesson 47

Critical Reading
    Answer: C

Solve
    A. x = David's present age. Karen's present age = x - 8. In 3 years this equation is true:
        $x + 3 = 2(x - 8 + 3)$
        $x + 3 = 2x - 10$
        $13 = x$
        Therefore, if David is 13, Karen is 13 - 8 = 5.
    B. 255/5 = 51 mph
    C. The average propane usage for the first six months: ${}^{21}\!/_6 = 3.5$
        The last six months: ${}^{24}\!/_6 = 4$

The greatest increase: 3—between November and December
The business spent: 45 tons x $100 = $4500

Lesson 48

Matching
__C__ deny
__E__ contempt
__D__ derivative
__A__ detached
__B__ obstacle

Critical Reading
1. Answers will vary, but Marsden would blame A, increased substance abuse among college students, on the university's penchant to wander from its Judeo-Christian moorings. The same for answer D, as the reason so many college students cheat. Ironically, B, the absence of courses on creationism, reflects the closemindedness that exists on many modern campuses—something that Pelikan would abhor. But, Marsden's point is that modern universities—with their rejection of their spiritual roots—are not as open as they think. And, finally, Marsden would be horrified that college students would not know who the great Christian writer John Milton was, C. Pelikan is not worried—they can find out who he was in the "discovery" of university life.
2. Belshazzar is a disrespectful, pretentious man who forgets his place before Almighty God (Daniel 7). Moses, however, is a man on his knees before an omnipotent God (Exodus 3).

Critical Thinking: Essay
Example:

Traveling the Back Roads

The sounds of a boisterous metropolitan area melt into the background as your car heads east to the foothills of the Cascade Mountains. Thoughts of suburban life soon vanish as towering Douglas fir trees flash by. Traffic eventually thins and fresh, cool mountain air replaces the need for air-conditioning. The mountains give way to a wide vista of hills, sagebrush and juniper, and you begin to explore the back roads of Oregon.

The trek may take you to the desert land once inhabited by an earlier civilization in Lake County in stark contrast to Portland's modern cultural melting pot. Or you can travel farther south and east to a wildlife refuge that rests in the lap of the towering Steens Mountain. Thousands of geese, ducks, swans and dozens of other species make this sanctuary their migratory stopping place unlike many of their cousins who reside in more populated areas of the state.

Farther north, you may stop in Halfway, a town of 350 people that once gained notoriety by permitting its name to be associated with a dot-com Web site. If you stop there overnight and ask for a key to your room, don't be surprised if you are told, "We don't lock our doors here."

The roads that lead east eventually end at one of the state's scenic wonders. In contrast to the buildings in cities that rise several blocks heavenward, the Snake River runs thousands of feet below the mountain rim of Hell's Canyon, the deepest gorge in North America. The back roads reach the northeast corner of the state known as the Wallowa Country, also referred to as the little Alps of America. A century ago, Chief Joseph, a famous American Indian, resided there. Today, tourists of many nationalities enjoy the lake and surrounding mountains.

Other options unfold year by year as you escape a pressure-packed life in the city to travel the back roads of Oregon. Next time, you may opt to explore the Oregon Coast, the Columbia River Gorge, the Crater Lake country, the Three Sisters mountains or former gold mining sites of central and eastern Oregon. No matter what the choice, the list of back roads you can explore in Oregon appears endless and promises to fill a lifetime of adventure.

Lesson 49

Vocabulary

purgatory (hell)
writhed (squirmed)
indifferent (apathetic)

Solve

A. They won $^{100}/_{125}$ = ⅘; They lost $^{25}/_{125}$ = ¼; The ratio of games won to games lost is $^{25}/_{100}$ or ¼.

B. Answer: x = 3
$2x^2 - 5X - 3 = 0$
$(2x + 1)(x - 3) = 0$
$2x + 1 = 0$
$2x = -1$
$x = -½$
$x - 3 = 0$
$x = 3$

Lesson 50

Grammar

Answer: who. Use the same case as the antecedent of the pronoun.

Solve

Perimeter = 14 + 3 + 14 + 2 + 2 + 3 = 38
Area of a = 3 x 5 = 15
Area of b = 5 x 3 = 15
Area of c = 6 x 3 = 18
Area is a + b + c = 15 + 15 + 18 = 48

Lesson 51

Critical Reading

A. The point of view is from Bilbo Baggins, but it is limited omniscient narration. Bilbo Baggins is the protagonist. Gandalf is a foil.

B. Answer: B

Solve

A. ⅓ [(2½ x ⅓) - (¾ x ½)] =
⅓ [(⁵⁄₂ x ⅓) - (¾ x ½)] =
⅓ [⅚ - ⅜] =
⅓ [²⁰⁄₂₄ - ⁹⁄₂₄] =
⅓ (¹¹⁄₂₄) = ¹¹⁄₇₂

B. Perimeter = 20 + 45 + 10 + 34 + 3 + 33 + 3 + 28 + 4 +
(45 + 34 + 33 + 28) = 320 meters = 32,000 cm

Lesson 52

Matching

 D disperse
 A disseminate
 I oppose
 H dissuade

   <u>G</u> eclectic
   <u>C</u> docile
   <u>F</u> dogmatic
   <u>B</u> eccentric
   <u>E</u> surpass
   <u>I</u> sanction

Vocabulary

genial (friendly)
recluse (hermit)
bleakness (dreariness)
secluded (isolated)
preparatives (preparations)
competent (able)

Solve

A. $3x + 1, 3x + 2, 3x + 3, 3x + 4$
B. .005
C. .035

Lesson 53

Critical Reading

A. shroud (death clothes)
  skirmish (fight)
  distinguished (celebrated)
  effeminate (having feminine qualities untypical of a man)
  incorrigible (stubborn)
  veiled (hidden)
  castigated (scolded)
  paternalistic (demeaning)
  diatribes (verbal attacks)
  exigencies (demands)

B. Examples:
1. Green was worried about "immoral" thoughts as the whole world watched with anxiety the integration of Central High School, Little Rock, Arkansas.
2. Dwight Washington could attend a revival service and remain quiet. But, once he did what his white leaders told him to do—confess Christ as Savior—he was kicked out.

C. Answers will vary. Here is one example:
In my Southern community, Palmer Green, a man distinguished by his mediocrity and who seemed to be an incorrigible sentimentalist, taught us to cry.

Solve

Answer: 8
½ BH = Area
½ (4) (2 X 4) = 16

Lesson 54

Grammar

Answer: they. Pretend that the sentence is complete. "Did you work as hard as <u>they worked</u>."

Solve

A. $x + y = 72 \qquad x = 24 + y$

   $(24 + y) + y = 72$

   $2y = 48$

   $y = 24$

   $x = 48$

B. xy

C. $\dfrac{30}{4a} = \dfrac{10}{24}$

   $40a = 720$

   $a = 18$

D. $45a = 3825$

   $a = 85$

E. $\dfrac{2225}{25} = a$

   $a = 89$

F. $56(a - 74) = a$

   $56a - 4144 = a$

   $-4144 = -55a$

   $75.345 = a$

G. $\dfrac{61,542}{78} = a$

   $789 = a$

H. $\dfrac{56,833,396}{4562} = a$

   $12,458 = a$

I. $32 + 89 - 67 + 34 \times 212 - 89 + 31 = a$

   $32 + 89 - 67 + (34 \times 212) - 89 + 31 = a$ Do multiplications first, then additions, etc.

   $7,204 = a$

Lesson 55

Solve

A. $x, x + 2, x + 4$

   $x + (x + 4) + 24 = 3(x + 2)$

   $2x + 28 = 3x + 16$

   $22 = x$

   $22, 24, 26$

B. $+4$

Critical Reading

A. Answers will vary. Here is an example: This is a story of a Nepali man whose perseverance, along with a faithful God, brought healing to his wife.

B. Answer: A

Lesson 56

Critical Thinking: Classification

instruments and sewing tools

Grammar

Answer: E.

Solve

    A. $8 + (7 \times 3)2 + 3(12 - 3) = 77$

    B. $50 + 20 + 50 + 20 = 140$ cm

Lesson 57

Vocabulary

    A. stern (rear of ship)

        flourished (waved)

        derision (scorn)

        discomfited (agitated)

    B. Synonyms:

        1. intensify

        2. aspiring

        3. inconsistent

        4. confidential

        5. advocate

        6. misapply

        7. possible

        8. facile

        9. blunt

        10. fortunate

Solve

    Answer: B

Lesson 58

Vocabulary

    interloper (intruder)

    intrudes (forces in or upon)

    smirking (taunting)

    flaunting (brandishing)

    venerable (old, distinguished)

    vicissitudes (uncertainties)

    sustenance (nourishment)

    overshadows (surpasses)

    grasping (clutching)

    torturously (painfully)

Grammar

    Answer: I

Critical Thinking: Summary

    Answers will vary. Example:

    The speaker is exploring the cosmological ambivalent feelings he has about a benevolent God who apparently took his father through death.

Critical Thinking: Literary Devices

    Personification. The pine tree is perceived as a person.

Lesson 59

Critical Reading

Answer: True

Solve

A. Two minutes.

B. 20 (2x - 10)

C. Find its dimensions if the length is 5 feet less than twice the width:
2 (w) + 2 (2w - 5) = w = 45, l = 85

D. BAG fits because all words can begin with the word sand.

Lesson 60

Critical Reading

1. A. The Baroque Sonata

B is too limiting, C is not true, and D is only part of the passage.

2. C. Sonatas were written only for religious purposes.

This statement is false because sonatas were also used to entertain kings.

Solve

Answer: D.

Critical Thinking: Essay

Example:

Move Over Dick Tracy

Comic strip characters of yesteryears would feel at home in today's world. In the 1930s Dick Tracy chased criminals with the help of a watch-sized television/walkie-talkie worn on his wrist much like many of today's photo/cell phones. Buck Rogers jetted around the universe in a space ship. These characters would be quick to join us in using computers, cell phones, palm pilots, e-mail, Web sites and other forms of instant messaging. And golly, gee, there's television.

Today, a computer puts us in touch with the world, principally via the Internet. Web sites of every stripe compete for our attention, or we can create our own. We invest untold hours chasing information and the associated expense of keeping pace with technological innovation. E-mail replaces snail-mail as the letter of choice. No stamps, paper or envelopes to buy. Time saved so we can speed up our surfing. We can do our banking, place orders, play games, watch television, chat with friends and participate in an increasing number of other activities without moving from a chair. Nothing beats being able to do it now. No waiting, no fuss, no bother, just do it.

Print media fight declining circulation and readership as a result of instant messaging. They countered by establishing Web sites, wondering whether business will meet the rising cost of harvesting trees to manufacture paper and of maintaining a staff. Meanwhile, newspaper journalists find themselves challenged to be more accurate, fair and truthful while competing with other voices on television, radio and the Internet who barrage the public with self-serving statements and with opinion that passes for fact.

For decades, newspapers served as the arbiters in separating fact from fiction, the objective report from editorial comment. Instant messaging and the entertaining emphasis in television programming continue to erode the role of the newspaper as society's watchdog over public affairs. Readers who believe that a newspaper is the handmaiden of some political party or some ideology would welcome their demise. An option, of course, is to surf the electronic media, which permits us to live in an uncluttered, non-threatening and simplistic world of our making.

Dick Tracy no longer is a step ahead of other police officers in solving crime. His tools are old hat. He's history. And so are we. Instant messaging reminds us that there's nothing new in the world, not even change. The pace of change rockets by at an ever-increasing tempo, one that would put Buck Rogers and his space ship to shame.

Lesson 61

Vocabulary

querulous (crotchety)
protuberances (bumps)
valise (suitcase)

Solve

A. 1) 88
    2) 582
B. 78 X 2 = 39 X 2 X 2 = 13 X 3 X 2 X 2

Lesson 62

Grammar

Answer: B. *Do you object to my being the…*

Critical Thinking: Classification

A. stones and styles of cooking
B. clothing fasteners and colors

Vocabulary

Answers will vary. Examples are:
A. *super*impose (to place above)
B. *ambi*dextrious (skilled with both hands)
C. *ante*cedent (preceding)
D. *anthropo*logy (the study of man)
E. *arch*rival (principal enemy)
F. *aqua*tic (having to do with water)
G. *aster*isk (starlike symbol)
H. *audi*ence (those who listen)

Solve

A. $40 x .20 = $8 profit
    $40 + $8 = $48.00 price he charged
B. 6 X 8 = $48
C. .3 X 80 = $24. $80 - $24 = $56

Lesson 63

Critical Reading

Answer: D

Sentence Completion

Answer: C

Solve

Pete lost money. He bought one boat for $5000 and sold it for $6000. The other boat he bought for $7500 and sold for $6000. He originally spent $12,500, but on the resale, brought in only $12,000.

Lesson 64

Critical Reading

1. Answers will vary.
2. *Origin of the Species* attacked the teleological basis of Judaism and Christianity.
3. Teleological means exhibiting purpose in nature.
4. God created them that way.
   They are in the evolutionary trail from fish to human being.
5. They were logical and gave people who did not want to believe in biblical creation an opportunity to believe in common sense. Also, just so you know, Darwin's ideas were part of the spirit of the age. At the end of the nineteenth century, philosophers and scientists were suggesting that nature was to be studied without God being mentioned.
6. Answers will vary.
7. Pandora was a Greek figure who opened a box full of all sorts of problems for humankind.

Lesson 65

Sentence Completion
Answer: B

Vocabulary
Synonyms:
1. foster
2. frail
3. futile
4. hamper
5. attend
6. hindrance
7. hostility
8. meek
9. misleading
10. hypothetical
11. exempt
12. handicap
13. neutral
14. imperceptible
15. insinuation

Solve

A. 2, 3, 11
B. Coin tosses are independent events because the result of one toss has no effect on the next toss. So, because the probability of independent events occurring in a designated order is the product of the individual probabilities, the answer is ½ x ½ x ½ = ⅛.
C. Each question is an independent event so the results of one question are unrelated to the previous question. Therefore, the answer is 1/5 (because there are five possibilities on each question).
D. $140y^6 / 28 y^3 = 5y^3$

Lesson 66

Vocabulary
A. *trans*portation
B. *pro*logue

C. *philanthropist*
D. *lunatic*
E. *scrib*ble
F. *bicycle*
G. *un*animous
H. *demo*graphics
I. *geo*graphy
J. *photo*graphy
K. *mega*phone
L. auto*graph*
M. socio*logy*
N. *video*tape
O. *aquarium*

Grammar
Answer: lie

Solve
A. 4.574
B. 5
C. 6.8

Lesson 67

Critical Thinking: Synthesis
Answers will vary, but these Scriptures develop these aspects of Christ's life: His deity, His humanity, and His resurrection. We know that He was the Son of God, but also a man. He was resurrected from the dead, so He was not like any person who ever lived. He was present at Creation and He is the Word.

Critical Reading
A. Answer: D. Monet and the Genesis of Impressionism
   A implies the article is only about Monet; it is about impressionism too. B refers to the technique of impressionism—it is too specific for a title. C is only a small part of the article.
B. Answer: D

Lesson 68

Solve
A. Barney was driving on the wrong side of the road. The cars he passed were going the opposite way!
B.
   1. $20 + 40 + 30 + 30 = 120$
   2. $20 + 40 + 30 + 30 = {}^{120}/_4 = 30$
   3. 333,333
   4. 30

Lesson 69

Critical Reading
1. Answers will vary. Example: This passage argues that government intervention through welfare is one of the major causes of the demise of the urban family.
2. The topic sentence is usually the first sentence.
3. I blame human depravity and the social welfare system for this problem.
4. Answers will vary.

5. Answers will vary. Example: The Runaway Social Welfare System.
6. See the answer to question 1.

Solve

Answer: B

Lesson 70

Grammar

Answer: had thought

Vocabulary

A. sarcastic (mocking)
   incessantly (ceaselessly)
   nerveless (without courage)
   emendation (alteration)
   sarcasm (mockery)
   vitriolic (caustic)
   ennobled (honored)
   exhortations (entreatments)
B. Synonyms:
   1. impetus
   2. incompatibility
   3. accuse
   4. indifferent
   5. persuade
   6. awkward
   7. inevitable
   8. clever
   9. change
   10. intricacy

Solve

A. A bar graph would work to represent the scores.
B. Math = 577.5
   Verbal = 560

Lesson 71

Critical Reading

A.
   1. Answers will vary. Example: Anger and Power in the Study of Race Relations.
      The cause of anger is disappointment in the lack of real progress in U.S. race relations.
   2. A feeling of powerlessness leads to anger.
   3. To compare the newness of anger as a socially acceptable emotion to a culturally established acceptable emotion.
      The origins of racism lie in comparativism.
   4. You will have about 3 minutes on the SAT.
B. Answer: A—The reader sees into the mind of only one character.

Solve

Answer: C

Lesson 72

Solve
Answer: B

Lesson 73

Critical Thinking: Comparison
1. I think so. As surely as Abram left the safety of home and entered a strange new land, likewise adopting an interracial child was a very new thing for me.
2. Rachel joined my entire history. This adoption was not merely an isolated incident. It had ramifications for my whole life.
3. Any time we do something that threatens our worldview we are taking a risk.
4. Answers will vary. A suggested title is The Promise and Risks of New Beginnings. A suggested précis is: Rachel, a new daughter, brought new beginnings to her father.

Lesson 74

Grammar
Answer: Having been wrong

Vocabulary
avowal (admission)
affected (influenced)
debated (argued)
involuntarily (uncontrollably)
countenance (face)

Lesson 75

Critical Reading
Answer: D

Solve
A. $\frac{4}{1} \times \frac{2}{16} = \frac{1}{2}$
B. $35A = \frac{38}{7}$
    $245A = 38$
    $A = \frac{38}{245}$
C. $56A = 6 = \frac{6}{56} = \frac{3}{23}$
D. If the ratio is 4 to 3, divide the total—175—into 7 parts. 175 divided by 7 = 25. Therefore, there are 25 x 4 = 100 dimes and 25 x 3 = 75 nickels.
E. $75 \times .05 = \$3.75$
    $100 \times .10 = \$10.00$
F. 72

Lesson 76

Critical Thinking: Comparison
1. Passage A is identifying the speaker and reflecting on the fact that the second coming of Jesus Christ rarely is mentioned in mainline churches (i.e., Methodist, Presbyterian, and so on vs. non-denominational fellowships). In passage B, Dr. Brueggemann analyzes the need for apocalyptic hope.
2. Answers will vary. An example is: "Whatever we think about the Second Coming, we cannot live without hope…"

3. Hope is necessary for us to remain healthy and strong. Take away hope and we will perish.

   The Second Coming of Christ reminds us that no matter how bad things may be now, in the end Christ and goodness shall reign.

   A history maker is someone who obeys God no matter what.

   History makers are incorrigibly optimistic about the future and uncompromisingly committed to telling the truth no matter how controversial that truth may be.

   "Apocalyptic hope" is a firm belief that ultimate good will triumph over evil.

Critical Thinking: Essay

Example:

The headless horseman

Several members of the seventh grade basketball team crowded into a car with the coach after a game in a nearby town. Even though I suffered a sprained ankle during the game, I scored the winning basket. So, I had reason to rejoice. As we returned home on a rural road that night I volunteered to save the team a few miles of travel by getting out of the car and walking a shortcut to my farm home. As the car pulled away I had second thoughts about my heroic gesture, especially when I remembered that this was the night before Halloween.

Granted, I was a seventh grader, and I no longer believed in ghosts and goblins. I did, however, recall the story of the headless horseman. To bolster my confidence I quickly tallied several attributes in my favor. I was brave, I was enterprising, I was strong and I was a basketball star. No doubt, I could easily trek across a couple of fields, a bridge and through a woods.

Resolute, I climbed over a wire fence and began the shortcut home. As I walked gingerly on my right ankle through the edge of a pasture, I saw dark objects blocking my path. With shortened breath I gingerly advanced. Then one of them snorted, and I ran a few steps before recognizing a neighbor's herd of cows.

Down the hill and over another fence I limped, reviewing my role in the night's game, how I made the winning basket and how the coach had praised me after the game. A wheat field interrupted my reverie. I edged near the fence to avoid trampling too much of the valuable wheat, which rattled as the heads ripe with grain brushed together in my wake. The sound reminded me of a rattlesnake. Step after step I awaited the dread sharp pain of fangs piercing my injured ankle, causing it to swell even larger. A fence loomed ahead, and I raced to reach it.

Now, if I could make it along an old wagon road, across a bridge made of logs and up the hill through the woods, I would be home. The evening stars watched my odyssey in the moonlight as I approached the bridge and saw the foreboding woods ahead. Then I remembered the headless horseman. Would he ride here tonight? Could I outrun horse and rider?

The race against death started a few yards from the bridge. As I bounded across the logs that spanned the creek I could hear what I thought were the pounding feet of a horse behind me and envisioned the eerie form of a man astride the steed, leaning down to grab me. I sprinted up the hill into the woods. At last, I stumbled to a stop, gulping for air and grimacing from the pain of the injured ankle. I had escaped the figments of my imagination, the ghosts and goblins of Halloween. Then I froze. Obscured in the darkness a few steps ahead stood the form of a man. Oh, no, I had lost after all. The headless horseman had dismounted and now threatened to ensnare me. As I stood petrified in the darkened woods, battered, bruised, exhausted and defeated, my father said, "Hello, son, I came to meet you."

Lesson 77

Solve

A. l = w + 10

   2(w) + 2(w + 10) = 380

   4w + 20 = 380

$4w = 360$

$w = 90$ yards

$l = w + 10$

$l = 90 + 10$

$l = 100$

Therefore, width = 90 yards and length = 100 yards.
B. 150 feet
C. $1000 x .10 = $100 profit; .15 x second investment amount = $600 = $4000 second investment; total profit = $700.
D. 84.5 cups at $.65, so the answer would have to be 85 or 84. 565 or 564 cups at $.90.
E. A

Lesson 78

Grammar
Answer: D. Looking is a linking verb and requires the use of an adjective not an adverb.

Solve
A. $35 - \{6 [8 (2a + 9) -7] -8\} = a$

$35 - \{6 [16a + 72 - 7] -8\} = a$

$35 - \{96a + 390 - 8\} = a$

$35 - 96a - 390 + 8 = a$

$-347 = 97a$

$-3.577 = a$
B. $28a + 3 = 1571$

$28a = 1568$

$a = 56$

Sentence Completion
1. A
2. C
3. B

Lesson 79

Vocabulary
mortal (transient)

vanity (vainglory)

abusive (offensive)

authority (influence)

Critical Reading
A. D. I and III only

They did not settle all over the city—they settled in ghettos.
B. C

Lesson 80

Critical Reading
A. Answers will vary. It could be argued that the author is understanding of both Tony and Ellen, showing how anybody can end up in a predicament.
B. wistful (longing)

uncemoniously (unpretentiously)
prestigious (impressive)
rancorous (malicious)
deteriorated (disintegrated)
surrealistic (dream-like)
hue (color)
persevering (persistent)
protruding (extending)
invulnerable (indestructible)

C. Answers will vary, but any or all could be argued.

Lesson 81

Solve

A. Eighteen. Because ten cars are involved, all the bumpers will have been hit except the front one on Charles' car and the back one on the last police car.

B. You get 100 candles from the tallow of the original 1000, plus ten more from the tallow of the 100, plus one more from the tallow of the ten. $100 + 10 + 1 = 111$.

C. $(a + 5)(a-3) =$ $ab - a = 2ab + a$ $33a = 66$
   $a^2 + 2a - 15$ $-2a = ab$ $a = 2$
                              $a = {}^{-ab}/_2$

D. Answer: For polynomials with one variable, this is the highest exponent on the variable.

Vocabulary

Synonyms:
1. addicted
2. nebulous
3. idealist
4. contradiction
5. ubiquitous
6. negativism
7. grouchy
8. humanitarian
9. inactive
10. lie
11. pattern
12. ostentatious
13. compliant
14. revelatory
15. captivating
16. passionate

Lesson 82

Grammar

Answer: really bad

Solve

1. E
2. B
3. A

Lesson 83

Vocabulary

   A. sentinel (guard)
       acuteness (sharpness)
       contagion (the spreading of disease)
       deafening (loud)
       clangorous (cacophonous)
       din (bedlam)

   B. incise
       incompatible
       intervarsity
       scientist
       itinerary
       security

Critical Reading

   Answer: A

Lesson 84

Critical Reading

1. A is decidedly sarcastic. B is more serious.
2. A does not like the book and argues that Gilder stereotypes everything. B doesn't necessarily like the book but is more sympathetic, saying that Gilder opens our eyes to new categories of discussion.
3. Answers will vary. I find A to be more convincing although B's analysis is more balanced.

Solve

   Answer: D.

Lesson 85

Vocabulary

1. C
2. A

Solve

   A. Area: = A + B + C + D
       = 4 + 6 + 84 + 102 = 196
       Perimeter: = 4 + 58 + 3 + 58 + 1 + 1 + 1 = 126

   B. Answer: The expressions + and - are said to be conjugates of each other. Similarly x + bi and x - bi are conjugates.

Lesson 86

Grammar

   Answer: A.

Sentence Completion

1. A
2. C

Lesson 87

Critical Reading
1. sacred (holy)
   subcontracted (hired out)
   wiry (sinewy)
   reticence (shyness)
2. Irony: ironical that I would meet Viola in Pittsburgh. Sarcasm: what Governor Faubus said to Uncle George.
3. Answers will vary, but this is a story of how God in His providence brings two old friends, once separated by race, now connected again for a moment on the streets of Pittsburgh.
4. The tone of this article is serious. My attitude toward Viola is sympathetic.
5. Uncle George would probably see her as just another derelict who got what she deserved.
6. "Stream of consciousness" is a literary technique that allows the reader to see into the mind of a character. Most of this passage is stream of consciousness—I am remembering the past.

Critical Reading
Answer: C

Solve
Answer: A.

Lesson 88

Vocabulary
extempore (off the cuff)
discourses (speeches)
dogmatical (dictatorial)
inculcated (imparted)
zealous (enthusiastic)
partisan (follower)

Solve
A. At 10 pm Mary has traveled 60 miles. At 3 am Mary has traveled 60 miles + (5 hours x 30 miles) = 210 miles. Harry has traveled 210 miles + 50 miles = 260 miles. His speed is 260 miles/5 hours = 52 mph.
B. $45/78$ = .58 and .60 is larger than .58

Lesson 89

Solve
A. Miss Patience simply gave nine of the children a cracker, and the tenth child received the jar with the last cracker in it.
B. Five buses: two will have 34 people, three will have 35 people.
C. Answer: B

Lesson 90

Grammar
Answer: B

Critical Thinking: Facts, Opinions, Inferences
A. opinion
B. I would say that it is a fact; but, actually it is seen as an opinion.

C. opinion
D. opinion
E. fact
F. opinion
G. inference
H. inference
I. opinion (Causation is usually a matter of opinion)
J. opinion (In our society, the Bible is not considered sufficient evidence for a fact; therefore, it is my opinion that it is a fact.)

Lesson 91

Critical Reading
Answer: A

Solve
A. 21. Most people would think there were 42 handshakes, but when A shakes hands with B, B has already shaken hands with A and will not do it again.
B. The nail would be at the same height because trees grow at their tops.

Lesson 92

Solve
1. False
2. True
3. False
4. False
5. False
6. True
7. False
8. True
9. False
10. True

Lesson 93

Critical Thinking: Worldview
Dr. Davis takes a decidedly evangelical view of the issue. Clearly the Bible is the ultimate authority to Dr. Davis. Furthermore, God to Dr. Davis is a loving, but just God. That means that God sanctions, even demands, that wrongs be righted by punishment similar to the infraction. Thus, barring mitigating circumstances, murder should be punished by capital punishment. The author in B has no—what he would call—rigid biblical view. The God in B is a God who loves but does not punish—at least not by killing. In any event, the author in B is unable to grant humankind the prerogative to kill another human being through capital punishment. B skillfully uses Dr. Davis' words to his advantage. B, though, does not share Dr. Davis' high view of Scripture.

Solve
A.
1. $B = 2A$
2. $A = 5B + 3$
3. $A = \frac{8}{B} - 16$
B. Answer: C

C. Answer: D

Lesson 94

Grammar

Answer: invented

Critical Reading

1. harbinger (precursor)
    continuity (progression)
    ubiquitously (pervasive)
    suspicious (distrustful)
    anonymous (unknown)
    citadel (fortress)
    unscrupulous (unrestrained)
    mischievous (prankish)
    eccentric (odd)
    ravaged (severely damaged)
2. "Preserver of continuity" means the bag lady reminded me that some things stay the same. This is not true for much of city life. "Harbinger of hope" means she gave me encouragement by her hopeful feeding of the birds.
3. Answers will vary. An opinion is: "For her work was sacred and important…" A fact would be: "She visited our corner almost every day." An inference is: "But she had no story."
4. No, I am not being critical of homeless people.

Vocabulary

vigorously (powerfully)
absorbing (arresting)
shudder (quake)

Lesson 95

Critical Reading

A. Answers will vary but one title could be "The Cost of Discipleship." If I only had this passage, I would see Jesus as a very demanding leader and a man with vision.
B. Answer: C

Solve

A. $^{94.7}/_{72}$ = 131.53%
B. $^{9}/_{63}$ = $^{1}/_{7}$ = 14.29%
C. $488^{3}/_{7}$

Lesson 96

Critical Thinking: Comparison

A is addressed directly to God. B has God speaking to Isaiah. The metaphors used to describe God are considerably different in each passage. The subject matter, of course, in each passage is different. Both passages present an omnipotent but compassionate image of God. There are other similarities and differences.

Solve

3.6 hours

Lesson 97

Vocabulary

Synonyms:

1. paradox
2. peaceful
3. lying
4. reticence
5. intrusive
6. negativism
7. belligerent
8. pattern
9. showy
10. introduction
11. prophecy
12. hermit
13. contradict
14. disreputable
15. disavow
16. resentment
17. isolation
18. delicious

Solve

A. 4 p.m.—1600 military time
B. 6 p.m. the previous day
C. Yes. ⅚ = 83.3%
D. Answer: D

Lesson 98

Grammar

Answer: effected. Effect as a verb means "to cause to happen."

Vocabulary

lingering (staying)
peasantry (underclass)
benignity (goodwill)
shadowy (vague)
induced (enticed)
recollections (remembrances)
perpetual (ongoing)
phantasm (specter)

Lesson 99

Critical Reading

Answer: B

Solve

Answer: B

Lesson 100

Vocabulary

scandalous (disgraceful)
inveterate (habitual)
discarded (cast-off)
svelte (well-built)

Solve

Answer: A

Lesson 101

Solve

A. $4A + 40 = 120$
$4A = 80$
$A = 20$

B. $2(2A + 50) - 137 = -A$
$4A - 37 = -A$
$-37 = -5A$
$7.4 = A$

C. $A (3) = \frac{1}{3}$
$A = (\frac{1}{3})(\frac{1}{3})$
$A = \frac{1}{9}$

D. $48" \times 12" = 576$ square inches

Lesson 102

Grammar

Answer: among

Vocabulary

complexion (general appearance)
diminutive (small)
intimate (close)
bristles (coarse hair)
comely (handsome)

Solve

A. $2x + 46 = -102$
$2x = -148$
$x = -74$

B. $5x - 84 = -x$
$6x = 84$
$x = 14$

C. $(2x - 13) 3 - 24 = -x$
$6x - 39 - 24 = -x$
$7x = 63$
$x = 9$

D. $(2x - 15) 2 - 10 = -x$
$4x - 30 - 10 = -x$
$4x - 40 = -x$
$-5x = -40$
$x = 8$

Lesson 103

Vocabulary

Antonyms:

ubiquitous—limited
harmonious—discordant
unconquerable—defeatable
immortal—temporal
cosmological—earthly

Critical Reading

Answer: C

Critical Thinking: Comparison

Notice that Luke's version is shorter than Matthew's. Also, Matthew emphasizes concepts that would be familiar to the primarily Jewish Christian Church. Both are careful about using the name of God—something a Jewish person would not do. To name God is to give Him limits. What a wonderful God we serve! He has given us two versions in these two inspired passages.

Lesson One Hundred Four

Vocabulary

Antonyms:

1. reverence—scorn
2. satirize—idolize
3. serenity—confusion
4. shrewd—guileless
5. stagnant—fluid
6. suppress—release
7. taciturn—vivacious
8. versatile—inflexible
9. withold—give
10. sarcasm—sincerity
11. scrutinize—ignore
12. sever—tie
13. skeptical—certain
14. subdued—excited
15. symmetrical—unbalanced
16. vigor—weakness
17. vivacious—taciturn
18. vulnerable—invincible

Solve

Answer: D
$4^4 \times 4^6 = 4^{10}$

Lesson One Hundred Five

Solve

A. 100. Working backward, the answer is easy: 9/10 of 1000 = 900, and 8/9 of 900 = 800, and so on, all the way down to the final answer of one hundred.

B.

1. $14 - 8 = 6$

2. 9 - 8 = 1
3. 12 blue, 4 green

Lesson One Hundred Six

Grammar

Answer: have, had

Critical Thinking: Analysis

1. Internal conflict
2. External conflict
3. Internal conflict
4. External conflict
5. External conflict
6. External conflict
7. Internal conflict
8. External conflict

Solve

A. $-3y = 3x - 6$

$y = -x + 2$

Therefore: $x = 6 + (-x + 2)$

$x = 8 - x$

$2x = 8$

$x = 4$

B. $4 = 6 + y$

$-2 = y$

C. Answer: C

Lesson 107

Vocabulary

faith (belief or complete trust)

improbable (unlikely)

atheist (one who does not believe in God)

rebellion (revolt)

Critical Reading

Answer: C

Solve

A. $\frac{4}{5}$

B. 4.35

Lesson 108

Solve

A.

¾	.75	75%
⅓	.33	33⅓%
$\frac{89}{100}$	.89	89%
$\frac{17}{100}$	.17	17%

B.
1. X(2A - 3Y)
   2XA - 3XY
2. 5 (2 - 4P)
   10 - 20P
3. 3 (X - 2Y)
   3X - 6Y
4. 24x - 6 (3x - 7) = 24
   24x - 18x + 42 = 24
   6x = -18
   x = -3
5. 14 (22 - x) + 34 = 8
   308 - 14x + 34 = 8
   -14x + 342 = 8
   -14x = -334
   x = 23.857
6. 46 = 67 - 3x
   -21 = -3x
   7 = x
C. 2 x 5 x 29

Lesson 109

Vocabulary

Synonyms:
   insightful (perceptive)
   consequences (effects)
   shrewish (mean)
   despicable (despised)
   perceived (seen)
   predictably (as expected)
   debilitated (broken)
   nightmarish (haunting)
   compromise (settlement)
   specters (spirits)
   lurk (wait)
   intolerable (unacceptable)

Critical Reading
1. Answers will vary, but Silent Spring espouses the view of evolution while Genesis 1 and 2 support creation.
2. Ms. Carson is an evolutionist.
3. I would disagree with Ms. Carson's basic assumptions, but I would still answer the question.

Solve
A. 18 x 4 = 72
B. Answer: D. The equation is a prime factor already.

Lesson 110

Grammar

Answer: fewer. Use before a plural noun.

Critical Thinking: Comparison
1. View One is that race should be ignored because the Bible is clear that a person's worth is not determined by his/her race. View Two agrees that a person should not be judged according to his/her race but adds that race cannot and should not be ignored because racism is such a large part of American society. The title is "Black Anger as an Obstacle to Racial Reconciliation."
2. The mutual criteria being considered by both sides are the socio-economic aspects of being black. "Marginality" means to be part of a racial/ethnic group that is consciously separated from mainstream America.
3. Answers will vary.

Solve
Answer: E

Lesson 111

Solve
A. They were all married.
B. 3 cm

Critical Reading
Answer: A

Lesson 112

Solve
A. Use A, A + 2, A + 4 to represent consecutive odd integers.
$A + A + 4 - 9 = A + 2 - 18$
$2A - 5 = A - 16$
$A = -11$
-11, -9, -7 are the three consecutive odd integers.
B. $N^N + N^D = 30$
$5N^N + 10N^D = 210$
$5(30 - N^D) + 10N^D = 210$
$150 - 5N^D + 10N^D = 210$
$5N^D = 60$
$N^D = 12$
Since $N^N + N^D = 30$
Therefore $N^N = 30 - 12 = 18$
Check your answer = 12 dimes = $ 1.20
18 nickels = $ .90
C. X = Original Price of Coat
$X - .32X = \$215$
$.68X = \$215$
$X = \$316.18$
D. $(9/2)\ 826 = 3717$
E. $30/60 = 1/2$
F. $90 + 85 + 77 + 44 + 89 = 385 \div 5 = 77$
G. $34/10 + 6/10 = 4$
H. 6.7

Lesson 113

Vocabulary

stern (rear of ship)
jagged (a sharp, uneven edge)
tiller (steering device that turns the rudder)
rudder (the part that turns the ship)
skiff (small rowboat)

Solve

Answer: F

Lesson 114

Grammar

Answer: emigrate

Critical Thinking: Worldview

1. Naturalism and Deism
2. Christian Theism
3. Naturalism
4. Christian Theism
5. Christian Theism—in this universe sin does not go unpunished! In other parts of the book, Wharton seems to be Naturalistic—as if nature dispassionately punishes those who dare to want to be happy.
6. Existentialism
7. Absurdism

Solve

A. 36
B. Answer: D

Lesson 115

Critical Reading

Answer: B

Solve

lwh = 8 x 6 x 6 = 288

Lesson 116

Critical Thinking: Literary Devices

Some examples from Romans 8 are verses 31 and 33. Other answers will vary.

Solve

A. Four
B. $\frac{5}{8} + \frac{4}{8} = \frac{9}{8} = 1\frac{1}{8}$

Critical Reading

1. A
2. C
3. B

Lesson 117

Solve

    A. $^{-13}/_{-1} = 13$

    B. $^{-1}3/4 + ^{25}/_{11} =$

        $^{-143}/_{44} + ^{100}/_{44} =$

        $^{-43}/_{44}$

    C. $-4 - -4(-3) =$

        $-4 - 12 =$

        -16

    D. $-2 [-3 (-8)(3)]$

        $-2 [24 \times 3]$

        $-2 [72] = -144$

    E. 4%

    F. Answer: Dog = 2; Man = 26

        Man's age now = M

        Dog's age now = D

        Man's age in 10 years = M + 10

        Dog's age in 10 years = D + 10

        M + 10 = 3 (D + 10)

        M = 26; D = 2

Sentence Completion

    Answer: C

Lesson 118

Grammar

    Answer: A

Vocabulary

    Answers will vary. Some examples are:

        chast*ity*, advers*ity*

        rational*ize*, steril*ize*

        pro*ject*ile, inter*ject*ion

        *jur*y, per*jur*y

        *labor*atory, laborious

        *leg*alistic, il*leg*al

        bio*logy*, anthropo*logy*

Critical Thinking: Worldview

    1. Absurdism and Deism

    2. Existentialism

    3. Christian Theism

    4. Answers will vary.

Lesson 119

Vocabulary

    subsequent (succeeding)

    encounter (a chance meeting)

    conclusive (definitive)

    impregnable (impenetrable)

Solve

-7, -6, -3, 0, 3, 8

Lesson 121

Critical Thinking: Analysis

1. It is not present.
2. One major cause of the Church's irrelevance to Western society is that it has not met the needs of modern culture. It is a sufficient cause.
3. The Church has lost influence is a fact; why that exists is an opinion.
4. Whether or not we can demonstrate a community that is countercultural. In other words, how can the Christian community be different in meaningful ways?

Solve

A. $2 + 3 (2 \times 4) =$
   $2 + 3 (8) =$
   $2 + 24 = 26$
B. $45 - 18 (34 + 3) =$
   $45 - 666 = -621$
C. Weigh three and three at the same time. If they balance, the light coin is the one not on the scale. If not, you set aside the heavier three and put one of the lighter three on each side of the scale. Again, if they match, the one left aside is the light coin. If on the second weighing the scales do not balance, you have found the light coin on the lighter side of the scale.
D. $-16/5$ divided by $7/3$ (or $\times 3/7$) $= -48/35$
E. $-3^{5}/_{40} + 1^{24}/_{40}$
   $-2^{45}/_{40} + 1^{24}/_{40}$
   $-1^{21}/_{40}$
F. $3/5 = .60$ which is larger than $.56$
G. $(x - 2/5)^2 = 4$
   $x - 2/5 = 2$
   $x = 2 + 2/5$
   $x = 5/10 + 4/10$
   $x = 9/10$

Lesson 122

Grammar

Answer: but

Solve

A. $68.90
B. 15%
C. 30%

Lesson 123

Vocabulary

inviolate (pure)
precipitately (suddenly and quickly)

Critical Reading

Answer: A

Solve

    A. 5, 6, or 7

    B. Answer: B

Lesson 124

Critical Thinking: Analysis

Answers will vary. One of the fascinating things about modern American thought is its existential bent toward experience. As a culture, we come by it honestly. I traced the beginning of this fascination to a Scottish philosopher named David Hume. Hume suggested that reality is really to be understood in human experience—not necessarily in any outside reality or authority (e.g., the Word of God). In the 1960s the psychologist Eric Erickson continued this tradition. Although the SAT folks are reticent to speak about feelings or experience, they will be part of the hidden agenda of SAT test-taking, and a part of life in a twenty-first century American university. Learn to articulate your feelings without allowing them to make decisions for you.

Solve

Answer: B

Lesson 125

Solve

    A. x = reciprocal of b

        $\frac{2}{5} + x = 2$

        $x = 2 - \frac{2}{5}$

        $x = \frac{10}{5} - \frac{2}{5}$

        $x = \frac{8}{5}$

        $b = \frac{5}{8}$

    B. B = 0

    C. $4(x - 12) = 2(-x) - 90$

        $4x - 48 = -2x - 90$

        $6x = -42$

        $x = -7$

Lesson 126

Vocabulary

obeisance (submission)

pogrom (physical destruction of a group of people)

Grammar

Answer: A. Dangling modifier.

Solve

Fraction	Decimal	Percent
$\frac{13}{20}$	.65	65%
$\frac{7}{10}$	.7	70%
$\frac{5}{4}$	1.25	125%

Lesson 127

Critical Reading

A. The main argument of this passage is that the separation between religious work and social work in the late 1900 evangelical movement does not exist.

B. The author uses primary source letters an other material to support his argument.

C. Revivalism is a form of Protestant Christianity, which emphasizes a privatistic faith joined with an overwhelming urge to share that faith with outsiders.

D. The mainline church leaders differed from the revivalists in that, unlike the revivalists, many mainline churches were preaching a form of populism, health and wealth Gospel.

E. The author does not really believe that Andrew Carnegie was a spiritual giant; this is an example of sarcasm.

F. An explanation of the quote might be: Notwithstanding the argument that there has been a wall between revivalism and social reform, in the late nineteenth century, there was already a natural link that was made stronger. In other words, not only were the revivalist preachers not obstacles to social reform—they themselves were the social reformers!

G. An "evangelical revivalist mind" is a form of conservative, biblical Christianity popular all over America in the late nineteenth century. It was popular with men like D.L. Moody.

Vocabulary

pietistic (religious devotion)
revivalistic (renewing religious interest)
holiness (piety)
innovative (original)
redevelopment (renewal)
profound (all-encompassing)
empathic (based on sensitivity)
unabashedly (without embarrassment)
systemic evil (evil within a societal structure)
congenitally (as born)

Solve

Answer: C

Lesson 128

Critical Thinking: Argument

1. The central argument is: The modern age begins with the assurance that the theory of relativity was indeed true.
2. The author does not employ any fallacious arguing techniques, but he does believe that relativity is evil. And, one wonders if one can really blame all of today's problems on Immanuel Kant!
3. The alternative position is that relativity is good—after all, don't we have to be open minded?
4. Answers will vary.

Lesson 129

Solve

A. 360 kilometers
B. 50 kilometers per hour
C. 9 hours;
9 hours - 6 hours = 3 hours = 180 minutes
D. Answer: ¼

Lesson 130

Vocabulary

cunningly (craftily)
conjectured (guessed)
protracted (drawn out)

Grammar

Answer: D. Avoids awkward shift in verb tense.

Solve

Answer: A

Lesson 131

Critical Reading

A.

1. The author is preparing for a sermon on Saturday night, so he must be a pastor.
2. Karen is his wife.
3. The couple is preparing for Christmas on a small budget.
4. Yes, the writing is sentimental. "Sentimental" means "maudlin" or "mushy." I am evoking all sorts of emotions—motherhood, Christmas, limited income—to affect my reader.
5. Titles will vary.
6. The setting is Christmas in an American pastor's family.
7. There is internal conflict—how do we serve the Lord and still provide for our family?
8. "Vicissitude" means "unpredictable aspects." If one is on the edge financially, or otherwise, one is inordinately vulnerable to the vicissitudes of life.

B. Answer: A

Lesson 132

Solve

A. $^{126}/_{15}$
B. 0.01395
C. $w - \frac{2}{3} = 3\frac{1}{3}$
$w = \frac{2}{3} + 3\frac{1}{3}$
$w = 4$
D. $3\frac{1}{2}a + 2 = 9$
$\frac{7}{2}a = 9 - 2$
$a = 7 \times \frac{2}{7}$
$a = \frac{14}{7}$
$a = 2$

Lesson 133

Critical Thinking: Comparison

1. Answers will vary, but A is in general a celebration of God's magnificent power and B is a powerful admission of anger toward God—both responses are appropriate. I must add, however, that before one judges Jeremiah harshly, one should read other parts of his book. Jeremiah was a great man of God—albeit an honest one too.
2. Answers will vary. But I would see a God who is great enough to create a world but also loving enough to take our honest questions.
3. In my opinion, Daniel was a sort of conservative, straight guy. I see Jeremiah as a more fluid, at times

moody believer. Both visions are important to our own theologies. It is also important to note the stylistic differences between a prophecy (Jeremiah) and a narrative section (Daniel).

Solve

$$\frac{5 \times 10^4}{88.514 \times 10^{-3}} =$$

$$\frac{50,000}{.088514} =$$

56,4882.39

Lesson 134

Grammar

Answers will vary. Here is an example: John Knowles was a master at creating internal struggles with his characters. In A Separate Peace Gene, the protagonist perfect student, struggles with his feelings about his best friend Finny and Gene's alter-ego/ antagonist. Knowles skillfully shows how Gene feels both love and hatred toward Finny.

Critical Thinking: Comparison

Answers will vary, but we know that the Holy Spirit is omnipresent (Psalm 139), one Spirit who is part of the Godhead (1 Corinthians 12). The Spirit can fill a person (Ephesians 5), seal a person (Ephesians 1), and stimulate gifts (1 Corinthians 12). There is paradox in the Holy Spirit: He brings unity and diversity (1 Corinthians 12). And so forth…

Lesson 135

Critical Reading

A.
1. False
2. True
3. False
4. True
5. True

B. Answer: C

Lesson 136

Vocabulary

resolve (purpose)
roused (excited)
silhouette (outline)
eddies (small whirlpools)
vain (useless)
dissipated (scattered)
strained (weakened)
fancies (illusions)

Solve

A. The formula for finding a slope = The difference in Y coordinates over the difference in X coordinates.
So, $\frac{-1 - 0}{-3 - 0} = \frac{1}{3}$

B. length = 2 times width; perimeter = 2 x length + 2 x width;

So, 2 (2w) + 2w = 30

4w + 2w = 30

6w = 30

w= 5

Critical Thinking: Essay

Example:

An American Nightingale

Frances Slager never dreamed of being the subject of a book while surviving childhood in World War I or later while growing up in the United States. Bob Welch didn't dream of such a book either until he learned about this unique woman while writing one of his regular columns for The Register-Guard daily newspaper in Eugene, Oregon. More than three years later, the book appeared and should please anyone who reads this account of the first American nurse to die in combat during World War II.

American Nightingale, which was published in 2004 by Atria Books, is the story of a heroine of Normandy who was largely forgotten until the book appeared. Slager, who fancied herself as an author, wrote a letter to Stars and Stripes, a military newspaper, praising soldiers, many of whom she helped treat as a nurse during the summer of 1944. Her letter struck a chord in the hearts of hundreds of readers who were touched by her humility and patriotism. Unfortunately, Slager was killed the day after she sent the letter when German troops shelled her field hospital.

Other compelling facets of this unique woman's life appear in Welch's well-organized narrative, one that moves smoothly from past to present and back again through the artful use of flashback. One story focuses on Slager, a Jewish girl who survived World War I in Poland and moved to the United States when she was 7. The family lived in Boston where Slager helped her father, a fruit vender. They lived in near poverty, but Slager religiously wrote about her dreams of a better life.

Slager defied convention in numerous ways. She refused to let poverty defeat her. She chose a nursing career and was accepted into nursing school against great odds. She graduated from Boston City Hospital in 1937 and was praised for her heartfelt concern for patients. The odds were even greater against her being admitted to a combat field unit that was shipped out of England to Normandy into battle.

In his 308-page hardcover book, Welch paints action-filled word pictures that bring the rigors of front-line combat action to life. He writes: "Onward the nurses trudged, wet clothes matted to their bodies. Too-large boots squished with salt water. Foot blisters formed, then popped and chaffed. The brackish smell of sea and diesel gave way to plain diesel, with occasional whiffs of dead bodies that Graves Registration hadn't gotten to."

The significance of Slager's story is underscored in the "afterword" section of the book and offers a reason why the book should experience a long shelf life. In September 2001, Welch visited Normandy while researching the book and tells about viewing the now placid and serene coast. While he was questioning "the relevance of the book about a World War II nurse who had died nearly six decades ago," he was informed about that day's attack on New York City, an event now referred to as 9/11.

Lesson 137

Critical Reading

1. D

2. A

Solve

A. Answer: A

B. Answer: D

Lesson 138

Grammar
Answer: Gus's

Solve
1. May, year 1, August, year 1, and February, year 2.
2. Between January and February, year 2
3. The first six months average is 2.58. The next six months average is 3.08.

Critical Thinking: Worldview
Both are egocentric existentialism.

Lesson 139

Critical Reading
A.
1. Christian Theist. Bunyan has created an allegory of the Christian life.
2. An allegory is a story that uses fictional characters and actions to symbolize truths about human nature. Bunyan's allegory is an effective portrayal of biblical theology in a non-threatening way. It is less subtle than most allegories.
3. The theme of Exodus (Exodus 3 ff) and Abraham's Journey (Genesis 12).

B. Answer: B

Vocabulary
tempting (enticing)
foiled (hindered)

Solve
A. 270%
B. ⅚ is equal to .8333.

Lesson 140

Solve
1. 24
2. 600 miles
3.
4. $1 + $3 = $4 cost for first seven pounds. $10 - $4 = $6 cost for all pounds over seven pounds divided by .25 = 24 pounds + 7 pounds = 31 pounds total
5. Answer: A

Lesson 141

Solve
A.
1. Line A: 1.5 inches; Line B: 2 inches; Line C: 4 inches; Line D: 1.75
   Average length: 2.3125
2. C in feet: $\frac{4}{12} = \frac{1}{3}$ foot
   Total length in feet: $\frac{9\frac{1}{4}}{12} = \frac{\frac{37}{4}}{12} = \frac{37}{48} = .77$
3. 4 - 1.5 = 2.5

B. Answer: C

Lesson 142

Grammar
Answer: stationery

Critical Thinking: Argument
1. Cities and city churches are in trouble.
2. One assumption is that city churches and cities are connected. Therefore, if cities are declining so are city churches. A counter assumption would be that they simply are not connected. To support that argument one would only have to point to thriving downtown churches in declining cities.
3. Bridgeport, Connecticut may be a fair representation of American cities; it may be too small.

Lesson 143

Critical Thinking: Argument
A. By 1600, notwithstanding European interpretations, Native Americans had an advanced culture. The author develops his argument by offering evidence that cities and societies existed that were very sophisticated.
B. Answers will vary, but you might have another interpretation of Native Americans. As a matter of fact, severe cruelty and violence were endemic to several Native American cultures.
C. The author's comparison of the Thirty Years War to the formation of the Iroquois Nation is not really a fair comparison. At the same time the Thirty Years War was occurring, Mozart was writing his marvelous operas. The author felt a need to denigrate European culture to enhance Native American culture. This technique—called dialecticism—is a frequent technique employed by debaters.
D. You could simply offer examples to show when they were not peaceful.

Critical Reading
Answer: A

Lesson 144

Critical Thinking: Analysis
Because I assume that you accept my basic assumptions (this is unabashedly a Christian statement), I am not arguing my viewpoint—the tone is not argumentative.

Solve
A. AC - AB = BC; therefore, $9\frac{3}{4}$ - $8\frac{2}{3}$ = $9\frac{9}{12}$ - $8\frac{8}{12}$ = $1\frac{1}{12}$ inches
B. Answer: E
C. Answer: D

Lesson 145

Solve
A. Green lettuce cost $\frac{80}{16}$ per ounce or 5 cents/ounce. Red lettuce cost $\frac{72}{12}$ or 6 cents/ounce. Green lettuce was the best buy.
B. 2
C. E

Lesson 146

Vocabulary
platitudes (clichés)

Grammar

Answer: C

Solve

Determine the value of each side. Then, add all the sides.

$10 + 10 + 5 + 30 + 5 + 10 + 10 + 50 = 130$

Lesson 147

Vocabulary

junctures (joint or connection)
debris (scattered remains)
mottled (blotchy)
recumbent (prone)
skittering (quick moving)

Critical Reading

Answer: A

Solve

A. .0177954
B. $C = 2\pi r = 6\ (2)$ x $3.14 = 37.68$ inches
C. 0.0001506
D. $^{28}/_3$ x $^2/_7 = ^8/_3$
E. $^{80}/_9 = 8^8/_9$

Lesson 148

Solve

A. The storm is about four miles away.
B. 8.5 x 16 = 136 ounces
C. $(-6) - (-9) = 3$

Lesson 149

Critical Thinking: Comparison

1. The obituary from 1889 is concerned about character and quality issues more than the obituary from 1996.
2. The differences tell us that the value of a person in 1889 was tied more to empathic criteria. A person was valued by what he accomplished in his church and family more than his job. The similarities tell us that death was understood as an important event in both eras. The first article tells us that in our atomistic society, individual achievement is valued more than corporate responsibility.
3. Obituary A portrays the most bias.

Solve

A. Answer: $x^2 = y^2$
B. Answer: E

Lesson 150

Grammar

Answer: South. It refers to a specific region of the United States.

Critical Thinking: Comparison

Answers will vary, but both Caulfield and Buechner emphasize that God is a "mystery." Caulfield's view would be a more orthodox view; Buechner opts for a more informal view.

Solve

A. Any even number is divisible by 2. So 2 is a divisor of 6, 32, and 3020.

The numbers that are divisible by 5 are those that have either a 5 or 0 as their last digit. 3020 is the only number in this group that is divisible by 5.

To be divisible by 10, the last digit must be 0. Thus 3020 is the only number that is divisible by 10.

To find if a number is divisible by 3 (or 9), add the digits in the number. If they equal a number divisible by 3, then the number is divisible by 3. Thus, 99 and 6 are the right answers.

B. Answer: D

Because the SAT is essentially a vocabulary and reasoning test you should work at developing your vocabulary. One way to do this is to keep vocabulary cards. When you encounter a new word, try to determine its definition from its use in the sentence. Then, look up the word in the dictionary to see if you were correct. Using 3 by 5-inch cards, write the new word on one side and the dictionary definition with the sentence showing its context on the back. These cards will be a quick way to help you increase your vocabulary for the SAT and will be useful throughout your college career.

At first, you will find this exercise to be very cumbersome. As time goes on and your 3 by 5-inch card stack grows taller, you will see that your vocabulary will grow, too, and it will not be necessary to look up as many words. At the same time, you must use these words in your spoken vocabulary twice a day for several days or you will forget them. Every Friday your parent or guardian or a friend can quiz you on the words you listed during the week.

A typical vocabulary card might look like the following:

pejorative	having negative connotations; tending to disparage or belittle "The man did not appreciate the pejorative comment."

Remember: The primary purpose of this exercise is not to enhance achievement scores or increase knowledge of literature. The purpose is to help you increase your reading speed, improve your comprehension level, and to increase your vocabulary.

Book List

The following list represents a fairly comprehensive cross-section of good literature—books, poems, and plays. There are hundreds of other pieces of literature that might be as good. Ask your parents and teachers for suggestions. These particular selections were chosen because a.) their vocabulary is challenging, b.) they will help you in college, and c.) they are interesting to read. Some of them are relatively easy to read, e.g., *The Adventures of Huckleberry Finn*, by Mark Twain. Others are easier than you think, like *War and Peace*, by Leo Tolstoy. And others are really difficult but good for you, such as *Of Human Bondage*, by Somerset Maugham. So…start reading and increase your vocabulary!

Freshmen and Sophomores

Austen, Jane

Emma

Emma Woodhouse is one of Austen's most memorable heroines: "Handsome, clever, and rich" as well as self-assured, she believes herself immune to romance, and wreaks amusing havoc in the lives of those around her. A humorous coming-of-age story about a woman seeking her true nature and finding true love in the process.

Sense and Sensibility

Sense and Sensibility tells the story of the impoverished Dashwood sisters who share the pangs of tragic love. Elinor, practical and conventional, is the perfection of sense. Marianne, emotional and sentimental, is the embodiment of sensibility. Their mutual suffering brings a closer understanding between the two sisters—and true love finally triumphs when sense gives way to sensibility and sensibility gives way to sense. Austen's first novel is a lively tale that deftly explores the tensions that exist in society that force people to be at once very private and very sociable.

Bolt, Robert

A Man for All Seasons

Bolt's classic play is a dramatization of the life of Sir Thomas More, the Catholic saint beheaded by Henry VIII at the birth of the Church of England. More refused to acknowledge the supremacy of England's king over all foreign sovereigns; he was imprisoned then executed in 1535. This is a compelling portrait of a courageous man who died for his convictions.

Bonhoeffer, Dietrich

The Cost of Discipleship

Bonhoeffer pulls no punches as he relates the Scriptures to real life and expounds upon the teachings of Jesus. He plainly teaches that there is a cost to following in the footsteps of Christ, just as Christ himself taught that Christ must be first and there is no compromise. This work is so intense that even Dietrich himself, later in life, wondered if he had been too blunt.

Bronte, Charlotte

Jane Eyre

Jane Eyre tells the story of a proud young woman and her journey from an orphanage to her role as governess in the Rochester household. A heartbreaking love story that is also full of mystery and drama: fires, storms, attempted murder, and a mad wife conveniently stashed away in the attic.

Buck, Pearl

The Good Earth

The Good Earth depicts peasant life in China in the 1920s—a time before the vast political and social upheavals transformed an essentially agrarian country into a world power. Buck traces the whole cycle of life—its terrors, its passions, its ambitions, and rewards—by combining descriptions of marriage, parenthood, and complex human emotions with depictions of Chinese reverence for the land and for a specific way of life.

Bulfinch, Thomas

The Age of Fable

Love, jealousy, hatred, passion—the full range of human emotions were experienced by the gods and goddesses of ancient Greece. This is a brilliant reconstruction of the traditional myths which form the backbone of Western culture, including those of ancient Greece and Rome that form a great and timeless literature of the past.

Bunyan, John

Pilgrim's Progress

The pilgrim Christian undertakes the dangerous journey to the Celestial City, experiencing physical and spiritual obstacles along the way. *The Pilgrim's Progress* captures all of the treacherous dangers and triumphant victories we encounter as we live the Christian life.

Carson, Rachel

Silent Spring

Silent Spring offered the first shattering look at widespread ecological degradation and touched off an environmental awareness that still exists. Carson's book focused on the poisons from insecticides, weed killers, and other common products as well as the use of sprays in agriculture, a practice that led to dangerous chemicals in the food source. Presented with thorough documentation, the book opened more than a few eyes about the dangers of the modern world and stands today as a landmark work.

Burdick, Eugene

Fail-Safe

Fail-Safe is a classic novel of the cold war and the limits we face. Although rather faint and shallow by today's techno-thriller standards, Fail-safe was for its day, THE story of the world on the edge of nuclear war. This is a good example of a best seller from the cold war crazy early sixties.

Christie, Agatha

And Then There Were None

Christie's mystery novel is the story of ten strangers, each lured to Indian Island by a mysterious host. Once his guests have arrived, the host accuses each person of murder. Unable to leave the island, the guests begin to share their darkest secrets of their past, and then, one by one, they begin to die.

Coleridge, Samuel

The Rime of the Ancient Mariner

One of the nineteenth century's most enduring narrative poems, *The Rime of the Ancient Mariner* has also been deemed one of the greatest of all English literary ballads. It is a strange and gripping tale of the ancient mariner who killed the friendly albatross and thereby committed an offense against nature—a ghostly adventure, of terror, retribution, and penance.

Conrad, Joseph

Heart of Darkness

This story reflects the physical and psychological shock Conrad himself experienced in 1890, when he worked briefly in the Belgian Congo. Compelling, exotic, suspenseful and far more than just an adventure story, this vivid picture of the moral deterioration and reversion to savagery resulting from prolonged isolation explores deep into the dark heart of its characters' souls.

Lord Jim

Conrad explores in great depth the perplexing, ambiguous problem of lost honor and guilt, expiation and heroism. The title character is a man haunted by guilt over an act of cowardice. He becomes an agent at an isolated East Indian trading post, where his feelings of inadequacy and responsibility are played out to their logical and inevitable end.

Cooper, James F.

The Last of the Mohicans

Hawkeye (Natty Bumpo) and his Mohican Indian friend, Chingachgook, share the solitude and sublimity of the wilderness until the savageries of the French and Indian War force them out of exile. They agree to guide two sisters in search of their father through hostile Indian country. Cooper incorporates massacres and raids, innocent settlers, hardened soldiers, and renegade Indians into his classic tale of romance and adventure.

The Deerslayer

A fine combination of romance, adventure, and morality, *The Deerslayer* follows the adventures of the brave and bold frontiersman, Natty Bumpo. The deadly crack of a long rifle and the piercing cries of Indians on the warpath shatter the serenity of beautiful lake Glimmerglass. Danger has invaded the vast forests of upper New York State as Deerslayer and his loyal Mohican friend Chingachgook attempt the daring rescue of an Indian maiden imprisoned in a Huron camp.

Crane, Stephen

The Red Badge of Courage

Crane vividly conveys the terror of battle and the slow-motion torrent of emotions pouring through soldiers under fire through the struggles of a raw recruit, Henry Fleming. Fleming simultaneously lusts for a glorious battle, and worries endlessly about the possibility of his own cowardice. When he finally comes face to face with slaughter, his romantic notions are stripped away as he witnesses brutal deaths and senseless maneuvers.

Day, Clarence

Life with Father

For everyone who has ever had a father.... This is a hilarious book about family life that will make everyone laugh out loud. It was first published by chapters in periodicals, and later produced as a Broadway play and a movie.

Defoe, Daniel

Robinson Crusoe

The first and greatest shipwreck/desert island story ever told, *Robinson Crusoe* is a unique fictional blending of the traditions of Puritan spiritual autobiography with an insistent scrutiny of the nature of men and women as social creatures, and it reveals an extraordinary ability to invent a sustaining modern myth. The title character leaves his comfortable middle-class home in England to go to sea. Surviving shipwreck, he lives on an island for twenty-eight years, alone for most of the time until he saves the life of a savage—an outcast Polynesian man whom he names Friday.

Dickens, Charles

Great Expectations

Pip, an orphan growing up in Victorian England, is a blacksmith's apprentice who dreams of a better life. Given the means to become a gentleman by an unknown benefactor, he learns from a dangerous escaped convict, a wealthy old woman, and a secret guardian that outward appearances can be deceiving. A mysterious tale of dreams and heartbreak, *Great Expectations* is widely regarded as one of Dickens' greatest novels.

Oliver Twist

This story of a street boy on the run is an archetypal adventure. Written shortly after adoption of the Poor Law of 1834, which halted government payments to the poor unless they entered workhouses, *Oliver Twist* used the tale of a friendless child as a vehicle for social criticism. While the novel is Victorian in its emotional appeal, it is decidedly unsentimental in its depiction of poverty and the criminal underworld, especially in its portrayal of the cruel Bill Sikes.

Nicholas Nickleby

This melodramatic novel tells the story of young Nickleby's adventures as he struggles to seek his fortune in Victorian England. Dependent on the so-called benevolence of his Uncle Ralph, Nicholas is thrust into the world to care for his mother and sister. Circumstances force Nicholas to enter the nightmarish world of Dotheboys Hall, a school run by the malevolent Wackford Squeers. Comic events are interspersed with Dickens' moving indictment of society's ill treatment of children and the cruelty of the educational system; Yet, with his extraordinary gift for social satire, Dickens gives us a light-hearted tale in which goodness and joy easily defeat the forces of evil.

A Tale of Two Cities

Set in the late eighteenth century against the violent upheaval of the French Revolution, this complex story involves one man's sacrifice of his own life on behalf of his friends. While political events drive the story, Dickens takes a decidedly antipolitical tone, lambasting both aristocratic tyranny and revolutionary excess—the latter memorably caricatured in Madame Defarge, who knits beside the guillotine. *A Tale of Two Cities* underscores many of Dickens' enduring themes—imprisonment, injustice, and social anarchy, resurrection and the renunciation that fosters renewal.

Doyle, Arthur C.

The Adventures of Sherlock Holmes

Sherlock Holmes, master of deductive reasoning, and his sidekick, Dr. Watson, solve four classic cases. "A Scandal in Bohemia" finds the sleuth committing a crime of his own to protect a royal reputation. Then, in "A Case of Identity," Holmes must unmask a devious disguise to trace a missing person. "The Red-Headed League" and "The Boscombe Valley Mystery" round out a quartet of diabolical deceptions sure to enthrall readers.

Dumas, Alexandre

The Three Musketeers

A historical romance, *The Three Musketeers* relates the adventures of four fictional swashbuckling heroes who lived during the reigns of the French kings Louis XIII and Louis XIV. The young and headstrong d'Artagnan, having proven his bravery by dueling with each, becomes a friend of Athos, Porthos, and Aramis, members of the King's Musketeers. He is in love with Constance Bonancieux and, at her urging, he and his friends head for England to reclaim two diamond studs that the Queen has imprudently given to her lover, the Duke of Buckingham.

Eliot, George

Silas Marner

Silas Marner is a friendless weaver who cares only for his cache of gold. After being wrongly accused of a heinous theft and secluding himself, he is ultimately redeemed through his love for Eppie, an abandoned golden-haired baby girl who mysteriously appears at his cottage.

Eliot, T.S.

Murder in the Cathedral

Eliot's dramatization in verse of the murder of Thomas Becket at Canterbury was written for the Canterbury Festival of 1935. Like Greek drama, its theme and form are rooted in religion and ritual, purgation and renewal. It is a return to the earliest sources of drama.

Fitzgerald, F. Scott

The Great Gatsby

The Great Gatsby offers a very human story about a man torn between the various pressures of life: conformity and individualism, facade and substance. Nick is a silent narrator, but he is also a participant as he wades through an insane and typical world, an outsider and a member. Fitzgerald makes no judgement of morality, grace, or sin, nor does he favor idealism or cynicism.

Tender Is the Night

Fitzgerald's classic story of psychological disintegration is a powerful and moving depiction of the human frailties that affect privileged and ordinary people alike. The world has recently fallen to pieces in what has become known as the Great War. Consequently, most of the characters are falling to pieces, too. Hints about this are to be found everywhere in the book, although Fitzgerald, with his knack for writing about the complicated nature of humans, often hides them in subtle ways.

This Side of Paradise

This Side of Paradise tells the story of Amory Blaine in his adolescence and undergraduate days at Princeton. Largely autobiographical, this classic novel of youth and alienation was written with a grace that captures the essence of an American generation struggling to define itself in the aftermath of World War I and the destruction of "the old order."

Foxe, John

Foxe's Book of Martyrs

Foxe recounts the lives, suffering, and triumphant deaths of Christian martyrs throughout history with a sense of immediacy and insight into suffering that few church historians can match. Beginning with the first martyr, Jesus Christ, the book also focuses on such men as John Wyclyffe, William Tyndale, and Martin Luther, and it is an exceptional historical record tracing the roots of religious persecution.

Frank, Anne

The Diary of a Young Girl

In 1942, with Nazis occupying Holland, a thirteen-year-old Jewish girl and her family fled their home in Amsterdam and went into hiding. Cut off from the outside world for two years, they faced hunger, boredom, the constant cruelties of living in confined quarters, and the ever-present threat of discovery and death. In her diary, Anne Frank recorded vivid impressions of her experiences during this period. It is a powerful reminder of the horrors of war and an eloquent testament to the human spirit. By turns thoughtful, moving, and amusing, her account offers a fascinating commentary on human courage and frailty and a compelling self-portrait of a sensitive and spirited young woman whose promise was tragically cut short.

Franklin, Benjamin

Autobiography

One of our most inspiring Americans comes to life in this autobiography. Written as a letter to his son, Franklin's account of his life from his childhood in Boston to his years in Philadelphia ends in 1757 with his first mission to England.

Gibson, William

The Miracle Worker

This is the inspiring story of Helen Keller and her teacher, Anne Sullivan—The Miracle Worker. Deaf, blind, and mute twelve-year-old Helen was like a wild animal. Scared out of her wits but still murderously strong, she clawed and struggled against all who tried to help her. Half-blind herself but blessed with fanatical dedication, Annie began a titanic struggle to release the young girl from the terrifying prison of eternal darkness and silence.

Goldsmith, Oliver

The Vicar of Wakefield

This story, a portrait of village life, is narrated by Dr. Primrose, the title character, whose family endures many trials—including the loss of most of their money, the seduction of one daughter, the destruction of their home by fire, and the vicar's incarceration—before all is put right in the end. The novel's idealization of rural life, sentimental moralizing, and melodramatic incidents are countered by a sharp but good-natured irony.

Hawthorne, Nathaniel

The Scarlet Letter

The Scarlet Letter is set in a village in Puritan New England. Hester Prynne, a young woman who has borne an illegitimate child, believes herself a widow, but her husband, Roger Chillingworth, returns to New England very much alive and conceals his identity. He finds his wife forced to wear the scarlet letter A on her dress as punishment for her adultery, and becomes obsessed with finding the identity of his wife's former lover. Hawthorne's greatest novel is a philosophical exploration that delves into guilt and touches upon notions of redemption.

The House of Seven Gables

Set in mid-nineteenth-century Salem, Massachusetts, Hawthorne's gothic masterpiece is a somber study in hereditary sin. It is based on the legend of a curse pronounced on Hawthorne's own family by a woman condemned to death during the infamous Salem witchcraft trials. The greed and arrogant pride of the novel's Pyncheon family through the generations is mirrored in the gloomy decay of their seven-gabled mansion, in which the family's enfeebled and impoverished relations live.

Hemingway, Ernest

A Farewell to Arms

While serving with the Italian ambulance service during World War I, an American lieutenant falls in love with an English nurse who tends him after he is wounded on the Italian front. He deserts during the Italians' retreat after the Battle of Caporetto, and the reunited couple flee into Switzerland. By turns romantic and harshly realistic, Hemingway's story of romance set against the brutality and confusion of World War I is full of disillusionment and heartbreak.

For Whom the Bell Tolls

For Whom the Bell Tolls tells the story of an American in the Spanish War. Robert Jordan has drawn the assignment of blowing up a bridge, but as he flees, a shell explodes, toppling his horse and breaking the soldier's legs. Thus, Jordan not only faces the loss of his life but the loss of his love for Maria, a woman he met and fell for during his mountain tour of duty.

The Old Man and the Sea

The Old Man and the Sea tells a triumphant yet tragic story of an old Cuban fisherman and his relentless, agonizing battle with a giant marlin far out in the Gulf Stream. In this short novel, Hemingway combines the simplicity of a fable, the significance of a parable, and the drama of an epic.

The Sun Also Rises

Set in the 1920s, Hemingway's novel deals with a group of aimless expatriates in the cafes of Paris and the bullrings of Spain. They are members of the cynical and disillusioned post-World War I Lost Generation, many of whom suffer psychological and physical wounds as a result of the war. Friendship, stoicism, and natural grace under pressure are offered as the values that matter in an otherwise amoral and often senseless world.

Heyerdahl, Thor

Kon-Tiki

Heyerdahl had heard of a mythical Polynesian hero, Kon-Tiki, who had migrated to the islands from the east. Further investigation led the scientist to believe that the story of the migration of a people across thousands of miles of the Pacific was fact, not a myth, and he decided to duplicate the legendary voyage to prove its accuracy. Limiting himself to a balsa log raft, *Kon-Tiki* is the record of his outrageous and daring expedition.

Hilton, James

Lost Horizon

Hilton's haunting novel takes place in Shangri-La, the valley of enchantment. Amid the towering peaks of the Himalayas, Conway could think only of his crashed plane and the home he might never see again. He couldn't fully realize that he was soon to enter a world of love and peace as no Westerner had ever known.

Goodbye, Mr. Chips

Full of enthusiasm, young English schoolmaster Mr. Chipping came to teach at Brookfield in 1870. It was a time when dignity and a generosity of spirit still existed, and the dedicated new schoolmaster expressed these beliefs to his rowdy students. Nicknamed Mr. Chips, this gentle and caring man helped shape the lives of generation after generation of boys.

Homer

The Odyssey

Odysseus wants to go home. But Poseidon, god of oceans, doesn't want him to make it back across the wine-dark sea to his wife Penelope, son Telemachus, and their high-roofed home at Ithaca. This is the story in Homer's epic poem written 2,700 years ago. *The Odyssey* is a gripping read.

The Iliad

Although typically described as one of the greatest war stories of all time, to say the Iliad is a war story does not begin to describe the emotional sweep of its action and characters: Achilles, Helen, Hector, and other heroes of Greek myth. The Iliad is one of the two great epics of Homer and reveals the history of the tenth and final year of the Greek siege of Troy.

Hudson, W.H.

Green Mansions

An exotic romance set in the jungles of South America, the story is narrated by a man named Abel who as a young man had lived among the Indians. Abel falls in love with Rima, a girl of a magnificent and mystical race, and is led to discover the greatest joy—as well as the darkest despair.

Hugo, Victor

Les Misérables

Set largely in Paris during the politically explosive 1820s and 1830s, this epic follows the life of the former criminal Jean Valjean—an outcast of society—and his unjust imprisonment. Valjean has repented his crimes, but is nevertheless hounded by his nemesis, the police detective Javert. Les Misérables is at once a tense thriller, an epic portrayal of the nineteenth-century French citizenry, and a vital drama of the redemption of one human being. Hugo achieved the rare imaginative resonance that allows a work of art to transcend its genre.

The Hunchback of Notre Dame

Hugo's haunting and tumultuous tale of the horribly deformed bell-ringer, Quasimodo, unfolds in the shadow of Notre Dame cathedral. The hunchback falls hopelessly in love with the beautiful gypsy girl, Esmerelda, and after rescuing her both from hanging and the evil archdeacon Dom Frollo, he reunites her with her mother.

Irving, Washington

The Sketch Book

The Sketch Book is a collection of short stories, most of them based on folklore. Of these, the tales The Legend of Sleepy Hollow and Rip Van Winkle are the most famous, both of which are Americanized versions of German folktales. In addition to the stories based on folklore, the collection contains travel sketches and literary essays.

Johnson, Paul

Modern Times: The World from the Twenties to the Nineties

This history explores the events, ideas, and personalities of the seven decades since the First World War. It is a superb discussion of the most relevant aspects of the twentieth century—including good discussions on the beginnings of the Soviet Union and its close cousin Nazism, Peronism in Argentina and how it destroyed that prosperous country, and the devastation of the third world by the collectivist ideologues.

Kipling, Rudyard

Captains Courageous

This novel of maritime adventure takes place on the *We're Here*, a small fishing boat whose crew members rescue the son of a multi-millionaire, Harvey Cheyne, when he is washed overboard from an ocean liner. The captain refuses to take him back to port and instead makes Harvey a member of the crew, where he quickly learns respect, toughness, and gratitude—and inspires the audience to do the same.

Kim

Kim is an orphan, living from hand to mouth in the teeming streets of Lahore. One day he meets a man quite unlike anything in his wide experience, a Tibetan lama on a quest. Kim's life suddenly acquires meaning and purpose as he becomes the lama's guide and protector—his chela. Other forces are at work as Kim is sucked into the intrigue of the Great Game and travels the Grand Trunk Road with his lama. How Kim and the lama meet their respective destinies on the road and in the mountains of India forms a compelling adventure tale.

Knowles, John

A Separate Peace

Knowles' beloved classic is a story of friendship, treachery, and the confusions of adolescence. Looking back to his youth, Gene Forrester reflects on his life as a student at Devon School in New Hampshire in 1942. Although he is an excellent student, he envies the athleticism and vitality of his friend Finny. Unable to cope with this insecurity, Forrester causes Finny to break his leg, sabotaging his athletic career. *A Separate Peace* looks at this tragic accident involving the two young men and how it forever tarnishes their innocence.

Lewis, C.S.

The Chronicles of Narnia

Lewis's mystical tale of adventure takes the reader on an extraordinary journey to far-off lands. *The Chronicles of Narnia* consists of seven books: *The Magician's Nephew*; *The Lion, the Witch, and the Wardrobe*; *The Horse and His Boy*; *Prince Caspian*; *The Voyage of the "Dawn Treader"*; *The Silver Chair*; and *The Last Battle*. An allegorical saga great for all ages.

The Screwtape Letters

Written in defense of Christian faith, this popular satire consists of a series of thirty-one letters in which Screwtape, an experienced devil, instructs his young charge, Wormwood, in the art of temptation. Confounded by church doctrines and a faithful Christian woman, their efforts are defeated when their subject—a World War II pilot—dies in a bombing raid with his soul at peace. *The Screwtape Letters* is a classic treatise on a human nature that is as old as the world. Through his satiric use of the demonic narrative persona, Lewis examines the opposing sides in the battle between good and evil.

Mere Christianity

In 1943 Great Britain, when hope and the moral fabric of society were threatened by the relentless inhumanity of global war, an Oxford don was invited to give a series of radio lectures addressing the central issues of Christianity. *Mere Christianity* never flinches as it sets out a rational basis for Christianity and builds an edifice of compassionate morality atop this foundation. As Lewis clearly demonstrates, Christianity is not a religion of flitting angels and blind faith, but of free will, an innate sense of justice and the grace of God. Lewis' lucid apologetics will challenge the faithful and convince those who have not previously heard the Gospel.

Llewellyn, Richard

How Green Was My Valley

In this nostalgic tale of a young man's coming-of-age, the Morgan family experiences the simple, vital pleasures of life in the coal fields of south Wales in the late 1800s. However, industrial capitalism takes its toll on the family and community. The Morgan boys are driven from their family home because of the stresses and wild cycles of early industrialism, and the town, once a community of friends, gradually becomes a mean, brutal place. Llewellyn looks critically at industrial capitalism from a conservative point of view.

London, Jack

The Call of the Wild

In his classic survival story of Buck, a courageous dog fighting for survival in the Alaskan wilderness, London vividly evokes the harsh and frozen Yukon during the Gold Rush. As Buck is ripped from his pampered, domestic surroundings and shipped to Alaska to be a sled dog, his primitive, wolflike nature begins to emerge. Savage struggles and timeless bonds between man, dog, and wilderness are played to their heartrending extremes, as Buck undertakes a journey that transforms him into the legendary "Ghost Dog" of the Klondike.

White Fang

White Fang is a wolf dog, the offspring of an Indian dog and a wolf, alone in the savage world of the desolate, frozen wilds of the Yukon territory. Weedon Scott rescues the fiercely independent dog from a cruel, ignorant master, training him to be a loving companion. When an escaped convict threatens violence, a savage beast transformed by human kindness must confront a man brutalized by society.

MacDonald, George

The Curate's Awakening

Originally published as Thomas Wingfold, Curate in 1876, MacDonald's tale is retold for today's readers in The Curate's Awakening. MacDonald masterfully weaves together an old abandoned house, a frightened young fugitive, a tragic murder, and a sister's love, as the Curate's confidence and faith are shaken.

Malory, Sir Thomas

Le Morte D'Arthur

The legendary deeds of King Arthur and his Knights of the Round Table follows Arthur's magical birth and accession to the throne as well as the stories of knights Sir Lancelot, Sir Tristram, and Sir Galahad. Malory's unique and splendid version of the Arthurian legend tells an immortal story of love, adventure, chivalry, treachery, and death.

de Maupassant, Guy

Short Stories

de Maupassant was indeed a great influence. His short stories are considered little masterpieces and have been followed as a model for short story writers since his time.

Melville, Herman

Billy Budd

It is a time of war between nations, but on one ship, a smaller battle is being fought between two men. Jealous of Billy Budd, known as the "Handsome Sailor," the envious Master-At-Arms Claggart torments the young man until his false accusations lead to a charge of treason against Billy.

Moby Dick

Melville tells this story through the eyes of Ishmael. A giant white whale took Captain Ahab's leg on a previous voyage, and now, driven on by the Captain's obsessive revenge, the crew and the outcast Ishmael find themselves caught up in a maniacal pursuit which leads inexorably to an apocalyptic climax.

Monsarrat, Nicholas

The Cruel Sea

The Cruel Sea presents the lives of Allied sailors who must protect the cargo ships and destroy the German submarines. Monsarrat vividly describes the savage submarine battles of the North Atlantic during World War II.

Nordhoff, Charles; Hall, James Norman

Mutiny on the Bounty

In this stirring sea adventure, Nordhoff and Hall tell the story of the historic voyage of the H.M.S. Bounty—a journey that culminated in Fletcher Christian's mutiny against Captain Bligh. This unforgettable, fictional tale of the high seas is so realistic it reads like truth.

Poe, Edgar A.

Poems

Poe revolutionized the horror tale, giving it psychological insight and a consistent tone and atmosphere. He invented the modern detective story, penned some of the world's best-known lyric poetry, and wrote a major novella of the fantastic. Some of his more famous works include: "The Raven"; "The Pit and the Pendulum"; "Annabel Lee"; "The Fall of the House of Usher"; and "The Murders in the Rue Morgue."

Remarque, Erich M.

All Quiet on the Western Front

Paul Bäumer and his classmates enlist in the German army of World War II, and they become soldiers with youthful enthusiasm. Through years of vivid horror, Paul holds fast to a single vow: to fight against the principle of hate that meaninglessly pits young men of the same generation but different uniforms against each other.

Potok, Chaim

The Promise

The Promise follows the story of Reuven Malter in his choices between traditionalism and his feelings. As Potok explores the themes of adolescence, morality, and our collective nature, he captures the essence of the Jewish customs and conflicts and puts them in laymen's term. This is an uplifting story realistically and dramatically told.

Sandburg, Carl

Abraham Lincoln: The Prairie Years, and The War Years

The definitive biography of one of America's greatest presidents recounts the fascinating log-cabin-to-the-White House success story. Sandburg aptly describes the complex individual who rose to become an outstanding leader.

Saroyan, William

The Human Comedy

Saroyan's autobiographical story centers around a family whose struggles and dreams reflect those of America's second-generation immigrants. Set in California during World War II, it shows us a boy caught between reality and illusion as delivering telegraphs of wartime death, love, and money brings him face-to-face with human emotion at its most raw.

Scott, Sir Walter

Ivanhoe

Set in twelfth-century England, Ivanhoe captures the noble idealism of chivalry along with its often cruel and impractical consequences. It follows the heroic adventures of Sir Wilfred of Ivanhoe as he and his fellow captives are rescued from Knight Templar's castle by Robin Hood; the wounded Ivanhoe's trial by combat with the powerful Knight to save the beautiful Jewess Rebecca from the stake; and King Richard the Lionhearted's aid in Ivanhoe's triumph at evil King John's tournament.

Sebestyen, Ouida

Words by Heart

Hoping to make her adored Papa proud of her and make her white classmates notice her "Magic Mind" and not her black skin, Lena vows to win the Bible-quoting contest. Winning does not bring Lena what she expected. Instead of honor, violence and death erupt and strike the one she loves most dearly. Lena, who has believed in vengeance, must now learn how to forgive.

Shaara, Michael

The Killer Angels

This novel reveals more about the Battle of Gettysburg—in which fifty thousand people died—than any piece of learned nonfiction on the same subject. Shaara's account of the three most important days of the Civil War features deft characterizations of all of the main actors, including Lee, Longstreet, Pickett, Buford, and Hancock. In the three most bloody and courageous days of our nation's history, two armies fought for two dreams—one dreamed of freedom, the other of a way of life.

Shakespeare, William

Hamlet

This powerful tale of ghosts, murder, and revenge takes on new meaning with each reading. The play begins as a ghost story, full of mystery and suspense. Then in Acts II and III, it becomes a detective story with Prince Hamlet seeking to find the murderer of his father. Finally, in Acts IV and V, it becomes a revenge story, as Hamlet seeks the ultimate revenge.

Macbeth

Shakespeare's tragedy revolves around destiny, ambition, and murder. It is prophesied that a Scottish lord "shall never vanquished be until great Birnam Wood to high Dunsinane Hill shall come against him." Macbeth luxuriates in his invincibility, knowing that woods don't climb hills. Or do they? As he and Lady Macbeth move from one heinous crime to another, a day of reckoning awaits them.

Julius Caesar

A crafty and ambitious Cassius, envious of Caesar's political and military triumphs, forms a conspiracy against him. After Caesar's assassination, Antony, seeking retribution against the murderers, drives them out of Rome. *Julius Caesar* is one of Shakespeare's greatest works.

Shaw, George Bernard

Pygmalion

The inspiration behind the popular musical and movie *My Fair Lady*, Pygmalion is a perceptive comedy of wit and grit about the unique relationship that develops between spunky cockney flower girl, Eliza Doolittle, and her irascible speech professor, Henry Higgins. The flower girl teaches the egotistical phonetics professor that to be a lady means more than just learning to speak like one.

Shelley, Mary

Frankenstein

After being rescued from an iceberg, Dr. Frankenstein relates his autobiography to the ship's captain. Dr. Frankenstein has been consumed by his desire to create a fully-grown living creature. When he reaches his goal, he perceives his creation as a monster, immediately regrets his work, and promptly abandons it. A story within a story, *Frankenstein* is a subtle and ironic prophecy that raises the question of who exactly is the real monster in this story.

Sinclair, Upton

The Jungle

In Sinclair's book we enter the world of Jurgis Rudkus, a young Lithuanian immigrant who arrives in America fired with dreams of wealth, freedom, and opportunity. And we discover, with him, the astonishing truth about "packingtown," the busy, flourishing, filthy Chicago stockyards, where new world visions perish in a jungle of human suffering. Sinclair explores the workingman's lot at the turn of the century: the backbreaking labor; the injustices of "wage-slavery"; and the bewildering chaos of urban life.

Steinbeck, John

Of Mice and Men

This tragic story, given poignancy by its objective narrative, is about the complex bond between two migrant laborers. The plot centers on George Milton and Lennie Small, itinerant ranch hands who dream of one day owning a small farm. George acts as a father figure to Lennie, who is large and simpleminded, calming him and helping to rein in his immense physical strength.

East of Eden

This sprawling and often brutal novel, set in the rich farmlands of California's Salinas Valley, follows the intertwined destinies of two families—the Trasks and the Hamiltons—whose generations helplessly reenact the fall of Adam and Eve and the poisonous rivalry of Cain and Abel.

The Grapes of Wrath

The Grapes of Wrath is the epic chronicle of man's struggle against injustice and inhumanity. It tells the story of the Joads and their journey to "the golden land." It is not so much just the story of one family and one time, but the story of the courage and passion of all men throughout history.

Stevenson, Robert Louis

Dr. Jekyll and Mr. Hyde

Stevenson's supernatural story of good versus evil centers around the well-intentioned, wealthy physician Dr. Jekyll. As he drinks the potion that is the culmination of his research, he unleashes the dark side of his nature, turning into the hideous Mr. Hyde. This book is one of the most horrific depictions of the human potential for evil ever written.

Treasure Island

When young Jim Hawkins finds a treasure map in Captain Flint's chest, he must outwit the dead Captain's collaborators if he is to keep it for himself. Only his two companions, Squire Trelawney and Dr. Livesey, share Jim's secret, and the three decide to set off on a seafaring adventure in this classic tale of exploits on the high seas.

Kidnapped

In this spirited saga, a young heir is seized by his villainous uncle and sold into slavery. Saved ironically in a shipwreck, he travels with a Scot expatriate until they become suspects in a murder. More than just a "boy's story," this is the tale of a brave young man and the amazing odyssey that takes him halfway around the world.

Stone, Irving

Lust for Life

Vincent Van Gogh was a tragic figure in his time, beseiged by uncertainty, disappointment, and a tortured mind. The heroic devotion of his brother was the most important sustaining influence on his life. In Lust for Life, Stone uses the techniques of a fiction writer and the approach of a biographer in recreating the storm and stress of this artist's life.

Stowe, Harriet Beecher

Uncle Tom's Cabin

This is a book that changed history. Stowe was appalled by slavery, and she took one of the few options open to nineteenth century women who wanted to affect public opinion: She wrote a novel—a huge, enthralling narrative that claimed the heart, soul, and politics of pre-Civil War Americans. It is unabashed propaganda and overtly moralistic, an attempt to make whites—North and South—see slaves as mothers, fathers, and people with (Christian) souls. In a time when many whites claimed slavery had "good effects" on blacks, *Uncle Tom's Cabin* paints pictures of three plantations, each worse than the other, where even the best plantation leaves a slave at the mercy of fate or debt.

Swift, Jonathan

Gulliver's Travels

This four-part, satirical novel is the story of Lemuel Gulliver, a surgeon and sea captain who visits remote regions of the world. Gulliver is shipwrecked on Lilliput, where people are six inches tall. His second voyage takes him to Brobdingnag, where lives a race of giants of great practicality who do not understand abstractions. Gulliver's third voyage takes him to the flying island of Laputa and the nearby continent and capital of Lagado, where he finds pedants obsessed with their own specialized areas of speculation and utterly ignorant of the rest of life. At Glubdubdrib, the Island of Sorcerers, he speaks with great men of the past and learns from them the lies of history. He also meets the Struldbrugs, who are immortal and, as a result, utterly miserable. In the extremely bitter fourth part, Gulliver visits the land of the Houyhnhnms, a race of intelligent, virtuous horses served by brutal, filthy, and degenerate creatures called Yahoos.

Tolkien, J.R.R.

The Lord of the Rings Trilogy

Tolkien's trilogy of fantasy novels, drawn from his extensive knowledge of philology and folklore, consists of *The Fellowship of the Ring*, *The Two Towers*, and *The Return of the King*. The novels, set in the Third Age of Middle Earth, formed a sequel to Tolkien's *The Hobbit*. The trilogy is the saga of a group of sometimes reluctant heroes who set forth to save their world from consummate evil. At 33, the age of adulthood among hobbits, Frodo Baggins receives a magic Ring of Invisibility from his uncle Bilbo. A Christlike figure, Frodo learns that the ring has the power to control the entire world and, he discovers, to corrupt its owner. A fellowship of hobbits, elves, dwarves, and men is formed to destroy the Ring; they are opposed on their harrowing mission by the evil Sauron and his Black Riders.

Tolstoy, Leo

War and Peace

This epic, historical novel is a panoramic study of early nineteenth-century Russian society. War and Peace is primarily concerned with the histories of five aristocratic families, the members of which are portrayed against a vivid background of Russian social life during the war against Napoleon (1805-14). The theme of war, however, is subordinate to the story of family existence, which involves Tolstoy's optimistic belief in the life-asserting pattern of human existence. The novel also sets forth a theory of history, concluding that there is a minimum of free choice; all is ruled by an inexorable historical determinism.

Twain, Mark

The Adventures of Huckleberry Finn

Twain's book tells the story of a teenaged misfit who finds himself floating on a raft down the Mississippi River with an escaping slave, Jim. In the course of their perilous journey, Huck and Jim meet adventure, danger, and a cast of characters who are sometimes menacing and often hilarious. This book's humor is found mostly in Huck's unique worldview and his way of expressing himself. Underlying Twain's good humor, however, is a dark subcurrent of cruelty and injustice that makes this a frequently funny book with a serious message.

The Adventures of Tom Sawyer

Twain's story of a mischievous Missouri schoolboy combines humor, terror, and astute social criticism in a delightful tale of life on the Mississippi. Written in 1876, Tom Sawyer became the model for an ideal of American boyhood in the nineteenth century, and many story elements—such as the fence-painting episode—are now woven into the fabric of our culture.

Verne, Jules

Master of the World

"It was seen first in North Carolina, or something was, smoking up from a mountain crater. With blinding speed, it roared past cars on a Pennsylvania road. It skimmed the Atlantic, then at the flick of its captain's will dove beneath the waves.... It was the 'Terror'...ship, sub, plane, and land vehicle in one and a letter from its inventor claimed that with it, he would rule the world." Long recognized as a truly prophetic science fiction classic, this adventure was also Verne's last novel.

Twenty Thousand Leagues Under the Sea

Professor Pierre Aronnax, the narrator, boards an American frigate commissioned to investigate a rash of attacks on international shipping by what is thought to be an amphibious monster. The supposed sea creature, which is actually the submarine Nautilus, sinks Aronnax's vessel and imprisons him along with his devoted servant Conseil and Ned Land, a temperamental harpooner. The survivors meet Captain Nemo, an enigmatic misanthrope who leads them on a worldwide, year-long underwater adventure. The novel is noted for its exotic situations and the technological innovations it describes.

Wallace, Lewis

Ben-Hur

This historical novel depicts the oppressive Roman occupation of ancient Palestine and the origins of Christianity. The Jew Judah Ben-Hur is wrongly accused by his former friend, the Roman Messala, of attempting to kill a Roman official. He is sent to be a slave and his mother and sister are imprisoned. Years later he returns, wins a chariot race against Messala, and is reunited with his now leprous mother and sister.

Washington, Booker T.

Up From Slavery

Illustrating the human quest for freedom and dignity, Washington's American classic recounts his triumph over the legacy of slavery, his founding of Tuskegee Institute, and his emergence as a national spokesman for his race.

Wells, H.G.

Collected Works of H.G. Wells

Wells is the founder of modern science-fiction. His stories include "The Crystal Egg," "The Strange Orched," and "The Invisible Man"—a serious study of egotism.

Wouk, Herman

The Caine Mutiny: A Novel of World War II

Generally, books about war fit their stereotype quite well—the hero is the commanding officer who leads his men courageously into battle. However, Wouk showed that even our most heralded commanders are human and make mistakes like the rest of us. Captain Queeg was unbalanced, but was he so unbalanced as to warrant a mutiny? That is one of the central themes of *The Caine Mutiny*, along with Willie Keith's change from an immature mama's boy into a man capable of commanding an entire ship in the United States Navy. Wouk shows how most men are vulnerable, and military men are no exception.

Juniors

Bellamy, Edward

Looking Backward

Bellamy's story, first published in 1888, is a passionate attack on the social ills of nineteenth century industrialism, Bellamy makes a plea for social reform and moral renewal; however, the action takes place in the year 2000. Julian West awakens after more than a century of sleep to find himself in twentieth century America—a land full of employment, material abundance, and social harmony.

Benet, Stephen

John Brown's Body

This is not the history of John Brown, nor a verse history of the civil war, but a narrative of the great and complex struggles between civilization, where nearly everyone is right and wrong. Benet's saga is an epic poem of the civil war.

Bronte, Emily

Wuthering Heights

The tempestuous and mythic story of Catherine Earnshaw, the precocious daughter of the house, and the ruggedly handsome, uncultured foundling her father brings home and names Heathcliff. Brought together as children, Catherine and Heathcliff quickly become attached to each other. As they grow older, their companionship turns into obsession. Family, class, and fate work cruelly against them, as do their own jealous and volatile natures, and much of their lives is spent in revenge and frustration. Wuthering Heights is a classic tale of possessive and thwarted passion, and it embodies Bronte's philosophy and spiritual quality.

Buechner, Frederick

Peculiar Treasures

In these short, pithy portraits of 125 Bible characters, Buechner has put together a humorous and entertaining bunch of folks who in most ways are just like ourselves. Buechner writes with a light touch, and his witty yet solidly instructive characterizations of these Biblical figures underscore lessons for Christians today.

Cather, Willa

My Antonia

Cather's novel honors the immigrant settlers of the American plains. Narrated by the protagonist's lifelong friend, Jim Burden, the novel recounts the history of Antonia Shimerda, the daughter of Bohemian immigrants who settled on the Nebraska frontier. The book contains a number of poetic passages about the disappearing frontier and the spirit and courage of frontier people.

Death Comes for the Archbishop

Death Comes for the Archbishop traces the friendship and adventures of Bishop Jean Latour and vicar Father Joseph Vaillant as they organize the new Roman Catholic diocese of New Mexico. Latour is patrician, intellectual, introverted; Vaillant, practical, outgoing, sanguine. Friends since their childhood in France, the clerics triumph over corrupt Spanish priests, natural adversity, and the indifference of the Hopi and Navajo to establish their church and build a cathedral in the wilderness. The novel, essentially a study of character, is considered emblematic of the author's moral and spiritual concerns.

de Cervantes, Miguel

Don Quixote

Humor, insight, compassion, and knowledge of the world underlie the antic adventures of the lanky knight clad in rusty armor and his earthy squire, Sancho Panza. The unforgettable characters they encounter on their famous pilgrimage form a brilliant panorama of society and human behavior.

Dostoyevsky, Fyodor

Crime and Punishment

Dostoyevsky's first masterpiece, the novel is a psychological analysis of the poor student Raskolnikov, whose theory that humanitarian ends justify evil means leads him to murder a St. Petersburg pawnbroker. The act produces nightmarish guilt in Raskolnikov. The narrative's feverish, compelling tone follows the twists and turns of Raskolnikov's emotions and elaborates his struggle with his conscience and his mounting sense of horror as he wanders the city's hot, crowded streets. In prison, Raskolnikov comes to the realization that happiness cannot be achieved by a reasoned plan of existence but must be earned by suffering.

Faulkner, William

The Hamlet, The Town, and The Mansion

The trilogy follows the origin, rise, and dominance of the Snopes family. The Snopes took root in Yoknapatawpha County and proliferated through and beyond it until they outmaneuvered and overpowered a society that had little defense against their invincible rapacity.

Go Down, Moses

Go Down, Moses consists of seven interrelated stories, all of them set in Faulkner's Yoknapatawpha County. From a variety of perspectives, Faulkner examines the complex, changing relationships between blacks and whites and between man and nature.

The Bear

The Bear is the story of a boy's coming to terms with the adult world. By learning how to hunt, he is taught the real meaning of pride, humility, and courage—virtues that Faulkner feared would be almost impossible to learn with the destruction of the wilderness.

Galsworthy, James

The Forsythe Saga

Galsworthy's saga chronicles the lives of three generations of a monied, middle-class English family at the turn of the century. Soames Forsythe, a solicitor and "the man of property," is married to the beautiful, penniless Irene, who falls in love with Philip Bosinney, the French architect whom Soames had hired to build a country house. The rest of the saga concerns itself with Soames, Irene, and Philip, and the generations that follow.

Justice

Justice is Galsworthy's tragic play about the irony of punishing by rule rather than helping or training the individual. It is full of both irony, justice, and injustice.

Loyalties

Loyalties treats incidentally the clash of classes and social groups. Its main purpose is to throw up into relief the incessant clash of differing loyalties, which makes the path of right action so difficult.

Hansberry, Lorraine

Raisin in the Sun

When it was first produced in 1959, *A Raisin in the Sun* was awarded the New York Drama Critics Circle Award for that season and hailed as a watershed in American drama. A pioneering work by an African-American playwright, the play was a radically new representation of black life.

Hardy, Thomas

The Return of the Native

This novel sets in opposition two of Hardy's most unforgettable characters: his heroine, the sensuous, free-spirited Eustacia Vye, and the solemn, majestic stretch of upland in Dorsetshire he called Egdon Heath. The famous opening reveals the haunting power of that dark, forbidding moon where proud Eustacia fervently awaits a clandestine meeting with her lover, Damon Wildeve. But Eustacia's dreams of escape are not to be realized—neither Wildeve nor the returning native Clym Yeobright can bring her salvation. Injured by forces beyond their control, Hardy's characters struggle vainly in the net of destiny.

Mayor of Casterbridge

This is a classic tale of a successful man who cannot escape his past nor his own evil nature. Michael Henchard is the respected mayor of Casterbridge, a thriving industrial town—but years ago, under the influence of alcohol, he sold his wife Susan to a sailor at a country fair. Although repentant and sober for 21 years, Henchard cannot escape his destiny when Susan and her daughter return to Casterbridge.

Hersey, John

Hiroshima

When the atomic bomb was dropped on Hiroshima, few could have anticipated its potential for devastation. Hersey recorded the stories of Hiroshima residents shortly after the explosion, giving the world firsthand accounts from people who had survived it. The words of Miss Sasaki, Dr. Fujii, Mrs. Nakamara, Father Kleinsorg, Dr. Sasaki, and the Reverend Tanimoto gave a face to the statistics that saturated the media and solicited an overwhelming public response.

James, Henry

The Turn of the Screw

One of the most famous ghost stories, the tale is told mostly through the journal of a governess and depicts her struggle to save her two young charges from the demonic influence of the eerie apparitions of two former servants in the household. The story inspired critical debate over the question of the "reality" of the ghosts and of James's intentions. Whether accepted as a simple ghost story or an exercise in the literary convention of the unreliable narrator, this story is classically, relentlessly horrifying.

Lee, Harper

To Kill a Mockingbird

Through the eyes of young Scout Finch, one of the most endearing and enduring characters of Southern literature, Lee explores with rich humor and unswerving honesty the irrationality of adult attitudes toward race and class in the Deep South of the 1930s. The conscience of a town steeped in prejudice, violence, and hypocrisy is pricked by the stamina and quiet heroism of one man's struggle for justice.

Lamb, Charles

The Essays of Elia

Lamb's personality is projected in all his literary work, but in *The Essays of Elia* it shines through. This collection of essays contains a vast deal of autobiographical material, and it is candidly personal in atmosphere and structure.

Lewis, Sinclair

Babbitt

Babbitt, a conniving, prosperous real-estate man, is one of the ugliest figures in American fiction. A total conformist, he can only receive self-esteem from others, and is loyal to whoever serves his need of the moment. Babbitt gives consummate expression to the glibness and irresponsibility of the hardened, professional social climber.

Arrowsmith

Lewis' book follows the life of Martin Arrowsmith, a rather ordinary fellow who gets his first taste of medicine at 14 as an assistant to the drunken physician in his home town. He is forced to give up his trade for reasons ranging from public ignorance to the publicity-mindedness of a great foundation, and becomes an isolated seeker of scientific truth.

Marquand, John P.

The Late George Apley

The Late George Apley is a wicked, brilliantly etched satire. A portrait of a Bostonian and of the tradition-bound, gilded society in which he lived, it is the story of three generations of Apley men, the maturing America, and the golden era of American security from 1866 to 1933.

Masters, Edgar Lee

A Spoon River Anthology

Masters introduces the reader to a selection of souls who describe their lives and their relationships (or lack thereof) through simplistic, poetic epitaphs. The collection of dramatic monologues by over 200 former inhabitants of the fictional town of Spoon River topples the myth of moral superiority in small-town America, as the dead give testimony to their shocking scandals and secret tragedies. Masters seems to place the reader in St. Peter's wings, inviting—almost daring—that reader to decide eternal placement for his characters.

Maugham, Somerset

Of Human Bondage

Maugham uses the tale of Phillip Carey, an innocent, sensitive crippled man in Victorian-era Europe as a front for his own autobiography. Phillip was left an orphan at a young age and was continually taunted for his club-foot and the limp that resulted. His early rejection from society gives him time to seek out his purpose in life and travel across Europe. This book is truly great for the in-depth examination of love and the human animal.

O'Neill, Eugene

The Emperor Jones

This play, as well as *Anna Christie* and *The Hairy Ape*, deals with the misery of man—not immediate, physical, or social, but metaphysical. The central character, a Negro, is insulted and injured. The "emperor" Brutus Jones, typifies all men with their raw ignorance and hysterical fear under the layers of intellect.

Orwell, George

Animal Farm

A farm is taken over by its overworked, mistreated animals. With flaming idealism and stirring slogans, they set out to create a paradise of progress, justice, and equality. Thus the stage is set for a telling anti-utopian satires—a razor-edged fable that records the evolution from revolution against tyranny to a totalitarianism dictatorship even more oppressive and heartless than that of their former human masters.

Paine, Thomas

The Rights of Man

The Rights of Man is unquestionably one of the great classics on the subject of democracy. Paines' vast influence on our system of government is due less to his eloquence and literary style, than to his steadfast bravery and determination to promote justice and equality.

Paton, Alan

Cry, the Beloved Country

Set in the troubled South Africa of the 1940s amid a people riven by racial inequality and injustice, *Cry, the Beloved Country* is a beautiful and profoundly compassionate story of the Zulu pastor Stephen Kumalo and his son Absalom. Everyone can relate to the pathos of Rev. Kumalo in his journey to reunite the tribe and his gradual awakening to the fact that there are changes that are occurring that his compassion and tears can do nothing for.

Plato

The Republic

In Plato's Republic exists a guide to life and living for every person alive. By trying to describe the ideal state, Plato creates the first "Utopia" and in the meantime questions our perceptions of reality. Through Plato's thought we can see the only way to judge fairness and equality is through the ideal state and what man could be, not what man is. Plato's look on justice and reality is unmatched despite hundreds of attempts to replicate his thought and style in the past few millennium.

Rolvaag, O.E.

Giants in the Earth: A Saga of the Prairie

This refreshingly stark view of pioneer life reflects the hardships, fear, and depression that one women experiences when her husband takes her from her Norwegian homeland and moves her steadily westward across the northern plains. This novel is gothic in dimensions—the physical landscape becomes the characters' mental landscape—the vast expanse of snow in winter and grass in summer become a metaphor for boredom and isolation. Rolvaag writes of a lifestyle and of motivations unimaginable to the modern American, and yet, he writes of a time that was shockingly recent in the history of the Midwest.

Rostand, Edmund

Cyrano de Bergerac

Set in seventeenth-century Paris, the action revolves around the emotional problems of the noble, swashbuckling Cyrano, who, despite his many gifts, feels that no woman can ever love him because he has an enormous nose. Secretly in love with the lovely Roxane, Cyrano agrees to help his inarticulate rival, Christian, win her heart by allowing him to present Cyrano's love poems, speeches, and letters as his own work, and Cyrano remains silent about his own part in Roxane's courtship.

Sophocles

The Three Theban Plays
  Oedipus Rex
  Oedipus at Colonus
  Antigone
This trilogy is Greek tragedy and compelling drama. It is the eloquent story of a noble family moving toward catastrophe, and dragged down by pride from wealth and power. *Oedipus Rex* raises basic questions about human behavior. *Antigone* examines the conflicting obligations of civic duties versus personal loyalties and religious mores.

Swarthout, Glendon

Bless the Beasts and the Children
Swarthout gives readers an opportunity to view six adolescents whom society has already labeled misfits from the inside out. As the book progresses, you gradually learn the history of each member of the group from past incidents, namely unintentional mental abuse by parents. The teenagers set out on a quest to free a herd of buffaloes from a senseless slaughter. Ironically, the freedom and fate of these animals parallel that of the young men. Their freeing the buffaloes symbolizes their own self-discovery, initiation into manhood, and entry into a realm of humanity that transcends the violent, "dog-eat-dog" society that has excluded them.

Turgenev, Ivan

Fathers and Sons
Fathers and Sons concerns the inevitable conflict between generations and between the values of traditionalists and intellectuals. The physician Bazarov, the novel's protagonist, is a nihilist, denying the validity of all laws save those of the natural sciences. He scorns traditional Russian values, shocks respectable society and, for the young, represents the spirit of rebellion. Uncouth and forthright in his opinions, Bazarov is nonetheless susceptible to love and by that fact doomed to unhappiness.

Thackeray, William Makepeace

Vanity Fair
Vanity Fair is a story of two heroines—one humble, the other scheming and social-climbing—who meet in boarding school and embark on markedly different lives. Amid the swirl of London's posh ballrooms and affairs of love and war, their fortunes rise and fall. Through it all, Thackeray lampoons the shallow values of his society, reserving the most pointed barbs for the upper crust. What results is a prescient look at the dogged pursuit of wealth and status—and the need for humility.

Vonnegut, Kurt

Cat's Cradle
Cat's Cradle is Vonnegut's satirical commentary on modern man and his madness. An apocalyptic tale of this planet's ultimate fate, it features a midget as the protagonist; a complete, original theology created by a calypso singer; and a vision of the future that is at once blackly fatalistic and hilariously funny. These assorted characters chase each other around in search of the world's most important and dangerous substance, a new form of ice that freezes at room temperature.

Wharton, Edith

Ethan Frome

Although Ethan Frome, a gaunt, patient New Englander, seems ambitious and intelligent, his wife, Zeena, holds him back. When her young cousin Mattie comes to stay on their New England farm, Ethan falls in love with her. But the social conventions of the day doom their love and their hopes. Ethan is tormented by a passionate love for Mattie, and his desperate quest for happiness leads to pain and despair.

Date:

Name of book: Name of author:

Publisher: Copyright date:

I.   Briefly describe:

     Protagonist:

     Antagonist:

     Other characters used to develop protagonist:

     Do any of the characters remind me of a Bible character? Who? Why?

II. Setting

III. Point of view: Circle one

     First person, Third person, Third person omniscient

IV. Brief summary of the plot

V.   Theme (the quintessential meaning or purpose of the book in one or two sentences):

VI. Author's worldview

     How do you know this? What behaviors does the character manifest that lead you
     to this conclusion?

VII. Why did you like or dislike this book?

VIII. List at least five new vocabulary words from this book. Define and use in a sentence.

IX. Name of next book I will read:

     Signature of parent(s)

A Thirty-Minute Prayer Devotional Journal

Date:

Passage:

1. Focusing Time (a list of those things that I must do later) (three minutes):

2. Discipline of Silence (remain absolutely still and quiet) (two minutes):

3. Reading Scripture Passage (with notes on text—this is not a time to do Bible study) (five minutes):

4. Meditating in Scripture (ten minutes):

A. How does the passage affect the person mentioned in the passage? How does he or she feel?

B. How does the passage affect my life? What is the Lord saying to me through this passage?

C. How has God spoken to me in the last twenty-four hours?

5. Prayers of Adoration and Thanksgiving, Intercession, and Future Prayer Targets (eight minutes):

6. Discipline of Silence (two minutes):

Possible Target Scriptures:

Job 23:10-12

Psalms 118:5-6

Psalms 119:33-37

Proverbs 2:1-11

Isaiah 12:2

Isaiah 26:3-4

Isaiah 41:10

Isaiah 43:1-3

Jeremiah 9:23-24

Jeremiah 17:7-8

Jeremiah 29:11

Matthew 6:33

Luke 8:15

Romans 5:1-5

Romans 8

Romans 12:1-2

Romans 14:7

1 Corinthians 6:19-20

2 Corinthians 5:15

2 Corinthians 5:17

2 Corinthians 9:10

2 Corinthians 12:9

Galatians 1:15-16

Galatians 6:7-8

Ephesians 1:13-14

Ephesians 1:17

Ephesians 3:16-21

Ephesians 5:1-2

Ephesians 5:15-16

Ephesians 6:10

Philippians 1:3-6

Philippians 1:11

Philippians 2:13

Philippians 3:7-11

Philippians 3:12-14

Philippians 4:4-7

Philippians 4:13

Philippians 4:19

Colossians 1:9-10

Colossians 2:2-3

Colossians 3:17

1 Thessalonians 5:16-18

2 Thessalonians 1:11-12

1 Timothy 6:12

1 Timothy 6:17-19

2 Timothy 2:3

2 Timothy 2:15

Hebrews 11:1

Hebrews 11:6

James 1:2-5

1 Peter 2:9

1 Peter 5:6-7

2 Peter 1:3-4

And more!

Test-Taking Strategies

1. I believe that your best scores will occur in May or June of your junior year. If you do not obtain the score you wish, you can always retake the exam during the next fall.

2. Take the SAT I reasoning test—morning exam—on a different day than the SAT II subject tests—afternoon exam. To take both of them together is too arduous.

3. Do not guess unless you can narrow the choices to two answers. I just did not guess at all. It is up to you.

4. Take at least six #2 sharpened—but slightly dulled—pencils. Don't use mechanical pencils.

5. Memorize the directions for every type of question on the math and verbal SAT.

6. Do not miss any of the first ten questions. Remember: Each question counts the same and the last questions are usually more difficult.

7. Sleep well the night before an exam, eat well the morning of the exam, and arrive at the test site thirty minutes before the exam begins.

8. Bring a good calculator and an extra battery. No need to have a calculator that can figure out the GNP. Just a basic calculator. Preferably one with big numbers. Use one with which you are familiar. Practice putting in a new battery. It would not hurt to have an extra calculator with you.

9. Bring a snack—no candy—something like a peanut butter sandwich. Eat the snack at or near 10:30 a.m. Most poor scores occur from 10:30–12:30.

10. Never have I known a student with an exceptionally high Critical Reading score to do poorly on the exam. Therefore, pay particularly close attention to those parts of your preparation. Remember! Forty percent of the verbal portion of the SAT I exam is related to reading passages.

11. Forget cramming. It will not help you. Better to relax and to pray. In fact, I recommend that you do not look at your preparation material the last two nights before the exam.

12. The SAT verbal exam is essentially a vocabulary exam. I want to tell you as plainly and forcefully as I can: If you do not consciously and deliberately increase your vocabulary base, you will not do well on the SAT I verbal exam.

13. Everyone knows how important stress reduction techniques are to enhanced SAT scores. Therefore, a target Scripture and devotional material have obvious value. At the same time, pay attention to your physical environment. You should find as comfortable a chair and desk as possible in which to take the test. If you are left-handed, find a left-handed desk. Before you began the exam, meditate on your target Scripture.

14. Do not let them psyche you out by giving you questions that have the same answer letter four or five times in a roll. It sounds silly, but if questions 1–5 have A as the correct answer you might be tempted to avoid answering 6 with an A too. But if A is the right answer, mark it! I don't care if you use A 99 percent of the time.

15. Fill out each circle grid on the test booklet—but only enough for the computer to catch. Give it a good mark and go on.

16. Develop a personal strategy before test day: Will you guess or not? How much time will you allow for checking the exams? Have you concentrated on your strong areas? Have you done the best you can with your weak ones?

Critical Thinking Skills

The Bubletown Detectives: A Critical-Thinking Book. NY: Time-Life Books, 1991.

Cassel, Jeris F., and Congleton, Robert J., *Critical Thinking: An Annotated Bibliography.* Scarecrow Publisher, 1992.

Edwards, Ronald R., Problem Solving Through Critical Thinking. Addison-Wesley, 1993.

Gifted and Talented: Puzzles and Games For Critical And Creative Thinking. Lowell House, 1994.

Lundquist, Joegil, *English from the Roots Up: Help for Reading, Writing, Spelling, and SAT Scores.* Bellevue, WA: Literacy Unlimited, 1989.

Olson, Carol Booth, ed., *Thinking/Writing: Fostering Critical Thinking Through Writing.* NY: Harper Collins, 1992.

Reasoning, *Logical Thinking, Problem Solving.* Princeton, NJ: Educational Testing Service, 1990.

Schwartz, L., *Analogy Adventures.* Learning Works, 1989.

Shermis, Samuel S., *Critical Thinking: Helping Students Learn Reflectively.* Bloomington, Ind.: Edinfo Press, 1992.

Solution Sleuth, Learning Works Staff. Learning Works, 1989.

Stice, James E., *Developing Critical Thinking and Problem-Solving Abilities.* Jossey-Bass Publishers, 1987.

Tuttle, Cheryl, and Paquette, Penny, *Thinking Games to Play With Your Child: Easy Ways to Develop Creative and Critical Thinking Skills.* Lowell House, 1991.

Virkler, Henry A., *A Christian's Guide to Critical Thinking.* Nelson Publisher, 1993.

Whimbey, A., Lockhead, J., Potter, P. B., eds., *Critical Thinking Through Math Word Problems.* L. Earlbaum Publishers, 1990.

Williams, Jane A., *The Young Thinker's Bookshelf: Books, Software, Music, Movies, Audiocassettes to Encourage Independent and Critical Thinking.* Not in print.

Remedy for College Admission Essay Jitters

The main purpose of the SAT, of course, is college admission. At this time, with the help of this book, and other factors, I am fairly certain that you will do well on the SAT. So what is next? College admission!

The following section will lead through the maze of college admission. You will learn how to create a strategic, college prep transcript. You will learn how to prosper in a secular university. Finally, you will learn how to write the very important college admission essay.

Enjoy the following section and be prepared to be all that you can be in Jesus Christ our Lord so that His Kingdom may come on earth as it is in Heaven!

To Harvard University-

While an intrinsic ardor prompts to write,
The muses promise to assist my pen;
'Twas not long since I left my native shore
The land of errors, and *Egyptian* gloom:
Father of mercy, 'twas thy gracious hand
Brought me in safety from those dark abodes.
Students, to you 'tis giv'n to scan the heights
Above, to traverse the ethereal space,
And mark the systems of revolving worlds.

Still more, ye sons of science ye receive
The blissful news by messengers from heav'n,
How *Jesus'* blood for your redemption flows.
See him with hands out-stretcht upon the cross;
Immense compassion in his bosom glows;
He hears revilers, nor resents their scorn:
What matchless mercy in the Son of God!
When the whole human race by sin had fall'n,
He deign'd to die that they might rise again,
And share with him in the sublimest skies,

Life without death, and glory without end.
Improve your privileges while they stay,
Ye pupils, and each hour redeem, that bears
Or good or bad report of you to heav'n.
Let sin, that baneful evil to the soul,
By you be shun'd, nor once remit your guard;
Suppress the deadly serpent in its egg.
Ye blooming plants of human race divine,
An *Ethiop* tells you 'tis your greatest foe;
Its transient sweetness turns to endless pain,

And in immense perdition sinks the soul.

-Phillis Wheatley

The Rise of the Secular University:
How to Thrive in Babylon Without Becoming Babylonian

Thousands of young Christian young people are praying about where God is calling them to spend the next 4 years of their lives. That is good news to the United States of America!

Growing up in southern Arkansas in the middle of the last century I never thought much about religion or colleges.

Southern Arkansas was a generous but exhausted land. Cotton, pampered by what are now illegal chemicals like EPN and DDT, grew to bountiful heights. Southwest winds permanently bent rice plants pregnant with pounds and pounds of offspring. Pecan trees cradled whole acres of antediluvian loam with their gigantic arms. Every spring, bayous and rivers deposited a rich delta gift along the banks of grateful farm land. It was a gift from Minnesota and Ohio, freely given by the ubiquitous Mississippi River, and gratefully accepted by tobacco chewing Arkansas delta farmers. This was really an unselfish land, a land that seemed to give more than it took.

The house in which I lived was a natural addition to this magnificent land. Built during the depression years of cheap labor, the House — so named by grandmother Helen (whom I affectionately called "Mammaw") — reflected my grandparent's unbounded optimism. They had built it with a profitable business and Depression-priced labor. They shamelessly flaunted their prosperity in a culture that was painfully impoverished. No one seemed to mind. The South has always been kind to its elitists. They were a chosen people, or so they claimed with every offering of ebullience. No one questioned their credentials-especially when my grandmother imported bricks from New Orleans streets, painted wicker chairs from replete Havana shops, and crystal chandeliers from abandoned Liverpool mansions. I remember that the bricks surrounding our fireplace evoked a faint smell of horse manure every winter as we enjoyed our winter fires.

The House was a testimony both to my grandmother's generosity and to her eccentricity. This special house had five thousand square feet, six bedrooms and five full baths, and a full basement-the only full basement in my below sea level community. The servant's quarters were above the kennel and they were better than many of our neighbor's houses. The kitchen was built of cool New Orleans bricks and attached to the house by a closed walkway.

As the reader can imagine, I hesitated leaving such a place. I remember thinking about my home as I traveled "North" to attend Harvard Divinity School. I had been North once–to a wedding in New York City–but I had successfully managed to avoid northern contagion. My Yankee-hating grandmother had filled my mind and fears with images of cigar-smoking, carpetbag toting (I never once saw a carpet bag) Yankees accosting me as I attempted to cross Harvard Yard. "Jimmy," my grandmother earnestly pleaded with me, "stay away from Yankee ladies. They are full of guile and no well-bred naïve southern gentleman has a chance against their wiles." I later met at Harvard and married my Yankee wife from New Jersey. Karen, my wife, in fact, is one of the most Godly, principled people I have ever met!

While my grandmother's characterization of the north, and the university, were full of gross exaggerations and untruths, I, an evangelical Christian, nonetheless found the university to be a hostile place.

To many evangelical Christians, the modern, secular, university is a hostile place. It was not always so.

American Evangelicalism has two distinctives: it emphasizes a personal commitment to Christ and the exclusive authority of the Bible above all other authority. The university, as we understand it, is "an institution of higher learning providing facilities for teaching and research and authorized to grant academic degrees." (Merriam-Webster Dictionary)

In fact, the American university was built solidly on evangelical principles. An early brochure, published in 1643, stated that the purpose of Harvard University (the oldest American university) was "To advance Learning and perpetuate it to Posterity; dreading to leave an illiterate Ministry to the Churches." Harvard's motto for 300 years was "Christo et Ecclesiae." In fact, most of the U. S. universities founded before the 20th century had a strongly religious, usually Protestant Evangelical Christian character. Yale, Princeton, Chicago, Stanford, Duke, William and Mary, Boston University, and Michigan had a decidedly evangelical Christian character in the early years of their existence and abandoned it in the 20th century. By 1920s, the American university had stepped completely back from its evangelical roots. This was true of every American university founded in the first 200 years of our existence.

Readers would be surprised to see how evangelical early universities were. They had pastors as presidents. These men closely tied the identity of their university to a strong Christian world view. The core curriculum included Bible courses and Christian theology. These were mandatory Bible courses. All American universities insisted on a doctrinally sound content for sensitive courses and often required that faculty be born again Christians! Imagine this: the famous historian Frederick Jackson Turner was refused a professorship at Princeton because he was a Unitarian! Chapel attendance was required at Harvard and Yale! It is more than coincidental that the architects who designed early universities designed them to look like churches. At the University of Pittsburgh, for instance, the most prominent building on campus is the Cathedral of Learning (J. A. Appleyard, S.J., http://fmwww.bc.edu/SJ/marsden.html).

Universities were founded because early Americans earnestly believed that American society should be governed by evangelical Christian people. They believed that American industry should be run by evangelical Christian entrepreneurs. They believed that American culture should be created by evangelical Christians. The desire to assure that America would be ruled by an evangelical elite was no doubt the primary reason that American universities were founded from 1636-1800.

The marriage of spiritual maturity and elite education is a potent combination and to a large degree assured the success of the American experiment. Its divorce may presage its demise.

Evangelicals became uncomfortable with the secular university as early as 1800. As modern science influenced the university, Christian evangelicalism maintained peace with it, believing that all truth was God's truth. In fact, Christian evangelicalism wed the Gospel to science. Evangelicals sought to maintain a commonsense epistemology that easily accommodated scientific advances (George Marsden, *The Soul of the American University*. Oxford, England: Oxford University Press, 1994). In a congenial, almost filial spirit, the colleges endorsed a broader, more moralistic, less sectarian Christianity. However, as science abandoned theism for naturalism, evangelicals grew uneasy. Eventually, by the 1880s, religion–including evangelicalism–was on the fringes of the American university. Eventually Christian evangelicalism was to be off the university radar screen altogether.

Universities were founded because early Americans earnestly believed that American society should be governed by evangelical Christian people, that American culture should be created by evangelical Christian people.

Universities now professed a vague commitment to a liberal, ethical Christianity which invited skepticism and indifference. Religious commitment was perceived as psychological phenomenon, and moved to the fringes of university life. In fact, religious commitment was perceived as a voluntary activity, an aberration rather than an expressed purpose of the institution. Christianity was taught along with other religious expressions in religious departments. Christian ministry was relegated to insignificant graduate schools or dropped altogether.

By the 1920s the university was not even loosely a Christian institution. Religion in the university and in public life was to be relegated to the private experience. So-called "academic freedom" became a sacrosanct concept and precluded anything that smacked of religiosity–especially old time religion that evangelicals so enthusiastically embraced. Religion was represented on campus in sanitary denominational ministries and token chapel ministries (that were hardly more than counseling centers). The separation has been so thorough that when the New York Times' reporter Ari Goldman spent a year at Harvard Divinity School he was pleased to find, after all, God at Harvard! (Ari L. Goldman, *The Search for God at Harvard*. NY: Random House, 1991).

At the same time, with growing persecution, evangelicals abandoned the secular university and founded their own universities. This whole process accelerated after the Scopes Trial in the 1920s.

To a large degree, then, the American university abandoned the evangelical and the evangelical abandoned the American university.

This created a crisis in the American university and in the evangelical community. The secular American university compromised its "soul" for naturalistic positivism (to use George Marsden's terminology); evangelicalism compromised its epistemological hegemony for ontological supremacy. In other words, the secular university became a sort of an academic hothouse for rationalism. Evangelicals abandoned the secular university, and, until recently, more or less compromised their academic base. Evangelicals even founded their own universities but some were poor academic substitutes for secular offerings. That is changing as we speak.

The true crisis of the university lies not in financial exigencies, political assaults from the left or right, or the myopia of modern life; it lies in the crisis of confidence within the university itself about its abiding nature/purpose (Alvin Neiman, Review of Politics, Winter, 1994). The university, as it were, is having an Ericksonian self-identity crisis. It is a modern crisis fairly gained by embracing the spirits of the age. The university has lost something, but like the main character in Camus' *The Stranger*, it (he) has lost its way, lost its identity, but he does not quite know where he has come, where he got where he is, or where he is to go from here. In any event, it is a quest for an existential goal-not a Judeo-Christian one.

Evangelicals are wandering in the wilderness—but they have a goal. The secular university is wandering in the wilderness with no goal. The difference is that evangelicals are on a journey; the secular university is just plain lost with no destination.

This author resonates with John Henry Newman's *The Idea of a University Defined and Illustrated* (1852). Newman's Idea of a University grew out of Newman's struggle with the rise of scientific learning—a struggle that continues today. Newman, it seems to me, is a 19th century evangelical trying to come to make sense of his culture. Most American universities are full of intellectuals coming to grips with their Christianity.

"A university," Newman wrote, "is not a birthplace of poets or of immortal authors, or founders of schools, leaders of colonies, or conquerors of nations. It does promise

The modern university may be on a search for the truth, but this author does not want to join the quest. This author knows exactly what/who the truth is: Jesus Christ is the Way, the Truth, and the Life (John 14).

a generation of Aristotles or Newtons. . . a university training is the great ordinary means to a great but ordinary end; it aims at raising the intellectual tone of society . . ." In other words, the purpose of an education is to enable a person to live a life rather than to earn a living. Jaroslave Pelikan, *The Idea of the University: A Re-examined* (1994) adds his own interpretation: the university is a place of teaching universal knowledge, but also of advancing knowledge through research and of diffusing knowledge through publication, as well as of relating such advancement, teaching, and diffusion to the training of professionals (Pelikan 1994, 88). Pelikan says nothing about character or moral development.

Pelikan examines Newman's thesis and agrees. There must be in a university, Pelikan argues, freedom of inquiry, intellectual honesty, civility in discourse, toleration and trust in rationality. To that end, therefore, the university is concerned with intellectual rather than moral ends. Knowledge must lead to "moral" virtues (Pelikan 1994, 44). But these moral virtues, it seems to me, are separated from their Judeo-Christian moorings. They are simply part of "Golden Rule" sort of morality—akin to Lawrence Kohlberg's Level Six morality stage. I find this idea most disturbing. As if the university and humankind can know so much truth!

The modern, secular university is King Belshazzar's feast (Daniel 7). A university should be a time on Mt. Horeb, humbly bowing before Almighty God, freely admitting limits and extolling His omnipotence (Exodus 3). While American students might read John Milton's *Paradise Lost* without knowing the outcome before they read it, Pelikan suggests that the excitement of discovery mitigates the sting of American spiritual paupery (Pelikan 1994, 41). And, in spite of himself, Dr. Pelikan is indeed showing us the problem of the American secular university. Pelikan's suggestions are merely another form of veiled Gnosticism dressed up in pretty language. Knowledge-its acquisition, its dissemination-even in a gentleman's way-is the god of the modern American university. As the cognitive-moral formation specialist, psychologist Lawrence Kohlberg, Ed Fenton, and others have so convincingly shown us, there is no value free education. And we better be careful if we claim otherwise.

Newman, a committed Christian, never embraced Hegelian notions of the dialectic. Truth to the born again, Catholic priest Newman was not to be found in the academic search. Jesus Christ is the way, the truth, and the life. The American secular university, on the other hand, deifies the "search." Both teachers and students are on the "hunt" because Truth is yet to be fully understood.

The university, if it has any value, must be involved in the communication of immutable, metaphysical truth. The American secular university is not about to accept such limits. It recognizes no citadel of orthodoxy, no limits to its knowledge. Newman is the champion of orthodoxy. It was his whole life! Faith is Newman's ultimate destination of knowledge. In *An Essay in Aid of a Grammar of Assent* Newman is comfortable having faith rise out of an epistemological base. But, like Jesus reminds Thomas in John 14, our hope lies not in what we know, but most assuredly whom we know.

My understanding of an efficacious university is a place that humbly admits that the Truth is already known. It is the job of humankind to be a good citizen by reflecting the glory of God. Many American secular universities see the university as a place for the advancement of knowledge; Newman sees the university as a place for the communication of knowledge and advancement of the Kingdom of God.

As previous explained, there are gods galore at the American secular university.

Chesterton who argued, "Tolerance is the virtue of a man without conviction."

The American secular university deified "toleration," "scientific inquiry," and "intellectual honesty." Today, though, there is considerable confusion about how we ought to live with our differences. The modern appeal to toleration begs the question.

In the modern secular university there is only one viewpoint that is deemed legitimate: that is the conviction of uniform toleration! The net result is that people are forced to choose between their epistemology and their cosmology. People are forced to give up convictions based on what they believe to be true and right if their views appear remotely intolerant. Thus, if an Evangelical believes that homosexuality is a sinful lifestyle he is accused of intolerance. But he believes it because his world view framework demands that he believe it. He believes that the Word of God is truth and cannot be militated or compromised by circumstances or exigencies.

The problem is, according to S.D. Gaede, *When Tolerance is no Virtue* (Downers Grove, IL: Inter Varsity Press, 1993) is that the university asks a question it has no right to ask and then offers no satisfactory answer. What is truth? The American secular university does not have a clue. Many secular scholars know it and they conclude that there is no truth. They have lost confidence in truth searching and have come to the conclusion that truth is unattainable. Universities conclude that holding to a plurality of truths and tolerating them is virtuous. I agree, however, with G. K. Chesterton who argued, "Tolerance is the virtue of a man without conviction."

The evangelical commitment to toleration and intellectual honesty grows out of a commitment to truth and justice. This toleration is expressed through love, which is inevitably misunderstood by the secular university as intellectual dishonesty and parochialism.

While attending a secular university, I remember discussing religion over lunch. Each person shared his faith position. There was much interest engendered among this enlightened university crowd! Compliments and affirmations flowed freely–until I, the token Evangelical was asked about his faith. I stated, "Jesus Christ is the Way, the Truth, and the Life."

"You mean, a way, don't you?" a conciliatory classmate helpfully asked.

"No, I mean Jesus Christ it the ONLY way to wholeness and life," I gently responded.

Well, the Evangelical ruined everyone's lunch–again!

False notions of toleration breed false notions of relativism. Relativism is defined loosely as "anything goes as long as it is embraced sincerely and injures no one else." Evangelicals are ringing a fire bell and warning American culture that there are significant dangers in living in a relativistic world. The fact is, a relativistic world has no universally held view of truth and goodness. Inevitably the modern university is intolerant of intolerance which makes everyone confused and inconsistent.

Recently my son, who is a student at a very strict Christian university, was forbidden to leave campus on the weekend to visit his brother who lived off campus. Now, in fact the reason my youngest son wanted to visit my oldest son was that they wanted to participate in a community mission outreach. My son was irritated, he was frustrated–but he was not confused. The decision of the university was exactly consistent with its world view.

Relativistic toleration makes justice impossible. Both Plato and the Apostle Paul agree; justice requires both a moral and an epistemological base. One cannot do justice unless one knows the difference between right and wrong. The fact is, the American secular university in its headlong pursuit of toleration is victimized by both injustice and

Human needs are greater than this world can satisfy and therefore it is reasonable to look elsewhere. The university has forgotten or ignores this fact.

relativism that leads to intolerance!

Most secular universities have concluded that abstract concepts like grace, hope, and especially faith are indefinable, immeasurable, and above all unreasonable. Not that God or the uniqueness of Jesus Christ can be proved, or disproved. There are certain issues which the order of the intellect simply cannot address, so we must rise above that to the order of the heart. Faith is our consent to receive the good that God would have for us. Evangelicals believe that God can and does act in our world and in our lives. Human needs are greater than this world can satisfy and therefore it is reasonable to look elsewhere. The university has forgotten or ignores this fact (Diogenes Allen, *Christian Belief in a Postmodern World*. Louisville, Kentucky: John Knox Press, 1989).

In the midst of so much uncertainty, it is good to serve a God who loves His creation. The American secular university would try to convince us that it is fun to be living in clashing relativities where the foundations and structures of thoughts are up for grabs. Every truth is negotiated. Truth emerges by virtue of persuasion and consent. Truth is democratized. Morality is based on objective truth from an inspired corpus of information (i.e., the Bible); morality is an outcome of human interchange (Kenneth J. Gergen, *The Saturated Self: Dilemmas of Identity in Contemporary Life*. NY: Harper Collins Publishers, 1991. p. 46).

I doubt, really, if a free, and open debate can occur in a community (i.e., the university) where there is no loyalty to a higher truth, where consensus is absent. The best the American secular university can generate is tolerance for the sake of tolerance. History is reduced to a "pleasure principle." Reality is not based on truth but on the latest political agenda of the reigning department head.

At the beginning of the 21st century there is truly an exciting phenomenon occurring in American society: a resurgence of evangelicalism. As sociologist Peter Berger accurately observes, evangelicals generally subscribe to two strongly held propositions: that a return to Christian values is necessary if the moral confusion of our time is to be overcome, and that the Enlightenment is to be blamed for much of the confusion of our time (Peter Berger, "At Stake in the Enlightenment," *First Things*, March 1996, p. 18).

In fact, 21st century evangelicalism is one of the most potent anti-Enlightenment movements in world history. The excesses of Enlightenment rationalism, exhibited so ably in the secular university, have sabotaged the certitude of classicism and Christian theism that so strongly influenced Western culture long before the formidable onslaught of the likes of David Hume.

The *Washington Post* in 1993 coyly observed that evangelicals are "largely poor, uneducated and easy to command." And, among our own, evangelical professor Mark Noll unkindly observed, "The scandal of the evangelical mind is that there is not much of an evangelical mind." Indeed. Not any more. While conceding that faith is not a makeshift bridge to overcome some Kierkegaardian gap between beliefs and evidence, Evangelicalism posits that it still is important that people look beyond their experience for reality. Human needs and aspirations are greater than the world can satisfy, so it is reasonable to look elsewhere for that satisfaction. Worth is the highest and best reality (a decidedly anti-Enlightenment notion) and its genesis and maintenance come exclusively from relationship with God alone.

Evangelicalism, then, moves backward in time, far back in time, when intellectualism was not separate from religion. It blows the claims of the Enlightenment to bits.

In summary, until 1800 the intellectual elite of the United States emerged largely from evangelical seminaries. Policy, programs, and culture were created from an educated evangelical base. This slowly changed as the American university implemented its own version of the Enlightenment. Toleration became the lodestone that drew the American university forward. Evangelicals were relegated to graduate schools, seminaries, and courses. They no longer were welcome in the core undergraduate secular university. At the same time, in response, evangelicals abandoned the American university. That decision was bittersweet.

The effect of that decision was brought vividly to this author's life when he entered graduate school.

I had looked forward to this day all my life.

Since I was 12 years old I had been told that I was going to Harvard. I had finally arrived.

It was late September and I was on my way to convocation. Now, keep in mind, convocation at Harvard University in the middle 1970s was convened by a homosexual Unitarian, so you can imagine how inspiring it was! But it was the only convocation that I had and I meant to make the most of it.

I lived outside Harvard Yard so I had to plan my trip over carefully. After referencing several Harvard maps, I had planned a perfect strategy to reach my destination. I set out.

However, along the way, I could not help noticing that several Harvard professors, the leaders in their fields, were going in a different direction. They were dressed in all their academic regalia. I tell you, they were impressive! I wanted those crows' feet on my robes! I wanted to be like these fellows!

Now, I had a choice to make. I could follow my own path–a path that I had carefully laid out. Or I could follow these robust paradigms of academia! One would think that these professors knew a better way than I. They lived here. They had Ph.D.s—I could trust these people.

Wrong! They were lost and we all were late.

What is remarkable to me, too, is that I decided to follow these men without any prayer–indeed, as I realized that afternoon, I was attending Harvard without praying about my decision! No prayer at all. I was a believer for 5 years, still young, true, but it never occurred to me to ask God where He wanted me to go to graduate school! I was the perfect candidate for the American secular university: I was making decisions from an existential base and not from a confessional base. I was drawing my information from circumstances and my own scenario generating equipment. I was not walking with God! Yet, the allure of the secular university is quite substantial!

One Harvard professor, the great evangelical author Fred Buechner resigned from Harvard Divinity School because he felt embarrassed to mention God in his classes. "The mere mention of God–an omniscient God, God as a transcendent being– when I was there . . . would be guaranteed to produce snickers," Ari Goldman wrote (*Atlantic Monthly*, Dec., 1990).

By 1920, with its reductionism mentality, the American secular university had become an inhospitable place for evangelicals. The mother turned and ate her young. The place that was founded by evangelicals, to prepare Evangelicals to be the elite of American culture is now a place of danger, risk, and struggle for its progeny.

Worse than that: Evangelicals seemed to accept willingly their own demise. Evangelical Christians in positions of formal power passively yielded to each stage in the advance of secularism. And, when they did resist, they failed.

Why? Douglas Sloan, in *Faith and Knowledge: Mainline Protestantism and American Higher Education* (Philadelphia: Westminster/John Knox) argues that the university looked to liberal Protestant Christianity to replace Evangelical Christianity. What no one understood, including Evangelical Christians, was that science, as understood in the late 19th century, was fundamentally at odds with Evangelical thought. The university was firmly in the camp of positivistic philosophy that basically had discarded the notion of supernatural from American intellectualism. Evangelicals tried accommodation, but, after the Scopes Trial, they abandoned ship, so to speak. So, if the secular university rejected evangelicalism, by 1920, evangelicalism abandoned the secular university.

In the end the university pulled back from affirming the real possibility of knowing God and of the existence of a spiritual world. What evangelicals learned, or thought that they learned, was that the secular American university was too dangerous a place to be. So they formed their own universities. It is unfortunate that there was no fight to the finish in the 1920s. If the issue had been forced who knows if we would live in a society dominated by secular-minded people. In the initial stages, though, Evangelicals did not muster the intellectual resources necessary to challenge the cultural assumption that knowledge comes only from natural sources (see Phillip E. Johnson , "How the Universities Were Lost," in *First Things* 51 (March 1995) 51-56). They never have–even until today.

Readers should not presume that I am arguing for a return to this parochial purpose of higher education, nor are readers to suppose that I would like to live in a country where everyone is forced to embrace a particular religious world view. Nonetheless, by and large, the marriage of American education and religion was assured for about the first 150 years of our existence. Its demise in the 20th century had disastrous results.

In fact, this author argues that a primary cause of the present unnatural American embrace of narcissistic, naturalistic secularism can be traced to the evangelical loss of the university. When American elitism was separated from its evangelical moorings, the cultural decline of American culture was assured. The divorce of the American university–the breeding ground of American elite culture—and Christian evangelicalism has created some of the cultural woes we presently are facing as a nation. Its reclamation—the evangelical campaign to reclaim the elite leadership of this nation—bodes well for the future cultural health of the United States.

Recalling again my time in Harvard Chapel in the middle of the 1970s and hearing the bold—but accurate I fear—assertion that the next generation of culture creators were attending this institution and institutions like it. We were told that we were the select few, the elite. That probably was true—evidenced by the cultural mess we find ourselves at the beginning of the next century.

That is all changing—and partly due to the popularity of the American home schooling movement. In massive numbers the American home school movement—initially and presently primarily an evangelical Christian movement—is depositing some of the brightest, capable students in our country into the old, august institutions like Harvard. And, what is more exciting, the flashpoint of cultural change is changing from Harvard, Princeton, Darmouth, and Stanford to Wheaton, Grove City, Calvin, and Liberty (all evangelical universities). Before long the new wave of elite culture creators will be graduating from American secular universities and Christian universities and they shall be a great deal different from the elite of which I was a part in the middle 1970s. I am not saying the secular university will change quickly—intellectual naturalistic reductionism makes that extremely difficult. However, I do see the whole complexion of university graduates to change significantly in the next twenty years. Never in the history of the world has such a thing happened.

Something similar occurred at the end of Augustine's life in the middle of the first millennium. Augustine lived in a time when the Roman Empire was collapsing. However, while the barbarians conquered Rome, the Church of Jesus Christ conquered the barbarians. Augustine and his elite Christian generation was used by the Lord to assure the future of the European church and European civilization.

Again, in the 1600s a new generation of evangelicals arose—the Puritans. Likewise this new generation of elites settled the New World and established the United States of America.

Young people, if you are part of this new evangelical elite, you have immense opportunities ahead of you. A new Godly generation is arising. Are they called for such a time as this to guide this nation into another unprecedented revival? We shall see.

Now, though, it is important that we look at more practical considerations. For instance, how is one accepted and able to thrive in the most competitive universities—secular or Christian? What does it mean to be a "Christian" university?

As this author argues, however one may feel about it, most of the culture creators of America graduate from 10 or 12 prestigious, competitive, mostly secular schools. That will change slowly as Christian universities become more competitive in attracting the best students (this author observed recently that the Christian evangelical university Grove City had the same acceptance rate as Princeton University!). In fact, many of the world's decision makers are graduates of these schools. And, praise God, evangelicals have more opportunities than ever to attend these schools. We have already discussed what the liberal 21st century university looks like.

What is an evangelical to do? An evangelical makes 1550 on the SAT and is invited to apply to Princeton or Rice or Stanford or Duke. Should he? And, if he is accepted, how does he survive—even thrive—in a secular prestigious/competitive college. Should you attend competitive secular colleges? Or do you attend Christian schools alone? I give an overview of how a Christian can prosper in an environment that is *ipso facto* hostile.

Under what circumstances would you perhaps decide to attend a secular college?

If you are a Daniel, or can exist and thrive in Babylon without being a Babylonian, you might choose to attend a secular college. Daniel was part of the elite culture in this hostile land. He was honored and respected, but he remained a worshipper of Yahweh (Almighty God). Even though he lived in a hostile, risky, dangerous land, Daniel was able to maintain his identity in the Lord. Remember: you can make bad choices in a Christian university as easily as in a secular University. The fact is, a better choice is merely to make Godly choices regardless of where you are!

When I entered Vanderbilt University as an evangelical freshman, before I began, I had decided to be obedient to Scripture. I decided that before I began my studies! And I am glad I did!

Over the next four years of undergraduate school, and then two years of graduate school, I was sorely tested. For example, I had decided to remain morally pure and chaste. That was no easy thing since I lived in co-ed dorms both at Vanderbilt and then at Harvard! But I persevered. Success was rooted, however, at the moment I committed myself to a discipline—before the actual temptation began. It wasn't that the temptation was mitigated; it was simply that the desire to be Christ-like was greater than the temptation. Again, though, it began before I went to college.

If you are a Daniel, you may be called to an academic discipline no Christian college offers. In that case you might choose a secular university.

Be careful: what is a Christian college? Only a very few Christian colleges offer Ph.D.s. This means that the majority of Christian College faculties are trained in secular universities. That means there is no guarantee that Christian faculty will have a world view different from secular university faculty.

As a rule of thumb, in my opinion, evangelical students should try to attend Christian colleges. The fact is, if you are planning to attend graduate school, undergraduate degrees (if they are accredited) are more or less perceived equally by most graduate schools. If you have any doubt, phone the school and ask where their students attend graduate school.

Finally, in many ways it is a moot point. The majority of evangelical parents prefer to send their students to local, state or community colleges. Why? Cost. You can save on tuition and housing costs. In fact, it is not a bad idea to take most of your basic courses at a community or junior college. Keep this in mind, though. Transfer students with two years of college (c. sixty credits) virtually never receive financial aid. So, if you have a chance to receive scholarship aid, it might be more financial feasible for you to attend a four year undergraduate school immediately after high school graduation.

Speaking of graduation, why don't some of you home school students consider a senior mission year? My son, Peter, finished his academic work junior year, obtained a good SAT Score, and spent his senior year suffering for Jesus at Maui (as in Maui, Hawaii) Bible College. It was a very positive experience for him. When he finished Bible College, he applied to college (his SAT scores were current) and he began his undergraduate education at Liberty University, Lynchburg, Virginia.

Some students wisely learn a trade before they begin undergraduate school. For instance, I have heard of a young man (home schooled) who learned how to wire houses. While an undergraduate and then a graduate student at Cornel University, he paid his way through college by wiring houses. When he graduated with a Ph. D. in electrical engineering he had no debt and obviously he was very employable.

Some of you will consider distance learning programs. Obviously these alternatives are growing very popular. With good reason. More and more of them are accredited. But be careful. Not all are accredited and some are actually more expensive than resident education. You should contact several graduate schools and ask them how they feel about admitting online students from your preferred undergraduate school.

There are four major components to college admission:
- An SAT or ACT score
- A Completed Transcript
- References
- An Admission Essay(s)

By far the most important component to college admission is the SAT/ACT tests.

It is important to understand that the SAT I is an aptitude test, not an achievement test (like the Iowa Basics or Stanford Tests). The SAT II or Subject Area Exams are achievement tests. The SAT I is a math and English test—there is no history, science, or any other subjects on the exam (although students will need these other subject for college admission).

The College Board® claims that almost 4 out of every 5 American colleges require the SAT I. That is not bad news. Christian students in general, home schooled Christian students in particular, are doing very well on the SAT I. Evangelical Christians should view preparation for the SAT I as an opportunity to grapple with an important question: *Can they become what God is calling them to be?* They won't have the whole answer to this vital question at the end of their SAT preparation, but this can be a first step.

Students usually take the SAT I during the second semester of their junior year or first semester of their senior year. It measures their potential success in college, but it does not necessarily measure their information acquisition and assimilation skills. It has absolutely nothing at all to do with a student's worth or esteem in God's eyes.

The math portion and the verbal portion of the SAT are much different from the SAT some of us took several decades ago. There are more analysis questions, vocabulary is understood almost entirely in context, and there will be exercises requiring students to compare two reading passages. They will even have to write in some answers, instead of just picking a letter! There will be no antonyms on the SAT I, but double the number of reading comprehension questions. Finally, students will be allowed to use a calculator to help them with the math portion of the exam.

Vocabulary development is critical. As a matter of fact, I judge that 40 percent of the questions on the 2004 verbal portion of the SAT are related to vocabulary. Since analogies will be dropped and vocabulary problems will be increased, there are indications that that percentage will decrease on the 2005 exam. But that does not mean that students should ignore vocabulary development. Therefore, more than ever, it is vital that students learn the Latin/Greek roots of words. Also they should learn to define words in context. It is a waste of time for students to memorize the 500 most frequently used words on the SAT I. A better approach is to read good books (a list is included in the back of *The SAT and College Preparation Course for the Christian Student*).

Higher level critical thinking is important to high SAT I scores. The SAT I is a cognitive, developmentally-based exam which assumes that students learn in stages. Bloom's Taxonomy is frequently a reference resource for cognitive developmental thinking. Bloom's Taxonomy argues that students learn in six stages. Most of the questions on the SAT I are based on the bottom and most challenging three levels: analysis, synthesis, and evaluation. As a matter of fact, unless students are able to function at these higher thinking levels, they are doomed to manifest scores below 1000.

Sixty percent of the 2004 SAT I concerns critical reading exercises. That percentage will increase to eighty percent with the 2005 exam. In fact, the College Board is renaming the verbal section of the SAT I "Critical Reading Section." This change in titling shows how serious the College Board folks are about critical reading. The verbal section will no longer include analogies. Instead, short reading passages will be added to existing long reading passages. A new section called the SAT writing section will be added. It will contain multiple-choice grammar questions as well as a written essay. That is good news to most classical-educated students who have spent years studying grammar and writing

Bloom's Taxonomy* (*Argues that people learn in stages.)

Knowledge: Remembering the material without understanding, using, or changing the material.

Comprehension: Understanding the material being given without comparing it to anything else.

Application: Using a general concept to solve a problem.

Analysis: Taking something apart.

Synthesis: Creating something new by putting different ideas together to make a new whole.

Evaluation: Judging the value of material.

Students do not have to know how to solve quadratic equations to do well on the math portion of the SAT I. Some algebra and basic geometry is helpful, but I have found that the key to high performance on the math portion is the same as it is on the verbal portion: critical thinking and critical reading skills. Thus, best scores come from individuals who think well and read well-even if their math skills are average. The 2005 SAT I math section will not only cover concepts from geometry and elementary algebra, it will contain concepts from Algebra II. The math computation on the SAT I is usually not difficult. What makes the math portion of the SAT I so difficult is that it is presented in a word problem format. Thus strong critical thinking and advanced critical reading skills will increase SAT I math as well as SAT I verbal scores. The addition of Algebra II computations should not alarm good students. Good students, especially good home schooled students, usually have had or are taking Algebra II before or during the junior year when the SAT I should be taken.

The best time to take the SAT I is May or June of one's junior year. This allows students to retake the SAT I October of their senior year if necessary. Preparation is very helpful if the student implements a long- term program–as advocated in The SAT and College Preparation Course. Without long-term coaching, there is no correlation between the frequency of taking aptitude tests (e.g., SAT I and IQ tests) and increased scores. Therefore, the author recommends that students take as many unofficial, old, real (i. e., from the College Board) SAT I tests as they can. Students should avoid the high cost of taking stressful official tests at their local high schools and universities. They are much better off if they take practice tests. Practice SAT I tests can be obtained by contacting me (www.whatisthebesttest.com) or they can be borrowed from some libraries. Remember, there is evidence that a small percentage of colleges average SAT I scores (rather than accept the highest score). Therefore, students should anonymously obtain as many unofficial scores as they can and then take the test one or two times officially.

The PSAT is the major determinate of the National Merit scholarship. As you know, for years I have advocated ignoring the PSAT unless students are legitimate National Merit Scholar possibilities. I observe that since 1% of Americans actually are National Merit possibilities, since there is no correlation between PSAT and SAT I scores, and since some students are discouraged by low PSAT scores, it is unhelpful or even harmful to take the PSAT. I argue that the best preparation for the SAT I is the practice SAT I and years of advance preparation. Students should use practice SAT I tests as practice for the SAT I. They should not use the PSAT.

Finally, my 30 years of coaching remind me how important stress reduction is to high SAT I scores. In fact, in my opinion, it is the most important preparation variable. For Christians, at least, stress reduction is best accomplished by a frequent and rigorous devotional and Bible memorization program and disciplined devotional time.

The best time to take the SAT I is May or June of one's junior year.

Here are a few common-sense sorts of things to know about college admission:

- Don't be discouraged by high tuition charges. Private colleges, for instance, especially the costly ones, usually have much more money to give away in financial aid than state-supported schools. While cost consideration is an issue, many competitive colleges are very generous with financial aid.
- Financial aid is offered according to SAT scores, need, race/gender, transcript/recommendations, zip code—in that order. The financial aid process is separate from the admission process.
- A college will look at your entire high school record, from ninth grade on. But a college knows that a transcript is subjective and still want an SAT I or ACT score.
- Keep good records of interviews. Use your prayer journal to record what God is doing in your life through the process.
- You should make sure that you have taken pre-algebra, algebra I, algebra II, geometry, and advanced math (optional). If the way is clear, for practical considerations, take a consumer math course senior year.
- Playing a musical instrument and participating in debate are two events that many colleges consider special, and applicants with special talents get special consideration, above and beyond those who do nothing in school but get good grades.
- A second language helps your college application but I recommend Latin as one of your languages. By all means, take at least two years of each language.
- The volume of your mail is an early indication of how desirable a college applicant you will be. Colleges only recruit students they really want. The more mail you get, the more colleges want you.
- Show interest in the college. Be assertive.
- Be creative on your transcript. Advanced Literary Analysis: Beowulf to Ben Jonson sounds a whole lot better than English Literature I.
- Take the SAT I in the spring of your junior year.
- Take the SAT II if necessary. The SAT II is a subject area exam. Besides many competitive colleges require that all students take 2-3 exams, it is a way to show special knowledge. For instance, engineering majors who wish to attend Georgia Tech may find it advantageous to take a subject area in physics.
- Consider taking a CLEP or AP test or two.
- In your junior year visit the college(s) you are considering.
- If you apply to a college, you want the admission officer to have a favorable impression of you, even before reading your application. The interview when you visit the campus is your shot at creating that impression. The interview is important-especially to a home school student.

Transcript of High School Record
Home Education Program

Name: _____ Date of Birth: _____ Soc. Sec. #_____
Address: _____ City: _____ ST: _____ ZIP: _____
Entrance Date: _____ Graduation Date: _____ Diploma Number: _____

	FRESHMAN YEAR 200?-200?			SOPHOMORE YEAR 200?-200?			JUNIOR YEAR 200?-200?			SENIOR YEAR 200?-200?		
	COURSE TITLE	Gr	Cr	COURSE TITLE	Gr	Cr	COURSE TITLE	Gr	Cr	COURSE TITLE	Gr	Cr
ENGLISH (4 years Required)												
MATHEMATICS (3 years Required)												
SCIENCE (3 years Required)												
SOCIAL STUDIES (3 years Required)												
ARTS AND HUMANITIES (2 years Required)												
OTHER AREAS (Not Required)												
SUPERVISOR'S SIGNATURE:												
EVALUATOR'S SIGNATURE: Teaching Cert. No. Psychology License No. or School of Experience												

I certify that this student met all of the requirements for graduation from a home education program, and that the home education program was in full compliance with [state] law at the time of graduation.

SIGNATURE OF SUPERVISOR _____

GR. = GRADE: A= Excellent, B = Good, C = Fair, D = Poor, P = Pass, F = Fail, I = Incomplete
CR. is Credit: Unit of credit is years. 1 = 1 year, 1/2 = 1/2 year

John Smith Student

	FRESHMAN YEAR 1999-2000			SOPHOMORE YEAR 2000-2001			JUNIOR YEAR 2001-2002			SENIOR YEAR 2002-2003		
	COURSE TITLE	Gr	Cr	COURSE TITLE	Gr	Cr	COURSE TITLE	Gr	Cr	COURSE TITLE	Gr	Cr
ENGLISH (4 years Required)	Rhetoric I	B	1	Rhetoric II	B	1	Medieval-Reformation	A	1	Classical-Church Fathers	A	1
	Literature: Reformation-Romanticism	B	1	Literature: Naturalism-Existentialism	A	1						
MATHEMATICS (3 years Required)	Algebra II	A	1	Geometry	A	1	Trigonometry & Pre-Calculus	A	1	Calculus I	A	1
SCIENCE (3 years Required)	Natural Science	A	1	Biology	A	1	Chemistry	A	1	Physics	A	1
SOCIAL STUDIES (3 years Required)	Reformation to the American Civil War	B	1	Gilded Age	A	1	Medieval History	A	1	Ancient History	A	1
	Civics	B	1	Post-modernism	A	1	Economics I	A	1	Spanish II	A	1
ARTS AND HUMANITIES (2 years Required)	Debate & Logic	A	1	Latin II	A	1	Spanish I	A	1	Summit Ministries	A	1
	Latin I	A	1	Art	A	1	Philosophy: World View	A	1	Bible & Theology	A	1
							Bible & Theology	A	1			
OTHER AREAS (Not Required)	SAT Preparation	A	1	SAT Preparation	A	1	SAT Preparation	A	1	SAT Preparation	A	1
	Soccer	A	1	Soccer	A	1	Soccer	A	1	Soccer	A	1
SUPERVISOR'S SIGNATURE:												

I certify that this student met all of the requirements for graduation from a home education program, and that the home education program was in full compliance with [state] law at the time of graduation.

SIGNATURE OF SUPERVISOR _____

GR. = GRADE: A= Excellent, B = Good, C = Fair, D = Poor, P = Pass, F = Fail, I = Incomplete
CR. is Credit: Unit of credit is years. 1 = 1 year, 1/2 = 1/2 year

As you make final preparations for college, consider this information. American society is manifesting:

- Increasingly dysfunctional culture.
- A pervasive and abiding concern about the future
- A serious breakdown of community.
- Confusion about individual responsibility.
- Confusion about what toleration is.
- Confusion about sexuality.

As we begin the new millennium, Robert Bork in his prophetic book *Slouching Toward Gomorrah* warns us that the out of control individualism and egalitarianism of the 1960s are very much with us. One merely has to recall the impeachment hearings several years ago to see evidence of this sort of morality where "if what he is doing harms no one (individualism) then it is ok to do it (egalitarianism). We are part of a therapeutic culture, where wholeness is replaced by holiness, sanctification is replaced by therapy. And even the heartiest pagan is getting really tired of this mess! And, as he does, he may very well choose home schooling as an alternative to public education.

Os Guinness warns us that at some point Americans will become fed up with the excesses and dysfunctional aspects of our culture. He says that as American mainline culture fails to sustain Americans in their hedonistic pursuit of self interest, they will want something more. It is now questionable whether America's cultural order is capable of nourishing the freedom, responsibility, and civility that Americans require to sustain democracy. Modernity (a word to describe modern American culture) creates problems far deeper than drugs. It creates a crisis of cultural authority in which America's beliefs, ideals, and traditions are losing their compelling power in society. William Bennett is right to warn us that there is a "death of outrage" in our country but he might add that there is a numbness spreading across the land that offers much opportunity for Christians in general and for home schoolers in particular.

Next, there is a pervasive and abiding concern about the future. To those of us who lived through the Cold War this seem ludicrous. But the tentativeness and fear that pervades American society are real. Witness the catastrophe at Columbine. Those two young men were angry, confused, but most of all hopeless. We have lost our way; lost our dreams. Harvard professor Dr. Harvey Cox writes: "We once had dreams and no technology to bring them to pass. Now we have technology but no dreams!"

In fact, most social critics argue persuasively that this generation is one of the most hopeless in history. Interestingly enough this hopelessness has made us rather sentimental. We have become very sentimental about the past. Even in our most creative creations it is more of the same. Even though Hans Solo is a liar, a criminal and a fornicator, he still is a do-gooder spreading George Lucas' version of truth and justice across the land. But God is totally absent. The Star Wars phenomenon is so appealing because it is about the past; not about the future. Luke Skywalker is more like John Wayne than he is like Tom Cruise.

To this hopeless generation history is not sacred; it is merely utilitarian. It is not didactic; it helps make them feel better. The modern psychologist B.F. Skinner, for instance, disdains history and gives M & M's® to monkeys. We have no actions—only fate driving us. We are rudderless. The fact is we Christians know, however, that God is in absolute control of history. We need to teach our children to be tirelessly hopeful. We need to make sure that we are not mawkish! We can easily do so by speaking the

It is now questionable whether America's cultural order is capable of nourishing the freedom, responsibility, and civility that Americans require to sustain democracy.

Truth found in the Word of God in places of deception.

One of the greatest problems in this generation is confusion about individual responsibility. It was Freud who told us that feelings of guilt were a sign not of vice, but of virtue. That our problems stemmed from our mothers, not from our sin. Perhaps our problem began with Goethe whose Faust escapes the consequences of his sin by sincerity and good humor. What does this say for poor theistic Gretchen? Look at the evolution of the American understanding of hero:

- 1930-1970 Traditional John Wayne . . . While he was not overtly Christian, Wayne exhibited Judeo-Christian behavior in all his actions.
- 1970-2000 Modern Clint Eastwood . . . Eastwood is moral but the end justifies the mean. He is motivated by a golden-rule sort of moral code.
- 2000-Present Post-Christian Tom Cruise . . . Morality to Cruise is defined by what is right in his own eyes.

Perhaps our movie icons best typify what America values and promotes in her culture.

If we are confused about what is right and wrong, about individual responsibilities, we are even more confused about toleration. S.D. Gaede, *When Tolerance is No Virtue*, says . . . "In our culture, there is considerable confusion about how we ought to live with our differences and a cacophony of contradictory justifications for one approach as opposed to another. All appeal to the need of tolerance, but there is nothing like common argument on what that means. The question our culture raises by nature and development is what is truth and what can we believe? Our culture doesn't know the answers. In fact, we have lost confidence in truth and have come to the conclusion that truth is unattainable. Thus, tolerance moves to the forefront."

Finally, in the years ahead, there will be real confusion about sexual roles. Sir Arnold Toynbee says . . . In the nineteen forties Toynbee studied civilizations and came to the following conclusions: Based on his study of twenty-one civilizations Toynbee found that societies in disintegration suffer a kind of "schism of the soul." They are seldom simply overrun by some other civilization. Rather, they commit a sort of cultural suicide. Disintegrating societies have several characteristics, Toynbee argues. They fall into a sense of abandon People begin to yield to their impulses-especially in the sexual area. They also succumb to truancy that is escapism seeking to avoid their problems by retreating into their own worlds of distraction and entertainment. There is a sense of drift as they realize that they have no control over their lives. Consciousness is adrift, unable to anchor itself to any universal ground of justice, truth on which the ideals of modernity have been founded in the past.

Evangelicals, therefore, must not merely talk the talk. They must walk the walk. They are seeking to create an alternative community of hope. We/they are sabotaging the conspiracy of hopelessness and self-centeredness that is so pervasive in our nation. Bring on the revolution!

Next, once we understand the world to which you are called there are several things I want to see happen to you.

Make sure that you know who you are and who your God is. "By faith, Moses, when he had grown up refused to be known as the son of Pharaoh's daughter." (Heb. 11:24)

Refuse to be absorbed into the world but choose to be a part of God's kingdom. You are special and peculiar generation. Much loved. But you live among a people who do not know who they are. A people without hope. You need to know who you are—children of the Living God—and then you must live a hopeful life.

Take responsibility for your life. Moses accepted responsibility for his life. "He chose to be mistreated along with the people of God rather to enjoy the pleasures of sin for a short time." (Heb. 11: 25) If you don't make decisions for your life, someone else will.

Get a cause worth dying for. Moses accepted necessary suffering even unto death. You need a cause worth dying for (as well as living for). "He [Moses] regarded disgrace for the sake of Christ as of greater value than the treasures of Egypt, because he was looking ahead to his reward." (Heb. 11: 26). Evangelicals know that we are crucified with Christ, yet it is not we who live but Christ who lives in us (Gals 2:20).

Never ever take your eyes off the goal. "By faith, he left Egypt, not fearing the king's anger; he persevered because he saw Him who is invisible." (Heb. 11:27). How long can you wait? How long can you persevere? What is your threshold of obedience?

The following are ten moral issues that must be clear in your mind before you go to college:

- Punishment and blame: What is fair punishment? Do you accept your authority's right to enforce laws?
- Property: What is property and who owns it?
- Affiliation roles: What is a family? What are the motivations and obligations of a good family/ community member?
- Laws and statues: When if ever should laws be disobeyed?
- Life: What makes life valuable? Is life inviolable?
- Truth & Contracts: What is the truth? Why is truth telling valuable? Are there inviolable covenants that human beings must make?
- Government: What is a good citizen?
- Social justice: What are basic political, economic, and social rights?
- Sexuality: Is sex merely a biological response or is it related to religious or social guidelines?

Practically speaking:

- Find a local church before you go to college. Go to the first service you can.
- Parents should meet the local pastor and introduce themselves.
- Participate in a local Christian group—Navigators, Intervarsity, et al. But that does not substitute for a local church.
- Purpose to live a Godly life before you face temptation.
- Set up a study schedule that is a priority only behind your devotional life.
- Practice courtship.
- Expect persecution. The main persecution you will receive will be about your profession that Christ is the only way, the only truth, the only life.
- Summer school can be a spiritual and financial opportunity for you. You can participate in mission trips that may count for academic credit and may also help you grow spiritually. Also, summer school may be a cost-effective way to accelerate your college experience and thereby save money for you and your parents.
- Avoid all appearance of evil.
- Write from a Christian perspective but do not allow your confessional stand to be an excuse for shoddy work.
- You will probably not be able to choose your roommate before you first arrive.

But you can choose your roommate for your sophomore year. Choose wisely.

- Pray for your unsaved friends.
- Know the Truth.
- Live the Truth.
- Work hard and be the best follower of Christ that you can be!

Finally, what does it mean to the future of America to have 4 million of its best, brightest, and spirit filled students graduating from the most prestigious universities in the world? What will it mean to have four million new business persons, artists, authors, military officers, business leaders, and government leaders who are spirit-filled evangelical Christians? I can feel the ground shaking!!!!

Fifty Examples of College Admission Essays

The following are fifty potential college admission essays-types. That is to say that these are fifty essays that will hopefully inspire you to write even better essays! These essays, no doubt, cover every conceivable essay topic that a college might assign you. Again, do not copy these essays—write your own. They are meant to stimulate creativity in your own writing!

This year alone, five hundred thousand college applicants will write college admission essays. Slightly less than one-half will be rejected by their first choice school, while only about ten percent will gain admission to the nation's thirteen top colleges. With acceptance rates at all-time lows, with admission committees exhibited well-founded concern about writing deficiencies among admitted freshman, high SAT/ACT scores are important. But the admission essay has gained more and more importance.

Whether you are applying to Harvard, Wheaton, or your local state school, you will write an admission essay. Your job is to distinguish yourself from thousands of applicants with similar skills and abilities.

Every college application requires one or two essays. Here are a few observations:

- Your audience is not your English teacher. Your audience is a college admission committee. While you need to give ample attention to syntax and grammar, the content is more important. Don't lose any sleep if you have a dangling modifier. The admission committee wishes to ascertain if you are going to be a successful college student, not that you are a perfect grammarian. That is not to suggest that you can employ shoddy writing; everything counts. But give attention to content more than anything else.
- Make your essay as personable as possible. Remember: this is a persuasive essay but you are not arguing a position. You are selling yourself.
- Do not write too much or too little. Most essays should be about 250-500 words (unless told otherwise).

Inevitably admission essays are based on one of the following topics:

- Evaluate a significant experience, achievement, risk you have taken, or an ethical dilemma you have faced and its impact on you.
- Discuss some issue of personal, local, national, or international concern and its importance to you.
- Indicate a person who has had a significant influence on you, and describe that influence.
- Describe a character in fiction, an historical figure, or a creative work (as in art, music, science, etc.) that has had an influence on you, and explain that influence.
- A range of academic interests, personal perspectives, and life experiences adds much to the educational mix. Given your personal background, describe an experience that illustrates what you would bring to the diversity in a college community, or an encounter that demonstrated the importance of diversity to you.
- Topic of your choice.

The fact is, almost any essay topic is acceptable. The following essays are typological examples of successful essays. Most are fictional. The reader will observe that some of the examples are rewritten pieces from my other published books. Remember: these essays are suggested templates—readers are invited to create their own successful types. These essays, of course are not to be copied!

Write on the Topic

- No matter how interesting or well-written an essay, you must write on the topic. Your argument and evidence must be relevant to the question. Your answer should demonstrate that you have understood what the question is asking, and that you have indeed answered the asked question. Feel free to actually tell the reader, "This paper is about . . ." and "Now the reader understands . . ." Leave nothing to chance.

Clear structure and Argumentation

- The connections between each stage of your argument and the original question should be evident throughout the essay. Essays should not be just a series of unsupported arguments. You must evidence thoroughly your arguments.

Appropriate style

- For an academic essay the third person is a more preferable style. In any event, never use the second person. Remember your audience. By all means, remember that your writing should be grammatically accurate. Poor punctuation and weak sentence construction will create a bad impression.

Originality

- Your essay should demonstrate originality. However, don't be maudlin or faddish–answer the question succinctly and clearly as possible. Cogency should never be replaced by verbose originality.

In summary, here are three elements of style that you will need to address in your essay:
- Content: ideas are specific, relevant to focus and fully developed.
- Organization: there is a logical order of ideas.
- Focus: awareness of an audience/task; a clear purpose.

How to Write Precisely:

- Use the active voice.
- Use action, colorful verbs.
- Use as few words as possible.
- Reduce prepositional phrases.
- Reduce expletive constructions.
- Avoid using vague nouns; leads to wordiness.
- Avoid big words—aim for precision, not haughtiness.
- Avoid noun strings

The following is an admission essay written for Yale University.

South Arkansas summers are hot and humid. The golf course is usually empty towards the afternoon as most of the golfers play in the cool of the morning. Miller, William, Joseph, and I have morning jobs, summer school, or volunteer projects, but we manage to get together for a nine-hole round of golf each afternoon around three or four o'clock. I found these afternoon outings to be not only a great source of stress relief but also a source of inspiration on how to conduct my life.

Miller teed off first. After marking his ball he bent down and repaired his divot. We all have had divots in life. Backing out of a driveway full of cars one afternoon, I ran into a neighbor's Honda. I thought of driving away, since no one else was outside, but I knew that the divot was my responsibility to fix. Instead of leaving, I went inside and told my neighbor what happened. All of my birthday money, and then some, went to repair her car, yet I knew I did the right thing. How could such a little bump cost $300?

Later, as William made an approach shot, a strong gust of wind carried his ball into the woods. Instead of teasing him, we helped him find his ball. Just as William could not control the weather, there is much in life we cannot control. William's sister is autistic and her condition is beyond his family's control. Many times, my friends and I have helped William watch or play with Susana. We do not control the gifts or challenges life sends our way as I have found out from my friends.

On the sixth fairway I found myself in the rough. I thought back to my previous shot and tried to discern what caused the ball to stray off course. I knew that if I did not fix my swing, chances were high the problem would get worse. Likewise, last year I found myself in the rough at mid-semester with a C in History. Just as I did with my golf swing, I analyzed what was causing the problem and fixed it. It took extra effort to pull that grade up but with hard work and endurance I earned a low A.

As we neared the end of the front nine, Joseph pulled out three golf balls and began to juggle them. He told me to lighten up about my bogies on the previous three holes. He suggested that if I would learn to juggle I might have a future in the circus. This made us all laugh. Joseph had open-heart surgery this summer for a heart valve defect. He reminded us to not sweat the small stuff.

At the end of each game we stop in the snack shop for a coke. As we sit around a broken card table, I remind myself to not take these moments for granted. Since moving to ----- seven years ago, I have known eight students who have died by auto accidents and one by cancer. I am reminded by them to be grateful for every day that I am given and to make the most out of each opportunity in life. Dave Matthews says in one of his songs that every day should be a good day to die. I intend to make every day count. (Robert)

The author chooses a common motif, a game of golf, to exhibit profound elements of life. Notice that the author is very vulnerable and personable. Admission committees like this.

Essay 2

Admission essay for Duke University.

------ is a small town in south Arkansas two hours from the nearest large city. Many choose to live elsewhere because it is a rural area with limited access to activities and resources, yet I have come to appreciate what my town has to offer me. Growing up surrounded by forests and farms has given me unique experiences that have defined and shaped my views and activities in life.

Living in such a rural area has given me a greater appreciation of nature. I enjoy sitting alone on a deer stand during the last of the predawn moments. Nothing is heard except an occasional call from a night bird or an insect. A hint of sunrise can be seen in the east creating a gray-lighted atmosphere. A low fog settles on the ground below me. I am completely alone with only my thoughts to keep me company. Slowly as the sun begins to rise, color fills my gray-lighted world. Each twig and leaf on every tree takes on a shape and brilliant color. Birds awaken and sing loudly their songs of the morning. Never before have I seen such beauty or felt such contentment in my life. All of this was achieved simply by sitting alone in the woods. Living in a small Southern town has allowed me to have experiences in nature that few living in a city will ever have. I wouldn't trade experiences such as these for all the entertainment any city has to offer.

Although ------ is small in size, many opportunities are available. We have an excellent Arts Center. I volunteered much of the summer there assisting with art shows, musicals and a children's art camp. Various types of sports are offered from Friday night football games in the fall to my soccer games in the spring. The community is very supportive of its athletes. The curriculum at ----- High School surprisingly mimics one of a larger city high school. Many AP courses have opened doors for me to gain possible college credit and prepare me to study biomedical engineering at a top tier university. ----- may be small, yet it still has many of the advantages of a much larger urban area.

By living here I also see the real world. ----- has wide racial and economic diversity. For example, I attend the public high school where whites are in the minority. Some of my classmates' families are multi-millionaires from the Arkansas oil boom in the 1920's, while others live is extreme poverty. In any career path that I choose, I will encounter a variety of people. Because of my upbringing, I will be better able to work with people different than myself.

-----, translated from Spanish, means "The Golden". The founders of my hometown were right in naming it that, because I feel that there is no better place that I could have been raised. ----- provides many of the opportunities that a large city would yet still has the friendly country atmosphere of a small town. I have been privileged to grow up with such cultural and economic diversity. This variety of experiences has given me a better understanding of different cultures and an appreciation of both urban and rural life. (Robert)

This author gives an appealing picture of his hometown. Admission committees like to admit happy students!

Essay

Admission essay for Brown University.

You may have found my application to be a little bit different-my situation isn't typical by any means. Coming from a home-schooled, Christian, large family environment, my application may stick out for better or for worse. I'm hoping to use this space to explain a little bit about myself, in the hopes that it will allay any reservations you may have. Having grown up in a large family, I believe, has helped me develop excellent social skills; consider the interests of lots of people, not just myself; and develop intellectually. In my family, one is allowed to discuss any topic. The smattering of takes on most problems has helped me to see that simple solutions are rare.

To live a full and balanced life, I think we need to take time to enjoy life, away from work and study. One of my high priorities is to spend time with family and friends, and to enjoy freeing pursuits, like flying, cycling, and reading. I have a lot of friends, several of them quite close. We spend a healthy-to San Francisco-I've adored flying. While I can't afford lessons, I hope one day to get my flying license, and perhaps even own a plane. Seven years ago, I began to enjoy cycling. Until I had enough money to get a good bike, I rode all over town on a $20 road bike. When I was twelve, I became the NC state champion on that bike. Being home-schooled has freed me up to read lots of wonderful books-my favorites are by Charlotte Bronte and C. S. Lewis. Reading and cycling are both ways that I refuel myself-intellectually, emotionally, and physically.

I am increasingly interested in theology and in philosophy. I believe that a society's underlying philosophy has a significant impact on its success or failure. Naturally, I'm interested in what philosophies and theologies are driving our society, and what effect they're having. I recently listened, with great interest, to a Congressional hearing, as Senators and Cabinet-level officials discussed prohibiting the political activism of radical Islamic groups in Middle-Eastern nations. It triggered a flurry of questions in my mind: Where do rights such as free speech, press, and religion come from? If these rights only exist inside a society of mostly good people, our nation's stability is endangered-suddenly these inalienable rights have become conditional. Are people mostly good, meaning those rights are indeed inalienable? I believe humanity is fallen-people have a proclivity to hurt others-we see it in our history books and hear it on the news. Perhaps those rights do need to be qualified. Needless to say, I'm very interested in our humanity, and what we can do to influence the direction that it's headed.

My mind floods with ideas when I think about what to do with my life. I enjoy doing many things-running a business, investing, reading about theology and philosophy, watching politics--these are all things that I love doing. I recently saw a friend, a physician's assistant, at a bookstore. While discussing our future plans, he reiterated something he had told me before: "I do several things, and love every one of them. I just happen to make a living at one of them." He writes plays and runs a website, but makes a living in the operating room. I'm hoping my time at college will offer opportunities to learn more about the areas that interest me and to explore new areas of interest. People laugh when I tell them this, perhaps because they think I'm joking or unrealistic, but I would love to be President of the United States, but I wouldn't consider myself any less successful if I decided I'd rather be a philosophy professor or an accountant. One of my biggest pet peeves is people who aren't interested in realizing their potential. I've had friends who have no desire to exploit any of their abilities-it drives me crazy. I love to see people recognize that they're gifted in something, then go on to do it well. For myself, I always look forward and image what I can do. Several years ago, I was working on my golf game with a wise, older man. On this warm, sunny Saturday morning, we were at the golfing range, hitting ball after ball into the field. Struck by the apparent arbitrariness of the direction of my hits, he said, "You've got to aim for something. If you aim for nothing, that's exactly what you'll get. Nothing." Of course, that applies to more than just hitting golf balls. I've set my sights high, because I'd rather aim high, and possibly succeed, than expect nothing, and get nothing. (Nat)

In this highly personal essay, the author sought to separate himself from other candidates. He threw down the gauntlet so to speak. It is risky to separate oneself from the crowd. In this case it worked!

377

Admission Essay for Georgia Tech

The largest obstacle in choosing a college is the large number of them. As I began contemplating which college to attend to further my education and procure my degree, I was confronted by a vast array of choices. The price tag on some of these choices made them less appealing, but does not make the final choice. Having decided upon a major helps narrow the selection process, but still leaves a many choices. I needed a template to which I could compare colleges and quickly evaluate them. Leaving a smaller number to be investigated in more detail.

The solution to this obstacle came in the form of three questions: What characteristics must the college have? What characteristics must the college not have? What characteristics do I not care about?

One way to sort through schools is to identify those characteristics, which are most important to me for my education and in my college. I must examine what factors (such factors as the size of school, distance from my home, academic programs, etc) are most significant to me. For instance, one program, which I would like to have available to me is a swim team. As I identify these characteristics, I have a template of what to look for in each school. If the school does not have my 'must-haves' then I can eliminate it from my list of prospective colleges, leaving a shorter list.

I also found that deciding what characteristics I do not want should be part of my template. There are some characteristics, which would really detract from my learning experience or my enjoyment of that experience. Also there are some things, which just will not work. If I wish to gain a bachelor's or higher degree, then attending a junior college can not be my final destination. Also, if I wish to become an elementary school teacher, then attending a four-year engineering school would not be a wise decision. Identifying options that will not work or which I would dislike, help compose the template and eliminate some from the myriad of choices.

The final part to making the college selections template is to decide what features do not matter. If I end up eliminating all colleges from my list, I have another problem. If one has put some consideration into the other two components, this should be fairly easy. I must evaluate my likes and dislikes as they materialize in colleges. Is there something, which I originally thought I could not live without, which, in the presence of other positive factors becomes less important? Or some other feature, which I thought I could not live with, which in the presence of other desirable factors, becomes bearable? As I compare colleges.

These questions helped me overcome the obstacle of choosing a college, because it gives me a template to more quickly evaluate colleges and narrow down the selection to a few choice colleges. (Ashley)

Admission essay for University of Denver.

Volunteering as a workshop assistant at the Denver Museum of Nature and Science has helped both the community and me in several ways. The children who come to the classes learn about science concepts in a fun environment. They examined specimens, dissected organs, and learned fun experiments. I learned how to dissect various organs and animals including the heart, eye, and frog dissections. I was able to observe how new and experienced teachers handled distractions in the classroom.

The Museum of Nature and Science has many specimens, which school children would never see because they are not available to schools. Museum classes give them a chance to examine these specimens up close. They also get to learn about different body systems and dissect organs, such as a heart or an eye, from those systems. They learn how fun science can be by performing exciting experiments, such as making a film canister explode. They learn about various topics in science and natural history from solids, liquids and gasses to various aspects of ancient Egypt culture. Whatever the topic of the class, the children learn in a fun environment.

The children are not the only ones who learn, however. I have learned many teaching techniques from my opportunity to observe different teaching styles. This has also been an opportunity for me to work with teachers of different levels, from new to very experienced teachers. Because I am a home-schooled student, I have not been in conventional classrooms much. This opportunity has given me a taste of both the challenges and joys of teaching. I have learned much about classroom control. This experience has strengthened my desire to become an Elementary school teacher.

Volunteering at the Denver Museum of Nature and Science has been beneficial for both the community and me. The children who come to the classes learn about the fun in science as they examine specimens, dissect organs, and learn fun experiments. I was able to observe how new and experienced teachers conducted themselves in the classroom. (Anna)

This is a highly personal essay. Admission officers like essays that are vulnerable and exhibit the personality of a student.

6
Essay

Admission essay to Liberty University (250 word limit).

My perspectives and morality line up exactly with Liberty's mission. I desire to live a life serving God, quite possibly on the mission field. To that end, I feel that God is calling me to a four year college so that he might better prepare me to be effective in following His will for my life. I know I need to be grounded in the word of God so that my values are steadfast. I also need knowledge and the skills that come from learning, that God may use these skills as a tool through me to further His kingdom. It is my prayer that Liberty will be one instrument that God will use to give me values, knowledge, and skills that God is telling me I need to serve Him better. (Peter)

Topic: Discuss a pivotal moment in American history.

The American Civil War was almost over. Lincoln had been reelected as president. But just because the physical war is over, does not mean the emotional war is. For, at the very time that Lincoln is contemplating peace his colleagues in the Congress—radical Republicans like Thaddeus Stevens—are advocating a harsh punishment of the recalcitrant South. Lincoln wants forgiveness and peace. Which will it be?

The north has won, and many want every Confederate to hang. Many want revenge for their dead fathers, sons, brothers, and husbands. And who can blame them? The Rebels must pay for their bad choices. It is not fair that they get off with out paying the price.

But Lincoln stands in the gap. As president he has more influence then any other person. He tried to show his forgiveness in the Gettysburg Address; however, the hint was not taken. Then in his Second Inaugural Address he came right out and said it,"... With malice towards none; and charity for all . . ."He did not say charity just for the north because they were on the "right side." He said, "charity for all," and he meant it.

Genesis 50:17 says, "...I ask you to forgive your brother the sins and the wrongs they committed in treating you so badly..."This is what he was asking the nation to do. He was tired of war and wanted peace and forgiveness. He was willing and wanted the north and the south to be willing too.

Lincoln knew that forgiveness was the only way to rebuild the "...nation that it might live..." (Lincoln's second Inaugural Address) (Jessica)

Essay 8

Topic: Define freedom.

One of the most precious gifts that Americans have is freedom. Our forefathers fought and died for these freedoms. For instance, we enjoy freedom of religion, freedom of speech, freedom to bear arms, and so forth. But, as Americans we understand that there are some freedoms that need to be limited by law. When is there a need for a higher law for determining when certain freedoms should be abdicated?

When our freedoms harm others, or even kill another person, then our freedoms must be limited. For instance, freedom of choice is an important freedom, no doubt about it. I want to choose where I live, whom I marry, where I work. But if I choose to kill another human being then I am going too far. My freedom of choice, in this case, must be limited by law.

There is another time when our freedoms should be limited by law. It is a law of love. When our freedom becomes an obstacle to another's growth in the Kingdom of God, then we need to give up that freedom (1 Peter 2:16). That is our choice and we do it to bring glory to God.

Freedom is one of the most important parts of being an American. Only saving a life and bringing someone into the Kingdom of God are more important. (Jessica)

Topic: Analyze your favorite poem.

"*I struck the board, and cried, "No more. I will abroad./What? shall I ever sigh and pine?*" (George Herbert, "The Collar") "The Collar" is a poem about a struggle between Herbert and his perception of God. It explores freedom and asks if it would be better to seize it go abroad than to "sigh and pine" in submission. Herbert blames his suffering first on the freedom he has left untouched and proceeds to blame it on God Himself. How is this struggle resolved?

A major theme in the poem is potential liberty, accessible only in rebelling against God. Herbert flirts with this freedom and protests, "*My life and lines are free; free as the road…*" He moves on to blame his suffering on this lack of freedom. "*Have I no harvest but a thorn/To let me blood, and not restore/What I have lost with cordial fruit?/Sure there was wine/Before my sighs did dry it; there was corn/Before my tears did drown it.*" Interestingly, this passage has Eucharistic overtones. Could Herbert be referring to the blood of Christ? Suggesting that the wine that is blood was joy to him before his sighs dried it?

Regardless, Herbert continues defiantly to announce that he will "*forsake…[his]… cage.*" "*Leave thy cold dispute/of what is fit and not…*" he exclaims passionately. He longs for *God* but confuses Him with the "cold disputes" that can never satisfy.

Herbert continues to rant and rave, describing his suffering and finally accusing God: "*…While thou didst wink and wouldst not see.*" "*Away! Take heed;/I will abroad,*" he boldly challenges. Then, perhaps not *really* wanting what he is choosing, he tries to justify it. "*He that forebears/To suit and serve his need/Deserves his load,*" he protests.

But even as Herbert turns away "*Me thoughts I heard one calling, 'Child…'* In an instant his soul turns, recognizing the voice of his Lord. He leaves his "cage…which petty thoughts have made" and remembers his God who offers not "cold dispute of what is fit and not," but Himself. "My Lord," he replies.

In conclusion, "The Collar" moves beyond doctrine and religion to a personal relationship with a God whom Herbert calls "Lord" or "Abba." The imagery of a thorn to let blood and wine dried by sighs is a strong contrast to the surrender and content in the conclusion. It is reminiscent of Psalm 23, as if Herbert is saying with David, "My cup overflows."

(Psalm 23:5) (Courtney)

For the last two years of her life, a Jewish girl hiding from the Nazis in Amsterdam, Holland, pours out her heart in the poignant book entitled, *Anne Frank: The Diary of a Young Girl*. She confides all her hopes, fears, joys, and sorrows. As she lives in hiding, seeing only her eight fellow fugitives and their four benefactors, much of her emotions are formed around them.

Hidden in a secret apartment, cut off from friends and nature, Anne and her fellow fugitives grow understandably distrustful and irritable towards each other. Seeing all the inmates through one girl's eyes, we could not expect a balanced, accurate report. An element of biased acrimony certainly exists in many entries. Nevertheless, Anne is a talented, devoted writer, and as kind, generous and caring as the average girl her age. As she matures into a more thoughtful young woman, her entries become more truthful, less based on outraged emotions and more on rational, self-controlled thought. All of these aspects of her writing help us to read between the lines, and give us an engaging, insightful look at Anne's companions.

Due to the Nazis' unrelenting grasp on Holland's freedom and resources, Anne and her housemates live poorly, dress shabbily, and subsist on unappetizing food. Mealtimes are a source of disharmony and avarice. With limited opportunities for the minds and bodies through the day, people speak out of their restiveness. Invariably, their words come across as spiteful, annoying, complaining, accusatory, etc. This seems to be the case regardless of the time of day. Each person is struggling to cope with a disrupted life, living day in and day out with the same people, in the same place, with the same routine, continuously fearing discovery and death. This battle against circumstances Anne clearly portrays, though never explicitly states.

But it is Anne's characterization of herself that most interests the reader. At first Anne seems like a normal thirteen-year-old. She goes to school, gets crushes, enjoys her family, and makes friends, yet like every girl she is unique. For example, she loves to write and records her life quite freely and well, thus giving us an excellent picture of herself. As time passes, however, and Anne continues to spend month after month growing up in a few small rooms, a change comes over her. Anne tends to ruminate a lot. Questions about such topics as life, death, happiness, and love she considers for herself, and resolves to the best of her ability. Over a long period of time she grows more caring and loving toward others, despite the fear and strife surrounding her. She loses some of her mutability and pride. She begins to think deeply about her mistakes and learn from them. Hers is an engrossing and well-presented story—the story of a girl maturing into womanhood.

Characterization is what makes this book so wonderful. There is no flashy plot, no thrilling tale, and no gripping chain of events. It is a story not of happenings, but of people, and particularly of one person, its author. Anne gives us her heart. And that is a precious gift. (Bethany).

Armed with collard greens, black-eyed peas and a sturdy dusting cloth, my Mammy Lee single-handedly maintained my fragile world. Mammy Lee was parent, servant, and benevolent despot all rolled up into one. This 250 pound, five-foot tall, black woman was an awesome presence. Chewing tobacco, limping slightly, and occasionally rubbing a lucky Mercury-head dime tied around her foot with kite string, Lee enveloped us in her arms and propelled us forward through all adversity; she protected us from reality, and gave us false security garnished with pecan pies and encouraging words. Lee set perimeters for all our lives. "Mistah Jim," she often scolded me, "I'se gonna spank yo' bottom if you don't pick up yo' toys." And many times she did exactly that!

I loved my Mammy Lee. I can still feel her as she held me and squeezed —as if a hug and a shake could cure anything! Lee showed me where to find the fattest fishing worms; she helped me dig for pirate treasure.

But there was desperation about Lee. Her world was changing quickly —too quickly —and her discomfort grew. I loved Lee, I loved my homeland, this way of life, and, in a way, they —Lee and my South —were one and the same. They were both grotesquely generous and subtly selfish at the same time.

The Brown decision, and federal soldiers entering Little Rock's Central High School, marched through our quiet land with as much destructive force as Sherman's march through Georgia. This appealing, seductive land was mercilessly, if slowly, being ripped open for the whole world to see. And inside this enlarging cauldron, a young white boy and a sweet black lady were growing up together —and apart —at the same time.

As I leave for college my Mammy Lee will remain at home. But she is in my heart forever!

The author is revealing many details about himself through this narrative. He is discussing someone who was very important to him: Mammy Lee. It is probably too long for most admission essays.

Revolutions are by definition radical departures from the status quo. They are de-marcations, not merely digressions. They are new beginnings in a culture or society. In this case, it is this author's argument that American is undergoing a cultural revolution partly spawned by the home school community—of which I am a part.

What is this home school community? "Home school" is defined differently by different schools but for our purposes "home school" is defined as a population group that teaches its children at home at least 51% of the time. Two things are obvious about this group: it is redefining education and more and more people will join this group.

Many of my friends thought I was spending my days goofing off. But I worked very hard! And I never got any snow days! But it is not that we are working more, it is that we are embraced more! The notion that education emanates from a filial relationship is a natural one, but absent from American education.

This is an essay that discusses salient elements about this current generation.

Essay

Topic: Describe a memorable person in your life.

The topic of this essay concerns one of the most memorable characters of my life.

Amid the blue, acrid haze of Pall Malls and the shiny, stainless steel coffee pots sit the fallen angels of my city. Street people languished in the dawn of an inner-city diner, mercifully permitted by the management to stay.

A country breakfast or the deluxe waffle belongs to the clean-shaven postman, but not to the street people. They wait for their 10 A.M. mushroom soup at the soup kitchen.

Street people are created slowly. A reposed car. An unpaid mortgage. A lost job. Eventually the street person is born, and all that remains of the former, everyday person are wistful excursions into the real world through long gazes at the television in the Sears showroom window.

Jessie is dying, and she knows it. Two months ago her left foot was severely cut when she stepped on a piece of a Pepsi Cola bottle thoughtlessly thrown against the library wall by youths. It still bothers Jessie that kids would waste a nickel. "Kids," she growls. "Everything is given to them!"

A St. Francis Hospital emergency-room physician sutured her wound, but the root-cracked sidewalks, her oversized shoes, and too many days without a shower have doomed her. Her friend Sidewalk Sally—so named because her home was a discarded refrigerator box placed over a sidewalk heat vent—suffered a similar injury last year, and her foot was amputated. Jessie would rather die, and the awful smell coming from her foot reminds her that she soon will. "Jesus loves his little Jessie . . ." she continues to sing.

Dawn is past, noon is over too, and the food closet just opened. Night is returning. Commuters rush by.

Street people must move now too. Jessie is stepping onto a downtown bus. She will sleep in a women's shelter tonight. A child on the bus is screaming. Jessie gives her a generic brand chocolate-chip cookie carefully saved in a napkin.

At the end of the bus ride, Jessie steps off into night. Tomorrow, if they're alive, the street people will again stagger into downtown to continue the endless, empty cycle of the people of the street.

Topic: Describe a person who affected the course of history but would not appear in headlines.

Who is one of the most courageous persons in history? Who affected the course of history but would not appear in newspaper headlines? Ruby Bridges.

Harvard University's Dr. Robert Cole in his book The Spiritual Life of Children describes a 1962 interview he had with a young African-American child, Ruby Bridges. Ruby Bridges was being accosted by angry segregationists as she walked to school. In the face of so much hatred, Cole wanted to know why she was smiling.

"I was all alone," she began, "and those people were screaming, and suddenly I saw God smiling, and I smiled."

Then she continued with these astonishing words: "A woman was standing there [near the school door], and she shouted at me, 'Hey, you little n----r, what you smiling at?'"

"I looked right at her face, and I said, 'at God.'"

"Then she looked up at the sky, and then she looked at me, and she didn't call me any more names."

Ruby Bridges remained hopeful in the face of hopelessness.

Jesus Christ is the Way and the Truth and the Life. And He loves all children, red and yellow, black and white. Period. As early as 1976 John Perkins was saying the same thing-only the Gospel can transform people (Romans 12:1). The goal was voiced by King: ". . . the sons of former slaves and the sons of former slave-owners will sit down at the table of brotherhood together." 'Ruby Bridges lived in this truth.

Today, in the backyard of my childhood home is a forty foot pine tree. Thirty five years ago this fall, next to an in ground concrete pond of mongrel fish bred from dime store gold fish and leftover fishing minnows, beside a generous apple tree and a pink dogwood tree, Dad, my older brother Bill, and I planted three pine trees. One died during our neighborhood football game--heartlessly crushed under an eight year old Dallas Cowboys' sneaker. Our yard man accidentally mowed down another the next summer. But one-the one now standing-grows and grows and grows. The interloper overshadows the apple tree (out of protest I've heard that the old tree gives sour green fruit), poisons the beautiful dogwood tree and gold-minnow hybrid fish with its deciduous toxin saps. And the darn thing continues to grow about a foot a year!

That pine tree intrudes itself into my soul. I saw it the last time I went to Arkansas (my family has moved to Tennessee). I also see my dad in the last moments of his life. Dad died of cancer last year.

Sticky, brown, ageless, untouched even by the coldest Arkansas winter, that pine try still quietly stands, smirking at all of us dying human beings. Flaunting its immortality, the venerable tree postures itself in silent mockery of the rest of us who are struggling to deal with the many vicissitudes of life.

I wish that pine was dead too. As it overshadows my old yard, robbing all other life of light and sustenance, so also it overshadows me. I see my simple, caring, innocent father, kneeling and gently placing that ungrateful pine tree into the Arkansas delta. Lovingly pouring water among its selfish, grasping roots, he squats in silent hope. He really expected to live to see that tree tower above our farm house. That tree gives me painful thoughts of what was and will never be again. What might have been but was not. What I want but what I have instead. He will not see me graduate this May. He is not here when I need him. As God or cancer or whatever it is that unmercifully, slowly, torturously stole life from Dad, I similarly would like to kill that tree--slowly painfully stripping it of life until every evil, uncaring, nasty pine cone and needle joins my poor dad in his grave.

"But the angel said to them, "Do not be afraid, I bring you good News of great joy that will be for all the people. Today in the town of David a Savior has been born to you..." (Luke 2:10). This simple Scriptural text gives me pause. It gives me hope!

Let the ancient pine trees in our lives grow, and grow, and grow! We are not afraid. Someday I hope to show that old pine tree to my children. To tell them about times that once were and shall never be again. About their grandfather who loved Jesus Christ and is waiting for them in heaven. Let the pine trees cover the sky! Let their arms reach beyond the world until they fill our souls, for, you see, we fear not. Our Savior has come.

This intense, highly personal essay is a sure winner with admission committees. That is if the author can keep the essay from becoming maudlin.

There is a wonderful lady who attended my church.

She visited our corner almost every day, though. Harbinger of hope, preserver of continuity. She gently lay neatly cut one inch squares of white bread under the blue and white sign that warned would-be villains that there was a "Neighborhood Watch" ubiquitously watching over this community.

Some said that this lady was crazy. We whose stories are so complete and well rehearsed are suspicious of those with stories we do not know or cannot comprehend. But she had no story. Or, at least she was not talking. She offered us very few hints-a frayed coat two sizes too large, her pockets stuffed with West Penn Hospital brochures entitled "Cancer-You can survive!" That was all we knew. She came to church once a year and she never spoke. The old woman who ruled Friendship and Roup remained an anonymous citadel.

She guarded her pieces of bread from unscrupulous ants, barking blue jays, and mischievous school children. Her face was all seriousness-no trace of a smile. For her work was sacred and important, even if no one else thought so.

But I did. I thought that her work was important. And even if I did not know who she was-she accepted my friendly "hellos" with a suspicious frown-I appreciated this eccentric lady who brought bird song to a community muted by hard luck. She stood alone at our corner next to two abandoned buildings ravaged and neglected by time. She brought beauty and hope to a community that desperately needed both.

One Easter this lady visited my church. Some of us have been here all year, week after week, struggling to beat the world back so that the birds will eat our pieces of bread. Others haven't been here since Christmas or even last Easter. We all are trying to make it. That is all—nothing fancy—just make it one more day. Passing that final exam. Balancing work responsibilities and school responsibilities. We are silent today. We have a story to tell, a story we need to tell, and someday we shall. But today we want to listen to the preacher, we want to hear the organ, we want to sing the songs of victory. Because we are the bread lady. We are bringing song again to a community muted by hard luck and hopelessness.

The author is revealing many subtle details about himself through this narrative.

Topic: Discuss an important truth about life.

My pet ram—Stonewall Jackson—is always trying to get out of the pen. He does not understand that fences are there to keep bad creatures out—like dogs—not to keep nice rams in! Hour after hour, he crawls along the fence looking for a broken fence wire. When he finds it he escapes! He thinks the grass is greener on the other side (and he also likes my mother's daffodils!).

Fence crawlers are dangerous. They create problems for everyone. Stonewall encourages his sisters, Sandi and Patti, to escape too. He is a mean ram. No wild dog would bother him. He can take care of himself. But his sisters can't. And if he isn't careful he could cause his loved ones to be hurt. Everyone looses when Stonewall escapes.

Inevitably, Stonewall finds his adventure—but he usually finds a wild dog or two, too. And I hope to rescue him if he is in trouble. I am afraid someday that his sisters will follow him and they might be killed.

In my own life I hope I remember that God has put rules in place—fences as it were—around me to keep me safe. I hope I will not be a fence crawler. As I go to college I hope that I stay inside that pen!

Essay

Topic: Describe an ordinary incident that became an extraordinary event.

At the last bend before the west entrance of Glacier National Park, the rubber straps holding our sky blue 1960ish American Tourister, whose longevity was extended by reinforced silver ducktape, snapped with a sickening pop and our luggage suddenly launched itself from the luggage rack into Glacier before our clashing deep red 1992 SUV ever made it. In front of curious travelers, our family collected our unwashed underwear and wrinkled shirts deposited among wild mulberry bushes. Finally, after traveling for 3 days and 2500 miles, our SUV joined us inside the gates.

The funny thing is, my mom had warned my dad a few hours before that this might happen. Two good things I learned from this incident: my dad admitted he was wrong (and he was) and my mom forgave him. I enjoyed the national park but I enjoyed more this life-lesson that greatly encouraged me on my own journey. It is a memory that will last a life time.

Topic: Discuss an incident where our perceptions and understandings of reality are often incomplete or inaccurate.

Our perceptions and our understandings of reality are often incomplete or inaccurate.

During my senior year, I visited my girl friend at her vacation home at Hampton Beach, New Hampshire. No one ever told me about the advantages of courtship!

Now I know that some of you probably think that Hampton Beach is beautiful—but I have to tell you, when I first visited it, it was as if all the superficiality in pristine, beautiful New Hampshire had flowed downhill to this cesspool of humanity that was called Hampton Beach to ultimately flow to the Atlantic Ocean. Why would anyone want to have a vacation house at Hampton Beach, New Hampshire, when Rockport, MA, or Boothbay, ME, were within easy driving distance?

Nonetheless, I thoroughly enjoyed spending the afternoon with my Arkansas girl friend—whose father's one million dollars and 1500 acres of rice somewhat mitigated her marginal good looks and bland personality. That is I enjoyed my visit until we returned to her headquarters to end our date the way we always ended our dates . . . we prayed!!!

"Oh Lord," she began as I, with one eye closed, surreptitiously poured polluted sand out of my Converse tennis shoes, "Thank you that some day I will marry a pastor."

I gulped. I had just told her that afternoon that God might be calling me to the ministry.

Well, I do not know if this young lady married a clergyman or not, but I knew that I had no intentions of marrying her—1500 acres notwithstanding—so I figured I better end that prayer and our relationship as soon as possible. My girl friend was operating from the wrong set of assumptions. All her sincerity, innocence, and good intentions—and they were legion—while they were laudable, did not help her get a husband.

As I look at college and life and what is ahead I hope I can keep an open mind and not make decisions from my own assumptions. I want to be more than sincere in the future—I want to walk carefully and prayerfully into the future!

Topic: Discuss an incident that changed your life.

September 11th, 1975, was a particularly warm, promising day even in the South where fall oftentimes is lost between tepid, late summer afternoons and frosty winter mornings. My heart was beaming too, for I was 16 and on my way to Fayetteville, Arkansas, and summer school for gifted students.

My trip began on Rt. 1 North, a rather boring road that wound through white, unharvested cotton fields and one-grocery store towns.

I stopped at MacArthur and bought a moon pie and RC cola. The morning sun had a tropic hue that matched my cheery spirit.

Before I had finished my moon pie and RC, my right front tire blew out, and my little red Fiat curved to the right, made a 45 degree turn, and hit a concrete bridge.

It was a dull bridge; besides having an occasional thoughtless Dairy Queen cup thrown over its side, this little fourteen-foot structure, built in 1962, had never known any excitement. In fact, my wreck was the most exciting event that happened that day.

But I never forgot this bridge, because against its rain-wasted side, my poor compact car crumbled like a cheap, flimsy pop can. At the same time, my dreams were similarly shattered.

Before that day was to end I was to experience horror as I had never known. Besides breaking my hand in two places, I had a severed right foot, compound multiple fractures in my right femur, and a painful fractured right hip.

As the antiquated ambulance sped me toward the hospital, I touched my cold, severed right foot lying beside me on my stretcher. As I gently wiped blood off my ankle I wept —not in pain, not in anger, but in incredulity, and profound grief. Incredulity because I could not believe that I would do such a stupid thing to myself; grief because I knew that I would never run on that foot again. My life was forever changed.

As I recovered in my windowless hospital room, I encountered an aspect of life that I innocently did not know existed. My 16 years on this earth had scarcely prepared me for the valley I now entered. For seven months I lay in traction and then in a full body cast. But, as my body healed my soul languished.

Today, I look back at that catastrophe as a watershed day in my life. Oh, I still feel the pain of my accident. And I have had, and may have even worse catastrophes in my life. It is not that I grew accustomed to the darkness. It is that I have found a light that shines into every darkness I can experience or imagine. I remember a scene in Scott Fitzgerald's novel *This Side of Paradise* where the protagonist is asked why he had so many insights into life. He responded, "Because I have suffered!" My suffering has given me a new hope and vitality.

She was my twenty-first client. An overall-clad toddler was attached to one hand, and a mini-cart was in the other. This middle age, slightly overweight black woman seemed ordinary enough as she requested a bag of groceries from a cooperative emergency food pantry where I was one of the afternoon volunteers entrusted with this sacred duty. I had received early dismissal from my high school.

"Hello," I offered without looking up from my work pad. "My name is Jim."

Number twenty-one replied with a quiet, defeated "Viola."

Unusual name, I thought. I once knew a Viola. When I was eight years old, in Arkansas, my family sub-contracted most of our game cleaning to a thin, tobacco-chewing young lady named Viola. For good luck, Viola had tied around her ankle a Mercury-head dime that I would have loved to add to my coin collection. And she would have given it to me if I'd asked. She was that sort of woman.

Viola's claim to fame, though, was her gift: She could clean, dress, and fillet black bass faster than any person alive. Her hands moved like wild birds.

Her gift generally unappreciated, Viola lived in poverty. Her house was a ply board shack, absent of indoor plumbing or electricity. She had never ridden in a car, never been ten miles from where she lived, and had no hope of doing either in her lifetime. She ate cornbread, mustard greens with a little lard, and great northern beans. She had never visited a dentist or a medical doctor, and she never would. Her world was full of poverty, hopelessness, and despair. And danger. Her brother Leroy was one of the last lynching victims of the Ku Klux Klan before Governor Faubus sent an aide to speak to Uncle George MacNeilly, the grand dragon of the KKK and a ruling elder in my church, and advised him to employ more "subtle ways to keep the n---- in line."

Viola had a shy granddaughter whom she affectionately called her "grandbaby." Every summer this child visited her grandmother, and for six days a week, she chopped old Man Farrell's cotton. With expertise and enthusiasm unmatched anywhere in Desha County, Arkansas, young Viola single-handedly massacred whole acres of crabgrass that threatened the young cotton. With her six-foot hoe, she effectively equalized the equation. My Uncle Sammy knew he owed his cotton-growing success to a wiry little chopper from Marianna, Arkansas, who happened to visit her fish-cleaning grandmother every summer.

"Viola. That's V-I-O-L-A," said the lady sitting in front of me. "Do you have any ground meat today?"

I was lost in a remembered cotton field.

This woman in front of me, number twenty-one, was my Uncle Sammy's cotton chopper.

For the next twenty minutes Viola, with great reticence, and I, with great anticipation, shared our stories.

How far the reality is from the expectation! Viola's life once consisted of ten hours of honest labor, a refreshing RC. Now, Viola had not had a job and an RC in thirty years. Once the Desha County chopping queen, now Viola was just another unwed mother who would eat generic peanut butter until her new food stamps would arrive. It was more than my teenage mind could comprehend!

For Viola and for all of us, the play is not yet over. We may only give or receive a loaf of bread or a smile but ultimately our lives are the responsibility of a loving God. That on some serendipitous afternoon someone will walk into my young life and remind me that there is continuity and strength in life. This is the hope that I bring with me to college.

The author is discussing the impact that a volunteering opportunity had on his life.

This essay concerns books that the author has read in the last year. This is a very common admission essay topic.

Seven Habits of Highly Effective People, by Stephen Covey was thorough in his analysis-if somewhat trite in his illustrations (e.g., pp. 81ff). And, I wonder if Habit 4 "Think win/win" is a Christlike weltanschuung. Nonetheless, the notion of restoring the character ethic-even by a secularist-is a laudatory goal.

Evangelical Ethics by John Jefferson Davis is a refreshing overview of evangelical ethical arguments. I disagree, however, with Dr. Davis' discussion of capital punishment. I find no strong biblical, New Testament argument to support capital punishment

Henry Fiarlie's *The Seven Deadly Sins* is a fascinating book, isn't it? It is so uncharacteristic of modern ethics/morality. Its candor and precise language are refreshing. Even the title makes a rationalist/utilitarian run for cover! How nice that a scholar uses the word avarice and thinks that it is a sin!

I have a problem with James Patterson and Peter Kim's *The Day America Told the Truth*. It is, in my opinion, pop statistics. I remember my high school history teacher said that we could use statistics to prove most anything—even it really was not true!! Every historian in America is trying to prove something with statistics. .

I find Neil Postman's book *Amusing Ourselves to Death* to be painfully accurate. It confirms my worst fears. There is a sense in which Postman's book is a polemic against mass media (I felt sorry for my hero Oscar the Grouch who along with the rest of the Sesame Seed crowd is bashed!). But, his arguments are persuasive. His flirtation with conspiratorial tendencies damages his case, but only slightly. Who can disagree with his chilling conclusion: "What all of this means is that our culture has moved toward a new way of conducting its business. . . the nature of its discourse is changing as the demarcation line between what is show business and what is not become harder to see with each passing day (p. 98)."

I am glad that I have finally joined millions of Americans in reading Bellah et al., *Habits of the Heart*. At the same time, I must admit, I find Bellah to be somewhat wordy.

Finally, who can forget C.S. Lewis' *A Grief Observed*. I must confess my seventeen short years hardly prepared me for these insights! This is a timely book-considering *Shadowland* is still in the theatres. This book coupled with Henri Nouwen's *In Memoriam* are two of the most valuable studies of grief that I know.

Topic: What will be your major in college?

What will be my major in college? And why?

I think that I would like to major in history. The writing of history is the selection of information and the synthesis of this information into a narrative that will stand the critical eye of time. History, though, is never static. One never creates the definitive theory of an historical event. History invites each generation to re-examine its own story and to reinterpret past events in light of present circumstances.

The creation of this story is more difficult than it seems. From the beginning the historian is forced to decide what sort of human motivations matter most: Economic? Political? Religious?

For instance, what causes the American Revolution? The historian Bernard Bailyn argues that ideology or the history of thought causes the American Revolution. No, the historian Oscar Handlin argues, the Revolution is caused by social upheaval (i.e., the dislocation of groups and classes of people). Sydney Ahlstrom argues that religion is an important cause of the American Revolution. And so forth. The student will look at several theories of history, primary source material, and then decide for himself what really happened.

"Every true history is contemporary history," historians Gerald Grob and George Billias write. I want to make the theories of historical events personal and contemporary.

While the historian knows that he can never be completely neutral about history, he must be committed to telling both sides of the historical story. He may choose to lobby for one view over the other, but the historian must fairly present all theories. He must be committed to the truth no matter where his scholarship leads him. At times the historian will discover unflattering information about his nation/state. He must not hesitate to accept and then to tell the truth.

After everything is said and done, the historian only is *studying* the past. He cannot really *change* the past. Theories about the past come and go, and change with each generation. However, the past is past. It is over. Historians will debate about history, but they can never change history.

24 Essay

Topic: What goals do I have for my life?

Several years ago, in Chicago, Illinois, an elderly lady died.

When she was discovered by her neighbors, no one seemed to know who she was. She was called "Sister Mary" because she was a nun and member of the Cenacle Sisters (Roman Catholic Church). But no one knew her last name.

So, the police investigated. It was more difficult than they thought it would be.

You see, Sister Mary, owned almost nothing. She had no credit cards, no automobile, and no television. People knew and loved her though. She was well known at the local food bank. And almost every homeless person in the neighborhood knew her. But, the police could not identify her until they contacted the Cenacle Sisters and sent them a photograph.

"I have no need of credentials," the Apostle Paul writes the Corinthian Church. "My life is written on your hearts." Paul owned almost nothing, but his value as a person was to be found in the persons with whom he had shared Jesus Christ. Those were the riches he carried with him to the Roman gallows.

What do people say about us? "He buys a new car every year." Or, "His front yard is beautiful . . ." If we died tomorrow, what would people say about us?

In America, unfortunately, we are most often known by what we own. By our job. By our possessions. Our success is determined by how much wealth we collect. You know the old joke—"Success is determined by how many toys we have at the end of our lives." Sister Mary owned very little. So she could not be identified by outsiders. But her life was written on the hearts of thousands of people. And you can bet that God will know her when she gets to heaven!

The question is what do I want to do with my life? I want to live my life so that it is written on the hearts of thousands of people! Even if I don't have many toys or money or fame.

Topic: What is your greatest fear about going to college?

The thought of attending college, to me, is like climbing Mt. Moriah.

Standing on Mt. Moriah is where God demands everything and nothing must be taken for granted.

Hebrews 11:17 says, "By faith Abraham, when he was tested, offered up Isaac, and he who had received the promises was ready to offer up his only son." This man Abraham was called by God into the Promised Land. And he went. He was promised many descendants. And he waited-even into his nineties. And God gave him a son . . . but now he must go to Mt. Moriah. In Genesis 22 God wants Isaac. He wants Abraham to sacrifice Isaac. The promise destroyed. God wants Abraham to do the unthinkable . . . to trust Him even when it seems impossible to do so . . .

William Willimon, Chaplain to Duke University and an ordained Methodist preacher, tells of a congregant who said to him one day, "I am looking for another church because when I look at that God, the God of Abraham, I feel I'm near a real God, not the sort of dignified businesslike god we chatter about here on Sunday mornings . . . Abraham's God could blow a man to bits, give and then take a child, ask for everything from a person and then want more. I want to know that God."

I will meet that God again at college on Mt. Moriah, where God demands everything.

This God who calls us to Mt. Moriah has no parallel, no analogy. This God we serve is not predictable, not safe, and not controllable. He loves whom He wants to love-even those whom we cannot forgive, cannot love. He saves those whom He chooses. He is a God who cannot be controlled by our minds, by our political situations, or by our religions. Nothing is impossible for the God who lives on Mt. Moriah.

On Mt. Moriah God does not merely patch up what is old. He makes something entirely new. And, on Mt. Moriah, we find that all that we once believed, all that once demanded our allegiance has come in question.

Attending college, then, for me will be a time of great testing and growing!

Topic: Describe your favorite novel.

One of my favorite books is called *War and Peace* by Leo Tolstoi. I like it so much because it celebrates the triumph of love and goodness.

Pierre, "shy, observant and natural looking," was distinguished by no particular gift of intelligence, good looks, or moral courage. And, while his physical appearance never changed, his character did. And he became a hero of epic proportions. He selfishly put himself in harms way numerous times and eventually married the beautiful and equally heroic Natasha. Somehow the love between Natasha and Pierre mitigated all the horrible pain that the Napoleonic invasion of Russia had wrought on their generation.

Everything-face, gait, eyes, voice-everything was at once transformed in her. To her own surprise, the force of life and hopes of happiness floated to the surface and demanded satisfaction. From that first evening Natasha seemed to have forgotten all that had happened to her. From that time she never once complained of her position; she said not one word about the past, and was not afraid of already making lighthearted plans for the future.

Natasha and Pierre looked back on their past, noted its impact, and then went boldly into the future.

When is loss gain? When we surrender our control and our search for security in tangible things, and we discover that trusting in God and God's design is ultimately more satisfying.

Human history is always reconstructed, it is never created. When someone gives me a theory of history-including his own—I ask what evidence does the person marshall to build his case. History is always reconstructed from evidence.

But last year God touched my life and created something new. He saved me. That it is really something new. Something is created that was not here. A New Birth. And that is worth more than all the knowledge, money, or prestige in the whole world.

Topic: What is friendship?

One of my favorite historical figures is John Mark in the Bible.

Everything was going so well. Paul, his friend Barnabas, and his companion John Mark (John was his Jewish name, Mark his gentile name) were leading so many people to the Lord. This was the beginning of their missionary journey and things couldn't be going better.

Paul and Barnabas invited John Mark to join them on a new missionary journey-a great privilege. But, suddenly, for no apparent reason, John Mark abandons his friends and returns home.

We do not know why. Perhaps Mark resented the deposition of Barnabas from the leadership; perhaps he was afraid of the proposed journey up into the plateau where Antioch in Pisidia stood, for it was a dangerous road; perhaps he was homesick. In any event, he was a man who failed his friends.

Whatever the reason or combination of reasons for John Mark's failure, Paul thought Mark's failure was serious enough to disqualify him from accompanying them on their next missionary trip.

Then Mark vanishes from history, although a tradition says he went to Alexandria, Egypt, and founded the church there.

When he re-emerges 20 years later he is the man who has redeemed himself. Paul, writing to the Colossians from prison in Rome, tells them to receive Mark if he comes to them. "Get Mark and bring him with you, for he is very useful in serving me" (2 Timothy 4:11). So, the man who was once a deserter became the person Paul wanted with him at the end of his life.

Mark, who failed but came back, who forgave and made friends again, is a great example of friendship.

Topic: Defend a controversial position. The author must be aware of his audience. If he is applying to a secular college he has to define his religious terms.

If you asked me, when I was an eight year old, what my favorite holiday was, I would have enthusiastically proclaimed: Halloween! Haunted houses, costumes, candy-it all captured my imagination. But that was when I was eight. I am now seventeen.

After I gave my heart to Christ—five years ago-until today, I have grown increasingly uncomfortable with Halloween. It clearly is not a Christian holiday. In fact it is anything but Christian. In fact, Halloween is a celebration of death . . .

The origins and traditions of Halloween can be traced back thousands of years to the Druids, a pagan tribe in the British Isles who regularly practiced human sacrifice. The eve of October 31 marked the transition from summer into the darkness of winter. On this night, the spirits of the dead rose up. Demons, fairies, and ghouls roamed about the town. They destroyed crops, killed cattle, soured milk, and generally made life miserable . . . unless an appropriate appeasement was offered. Namely, a human sacrifice. So, anticipating these goblins, Druid towns annually, on October, chose young maidens and sacrificed them in honor of the pagan gods. . .

It is not funny, it is not harmless. This is not the same as having a Christmas tree, or believing in the Easter Bunny—Halloween is a celebration of death, destruction, and hell. I know that Halloween is a popular holiday and I imagine some will resist if you ask them to give up this hedonistic celebration, I at least, have enough nightmares in Hometown, USA, without having one that occurred on Elm Street.

Topic: If you had one thing to say to your generation, what would it be?

Moses walked along across the plain to the foot of Mount Pisgah. Slowly he climbed up the steep rocky mass, higher and higher, until he finally reached the summit.

Looking back, he could see his people camped far below him on the plain. The sun had begun to set, and the evening fires flickered among the tents. His eyes finally rested on the sacred encampment. Smoke was rising in black clouds from the altar, where the priests were sacrificing a lamb.

Reluctantly he turned away and looked westward, out over the far side of the mountain. There in the light of the setting sun lay the land of Canaan. Directly below he could see the fertile green valley of the Jordan River and, just beyond the Canaanite town of Jericho. To the south he saw the waters of the Dead Sea, glimmering red and gold in the sunset, and the purple Judean hills rising steeply westward toward Jerusalem (not yet so named). His eyes followed the winding course over the rough, rocky hills of central Canaan. This was the land that was soon to belong to the young nation of Israel...but not Moses.

Except from distant Mt. Pisgah and later Mt. Nebo, Moses was not to enjoy the Promised Land. Even after Moses pleaded with God whom he had loved so long and served so well, God responded "That is enough-do not speak to me anymore about this matter." (Deu. 3:26).

So what could he leave with them? What could he tell them that would summarize his own life?

Obey. "Follow these commands so that you may live and may go in and take possession of the land that the Lord, the God or your fathers is giving you." (4:1)

I remember this story when things are hard. I remember this story when I want to give up. After all, the world is bigger than my little corner in it. And there are more important things than my own comfort. When I reach the end of life and I look over into the Promised Land I hope I can find the strength to give thanks to God no matter what has happened.

Topic: Why do bad things happen to good people?

Joni Erickson was an attractive, popular, athletic teenager. A potential Olympic skier, Joni was riding a wave that apparently would never crest.

She was also a good person. But, Joni, by her own admission, was far from what God intended her to be. Her life revolved around her ego and desires. This changed when Joni broke her neck in a diving accident. She permanently lost the use of her arms and legs. How could a loving God allow such a tragedy? Joni struggled tremendously with that question for the first few months. Then, gradually, she began to realize that God really wanted to draw her closer to Himself. God was breaking down the old Joni so that the new Joni in Christ could become a blessing to others. And what a blessing she became! Today, Joni's beautiful relationship with God radiates from her wheelchair to thousands of people. Completely fulfilled in Christ, and in Christ alone, Joni confesses that she would not want her life any other way.

In World War II London, beautiful flowers, unknown since the great fire in 1666, brought to life by nitrates from the burning bombs —life blossoming out of death; beauty, out of pain; the past from out of the present —grew out of useless, grotesque bomb craters.

I don't know why bad things happen to good people but I know that it is not because God is weak or uncaring. He knows. He cares. He is in control.

Essay

Topic: If you could say one thing to your peers, what would it be?

If I could say one thing to my peers, what would it be? Have hope!

In Hal Borland's *When the Legends Die*, the protagonist, an Indian who had lost his home, ". . . stood among the ashes and whispered his sorrow chant, not even saying it aloud. For small griefs you shout, but for big griefs you whisper or say nothing. The big griefs must be borne alone, inside."

I am truly shocked at how much despair there is in America. The theologian Walter Bruggemann, in his book Hope Within History argues that "failure to hope-hopelessness-happens among the affluent, the prosperous, the successful, the employable, the competent for whom the present system works so well. We are the ones who are likely to be seduced into taking the present political, economic, intellectual system too seriously and to equating it with reality." This false complacency ill prepares us for the exigencies of life-a death, divorce, unemployment—so that we easily lose hope. Indeed, in the "you only go around once" generation, hopelessness is epidemic. We have benefited so well from the Great Society, that we falsely think it is the only game in town.

At the end of World War Two, many of the victims of Nazi atrocities would not leave the concentrations camps. In spite of horrible conditions, and terrible memories, the victims preferred the familiarity of bondage rather than the risk of freedom.

The one thing I want to say to my peers is to take a chance, to let go of those places of bondage and reach out to freedom! And have hope!

405

Topic: Describe a memorable character.

Roshanna was never subtle. Roshanna had an uncanny ability to find, sit next to, and irritate the most irascible congregants in my little Methodist Church.

This particular morning Roshanna, a child from the neighborhood, was sitting next to Mrs. Musick—a vintage grouch. With adeptness unparalleled in my neighborhood, Roshanna had marked her victim. Roshanna often timed her sneak attack during the silent prayers of confession, while her victim was most contrite and vulnerable. Before the Assurance of Pardon was pronounced, poor Mrs. Musick was hanged and quartered. At the end of the doxology-in celebration of the midpoint of our service—Roshanna deposited her used Bazooka bubble gum on Mrs. Musick's open red-letter Bible. The awful mess was placed between "He" and "multitudes" in Matthew 5:1. Poor Mrs. Musick's Bible would sport Bazooka bubble gum for generations to come.

There would be no peace this Sunday morning.

Mrs. Musick, who never suffered in silence, accosted our pastor at the back door. "Pastor, you have to do something about Roshanna. What are we going to do with these people."

Twelve year old Roshanna grew up on the city streets. Her mother was a Caucasian who worked two shifts at a local restaurant during the week and turned tricks at the Horoscope Bar on Friday nights; her father was mostly absent. Roshanna, if she lived anywhere, mostly lived with what appeared to be a wizened old grandmother.

Every summer morning Roshanna was given a wrinkled dollar and told to disappear until bedtime. Often she stood forlornly in front of her house, as if she was hoping her grandmother would change her mind. But she never did.

Roshanna never owned a doll. She never felt the touch of a kind adult. Her world was full of broken, glass-filled alleys and abandoned smoke scarred brick houses. Her favorite silver slide with a paint chipped clown on its ladder was once the final resting place of an overdosed addict. Roshanna had found him one morning while wasting time at the park. She was a tough street veteran acutely aware that she belonged to no one and to no place.

Roshanna changed my life—forced me to rethink what really is important in life.

Topic: Describe what September 11, 2001, means to you.

This essay is about when we should cry.

At times we are called on to deliver messages we do not want to deliver. When in the Bible Elisha was sent to Syria by God, he met Hazael, who at the time was very sick. As he looked into the face of this future ruler of Syria, Elisha saw that Hazael would get well and how much Israel would suffer at Hazael's hand in the future! Hazael was to destroy Elisha's nation.

No wonder the prophet, who loved his people, wept. It is always good news to hear that a sick man will be well . . . unless the man who gets well will kill your children.

Elisha wept . . .

After September 11, 2001, we in America are especially somber. I am not in anyway mitigating the horrendous crime that was committed on September 11, 2001. It was a great disaster. However, may I suggest, that we have looked into the face of Hazael. We are both the perpetrators and the victim in our present situation.

In our own country, at the beginning of the millennium, in spite of unprecedented prosperity, we see the seeds of our destruction everywhere. Increased crime, poverty, and unemployment. Hopelessness and domestic violence. Some of us wonder whether our American covenant is being recklessly compromised by some leaders who are choosing to condone practices that we see as immoral. We see Hazael. He will survive . . . but will we? Will the American dream survive?

Edward Gibbon in his seminal work *The Decline and Fall of the Roman Empire* says that the following five attributes marked Rome at its end. First, a mounting love of affluence. Second, a widening gap between the very rich and the very poor. Third, an obsession with sex. Fourth, freakishness in the arts, masquerading as originality, and enthusiasms pretending to be creativity. Fifth, an increased desire to live on welfare. Sound familiar? Are we looking at Hazael?

And Elisha wept . . .

Topic: Describe a person whom you greatly admire.

Some people seem to feel that they are free to do with their life what they wish, as long as they do not harm anyone.

I doubt that this thought occurred to my medical doctor Dr. David Hall, MIT graduate, adjunct professor at the University of Pittsburgh Medical School, and board certified family practice physician. Ten years ago Dr. Hall and several other Christian medical professors established a clinic that was housed in a basement of a church and they offered medical services on the basis of people's ability to pay. This was quality care, mind you. I and hundreds like me went to Dr. Hall. We went because it was the best medical care in town. But thousands went because it was all they could afford. Dr. Hall could have been a millionaire. He is not. Dr. Hall and his wife Susie and their family (five children!) live in a modest house in one of the worst parts of town. But Dr. Hall is called to this place. He, therefore, quietly does his work. Day after day. Quietly with no expectation of reward.

Topic: What are bad choices?

The road to failure begins with bad choices that grow out of our best intentions but not out of obedience to what is right.

And we begin our road to failure when we take the easy road, the road that fits our agendas and our pleasure. And we have all sorts of rationalizations! One of my high school teachers once told me that the mark of maturity is delaying my pleasure. Very few of my friends, I fear, have delayed their pleasure in the place of sexual purity. Elizabeth Eliott, a great Christian teacher, warns young people that intimacy does not show us one thing about the character of a person. We should not use sexual intimacy as an excuse to know people better. Some of my friends erroneously make the wrong assumption that sexual intimacy will be a good preparation for marriage. Therefore they choose to live together before marriage. The road of failure is paved with good intentions and wrong assumptions.

Topic: Define a term.

In general, we don't like being lost. We especially don't like being lost in the wilderness. What does it mean to be in a wilderness?

In the Bible people did not like the wilderness. They always thought of it as harsh and unnerving. There references to it were usually uncomplimentary.

But the pilgrimage of the Israelites through the wilderness of Sinai figured as one of their most cherished motifs. They remembered it with pride and fondness. It was their years in the wilderness that forged them as a nation, which had developed their character and marked them as the people of God.

The wilderness is a place of diminished resources but increased possibilities. There is a sense of abandonment. Yet, even in the midst of hard times, the Israelites sensed God's presence. And that made the hard times worthwhile.

When I enter college next year, I am entering a wilderness of sorts. It is scary to think about being away from home for the first time. It will be a place of diminished resources—how I will miss my mom's cooking!—but it will also be a place of great possibilities. And, to me, it will be a place where I can feel God's presence in a new place. That is important to me.

Topic: Discuss your favorite poem?

My favorite poem is Psalm 23.

Charles Allen, pastor emeritus of First Methodist Church, Houston, Texas, in his book *God's Psychiatry* tells how the Allied armies, in wartime, gathered up homeless children and cared for them. But at night the children were restless and afraid. A psychologist hit upon a solution. He gave each child a slice of bread to hold, and the child would go to sleep immediately knowing that he/she would have something to eat the next day. Likewise, in Psalm 23, we are given a slice of bread that we can hold through the night times of life. Hope that will carry us through.

The attraction of the 23rd Psalm does not lie in its profound in its comforting lyrics or pastoral metaphors. But comfort lies in the simple way we meet a loving Shepherd/God face to face.

I have heard that I will have a resident assistant while in college. That is some comfort. My RA no doubt will mitigate some of the uncomfortable moments in dorm living. Also, I know that I will have an academic advisor. Surely I will need help in choosing and scheduling classes.

But what I will really need next year is what I needed this year: A good shepherd. "The Lord is my shepherd, I shall not want . . ."

Topic: Describe one of the most tragic characters in your life.

Elie Wiesel in the book *Night Laments*, "I lost my faith in the shadow of the gas chambers." Wiesel, a survivor of a Nazi concentration camp was not an agnostic, nor an atheist; he was a believer who decided to stop believing because God seemed to be cruel and unloving. The compassionate God Wiesel had known in youth seemed to have turned into a vindictive, destructive, vengeful creature. Wiesel echoed the words of Aeschylus in his Greek tragedy *Agamemnon* (lines 183-184), "From the gods who sit in grandeur/grace comes somehow violent." In the midst of tragedy, Jeremiah, the author of Lamentations, honestly began to question if God really loved Israel, if He would ever show them grace. And worse than that, while Israel floundered, while Jerusalem lay in ruins, sinful, heathen adjacent nations prospered. Jeremiah complained, "All my enemies have heard of my distress; they rejoice at what you have done." (Lamentations 1:21)

I once saw a Peanuts cartoon strip. With his typewriter, Snoopy is writing a novel. The first words are, "It was a dark and stormy night." In Lucy's characteristic forceful manner, she sees what is on the page and gives Snoopy some advice.

"You stupid idiot! That's the dumbest thing I've ever read. Who ever heard of such a silly way to begin a story? Don't you know that all the good stories begin, 'Once upon a time.'"

Snoopy, taking her advice, began his novel, "Once upon a time, it was a dark and stormy night."

If that were our lives, would it begin the same way? It seems that our lives, that begin so promising, always end in dark and stormy nights. Our fairy godmother never appears and we never wear glass slippers.

Other people seem to have it so easy-especially wicked people! A survivor of the Lodz Ghetto, a Jewish internment camp in Poland during World War II, describes how devastating it was to look through barbed wire at laughing, fat, healthy sons and daughters of his Nazi captors playing on a merry-go-round while the Lodz emaciated children had to work from dawn to dark. The protagonist in *Fiddler on The Roof* shakes a half-cynical fist at God in the wake of another Russian pogrom, "And you call us the chosen people!"

Well I am very young, I know, and what do I know? But I know this: There will be Lodz Ghettos and gas chambers. But I know that hope lives yet. That there is no tragedy that cannot be overcome.

Topic: Discuss a family member who affected your life.

Shortly before my maternal grandmother died—I called her Big Momma (not mother!)—she recorded on paper her earliest memories. Besides making the best cream gravy and biscuits in Desha County, Arkansas, Big Mamma's memory was strong and clear.

Surprisingly, her favorite memory was not graduation from high school, or attending college, not even her wedding day. No, her favorite memory was a visit to her own grandmother.

Big Momma's grandmother lived in a two-room, unpainted pre-Huey P. Long poor North Louisiana clapboard house.

"The good old days," she began, "were when beans and hash tasted good."

"On top of the stove sat a black iron three-legged pot," she began. "Sometimes it overflowed with chicken and dumplin's, or enticed me with homemade vegetable soup, or-even better-appetizing whole squirrels bouncing around in boiling gray stew water."

At that point I felt the same way you do!

Boiled squirrel. Yuk! While I am an enthusiastic fan of those furry critters, my ardor does not lead me to the soup pot!

But, what attracted my grandmother to the squirrel stew was not the squirrel stew; it was her own grandmother. She loved her. Her grandmother Kolb (Big Momma's maiden name) was an affirming presence in her life. Even in her memory, my grandmother enjoyed remembering Great-Great-Grandmother Kolb.

As we gather at family holidays we remember Big Momma. She taught us all how to cook squirrels and how to love one another. Even when we have very little, even on those hard days. Memories of Big Momma sustain us.

Topic: Discuss how one should handle a bad situation.

Craig Masback faced a bad situation. In 1976 Craig Masback missed qualifying for the Olympics by one tenth of a second. In 1980, he was ready and sure that he would win. Probably would have, too, but the Olympics were canceled. In 1984, poor Craig, now the fastest human being in the world, was sick with the flu during the Olympic Games. Craig never won an Olympic medal.

C. S. Lewis faced a bad situation. In April 1956, C. S. Lewis, a famous English Christian philosopher, a confirmed bachelor, married Joy Davidman, an American poet with two children. After four brief, intensely happy years, Lewis found himself again alone, and inconsolable. His beloved Joy died of cancer. . . "No one ever told me that grief felt so like fear . . . "Lewis writes. "Talk to me about the truth of religion and I'll listen gladly. Talk to me about the duty of religion and I'll listen submissively. But don't come talking to me about the consolations of religion or I shall suspect that you don't understand (from *A Grief Observed*)." The cry of absence was deep in the heart of C.S. Lewis.

Tillich affirmed the importance of "the courage to be" as an essential resource for authentic living. I am more persuaded than ever that the key to handling a bad situation is merely "to be." To be courageous in the face of adversity. To live in tentativeness. That is the way to handle a bad situation!

Essay

Topic: Who are two philosophers who greatly affected world history?

Rene Descartes applied the rational inductive methods of mathematics, to philosophy. Before his time, philosophy had been dominated by the method of comparing and contrasting the views of recognized authorities. Rejecting this method, Descartes held nothing true until it seemed true to him. This phrase summarized his views," I think, therefore I am." After Descartes, mankind replaced God as the center of the universe in the midst of many. This was an ominous moment in Western culture.

It did not get any better when G. Hegel, a decidedly modern philosopher, vigorously attacked everything scientific. Hegel believed strongly in the dialectic and polarity. Truth had no application if there were not opposites warring for its reality. For instance, if there was no evil, there was no good. There could be no good in the universe if there was no evil in the same universe. From the struggle between these polarities, or in the dialectic, there emerged truth. Hegel began with a thesis (a position put forward for argument). Opposed to this was a contradictory statement or antithesis. Out of their opposition came a synthesis which embraced both. Since the truth lay only in the whole system, this first synthesis was not yet the truth of the matter, but became a new thesis, with its corresponding antithesis and synthesis. And so on. Truth, then, was not absolute and always open to interpretation. Truth lay in the "search" of the "system."

Both Descartes and Hegel were important philosophers for negative reasons. Like the blind men who felt part of the elephant and thought it was the whole thing, these two men saw a little bit of truth and offered broad generalizations.

415

Topic: What is the greatest need that you see in contemporary American society?

The greatest need in American society today is the pervasive and abiding need to belong to a community.

Jimmy goes to my church.

"O God," I complained rather than prayed, "there is Jimmy."

Jimmy, one of our "adopted" street people, sat in a corner of our tired inner-city church basement. Unshaven, polluting the room with his pungent body odor, he pulled his moth eaten (but nonetheless impressive) Harris Tweed jacket around his shoulders.

With a sigh, I issued a polite hello.

Jimmy was the last person I wanted to meet this early December morning. I had come to my volunteer position at our homeless ministry to grab a few quiet moments, but I had been greeted by light leaking from beneath our poorly insulated basement door.

I found Jimmy, who had managed, somehow, to enter the church last night. My parents had warned me never to be alone with street people but I thought I would take a chance with Jimmy.

Jimmy was the kind of person who would disappoint even the most dedicated humanitarian. "I need two bucks," he would plead. "Pay you back next week," he lied.

It was not the money or the lying that bothered me; it was his persistent, unmitigated gall. While the rest of us lived with limits, Jimmy, by lying, stealing, and conning, managed to exceed the limits.

Jimmy had never joined our church, but he had not missed a service in more than a year. Of course not! Church services were an entrepreneurial venture for Jimmy! He worked the north door during Sunday school, the basement door between services (to catch recalcitrant smokers who were more than willing to do penance for their nasty sin), and brazenly worked the front door after church services. When he was seriously conning Jimmy could make $40 an hour!

Now Jimmy had decided to camp in our church basement. He wheezed, and as he moved, a urine bag peeked from beneath his Harris Tweed. Then it hit me: Jimmy's not here to sleep, eat, or con anyone. His colon cancer has finally caught up with him. He's come here to die.

"Did you hear that the Pirates took the Expos last night?" Jimmy asked me. He knew I was caught.

Jimmy had come home to die. And he knew that home is the place where you go when you have to go there and a place where they have to take you in (from "Death of a Hired Hand," Robert Frost). He was my family and I was suddenly glad to enjoy this early morning with him.

Topic: What is the most important need of contemporary American society?

What the world needs now is love, true love—where have I heard that? While I know the Coca Cola people were trying to sell their soft drink, they nonetheless chanced upon a very important need in American society: love. The Christian counselor, Morton Kelsey once observed that the greatest need in America is not to love but to know that we are loved.

The following article was in the *Pittsburgh Press* several years ago:

Italian porn star and Parliamentarian Ilona Staller and U.S. sculptor Jeff Koons have fallen in love via trans-continental faxes and plan to tie the knot on Valentine's Day, a colleague said in Rome yesterday.

Staller wants to get married in Rome's city hall, said Sabrina Innocente, the secretary at the parliamentarian's porn agency, "Diva Futura." "They are madly in love," she said, "We are all happy." Koons has painted a series of pictures of himself with Stalle displayed at the Biennale art show in Venice.

According to the Italian news agency, AGI, love blossomed between the pair at the show. The relationship developed "Via fax, but he's also come here many times," said Innocente.

Staller's parliamentary group, The Radicals, said they had no information about the report.

According to her parliamentary biography, the Hungarian-born Staller is 39 and was married once before, to an Italian who worked in Hungary. The brassy blonde star of such films as "Boiling Flesh" and "Chocolate Banana" has campaigned for an end to obscenity laws and for the spread of free love.

And, so, we finally know what true love is . . .Not!

I am not sure that we in American have an inkling about what love is.

I like Valentine's Day. I love to receive all those construction paper, magic marker soaked cards from my nephews. I love to buy my girl friend a mushy, cellophane over-priced Valentines-I paid $4.75 for my card this year!-with someone-presumably some-one's sweetheart-on the cover-you know, the couple is always holding each other's hands and staring dreamily into each other's eyes. Ah, isn't love wonderful!

Valentine's Day is, unfortunately 100% American, 100% cute, and 100% pagan. Love, as we see it today, is a mindless, emotional, knee jerk, glandular reaction between each two persons. It is a selfish, self-serving arrangement-we fall in and out of love and the sack with hedonistic abandon. That is, of course, not love.

God is love and He is most accurately and vividly presented in the person of His only begotten son—Jesus Christ. If we know Him, then we truly know love.

Topic: Who is your favorite poet?

My favorite poet is Phillis Wheatley. Phillis Wheatley was born in Africa in 1753. At the age of eight she was brought on a slave ship to Boston where she was bought by John Wheatley a wealthy tailor. Her real gift, though, was in writing. At the age of thirteen Phyllis began to write poetry.

It is believed by some critics that Phyllis Wheatley should have used her influence as a black poet to enlighten the people of her day of the worth and dignity that was in the African heritage. But is that how Miss Wheatley thought of herself? Was she a black poet, or a Christian poet?

For example, her Christian faith is manifestly evident in her poem," To S.M.—A Young African Painter on Seeking His Works." Wheatley encourages S.M to paint things of the "realms above". She also reminds S.M of his permanent home. When these "shades of time are chased away,/And darkness ends in everlasting day,/On the seraphic pinions shall we move,/ And view the landscapes in the realms above.

She was a woman of God first and that is how she saw herself. To Wheatley writing poetry was not a matter of bringing worth and dignity to the African race, but rather to bring glory to God Almighty. In that sense, Wheatley was closer to white Christian poets, like Anne Bradstreet, than black non-Christian poets.

So the defense in which I would pose for Miss Wheatley, is that yes she could have benefited the race of which she was a part. By writing things that honored them. However she chose instead to honor God. It was more important to her to please God than it was to please men. What could be more important than that? (Jessy)

Essay

Topic: What is love?

During the winter my family heats our house with a wood burning boiler/stove. As far as I am concerned, I would not like it to be any different. I love the smell of apple, ash, and oak smoke wafting into the gray winter sky. But there is one problem with wood heat and it occurs about 3 A.M. every morning: the fire dies down to the point where the house is dangerously cold. So, my dad solves this problem by setting his alarm and waking up about midnight and adding more wood. He tends the fire so that his whole family will stay warm.

The point is, though, no one knows it. Every morning we wake up and the house is as warm as it was when we went to bed.

I guess that is what love is—getting up at 3 AM and tending the fire. And not caring who knows. Just doing it for love.

The theologian Carl Henry has observed that while love is personal, it is never private. The inner fire of devotion must burn brightly for the outer life to reflect in deeds and word love to the world. For love to burn within our hearts that we must be involved in the world, not withdraw from it.

I read a story once about a boy who loaned a quarter to his mother to put in a parking meter. Later, the conscientious mother tried to repay the quarter. The little boy put up both hands and exclaimed, "Oh, no, Mom. You owe me nothing. I did it for love!"

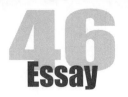

Topic: Discuss someone who influenced your life.

My mother's father, James Jesse Bayne, I called him Big Daddy, ran away from his two room, Louisiana pine barren home when he was eight. For the next 7 years he lived in woods and swamps in the wild Delta bottoms. Living on the outskirts of early 20th century southern towns, he experienced poverty that was sublime in its intensity.

Southern cuisine and lifestyle are the epitome of conservation and economy. Practically nothing is discarded from any animal: intestines, gizzards, stomachs-it all was eaten. There was precious little left for hoboes like Big Daddy, who ate crawdads and red-bellied brim.

There was not much that was big about Big Daddy. At 16 His blond, almost white-hair blue-eyed head oversaw a body that was not symmetrical. His left arm was at least 2 inches longer than his right.

It was not easy being a vagabond in the South. There was not much left for Big Daddy. Therefore, in those early years—far too early—Big Daddy lost all sentimentality and forgot the meaning of metaphor. Life was harsh and unforgiving.

Big Daddy taught me that almost any obstacle could be overcome.

One huge, black and red king snake named Uncle Roy, lived under the old piano in Big Daddy's house. Actually the piano didn't carry a tune at all. Big Momma kept it around to house Uncle Roy. An aggressive king snake brought all sorts of advantages to my mother's family-mice were noticeably absent. And no moccasin would dare bare his fangs!

Enjoying the only cool place in Big Momma's house, occasionally Uncle Roy slept behind the family toilet during the inferno Arkansas summers. This very nearly was his undoing, however. Once, when Big Daddy was enjoying a respite and the latest Back Corner Times, Uncle Roy affectionately licked Big Daddy's right achilles' tendon.

Such unfeigned, if unsolicited affection was even too much even for Big Daddy, Uncle Roy's most fervent supporter. While his admiration for Uncle Roy's rodent venery skills were second to known, he could not tolerate this violation of his most private savoir faire. Saltating with no thought of modesty, Big Daddy, in his entire sartorial splendor, quickly hopped out of the bathroom into the dining room where the whole family was gathered for supper. Then, with his pin-stripped railroad overalls around his legs, he ignobly fell to the ground with his uncovered derriere signaling his unconditional surrender to man and to reptile alike. Uncle Roy coyly retreated behind an old ceramic garbage can.

With surprisingly little compunction, Big Daddy banned Uncle Roy not only from the bathroom but also from the house.

Big Daddy also taught me always to look behind the toilet!

Topic: What is love?

Love is forgiveness.

A sixteen year old Westbury, Long Island boy was picked up by the police several years ago for defacing a synagogue. It seems that the boy went on a Halloween tear with some friends. They sprayed obscenities on the front door of the synagogue while a service was going on.

The young man, a Roman Catholic, was caught. He was fined $150 and ordered to give one hundred hours of service to his hometown church. His parents publicly deplored what their son had done. Their pain drew letters of understanding support from people near and far.

But most touching of all was a letter that had to do with court costs and expenses of legal counsel. The family incurred a deficit of $1,000 to defend their son. They were finding it hard to come up with the money. One day a letter arrived. It contained a check for $1,000. It was from a Jewish lawyer in Manhattan.

We consciously, deliberately, choose to love or to hate; love is not something which we unconsciously wander into.

A train pulls into Auschwitz concentration camp. Even before the steam has ceased hissing from the brakes of the engine, the hapless, forlorn Jews are being unloaded. An SS Captain stands erect with two ominous police dogs at his side. A motion with his right hand to the right means life in the work camp nearby, called Birkenau. A motion with left hand means instant death in the gas chambers. The Jews knew what was up-no one could ignore the ominous smoke billowing from the stacks of the crematorium. The awful stench of flesh burning was unmistakable. Yet, no one could move. Everyone hoped to be motioned to the right--the effort of escape should at least be postponed until one saw to which side he would be sent. The line moved ever so slowly toward the captain. Right, right, and then a whole series of people were sent left. A couple was perceivably nervous as the line moved closer to the captain. The couple had been newly married only a month before. What a honeymoon! The persons ahead of them were sent to the right. They felt hope! And then, the horror of hopelessness hit them. The woman was sent to the right and the man to the left.

Suddenly a man, a prisoner, approached the Captain. He interjected, "Excuse me, Herr Captain, but may I take the place of the young man you are sending to the left? I am a broken, unhealthy, man. He is strong. Wouldn't it be better if he lived and I died?" The young man was spared.

The prisoner was gassed. Recently, the man and his bride, now old people, attended a ceremony where the young prisoner, a priest, was honored.

Topic: Describe someone who changed your life.

He was an ordinary pastor, Brother Garner, the sort of pastor you would expect a Methodist bishop to send to my hometown.

A pastor distinguished only by his mediocrity, Palmer Garner seemed committed to irrelevance.

His breath always smelled of juicy fruit gum. He was trying to hide his cigarette breath everyone knew that he smoked Pall Malls.

Brother Garner dutifully remained irrelevant. That is to say, his sermons always concerned vitally important subjects such as "Sanctification" or "Soteriology." Most of us had not had an "immoral thought" since Elvis Presley played in the old VA gym.

The only redeeming feature of Brother Garner's sermons was that they were mercifully short. They allowed us to get to Lawson Cafe's hickory—smoked pork ribs before the Baptists!

Garner was, however, a greater threat to our fragile equilibrium.

Dwight Washington, a high school scholar and track star, had a conversion experience at one of our revival services.

I never told anyone, but I had invited him. It was my fault.

Above the choir loft in our church, directly behind Brother Garner, was a stain glass image of Jesus praying in the Garden of Gethsemane. When I kneeled at the communion rail I remember looking up at Jesus and wondering what it was like. I wondered what he was doing in that window. I imagined he had just finished brushing his teeth. Why not? My mother had told me that good people brushed their teeth twice, sometimes three times/ day. Jesus was, without a doubt, the best person who ever lived. So, if my sources were correct Jesus must be brushing his teeth right up there. Oh, that stain glass window implied that he was praying all the time but I knew better. I knew that he had to have been brushing his teeth a lot.

Now I did not know much about Dwight's soul, but everyone could tell that he needed to brush his teeth a lot more than he was, so when Brother Garner mentioned that we were going to have a revival service next Wednesday night I was very careful to invite Dwight.

The problem was Dwight was converted on Wednesday night and thought he would visit us again on Sunday morning. He foolishly thought that since Jesus loved him all the time, and we appeared to love him on Wednesday night, that we would love him on Sunday morning too.

So, he attended our Sunday morning worship service.

Dwight arrived promptly at 10:45 and shook Tommy Somerville's hand. Without looking up, Tommy Somerville, who ushered the faithful to their pews, handed Dwight a bulletin. Dwight smiled. Then Mr. Somerville forbad Dwight the right to enter our church.

Garner saw everything and was obviously displeased. Not that he castigated us. We could handle that. We enjoyed pastors who scolded us for our sins. We tolerated, even enjoyed his paternalistic diatribes. No, Garner did the intolerable: he wept. Right in the middle of morning worship, where our children were baptized, Garner wept! Right in the middle of morning worship, as if it was part of the liturgy, he started crying! Not loud, uncontrollable sobs, but quiet, deep crying. Old Man Henley, senile and almost deaf, remembering the last time he cried-when his wife died-started crying too. And then the children started.

Brother Garner taught me and others when to cry. There is a time when things seem so bad, overwhelming, all we can do is cry! Cry for injustice. Cry for justice!

Topic: Describe someone who changed your life.

My mom was obviously defeated by the cancer interlopers who had completely subdued her body and were now skirmishing with her spirit. With her blonde frosted wig slightly askew on her forehead mom very much appeared the defeated warrior.

She needed the bright color in the afghan to tease vigor from her emaciated frame and color from her pallid skin. My mother's body, naturally big boned but until recently pudgy, unnaturally jutted out from loose knitted afghan perimeters.

By the time our family surgeon and good friend Dr. Johnny Joe Jones, one of Dr. Donahue's cardinals, called the hogs with mom one last time before she went into the operating room and opened her up with his scalpel, mom was mellifluent with metastatic carcinoma.

Dr. Johnny Joe was the best surgeon in Arkansas. Trained in Houston, TX-the medical school Mecca of the South-everyone wanted a doctor trained in Houston-he must be good if he was from Houston-Dr. Johnny Joe was a brilliant, skilled surgeon. He had assisted in the first heart transplant attempt (the patient died) in Arkansas. He was also a Presbyterian. Everyone knew that the best doctors were Presbyterians who went to medical school in Houston. In spite of one nasty habit-Dr. Johnny Joe chewed Red Chief Tobacco during surgery-he was much sought after. "Wipe my mouth, nurse," Dr. Johnny Joe often asked.

No, my mother was fortunate to have him. He was pretty busy but since he was a good friend of my mother's old neighbor Josephine Mae Stuart, he agreed to take my mom's case.

Mom's tumor infected gall bladder was sent to Houston for tests but Dr. Johnny Joe had already announced my mother's death sentence. It was over just that quickly. With buck season in full swing, Dr. Johnny Joe was still able to kill a four point later that afternoon. Mom went home to die. Mom did not know that her gall bladder had been removed until she received her hospital bill. She thought it would be impolite to say anything. Dr. Johnny Joe could have taken out her heart and she would have still been grateful.

Mom died later that year but there was something inspiring about her simple, unpretentious courage in the face of overwhelming odds!

Essay

Topic: Give a brief biographical sketch. Do not discuss your entire life, but share one particularly interesting part of it.

In the summer of 1965 I was 12 years old. On this particular morning my family was asleep. It was 6:30 A.M. when I stepped into our back yard. The doughty St. Augustine grass irritated my virgin feet too long the captive of black Keds. The uninvited crabgrass surreptitiously invading our lawn, unobserved by our 68 year old colored yard "boy" Aubry, vexing my feet reminded me that neither I nor the crab grass belonged here this morning. I walked to the garden.

A southern garden was both afflicted and blessed by a ten month growing season. It was constantly battling interloping Johnson grass and ravenous rodents. As a result, while northern flowers, shrubs, and perennials sporting vivid colors and vigorous stems were nurtured by cool summer evenings and short growing seasons, southern Arkansas begonias and roses had to endure endlessly long, hot summer days. Their paleness was the result of too much sun, not too little. However, commitment to task assured ardent redolence if not inspired accretion.

I loved my grandmother's arsenal of yellow daffodils and I loved the skirmish line of Black-eyed Susans that allegedly guarded my father's tomato patch from unscrupulous felines and their hygienic practices.

As I stepped into our yard I quietly moved toward my dad's kennel. Dad's prize winning bird dogs, Sandy and Jim (my namesake), were delighted to see me.

Jim was a pure bred boxy male setter with caramel colored spots on a short white hair base. His most distinguishing feature was his voice that sounded more like a bloodhound than a prize winning quail dog.

Sandy was an impressive black and white long hair bitch setter who my father claimed was smarter than my dim-witted Uncle Homer. Sandy could locate a covey of quail faster than any dog I had ever known; Uncle Homer diurnally could barely locate his false teeth.

On this morning they wanted something I did not have: they supposed that I was a harbinger of a bird hunting expedition or at least a romp over to Mr. Stalling's pasture to harass his two yearlings. But they were wrong.

I sincerely apologized to Jim and Sandy and I vigorously scratched their prickly ears. Sincere appeasement accomplished nothing. Sandy and Jim rudely snubbed the young offspring of their master by turning their backs and growling.

They were my father's bird dogs; I was merely his son. They pressed home their advantage.

They were acutely aware of the differences of our station and pushed it to their advantage at every occasion that offered itself. They knew full well that no little league game or school activity could compete with a bird hunting excursion.

There was no advantage to be gained this morning, however, and my father's canine wonders had nothing else to do with this pretentious interloper except ignore him.

These dogs trusted my father to take care of them. I remember once during a storm that the dogs ran to my father—in the rain, in the wind, in the lightening—instead of into their houses. They sought their safety in the presence of their master, not in the place of a house. As I leave for college God help me to trust Him in that way!

Diogenes Allen, *Christian Belief in a Postmodern World*. Louisville, Kentucky: John Knox Press, 1989).

Peter Berger, "At Stake in the Enlightenment," *First Things*, March 1996, p. 18.

S.D. Gaede, *When Tolerance is no Virtue* (Downers Grove, IL: Inter-Varsity Press, 1993).

Kenneth J. Gergen, *The Saturated Self: Dilemmas of Identity in Contemporary Life*. NY: Harper Collins Publishers, 1991. p. 46.

Ari L. Goldman, *The Search for God at Harvard* (NY: Random House, 1991).

Phillip E. Johnson , "How the Universities Were Lost," in *First Things* 51 (March 1995) pp. 51-56.

Eric H. Monkkonen, *America Becomes Urban* (Berkeley: University of California Press, 1988), pp. 71-72.

George Marsden, *The Soul of the American University* (Oxford, England: Oxford University Press, 1994).

Gary Nash, et al., *The American Nation* (New York: Harper and Row, 1990), p. 608.

John Henry Newman, *The Idea of a University Defined and Illustrated* (1852).

Jaroslave Pelikan, *The Idea of the University: A Re-examined* (1994).

Douglas Sloan, *Faith and Knowledge: Mainline Protestantism and American Higher Education*, Philadelphia: Westminster/John Knox).

Patricia Waugh in Gene Edward Veith, Jr, *Postmodern Times: A Christian Guide to Contemporary Thought and Culture*, p. 45).

Prepare

Study Rhetoric, Writing, Literature & History

Master Books® and Dr. James Stobaugh are working together to provide curriculum to help junior and senior high school students excel as adult Christian leaders.

Written by Dr. Stobaugh, a Harvard, Vanderbilt, Princeton & Gordon-Conwell graduate, these studies offer the highest quality of education with a focus on devotion to God, our Creator. Since 1975, Master Books® has provided creation-based material for all ages; including apologetics, home-school resources, reference titles, and quality children's literature.

Connect with Master Books® online for updates on new releases by Dr. James Stobaugh.

masterbooks.net   facebook.com/**masterbooks**

to Lead

Prepare to Make the _right_ Decisions at College

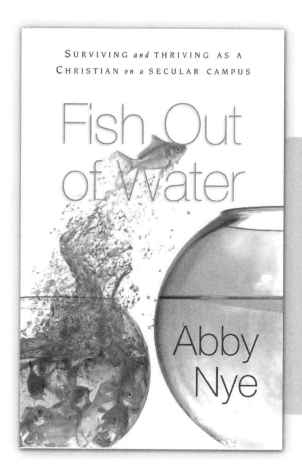

Fish Out of Water

- a valuable handbook for parents, teachers, and students

- addressing treatment of science and faith in the classroom

- difficult professors and real life solutions

- the many forms of liberal "indoctrination."

$12.99 | 978-0-89221-621-5

Where Do I Go From Here?

- focusing on the right motives

- looking ahead to potential outcomes

- turning to Jesus Christ for guidance.

$11.99 | 978-0-89221-515-7

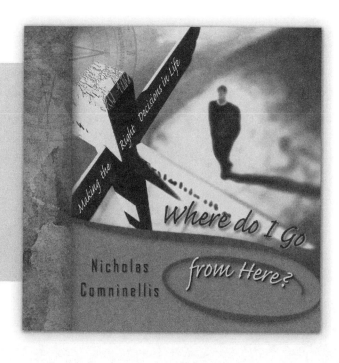

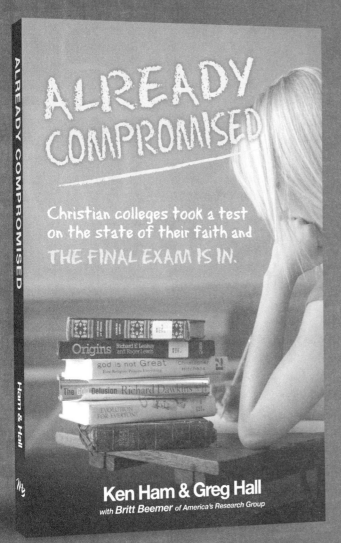

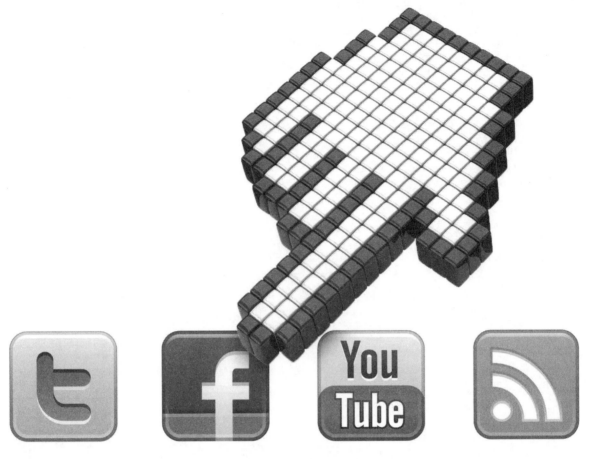

Connect with Master Books®

masterbooks.net

An imprint of New Leaf Publishing Group

facebook.com/**masterbooks**
twitter.com/**masterbooks4u**
youtube.com/**nlpgvideo**

nlpgblogs.com and **nlpgvideos.com**

Join us at
CreationConversations.com
Connecting Christians who believe in Biblical Creation

An experienced teacher and parent of four home-educated adult children, Dr. Stobaugh is a recognized leader in homeschooling and has published several books for students and teachers. Some are in the series *Preparing Thoughtful Christians to be World Changers*, with both student and teacher editions: *Skills for Literary Analysis* (2005), *Skills for Rhetoric* (2005), *World Literature* (2005), *American Literature* (2005), and *British Literature* (2005). Stobaugh has also published *Fire That Burns but Does Not Consume* (2003) and *A Gathered Inheritance* (2004). Most recently Dr. Stobaugh finished a seven-volume world social history.

Stobaugh is a Merrill Fellow at Harvard University and holds a B.A. cum laude from Vanderbilt, an M.A. from Rutgers University, a M.Div. from Princeton Theological Seminary, and a D.Min. from Gordon-Conwell Theological Seminary. Jim and his wife Karen have a strong burden for the new leadership group that God is calling forth from the home-schooling community. They travel widely to speak about literature, teaching, SAT/ACT Preparation, and education.

Other books by James P. Stobaugh coming soon to Master Books®:

Skills For Rhetoric

Skills For Literary Analysis

An American Literature Critical Thinking Course

An English Literature Critical Thinking Course

A World Literature Critical Thinking Course

American, British, and World History Companion to Literature

Epoch I, II, and III World History Companion to Literature

A Gathered Inheritance

Fire That Burns but Does Not Consume: A 52 Week Devotional

A Companion to 50 Classics

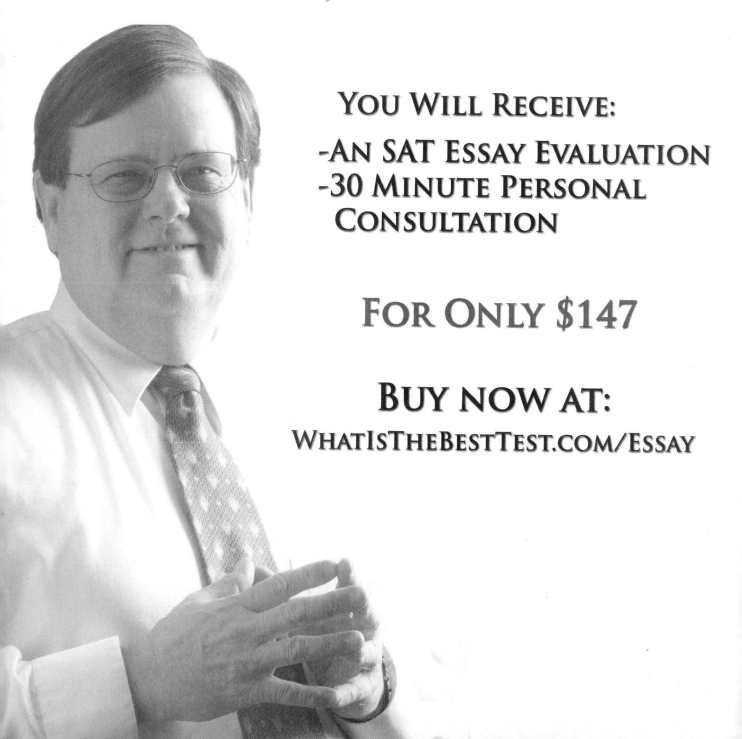